DRAWING REALISTIC

Pencil Portraits

STEP-BY-STEP

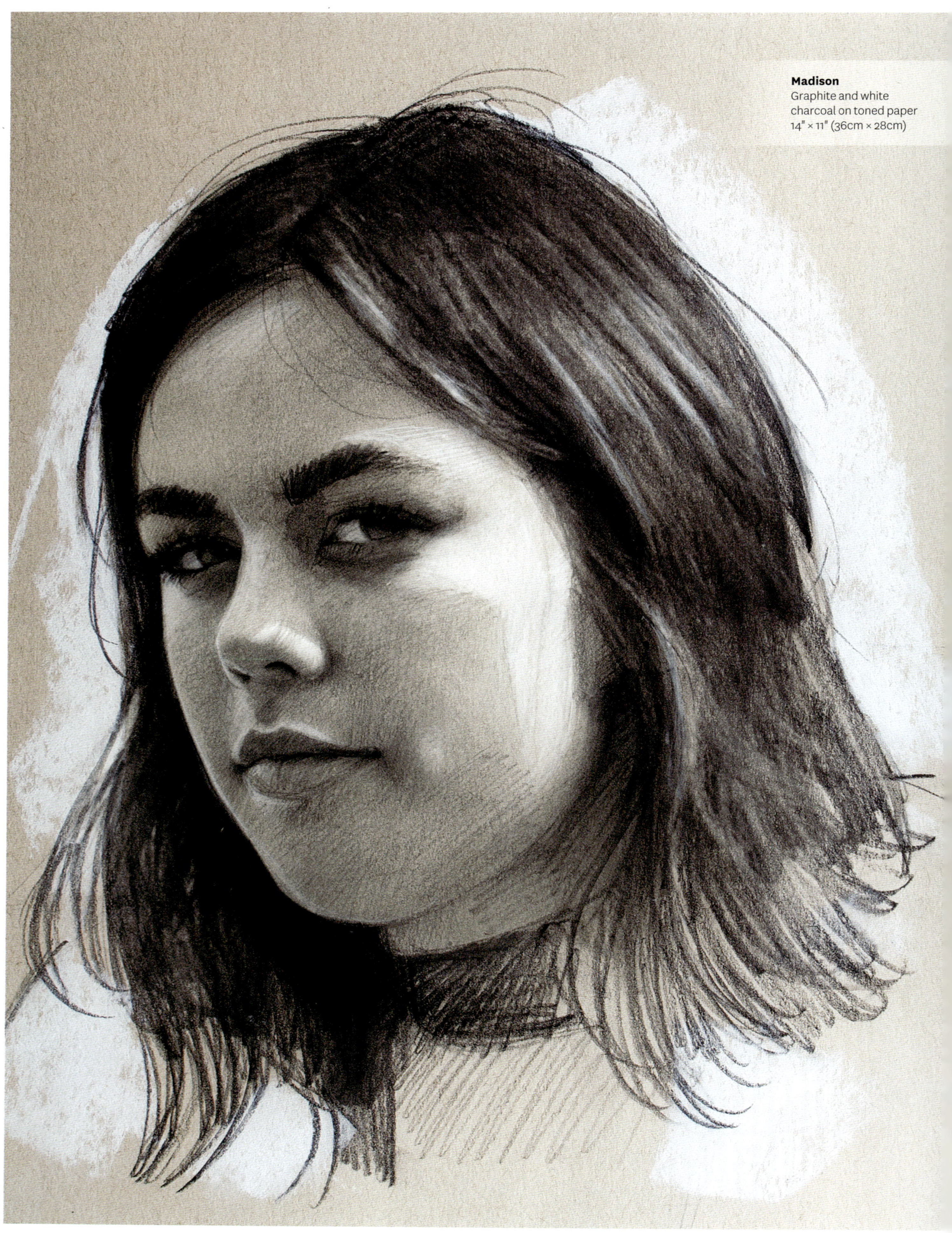

Madison
Graphite and white charcoal on toned paper
14" × 11" (36cm × 28cm)

DRAWING REALISTIC

Pencil Portraits

STEP-BY-STEP

JUSTIN MAAS

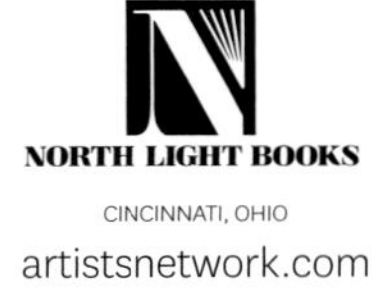

NORTH LIGHT BOOKS

CINCINNATI, OHIO

artistsnetwork.com

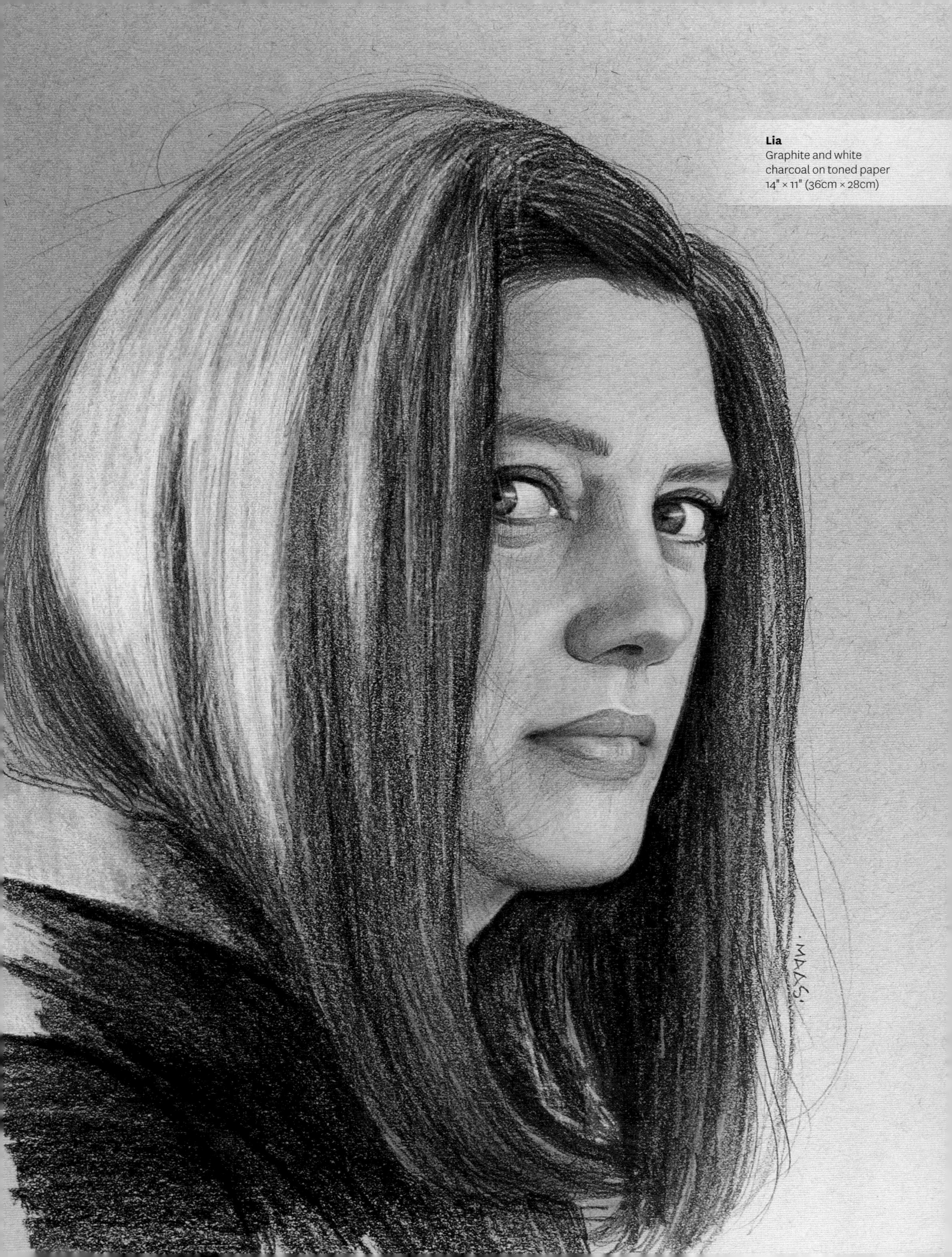

Lia
Graphite and white charcoal on toned paper
14" × 11" (36cm × 28cm)

CONTENTS

What You Need

SURFACES

- pastel paper
- toned tan sketch paper
- white sketch paper

PENCILS

- ebony pencil
- HB, B, 2B, 4B, 6B and 8B woodless and standard graphite pencils
- pastel pencils
- white charcoal pencil
- white Conté stick

MISCELLANEOUS

- click eraser
- kneaded eraser
- pencil extenders
- pencil sharpener
- tortillons (for both white and black tones)

OPTIONAL

- craft knife
- draftsman's brush
- ink pens
- painter's tape (green)
- ruler
- spray fixative
- transfer paper

INTRODUCTION

I visited London for the first time as a twelve-year-old boy. My family and I enjoyed all that the United Kingdom had to offer, but the art galleries interested me the most. The masterworks in the Wallace Collection, the Tate and the National Portrait Galleries mesmerized my young artist's brain. But it was the National Gallery—and one piece specifically—that changed me forever.

The masterpiece I am referring to is Leonardo da Vinci's *The Virgin and Child with Saint Anne and the Infant Saint John the Baptist*. Often referred to as "The Burlington House Cartoon," this drawing is hypnotizing in its beauty. It features passages as finished as any oil painting and others that are rough, loose and energetic. In the faces, the arms and the clothing we see da Vinci's trademark sfumato technique—the gradual blending of areas to create believable three-dimensional forms—while the hands and feet are composed of simple scribbles or a few well-placed lines. This drawing showed me that it was possible to combine the aesthetics of high realism with the energy of a loose sketch.

Over the years, materials such as oil, watercolor and acrylic have taken the spotlight as the "serious" mediums. But compared to drawing, the one thing they can never do as easily (or usually as well) is communicate energy. Drawing is the most essential of all visual art skills. I have met plenty of sculptors who don't paint. I have met plenty of painters who don't weave. I have met plenty of printmakers and designers and fabric artists that don't do etchings. But the one thing they all do, to some extent, is draw. Drawing is the most simple of all visual art forms: one tool, one surface and you are ready.

At the same time, it is one of the broadest. One can create a simple contour line drawing or a very finished rendering.

Drawing is also an incredibly visceral and raw form of art. Unlike oil, watercolor or acrylic, you are not

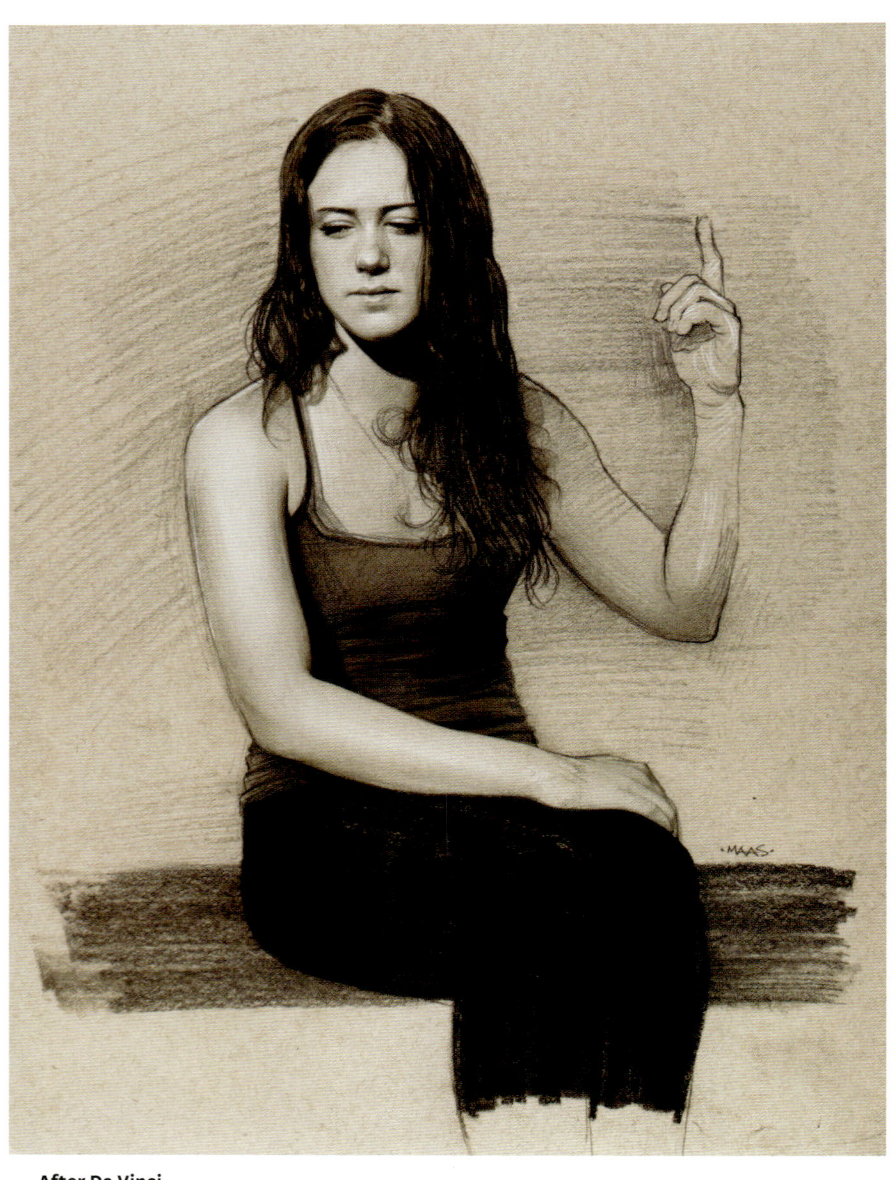

After Da Vinci
Graphite and white charcoal on toned paper
14" × 11" (36m × 28cm)

This image, highly influenced by da Vinci's "Burlington House Cartoon," shows areas of great detail and others of just a few lines of indication. This creates an image that is high in both energy and detail.

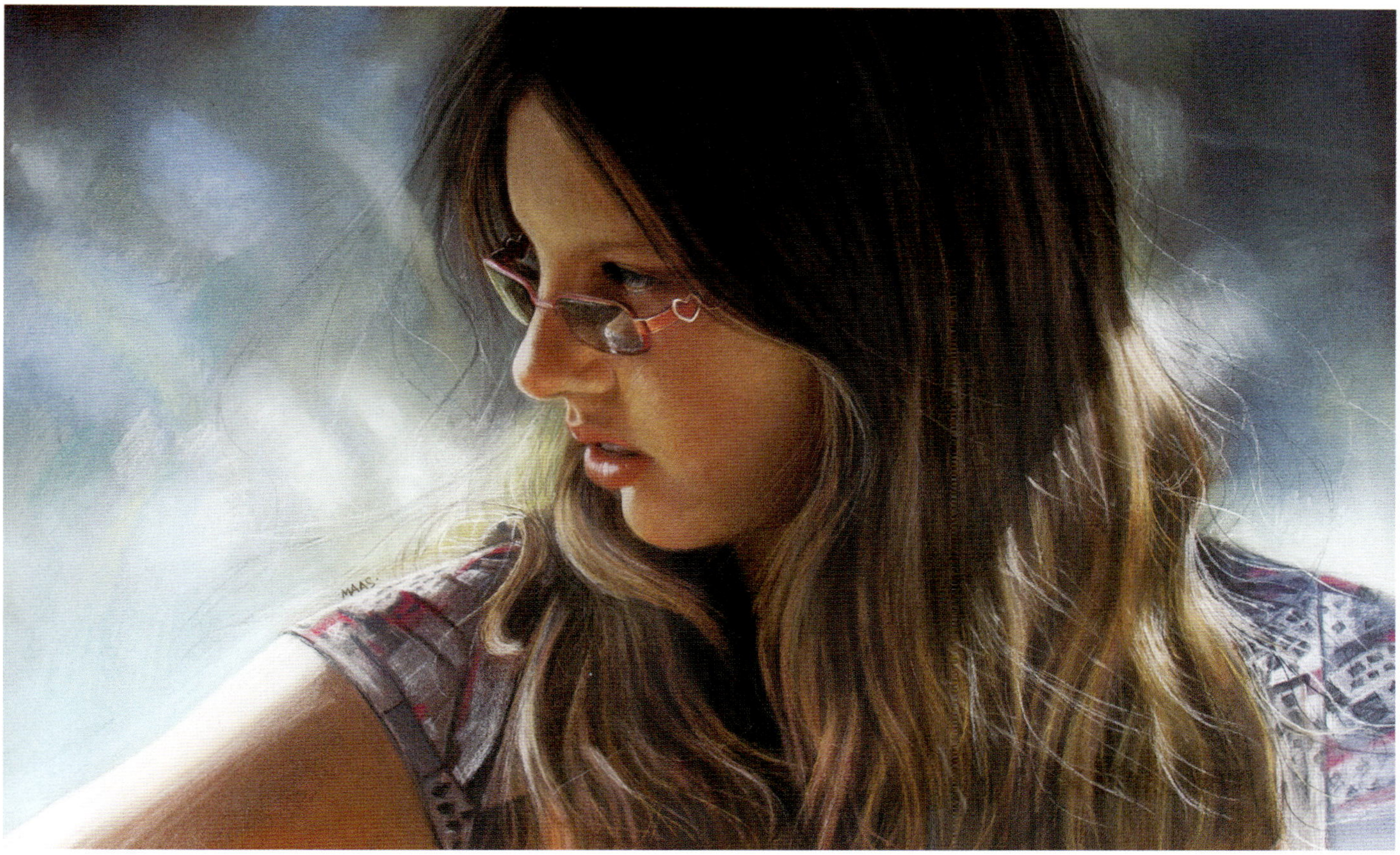

Some Day Never Comes
Pastel on paper
14" × 24" (36cm × 61cm)

distanced from the surface of your paper with a brush. You push and pull and mark the pages with your art tool right in your hand. Often you use your fingers themselves to push around pigment and tone. There is a sense of intimacy that you can get with drawing that is hard to match with any other medium.

Whether you use this book to help you get better at drawing as your medium of choice, or as a stepping-stone for painterly mediums, I hope you find it useful and inspiring.

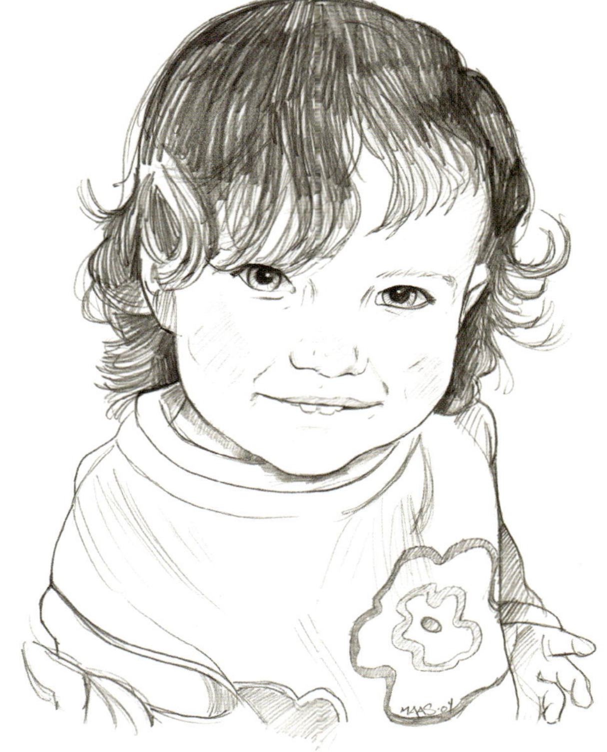

Jada, Day 1
Graphite on paper
12" × 9" (30cm × 23cm)

1 GETTING STARTED

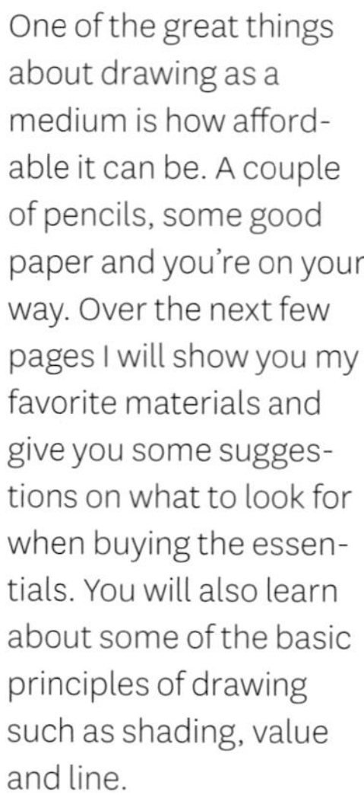

One of the great things about drawing as a medium is how affordable it can be. A couple of pencils, some good paper and you're on your way. Over the next few pages I will show you my favorite materials and give you some suggestions on what to look for when buying the essentials. You will also learn about some of the basic principles of drawing such as shading, value and line.

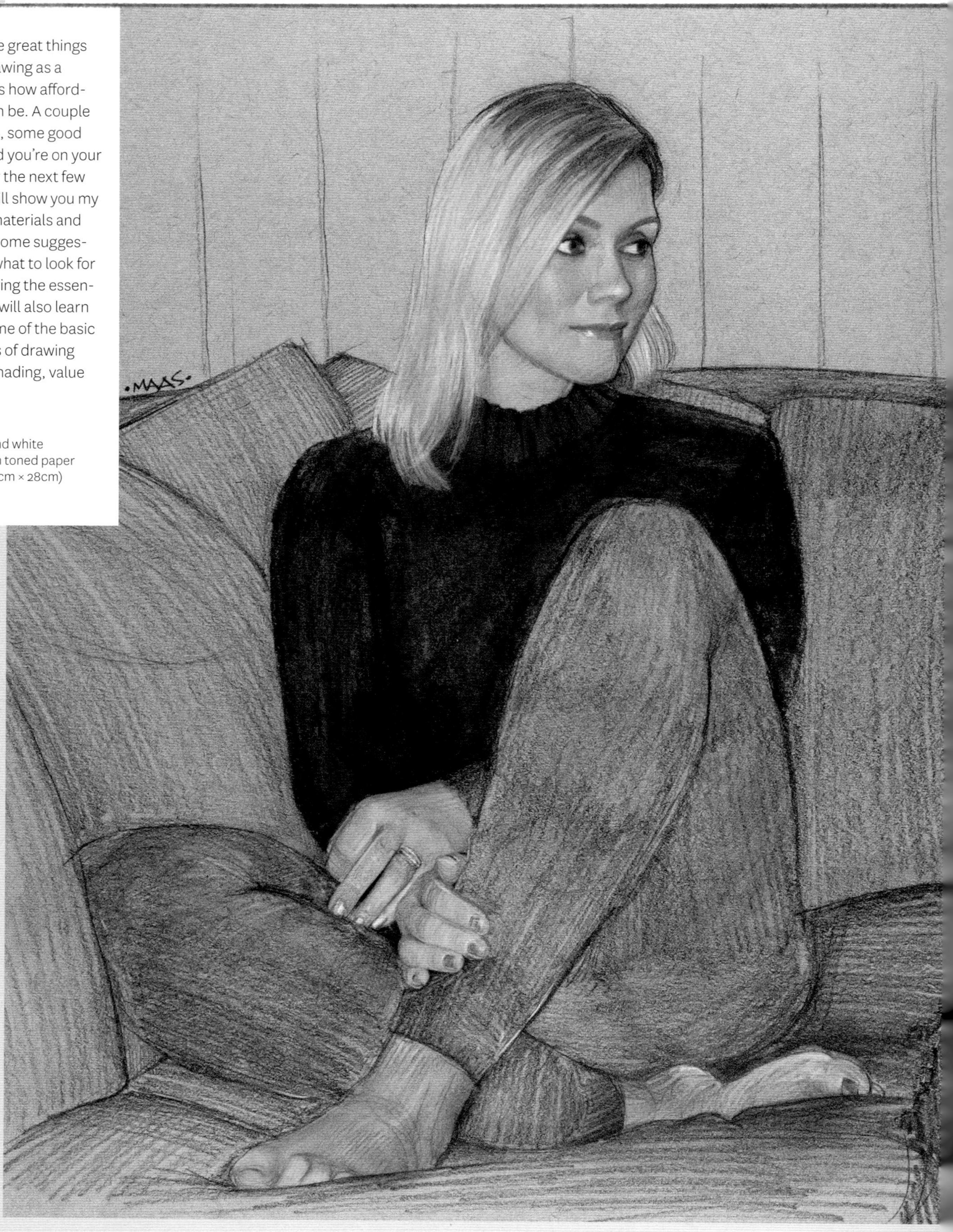

Carinna
Graphite and white charcoal on toned paper
14" × 11" (36cm × 28cm)

BASIC DRAWING SUPPLIES

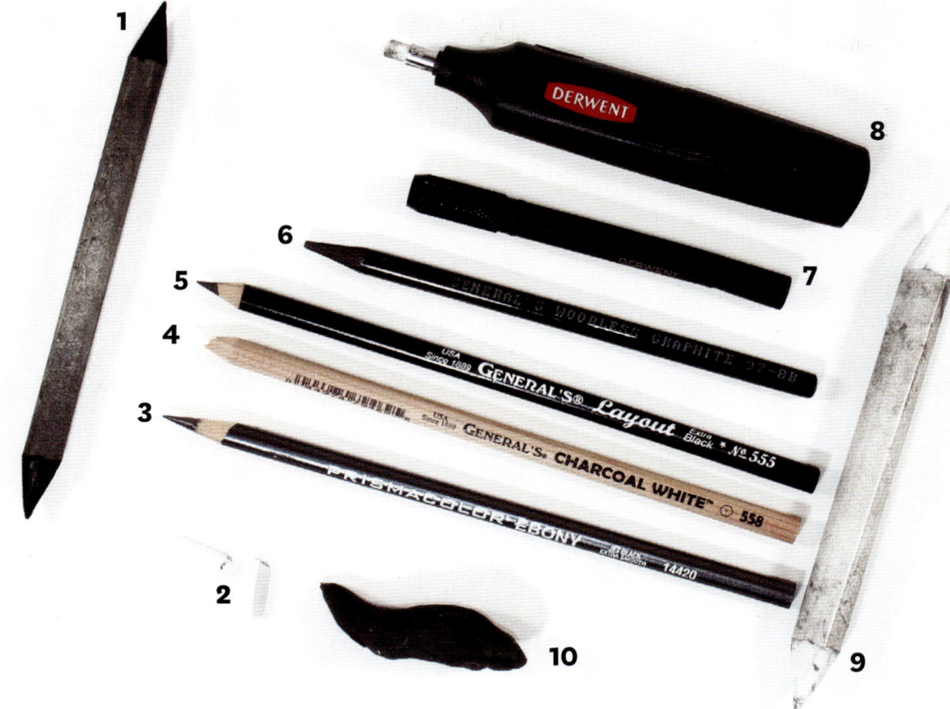

Main Tools

Here are the key items I use to create my pencil sketches and drawings.

1. tortillon (used for black)
2. white Conté stick
3. ebony pencil
4. white charcoal pencil
5. layout pencil
6. woodless pencil (8B)
7. pencil extender
8. electric eraser
9. tortillon (used for white)
10. kneaded eraser

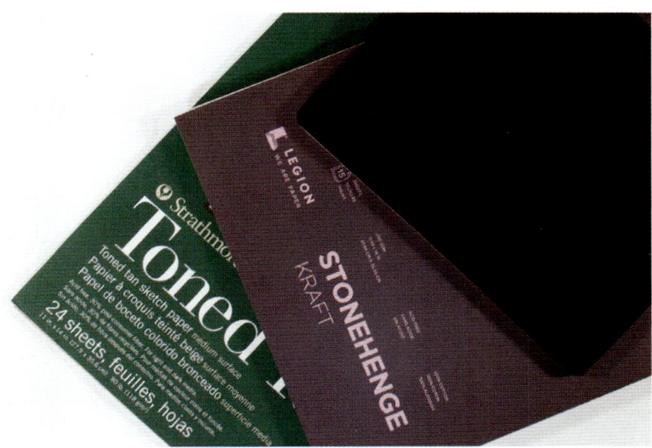

Paper

Most of the drawings in this book are done on toned paper. I like working on paper that is not white because it allows me to work both lights and darks simultaneously, creating an almost sculptural feel.

The toned papers I prefer are made by Strathmore (400 Series Toned Tan Sketch) and Stonehenge (Kraft or Fawn). There are other brands, and I urge you to explore them until you find the paper that is right for you.

I don't have a huge preference on white paper as long as it is good quality and a decent weight. I often use a Robert Bateman pad, but good quality sheets from Strathmore, Canson, Bienfang and other major brands work fine, too. Look for something that is 80 to 100-lbs. (170gsm to 210gsm) or more and has a bit of a tooth, but not too much.

ESSENTIAL TOOLS FOR DRAWING

Below is more detailed information about the supplies I like to use.

PENCILS

In my experience, almost all artist-grade pencils are good, so the decision about brands is an entirely personal one.

I use a wide variety of brands and types. For basic drawing, I often use regular student-grade pencils (rated HB), which I buy by the box. I use these during the block-in stage because they produce a line that is not too dark and not too light. They are easily erased and resist lead breakage better than softer pencils.

The bulk of my rendering is done with a pencil in the 2B to 4B range. I generally prefer a Prismacolor Ebony, which comes in only one softness but feels similar to a 3B. It is higher in carbon content, which is important when working with white charcoal. Staedtler's Mars Lumograph black line creates the very darkest darks.

In addition to the pencils listed above, I like to use a 6B or 8B woodless graphite pencil. This is the same type of graphite as any normal 6B or 8B pencil, but rather than being encased on wood, it's wrapped in a thin layer of plastic. These are great for large areas of dark or tone. I often use them for rendering hair.

WHITE CHARCOAL

I also use white charcoal in some of my portraits. The name is misleading because it is actually not charcoal, but a mix of calcium carbonate and binder—but for better or for worse, this is the name that has stuck. The brand I use is General's and they work beautifully for laying down bright or soft whites.

The caveat is that graphite and white charcoal do not work particularly well together. Unfortunately, no white medium (pastel, chalk or ink) works especially well with graphite, but I will offer suggestions on ways to make them work together.

ERASERS

A kneaded eraser is my go-to tool for lifting tone, as well as for removing unwanted lines. I also like to "draw" with the eraser when working with areas of tone, such as hair or a dark shirt. This eraser can be kneaded into various shapes, which makes it ideal for lifting graphite in specific shapes or sections.

A click eraser looks similar to a pen and is terrific for erasing small areas. Because it is harder and rougher, this tool can remove mistakes or overworked areas better than a kneaded eraser. It also comes in different sizes.

An electric eraser is very good for erasing large areas fast. Be careful that you don't damage your paper when using one, though.

SHARPENERS

One of the most important tools you can have is a good sharpener. Some artists prefer to sharpen with a craft knife, but my preference has always been an electric sharpener. I strongly recommend looking for a used model from the 1980s or 1990s (made in Japan or the USA) since they will almost always outlive newer models, which are made with a lot of plastic parts. If you can't find or afford an electric eraser, a simple hand sharpener will do the trick. I like the heavy brass sharpeners that allow you to replace the blades as they dull.

TORTILLONS

Tortillions are my preference for blending. They are tapered at one or both ends and are typically made from rolled paper or compressed fibers. I keep several on hand, dedicating some to dark tones and others to white tones to keep the drawings from getting dirty and muddy. In addition, a tortillon that has previously been used for black will help you achieve really rich dark.

INK PENS

Ink pens are fun to play with and help add layers of light lines (like hair wisps) over your finished drawings. Try different brands; some work better than others on top of graphite.

PENCIL EXTENDERS

The pencil extender is an invaluable tool for anyone that draws a lot. They may seem expensive at first—usually four or five dollars each—but because you can get several inches of additional use out of each pencil, they pay for themselves in just a few pencils. I like the grip on the Derwent holders so much that I actually put new pencils in them as soon as I start.

PASTEL PENCILS

Most of this book features work in gray tones. However, a lot of the principles and techniques apply to color, too. One of the nice things about working on toned paper is that it gives you a foundational set of skills that you can apply to working with color. I prefer pastel pencils for adding color, but you could also try regular wax-based colored pencils, watercolor pencils or even crayons.

Pastel pencils are pastels in pencil form. They offer the color and texture of pastels but the control of a pencil. They also mix well with regular soft pastels. My favorite brands are CarbOthello, Bruynzeel and Koh-I-Noor Gioconda and Conté.

MISCELLANEOUS TOOLS

There are a few other items that are useful but not absolutely vital. A ruler is helpful for straight lines (and working with the Maas method as explained in chapter 4). A draftsman's brush keeps your surface clean. Spray fixative can eliminate smudging. A craft knife can be used for general cutting and sharpening. Green painter's tape will not damage your paper the way regular masking tape can. And transfer paper is important if you are going to trace your reference or your own sketch onto your drawing paper.

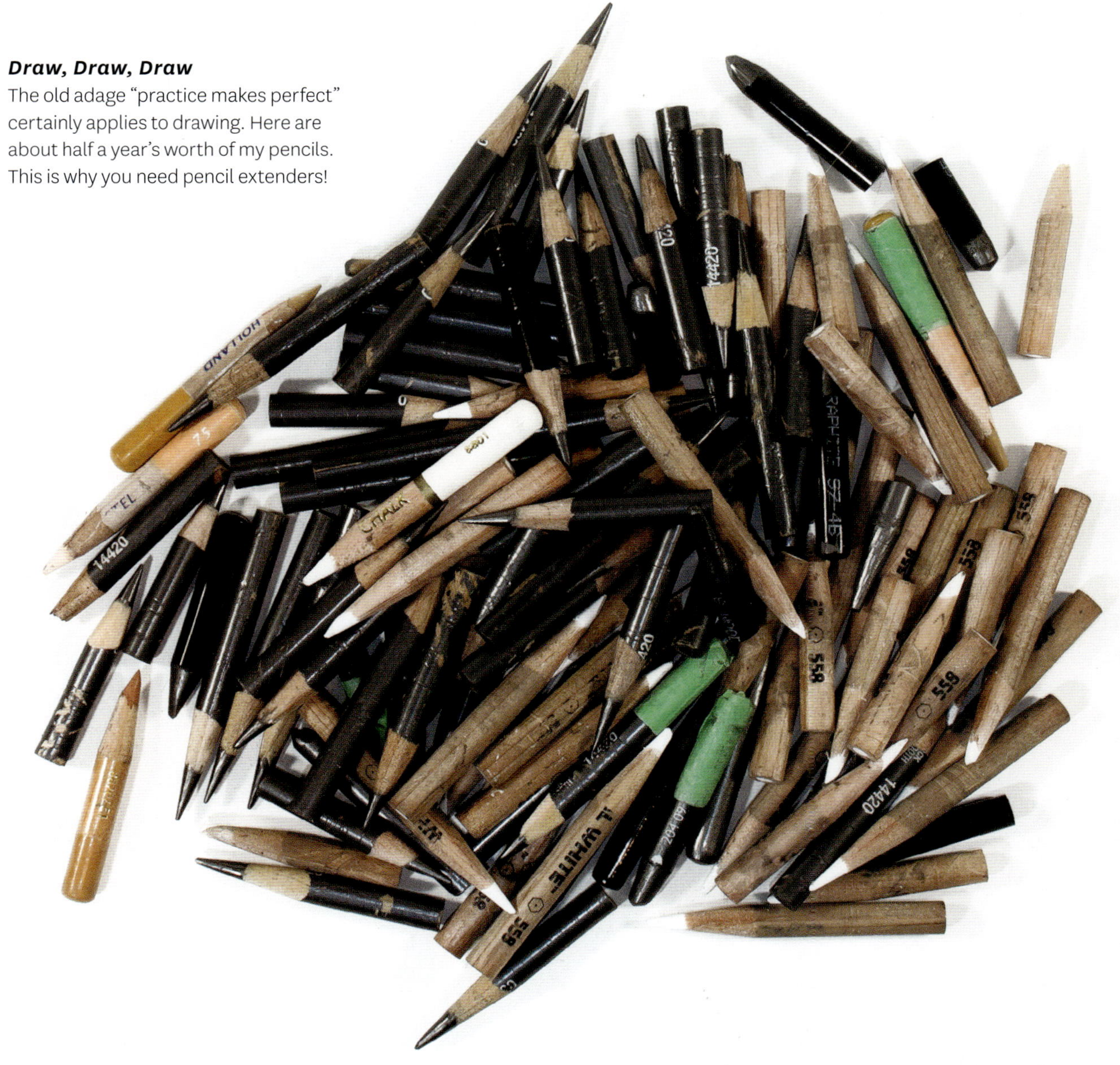

Draw, Draw, Draw

The old adage "practice makes perfect" certainly applies to drawing. Here are about half a year's worth of my pencils. This is why you need pencil extenders!

VALUES: LIGHTS AND DARKS

Values—that is lights, darks and everything in between—are crucial for all works of art, but they are the number one tool when it comes to drawing. While line helps us define the shape of an object, it is value that allows us to define its form. If we break down a drawing in terms of geometry, think of line as the circle and value as the sphere. You can't have a sphere without a circle, but you get much more information out of a sphere.

TWO WAYS TO VARY VALUES

There are two ways to achieve varying values using graphite. The simplest is to vary your pressure. Press harder and you get a darker line. Use a lighter touch and you get a lighter line. But pressing harder has two disadvantages: It can damage your paper, and it can cause graphite shine by creating a reflective layer of graphite.

The other way to vary your values is to change pencils. If you need light areas, use harder pencils. If you want dark passages, use softer pencils.

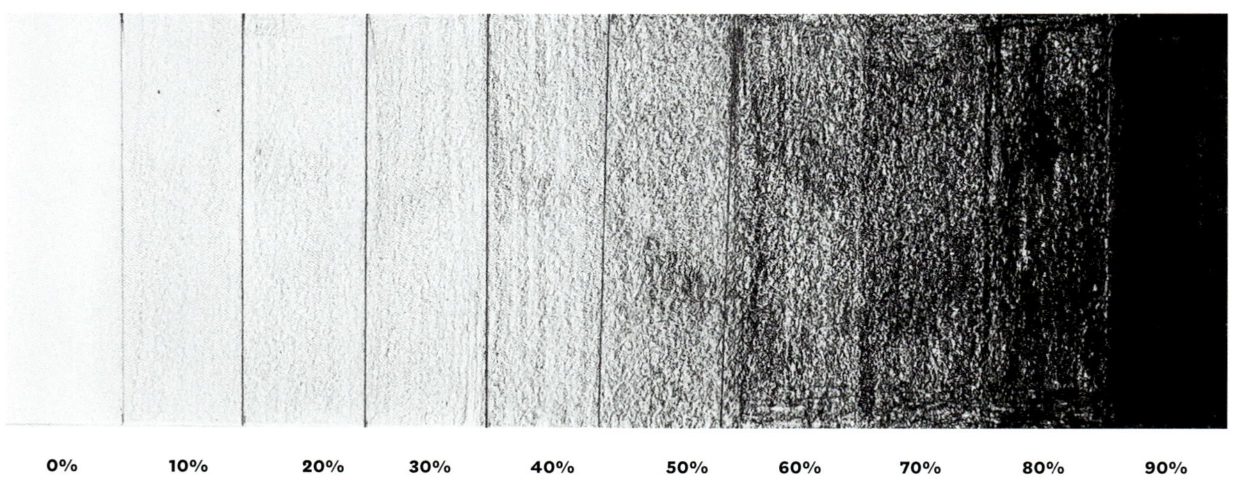

Create a Grayscale Finder

Create your own grayscale finder (or buy one readymade) to help discern and understand value. This simple tool is a great help to see just how much variation there is between the lights and darks in a drawing. A great deal of a drawing will often fall within the 30 to 70 percent area. However, it is crucial to pay attention to your darkest darks (80 to 100 percent black) and lightest lights (0 to 20 percent white).

DRAWINGS VS. PHOTOGRAPHS

As artists, we are able to show more subtle values than a camera because we are completely in control of the focus and the focal point. Compare the photo reference and the graphite drawing below, paying special attention to the values.

In the photo, the camera captures exactly what is there—namely, a lot of 30 to 70 percent values. In the drawing, I adjusted the key elements (eyes, nose, mouth and hair) in the darkest dark, midtone and lightest light areas. This allowed me to control the value and give the drawing more visual impact than the photo.

When someone asks you "why not just take a picture?" this is why.

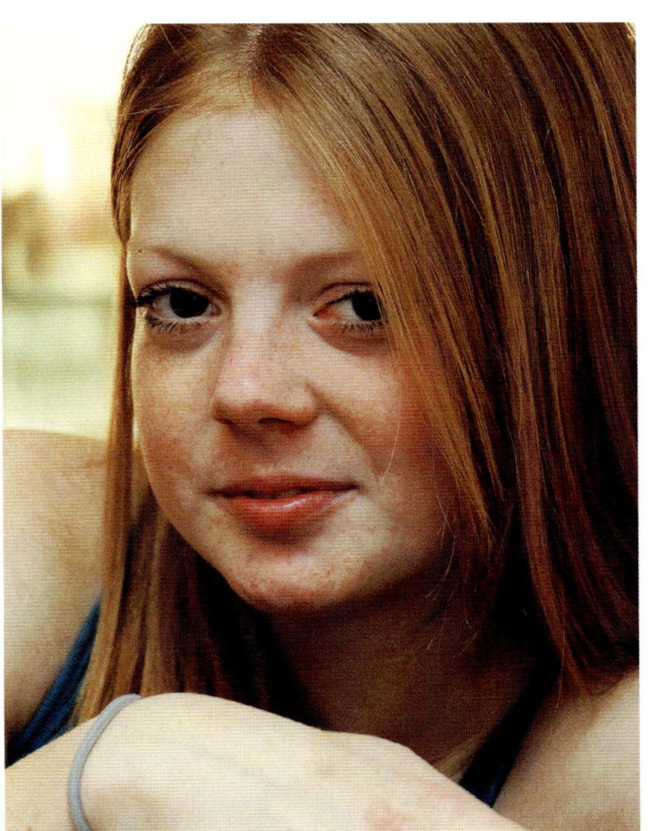

Photo Reference

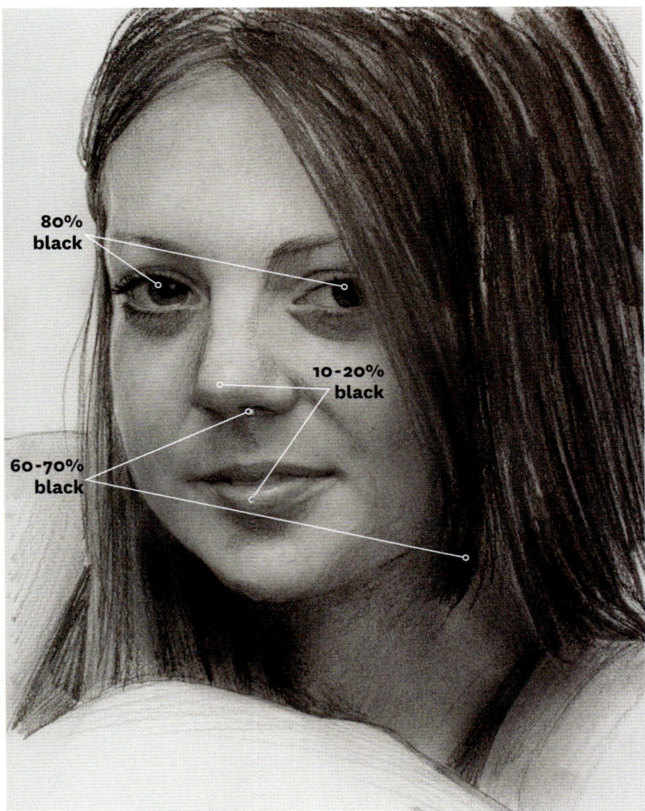

Graphite Drawing

THE MEANING OF HB

You'll notice on almost all pencils there is a designation with one or two letters (usually H or B) and numbers. The exact meaning of these letters is sometimes disputed. One common definition comes from Nicolas-Jacques Conté, the inventor of the modern pencil. In French, the H stands for *haute* (or high) and the B stands for *bas* (or low). Another less common but accepted definition is that B stands for *black level* and H stands for *hardness*. Regardless of the exact definition, the higher the number next to the letter, the more it displays the properties of H or B. So a 2B is relatively soft (or dark), a 4B is darker and an 8B or 9B is the darkest (although some brands only produce up to 6B). Likewise 2H is hard (and produces a light line), and 6H is almost impossible to see. Most artists stick with HB and softer. The H lines are often preferred by draftsmen and architects.

SHADOWS AND HIGHLIGHTS

Shadows and highlights are the most important parts of the value scale.

If you walk into a crowded gallery and do a quick survey, you will usually be drawn to one or two pieces. Chances are, those pieces are the works that handle shadows and highlights the best. They have the most appealing contrast and they immediately draw you in.

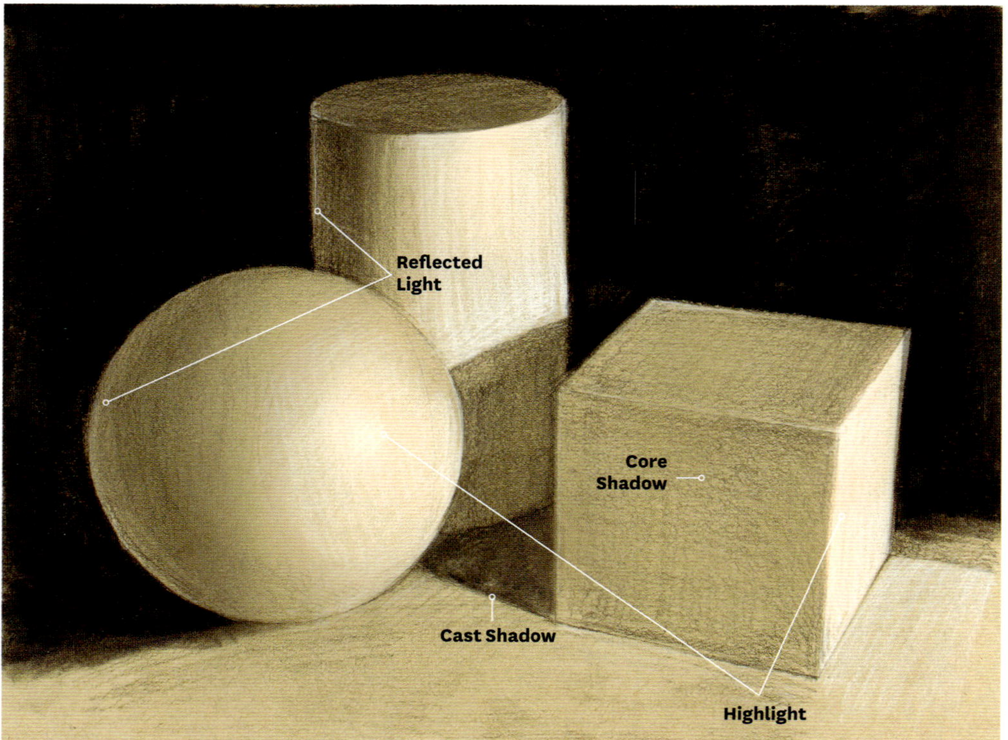

Shadow Basics

This drawing of basic shapes shows how shadows are cast on surrounding objects. The laws of shadows that apply to these rudimentary geometric items apply to *all* objects because ultimately everything is made up of these simple shapes.

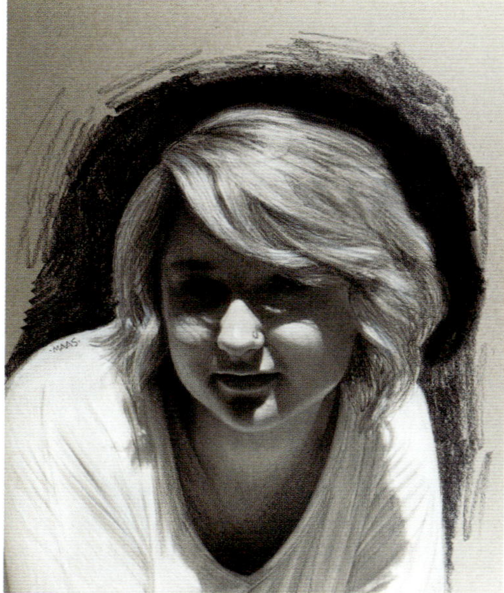

Original Drawing

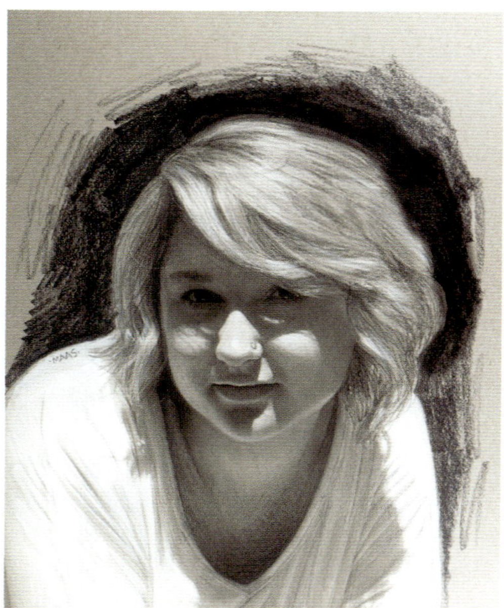

Digitally Altered Drawing

Maximize the Impact of Shadows

Here is a drawing I did that features very strong shadows. Notice the impact of the brightest parts of her nose and cheeks. In the altered version, I adjusted the contrast in Photoshop so that more details are visible but a lot of the impact is gone from the piece. Your job as an artist is to find the subtle balance between impact, detail and what you are trying to say. What is your story?

COLOR VS. BLACK-AND-WHITE REFERENCE

Assuming that most of the time you will be working from photos and that you are drawing primarily using graphite, does it make sense to print your reference (or view it on screen) in grayscale? Or should your reference be in color?

I usually prefer to work with a color reference, even if I'm working in monochrome, because I can see more information in a color photo. However, you may find that some of the guesswork is gone if you use a black-and-white reference.

Ultimately, the decision to work with color or black-and-white reference is entirely yours. My recommendation is to try both. It's easy to make any photo grayscale using digital software or an app. Just be sure you don't get rid of the color on your only copy of the file!

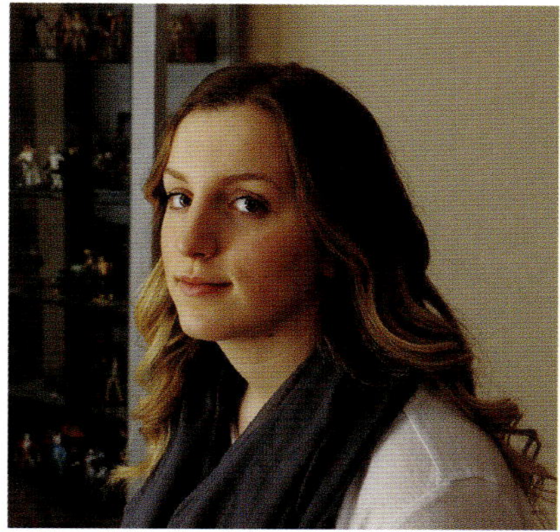

Color Reference
If you work with a color reference you will see shapes better. In the color photo it is easier to see the form in the cheeks and where the hair meets the face.

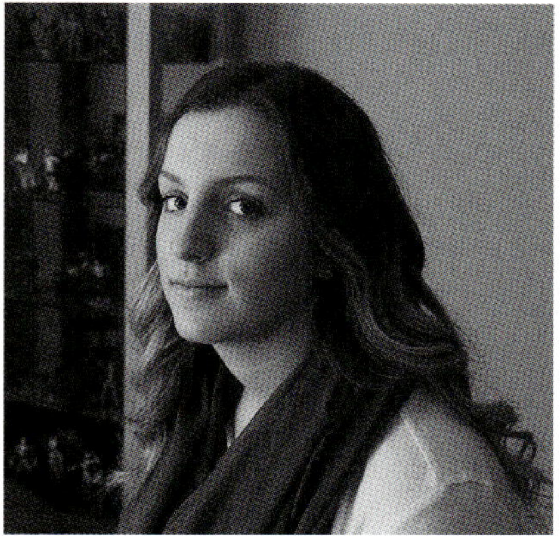

Black-and-White Reference
Some shapes are easier to define without the distraction of color. Here we're better able to see how dominant her eyes are than in the color version. I ended up making them the focal point in my drawing.

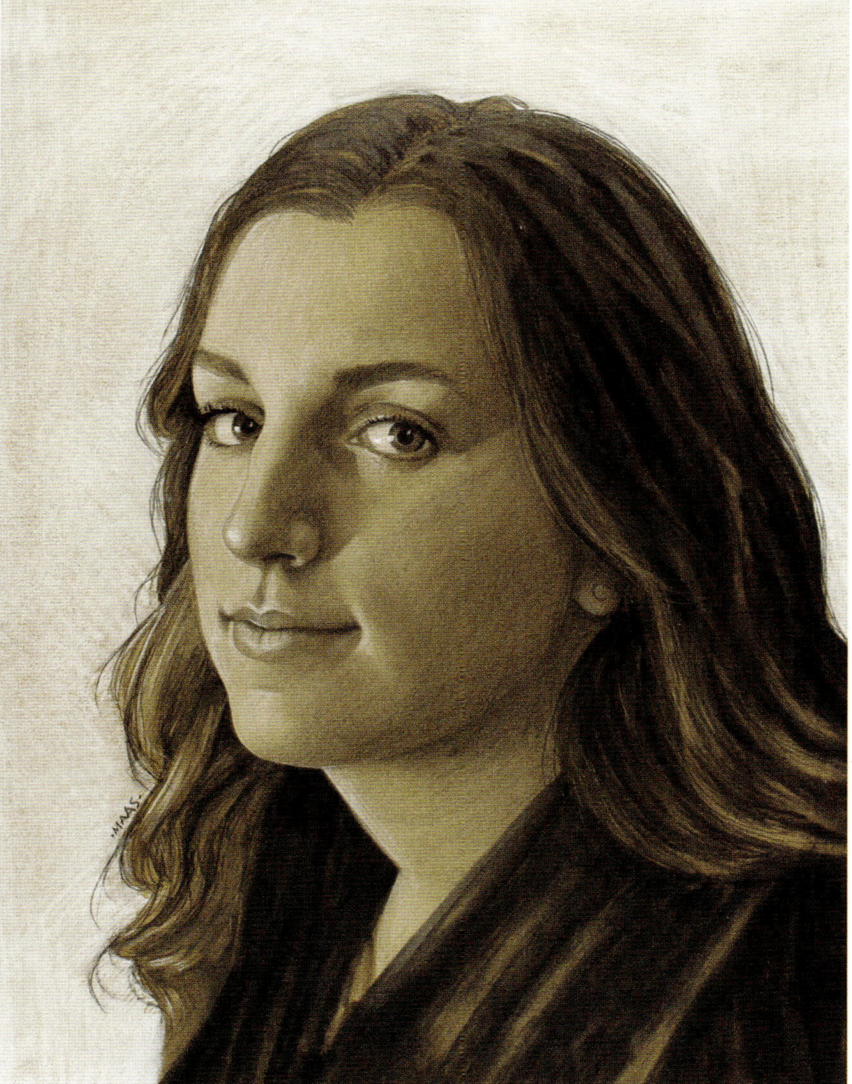

Finished Drawing
Study the two photo references I used to create this drawing to see the advantages of each.

Marley
Graphite and white charcoal on toned paper
15½" × 11½" (39cm × 29cm)

THE VALUE STUDY

There may be no better first step, especially when you are learning to draw, than the value study. This can be as simple as a few quick thumbnail sketches on a page—no more than 2 or 3 inches (5cm–8cm) tall—where you work out your basic lights and darks and also figure out how you will crop or focus your drawing.

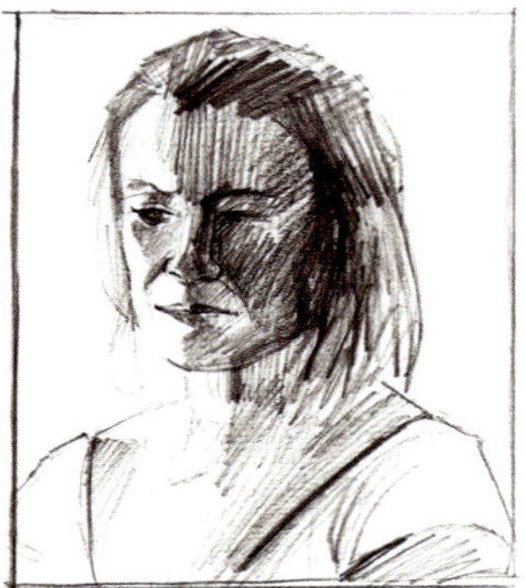

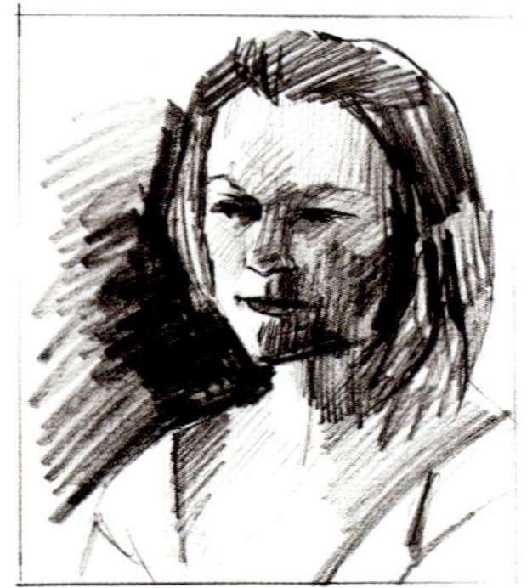

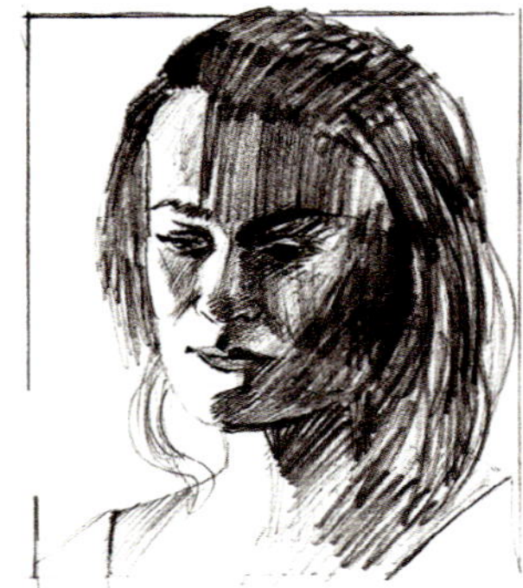

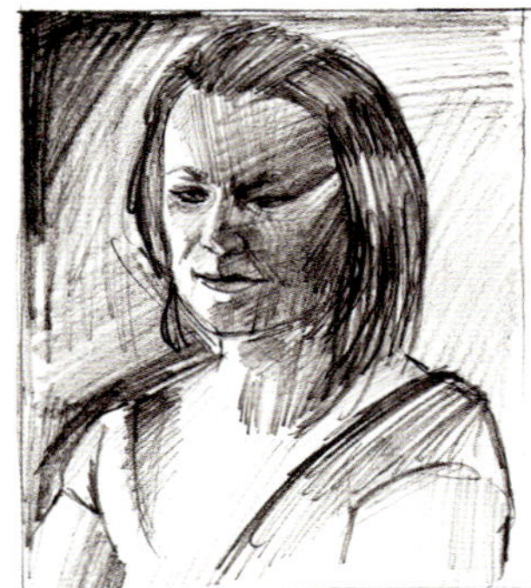

Value Sketches
In these four value sketches, I have quickly laid out the shadows and highlights to figure out my focal point. I settled on a more close-up view with most of the dark shadows on the model's left side (viewer's right). This creates a strong focal point along the centerline of her face with her right eye as the main part of the drawing.

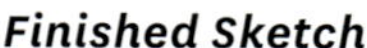

Finished Sketch
In this more finished sketch, I chose to combine some elements from several of the value studies before I spent more time on a larger drawing.

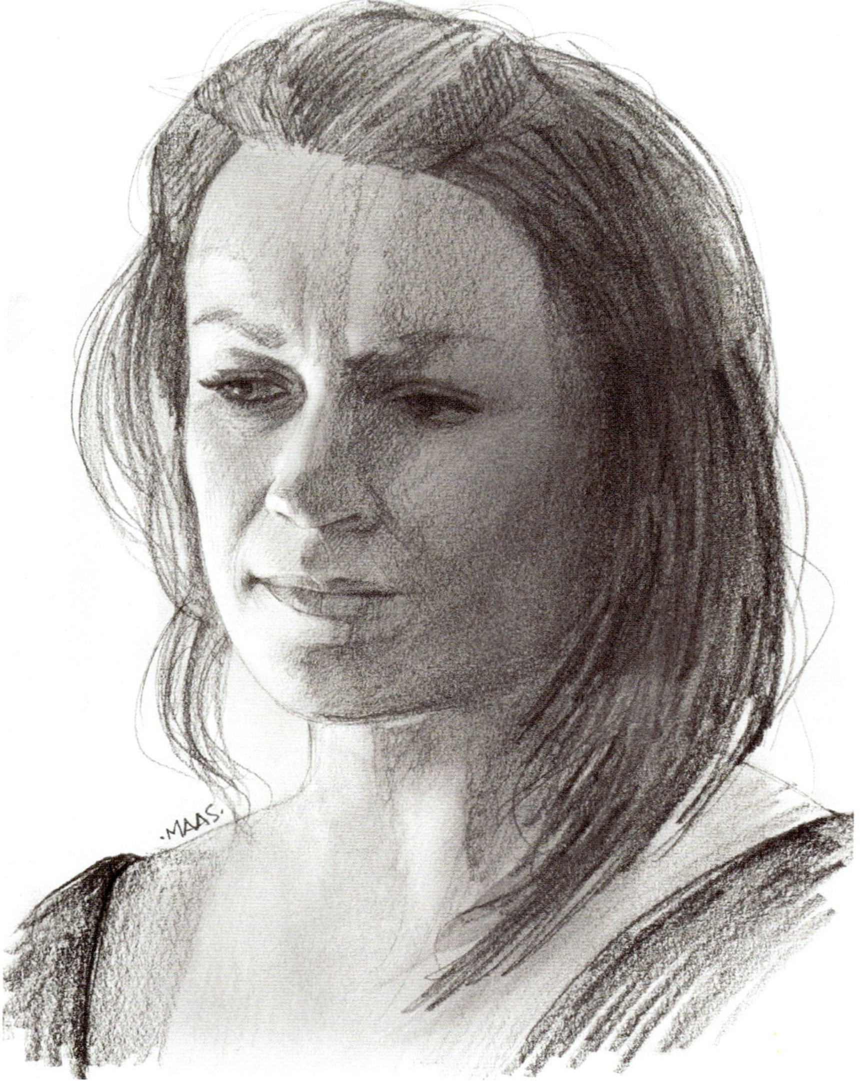

Asia
Graphite and white charcoal on toned paper
12" × 9" (30cm × 23cm)

QUALITY OF LINE

We have talked a lot about the importance of value and tone, but what about line? Tone is the shading and the highlights in a drawing, but the drawing itself is contained by line. Some artists choose to filter out (or blend) all their lines, but I enjoy leaving some of the framework of my initial drawing. If you choose to do this, too, then it's very important that you pay attention to the quality of your line. What do I mean by that? Here are two examples.

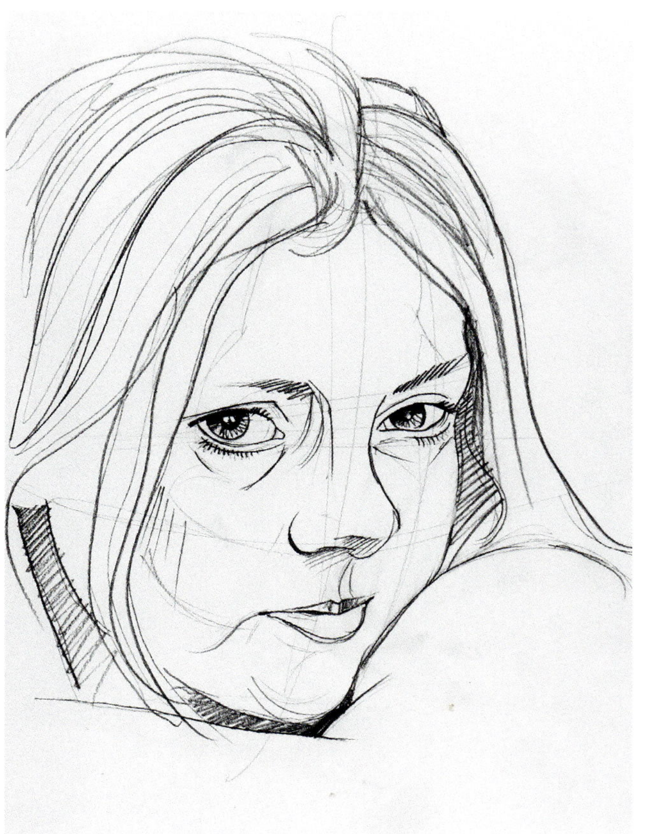

Unvarying Lines
This drawing has an unvarying line. See how every stroke is virtually the same level of darkness and thickness? Proportions are correct and everything is in the right place, yet it looks dull and boring.

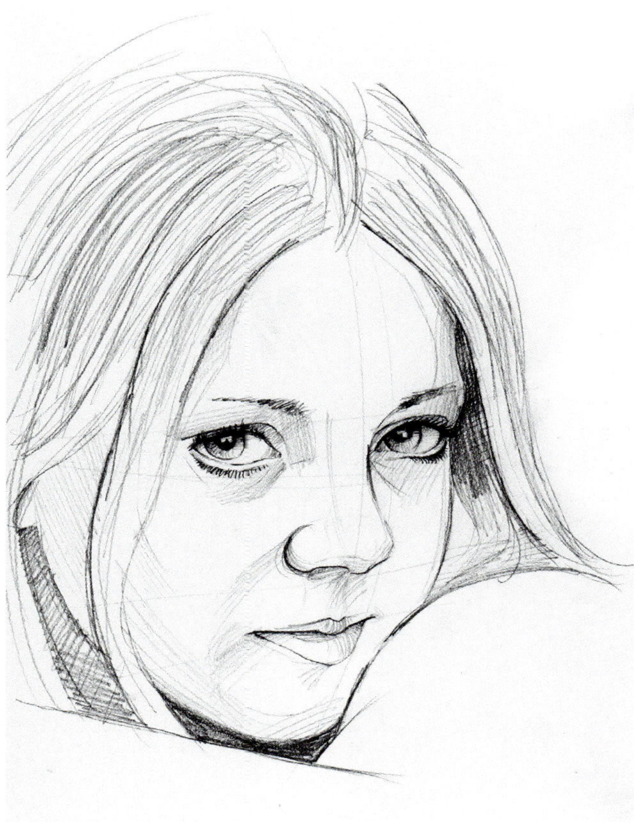

Distinctive Lines
Here is the same drawing but with a focus on line quality. I varied my line by pressing harder in some places and making lines thin and thick in others. Notice that even in this very simple line drawing things become so much more interesting because I paid attention to the lines themselves.

2 SELECTING YOUR SUBJECTS

So, now it is time to draw, but what? Or, since we're talking about portraits—whom? Whomever you want! Often we start with family, friends or someone that means something to us. Only you can choose why someone is important enough for you to want to draw. Often I ask someone to model for me and when they ask "why me?" I usually can't give a specific reason. We artists often choose such things on a subconscious level, so don't fight it—chances are that somewhere in your brain you know why even if you can't quite put a finger on it.

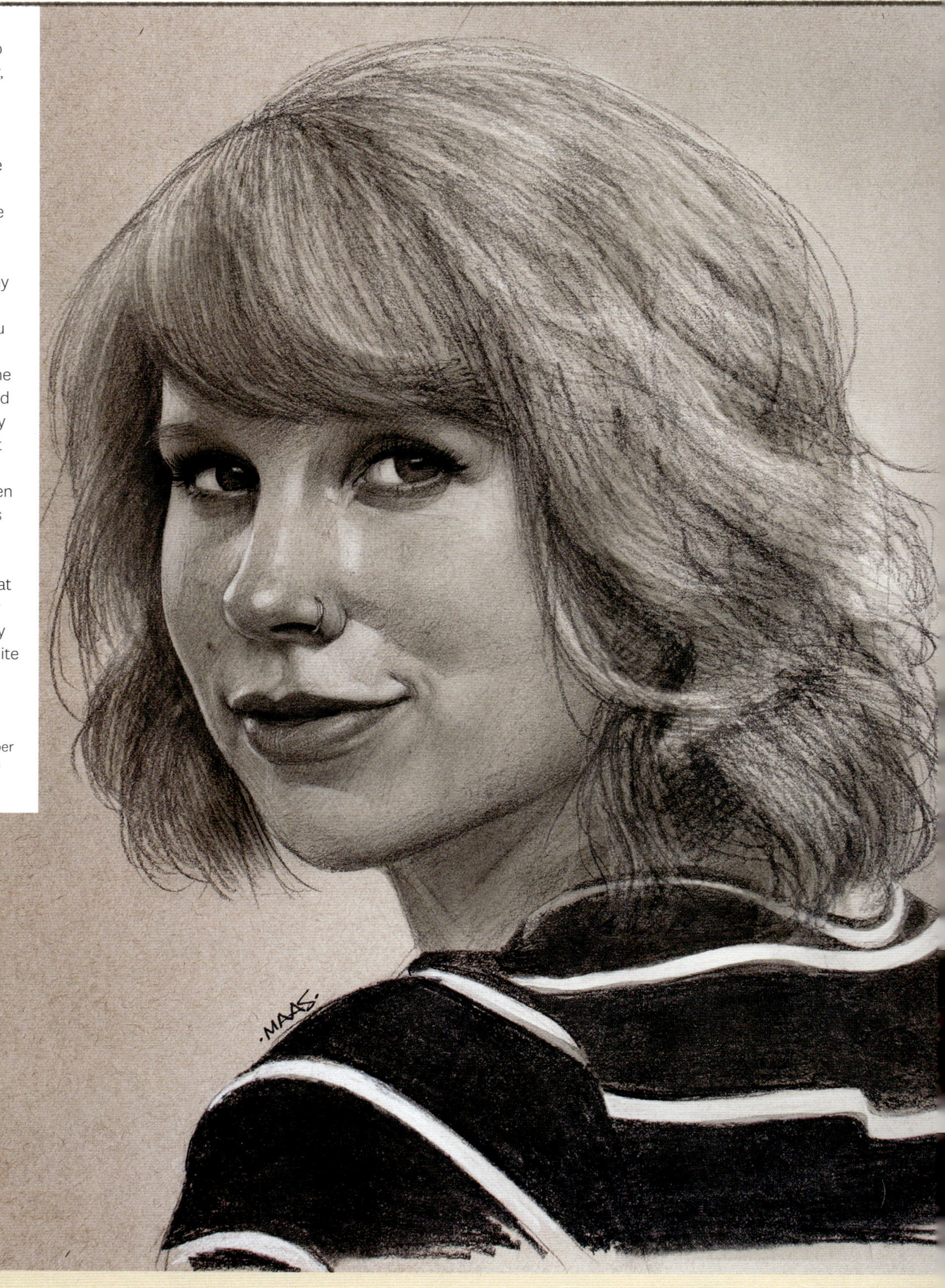

Grace
Graphite and white charcoal on toned paper
14" × 11" (36cm × 28cm)

WORKING FROM LIFE VS. PHOTOGRAPHS

Your references—whether photo, life or memory—are your means of getting the information necessary to draw your portrait. Drawing from life offers the greatest opportunity to get that information. You can walk around, see and sometimes even touch your reference. If you start your drawing and realize that you need to be just a few inches closer or at a slightly different angle, you can do this when you work from life. But working from life is often not practical. We all lead busy lives and even if you have the time to work with a live model, most of the people you ask to model will not!

There are many advantages to working from photos. The biggest advantage is that they don't move! Even the best model in the world will show some movement from start to finish in a session. Photos will always be the same, no matter how long it takes you to finish.

My personal preference is to do a series of sketches from life, get a feel for the model and what I want to express, then take photos for later. Then I work from the photos and my sketches back in the studio.

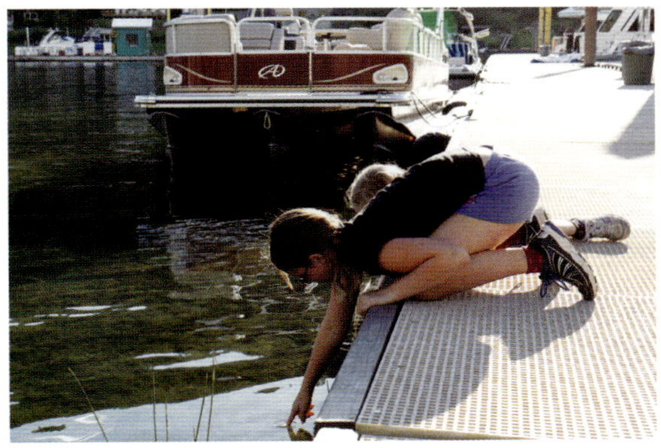

Be Aware of a Photo's Limits

Photos are a wonderful tool for the portrait artist but we must be aware of their limitations. Cameras capture what they see, but they also flatten things out and darken areas.

In this photo of my daughters, I like certain elements but would have to simplify and edit parts out of the background to keep the focus on the figures.

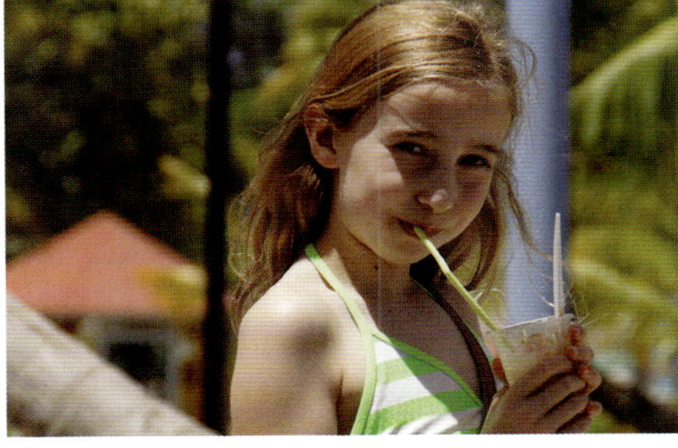

The Three-Quarter Turn

Most of the portraits in this book feature the subject with a slightly turned head. This is not a coincidence. When drawing a portrait, there is always more visual interest in a slightly turned head—often called a three-quarter turn.

In this photo of Ashley, you can see how by turning her a little (so she's not facing straight forward) we get a beautiful shadow down the side of her face, her shoulder and the tip of her nose. These elements create a strong foundation for a portrait.

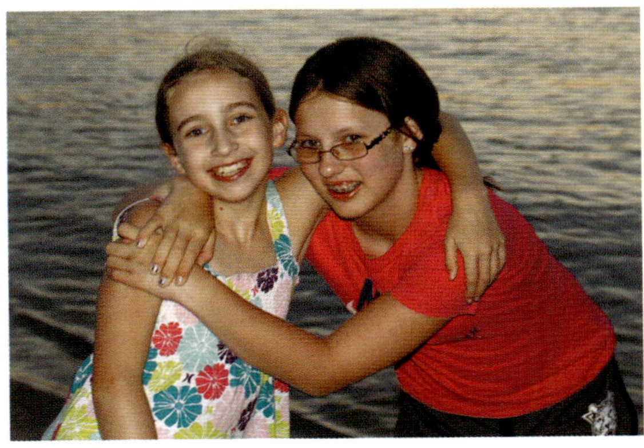

Choose Your Photos Carefully

One of the most common problems I see is when artists use reference photos that don't really look like the person in question. We've all seen photos of ourselves and thought, "Wow, that doesn't look like me." Various things can cause this, such as lighting, angle or posture. But let this be one of the first things you look for in a reference photo. Make sure your subjects look like themselves.

While this is a great family photo, it's not ideal for a portrait. The lighting isn't great, and the pose looks a little unnatural. There's a great family feeling in this photo that I would love to capture, but I would likely start with a different reference shot to achieve that sentiment.

WORKING FROM MULTIPLE PHOTOS

If you can't work from life, one of the things you can do to breathe life into your work is use a series of photos. This allows you to select certain aspects of your model from different images to achieve a composition. It also stops you from trying to make an exact copy of a photograph.

Most of the demos in this book use a single photograph, but when I work on my own pieces, I often use many references at once. In the example here, I used elements from five different photographs shot during one session with my model, Tovah. Here is the breakdown of how I combined them.

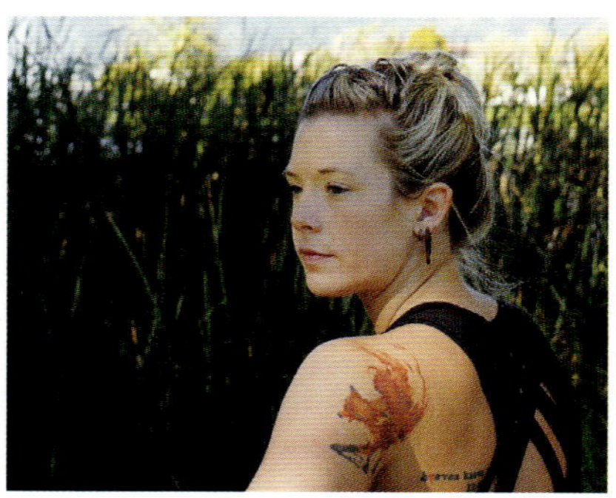

Photo 1
By keeping Tovah sharp in the foreground, the background takes on some mystery. I knew I wanted a more sweeping scene, but this sets up the idea for the background in my head.

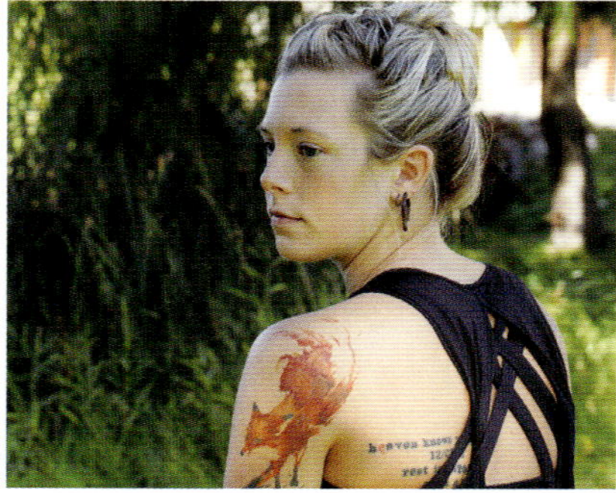

Photo 2
I liked how interesting the side of her face appears with the focus on the way the sunlight puts a sharp edge on the side of her face.

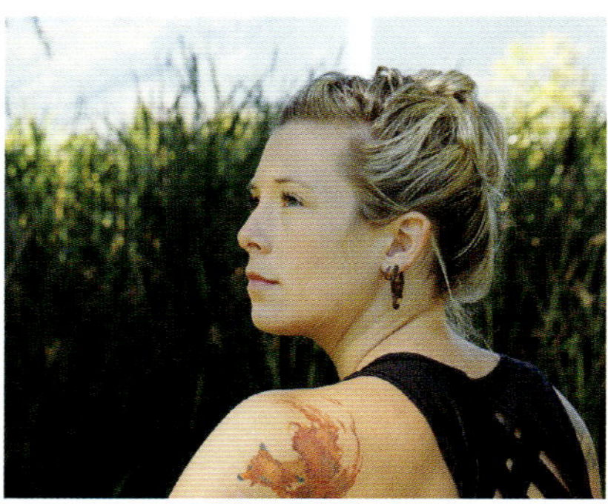

Photo 3
This is the expression I wanted to capture. Tovah looks focused and leaves us wondering what she is thinking.

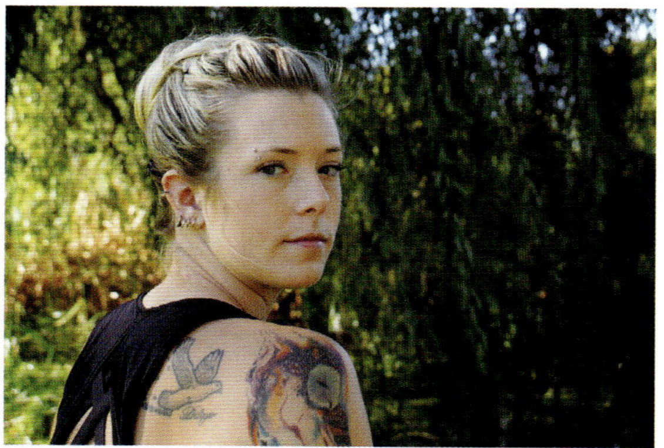

Photo 4
Here she looks directly at us. It's a nice photo but not the type of pose I had in mind for this piece. However, I liked the way the light is coming in strong from the left, highlighting the back of her hair.

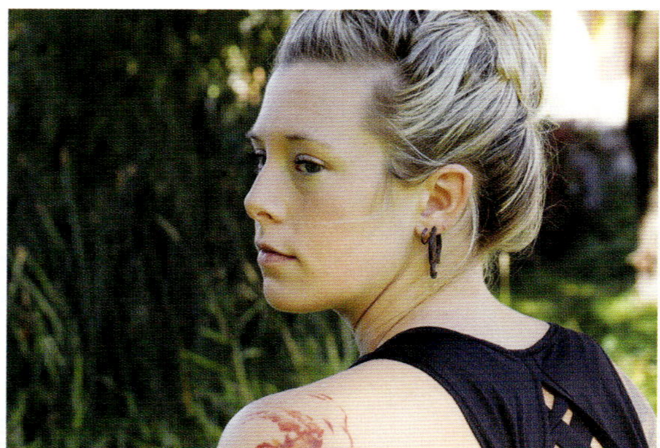

Photo 5
In this close-up photo, you can see wisps of hair as they cut across her face. This gave me the main focus for my drawing.

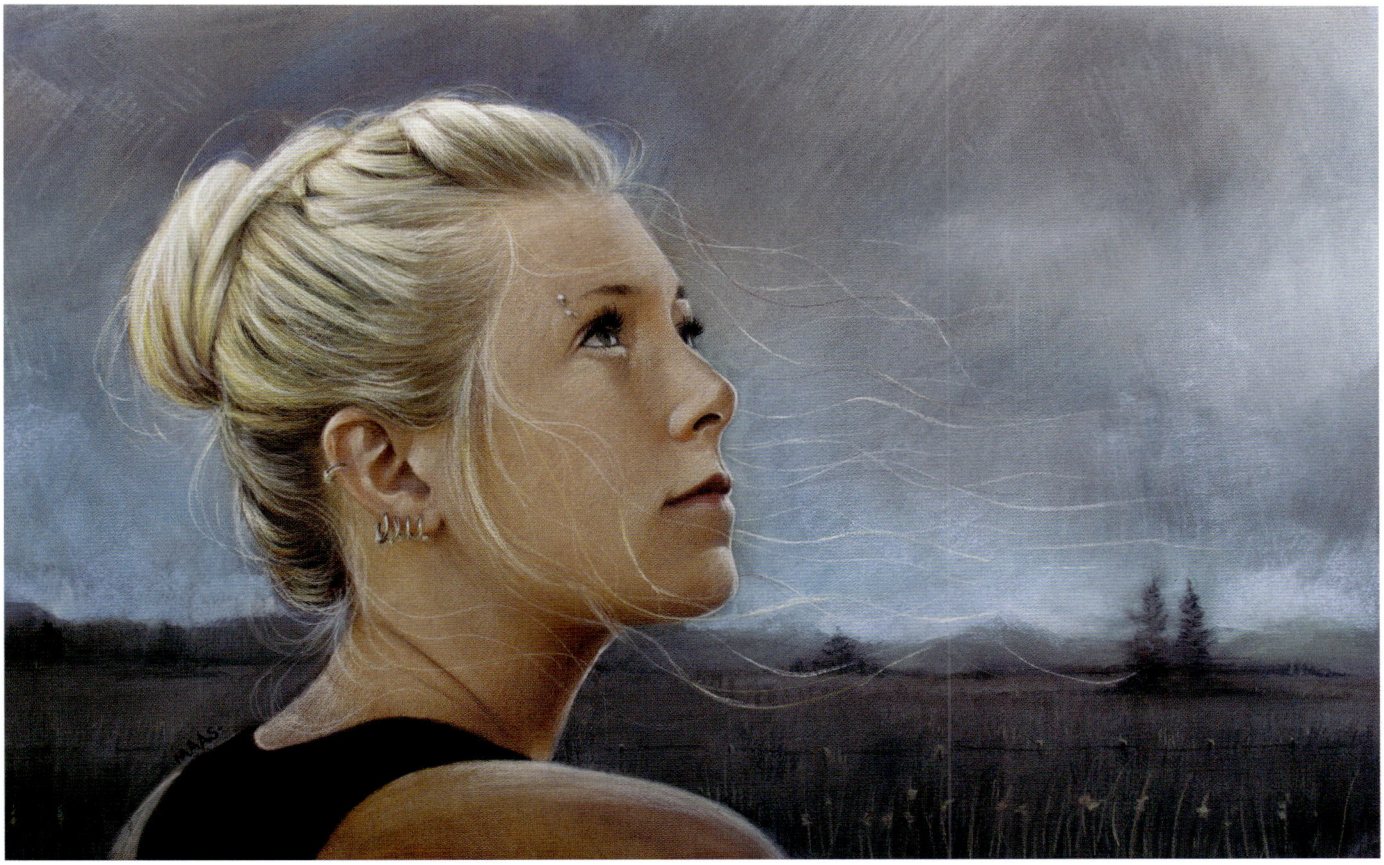

Finished Drawing

For the final piece, I decided to combine the enigmatic background from photo 1, the focus from photo 2, the expression from photo 3, the strong edge light from photo 4 and the wisps of hair from photo 5. In the end, I was able to achieve a successful piece by combining elements that I otherwise would have been unable to capture all at once.

Shelter from the Storm
Pastel on paper
14" × 24" (36cm × 61cm)

WORKING WITH A MODEL

Anyone can be a model! Most of us start with friends or family. The most important thing to remember when working with models is to keep them comfortable. An uncomfortable model will always yield unnatural results. Make sure your model is happy and having fun and you should get good results.

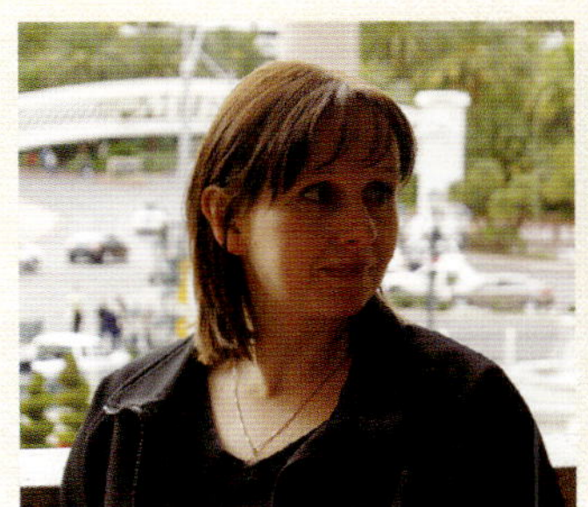

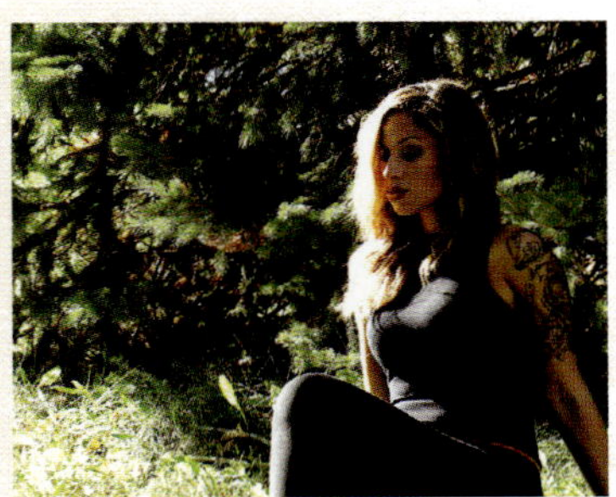

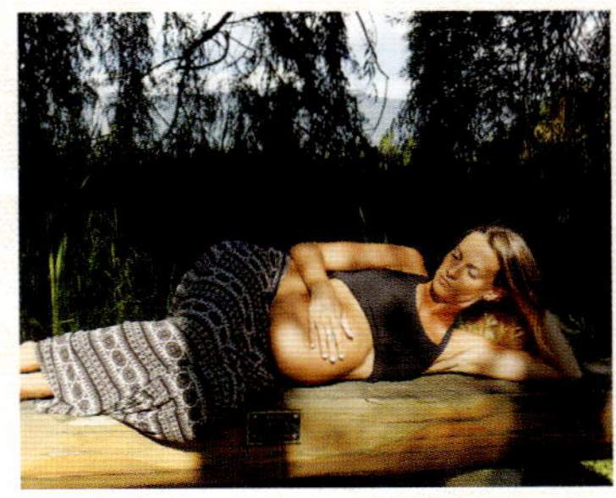

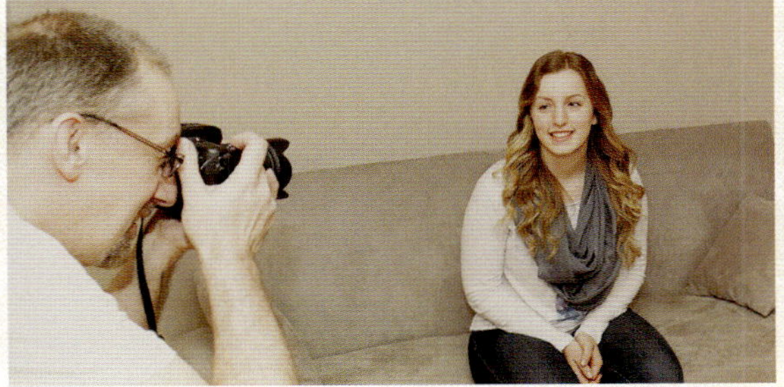

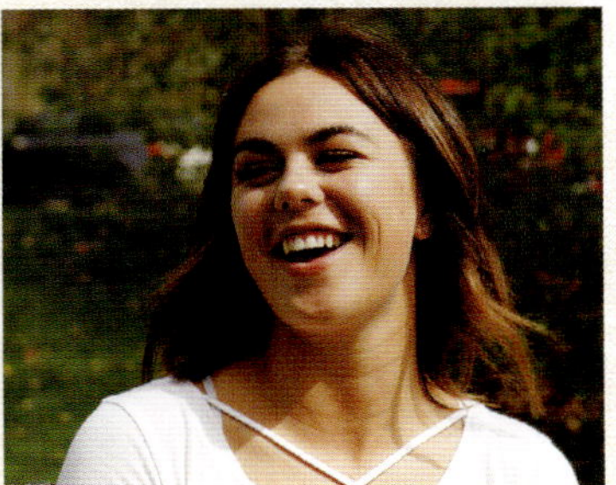

WORKING FROM LIFE

Asking a friend or family member to sit for a few photos is usually pretty easy. Asking them to sit still for an extended time so you can draw them from life is a lot harder; however, the reward is probably worth it.

These days I do the majority of my work from photos, but I have spent hundreds of hours working from live models. This is a step that can't be undervalued: drawing from life is very important in your development. So, what can you do to build this skill?

Try to draw people candidly: a friend watching TV, people on your daily train commute or passersby on your lunch break. Just keep it simple and fun.

You might also join a life-model session. Most cities and towns offer these, sometimes though a college, art museum or school. Many meet weekly and offer a variety of models. These sessions are invaluable for learning to draw from life and to help you practice. They are almost always fun, open to all skill levels and professional, so give one a try!

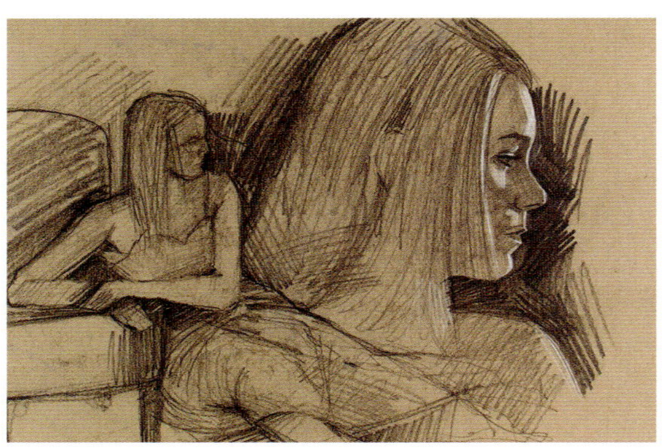

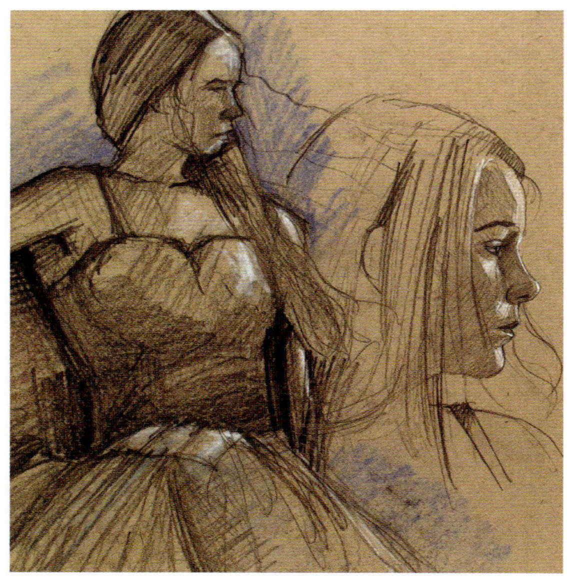

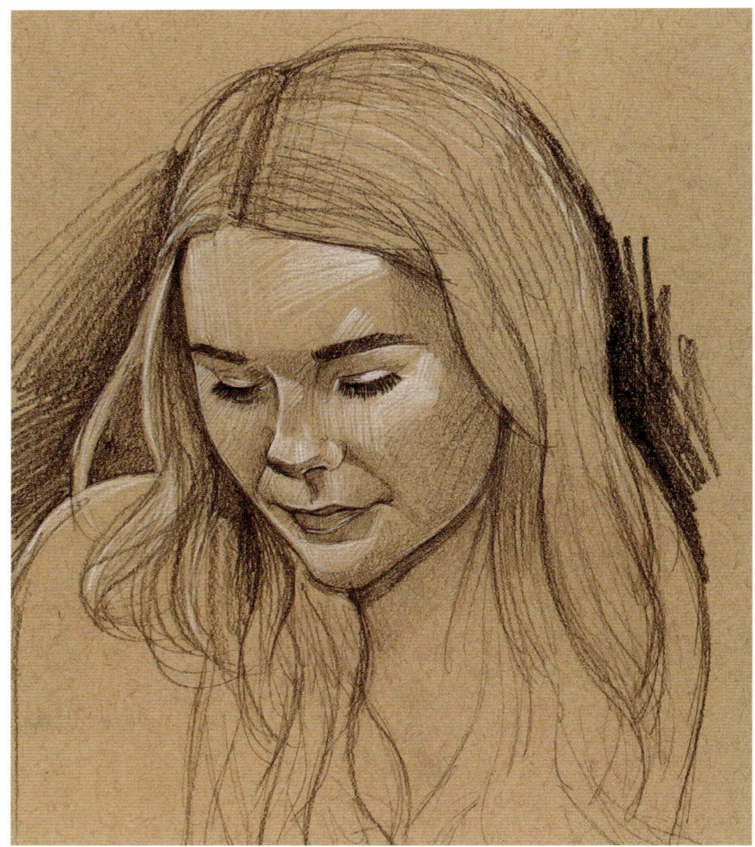

Sketching from Life

These sketches of Cassie were done during different life drawing sessions. Loose and fast, they capture her essence without worrying too much about detail. Because a live model always has the possibility of moving, artists will inherently work more quickly, which means they have less time to think and analyze, and more time to actually do it.

THE SELF-PORTRAIT

It goes without saying, but you've always got a model right at your fingertips: You! All you need is a mirror and you're all set. I prefer a wall-mounted mirror that you can position and move as you wish.

Drawing a self-portrait is not only a useful exercise for improving your overall skills, it can also be cathartic. Self-portraits are, in many ways, artists at their most vulnerable. We put ourselves on the page, both figuratively and literally. While I show almost all of my work publicly, my self-portraits sometimes aren't seen by anyone but me. Not even my family has seen all of them.

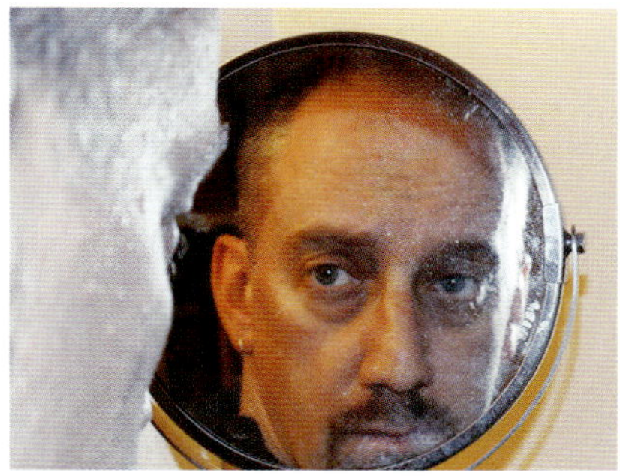

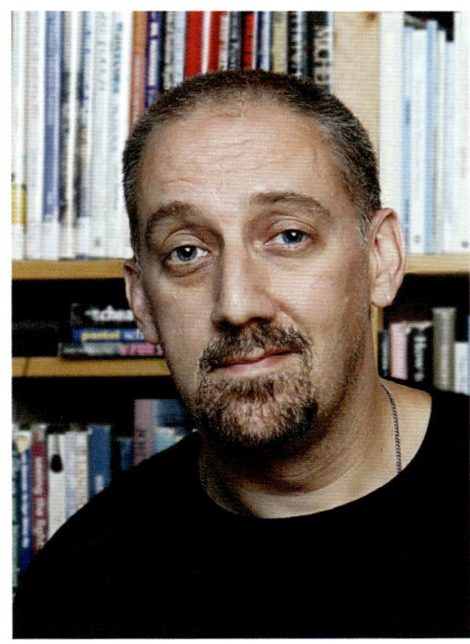

An Instant Model
Using an adjustable wall mirror and other photos of myself, I am able to explore expressions, decipher composition and understand lighting for both self-portraits and portraits of other people where I would like to adjust or change an aspect of the reference.

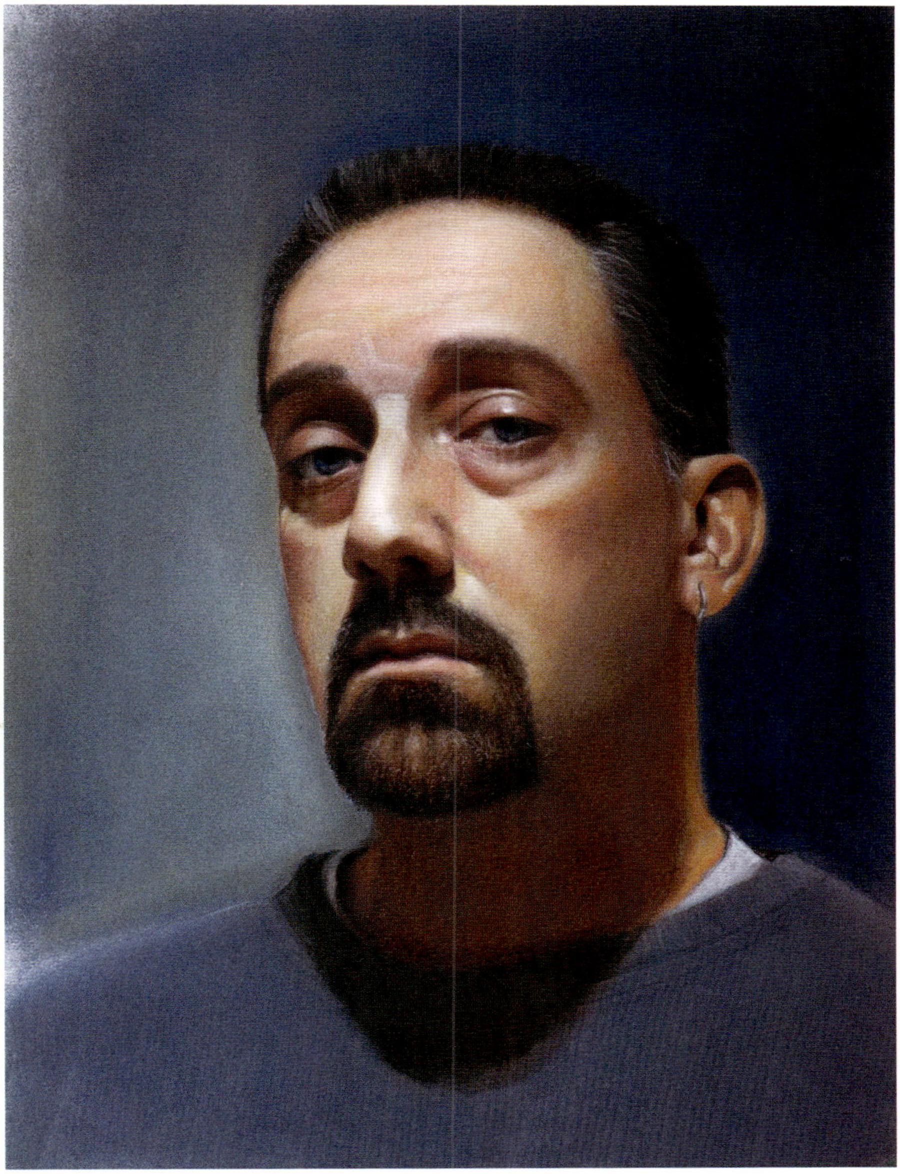

Just in Time
Pastel on sanded paper
16" × 12" (41cm × 30cm)

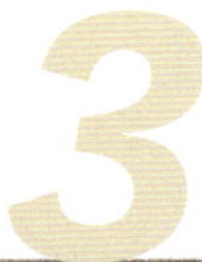

DRAWING THE HEAD AND FACE

The face is, for most people, the hardest subject to draw. Anatomically, the head and face are some of the least complex parts of the human body. The human skull consists of twenty-two bones with fourteen facial skeleton bones and eight cranial bones. By comparison, your two hands and arms have a total of 128 bones.

So if the face is so simple compared to the rest of the body, it should be relatively easy to draw, right? Wrong.

But why? The main reason is familiarity. If you draw an elephant 70 percent right, people will look at it and say "great elephant." But if you draw a person—especially a subject known to the viewer—even 1 percent wrong, they will say "looks good but something is not quite right." The average person does not see elephants very often, but we see human beings every single day.

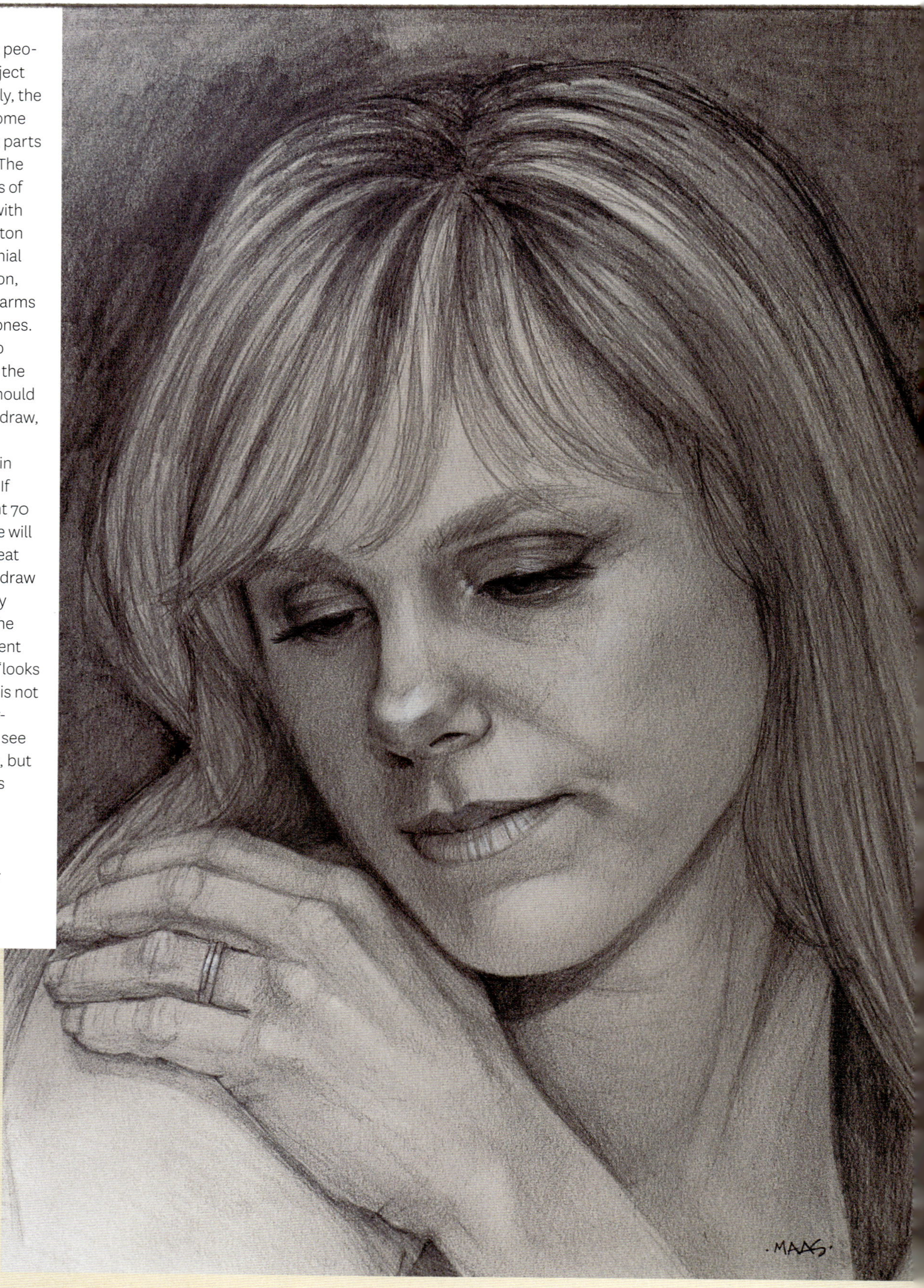

Melissa
Graphite and white charcoal on toned paper
14" × 11" (36cm × 28cm)

PRACTICE DRAWING A SKULL

Good drawing starts with the underlying structure. We've all seen movies where the stereotypical artist has a skull in her studio. There is a reason for this! Understanding underlying anatomy is crucial for mastering the drawing of the face.

Drawing a skull is not only an interesting exercise, it helps you break down the basic shapes of the human head without the distractions of features. Thus, by understanding the anatomy of the skull, you will be able to understand the placement of features better. It's a process that should not be skipped.

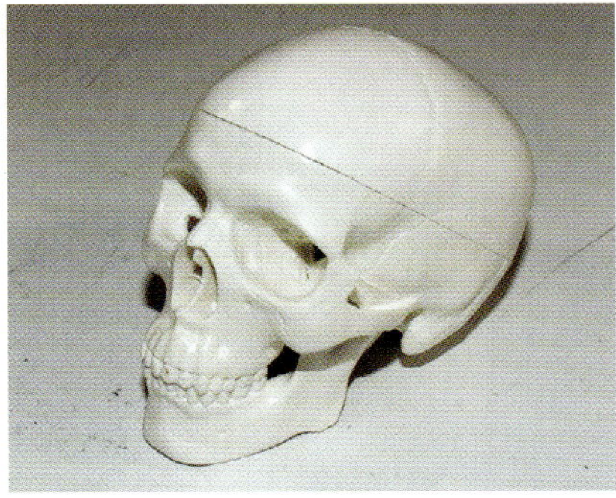

Invest in a Prop Skull
A mannequin or prop skull is a worthwhile investment for your studio. Many art stores sell various models ranging in size, detail and cost.

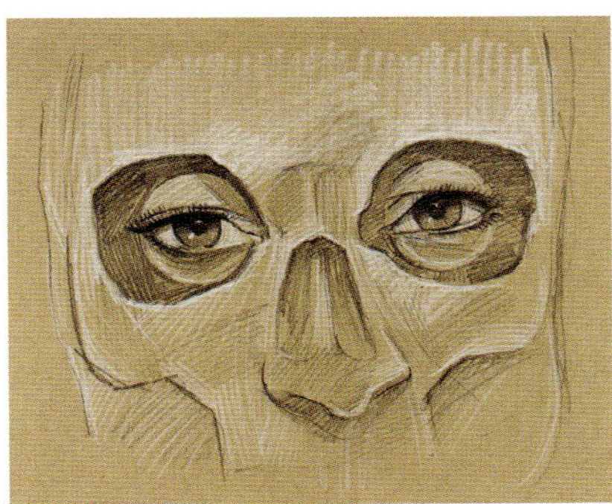

Understanding Skull Structure
On a skull it's easy to see that the eye sockets are roughly halfway up the face. On a human, this can be trickier because we get distracted by the hairline or by things like eye makeup and lipstick. All of these additional features fool our eyes into believing that the eyes are much higher up the face, which is how many people draw them.

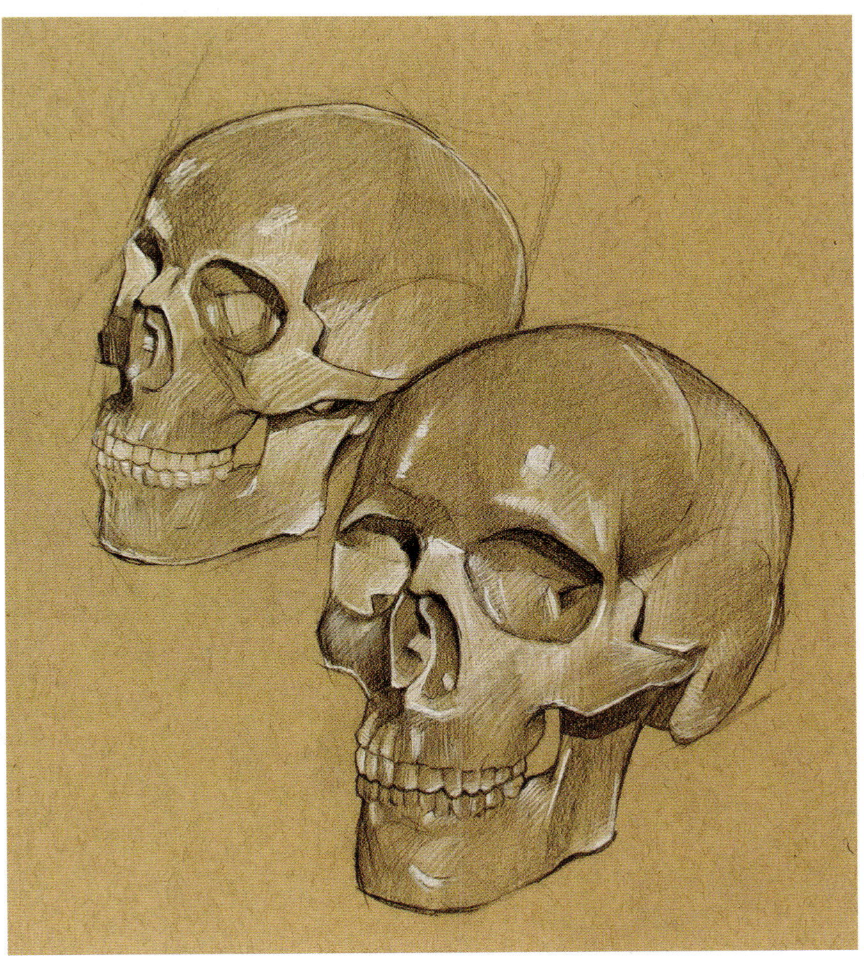

Skulls Aren't Just for Halloween
Aside from being fun to draw, skulls offer a myriad of lessons for the artist. Shape, proportion and visual planes are all understood better by drawing skulls. The added bonus is that, as you draw a skull, you are learning about facial anatomy without even realizing it.

BASIC FACIAL STRUCTURE

It is important to remember that every face is different. Even the slightest nuance can drastically change your appearance—and therefore recognizability.

So how do we create a portrait that looks correct? The first step is to understand the basic structure of the average human face. There are general guidelines that apply to the proportions of most faces. These guidelines allow us to measure the space between features and create a sort of roadmap to the face. Study the lines in the photographs and the key features in the sidebar to understand the basics.

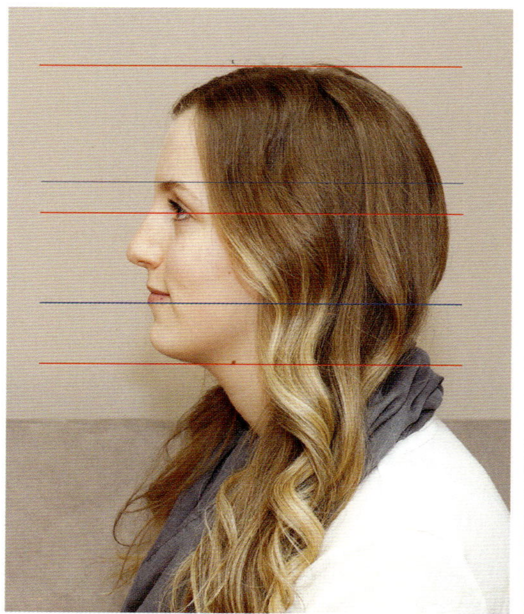

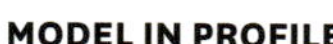

MODEL IN PROFILE

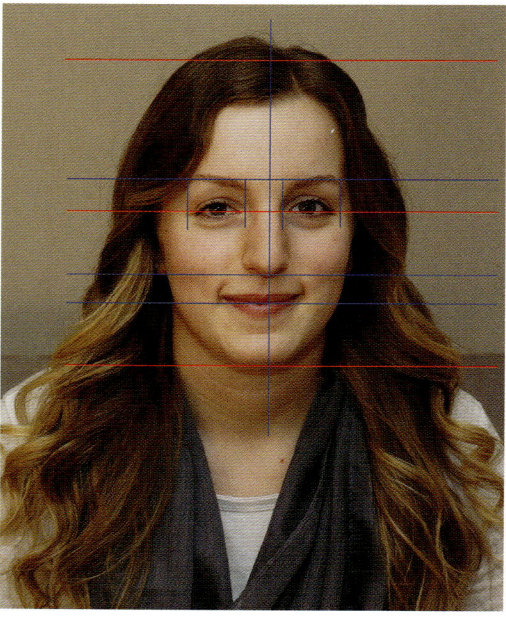

MODEL STRAIGHT ON

Guidelines for Facial Features

In this side-by-side comparison, you see the model straight on as well as in profile. Closely examine the lines placed over these photos. See the relationship between features such as the brow and lips, and the hairline, eye line and base of the chin. For instance, if you look at the lines indicating the top of her head (note that if your model has thick hair this can be just below the hairline) and her chin, you will see that the eye line is almost halfway between those two points. This gives you a good starting point for placing features.

BASIC RELATIONSHIPS OF FACIAL FEATURES

Keep in mind that these are *generally* true for most faces. Many measurements can vary slightly, which is what creates our own unique looks. Most faces are close to these averages, but never exact. These rules offer a good starting point and if you look at your drawing and notice something looks wrong, there is a good chance one or more of these relationships is off.

- The nose bisects the face almost in half. The curve at the top of the nose is generally in the middle of the face, right between the eyes.
- The eyes are roughly halfway between the top of the head (below the hairline) and the chin.
- The bottom of the nose is halfway between the eye line and the bottom of the chin.
- The mouth is almost halfway between the bottom of the nose and the chin.
- The ears line up with the mouth and the eye line (or just below it).
- The edges of the nostrils line up with the (inner) edges of the eyes.
- The eyes are one eye width apart.
- The base of the nose (including nostrils) is typically one eye width.
- The corners of the mouth line up with the centers of the eyes.

PROPORTIONS AND SYMMETRY

If you were to follow the guidelines in the Basic Relationships sidebar using those exact generalizations, this is what our results would be. One of the things you notice immediately, besides the obvious perfect proportions, is the symmetry of the facial features.

If you were to split each drawing in half and mirror it, both sides would look the same. This is not true of most human faces. Usually we have bends in our noses and eyes that are different shapes or sitting at a different height.

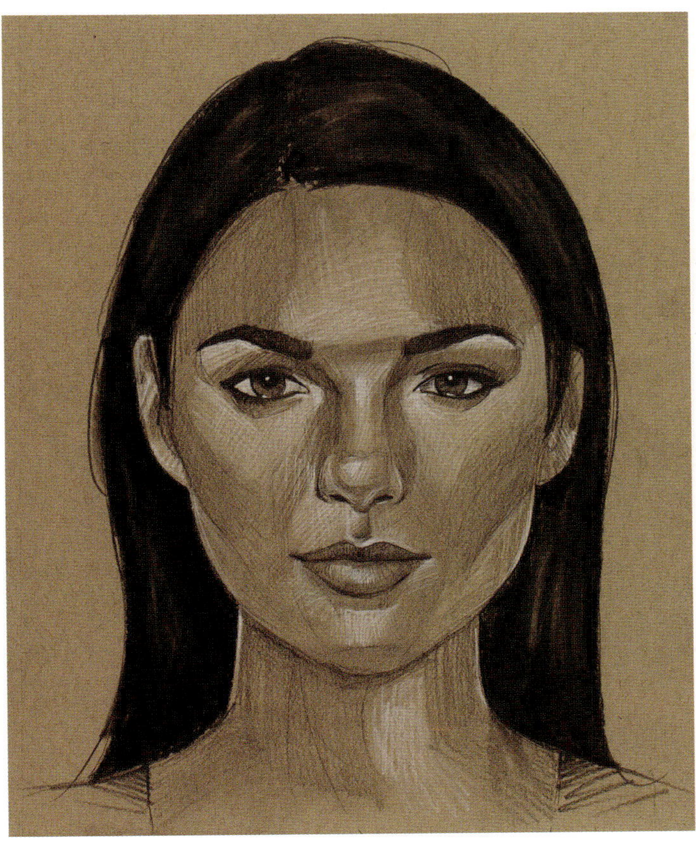

Symmetrical Female Portrait
Features are generally smaller and softer (having fewer sharp edges) on a female than on a male. The chin recedes and tapers, the cheekbones are lower and more curved. The eyes are usually larger but softer with more value changes, and the eyebrows are higher and curve more.

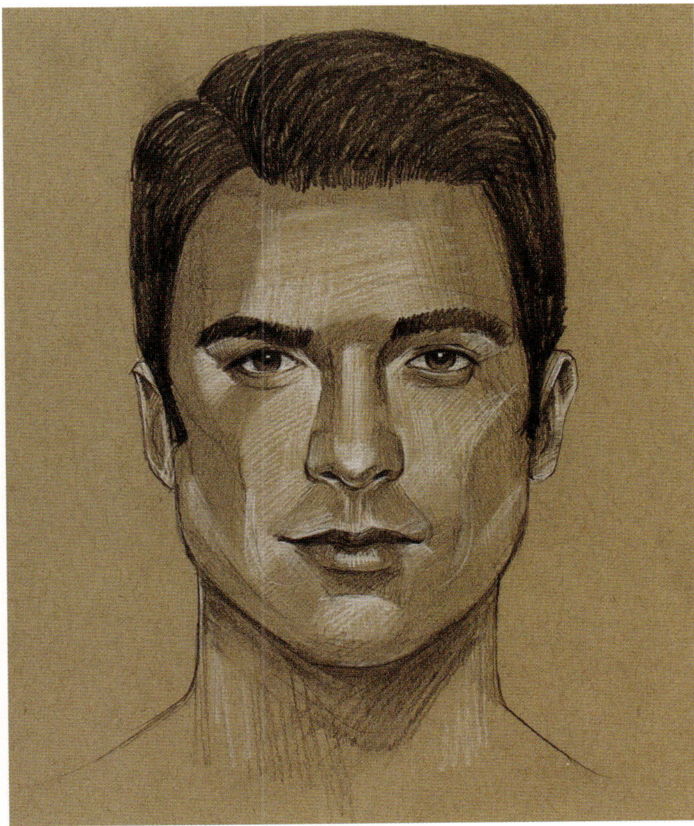

Symmetrical Male Portrait
On males, features are generally larger and sharper. The chin protrudes and is wider, the cheekbones are more angular, and the eyes are usually smaller. The eyebrows are usually straighter.

WHAT MAKES A LIKENESS

Many elements go into creating a successful portrait. But while we often spend a great deal of time and effort focusing on individual features, it is the *placement* of those features that is the most important principle in achieving a likeness.

If you find yourself fixating on the details of a nose or mouth, stop yourself and remember that it is the overall shape, form and placement of these objects that is more important. This is why you can still recognize a friend from a distance or when they are wearing sunglasses. It's why when your neighbor grows a moustache (or shaves one) you still know it's him. We see overall shapes long before we see singular features.

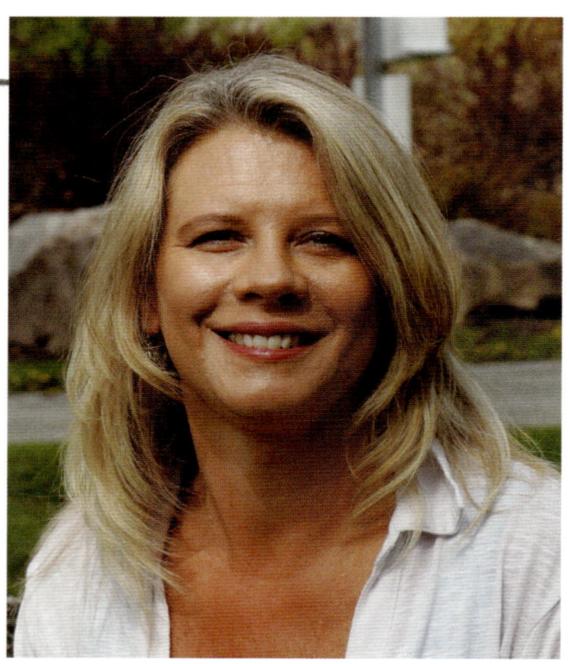

Photo Reference: Sharon

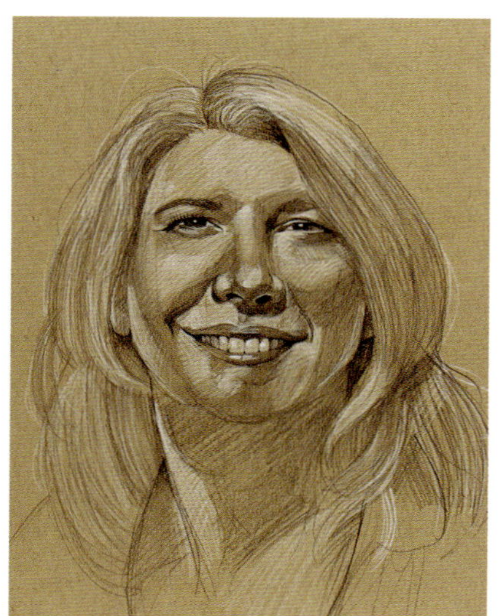

Detailed Features/Inaccurate Placement

This is an odd-looking portrait. It looks a little like Sharon, but in alien form. Surprisingly, the features are 100 percent accurate in this portrait. Her eyes, nose and mouth are exactly the right size compared to the reference. The problem is, they are not in the right places. This shows you how important placement is.

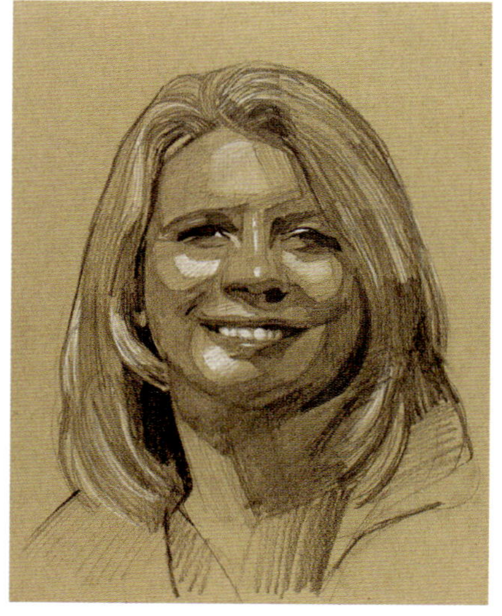

Loose Features/Accurate Placement

Here is a simple form-only portrait. Her features are loosely defined, yet her likeness is recognizable. This demonstrates how overall placement is more important than getting the individual features exactly right.

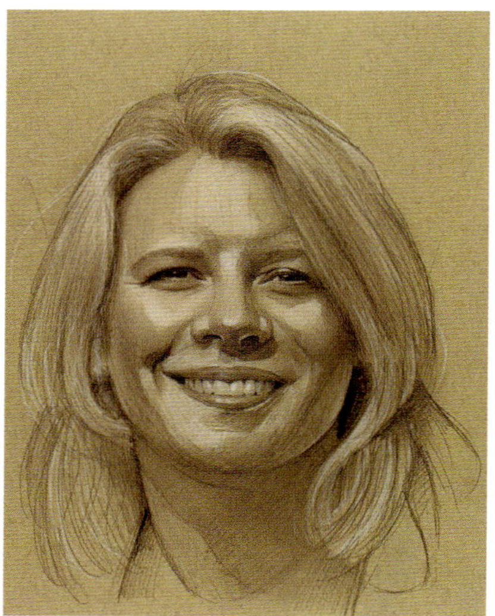

Detailed Features/Accurate Placement

In this example, we have detailed, accurate features that are also in the correct places. It captures her likeness well. To achieve portrait results like this, it is crucial to spend time getting your proportions and the relationships between features just right.

FACIAL EXPRESSIONS

This series of quick sketches shows how much a face can change depending upon expression. We often think that an expression changes entirely based on the mouth, but in fact most of the features in the face are affected by different expressions. The eyes, the mouth and the nose, even the shape of the face, can vary a lot when someone changes expression.

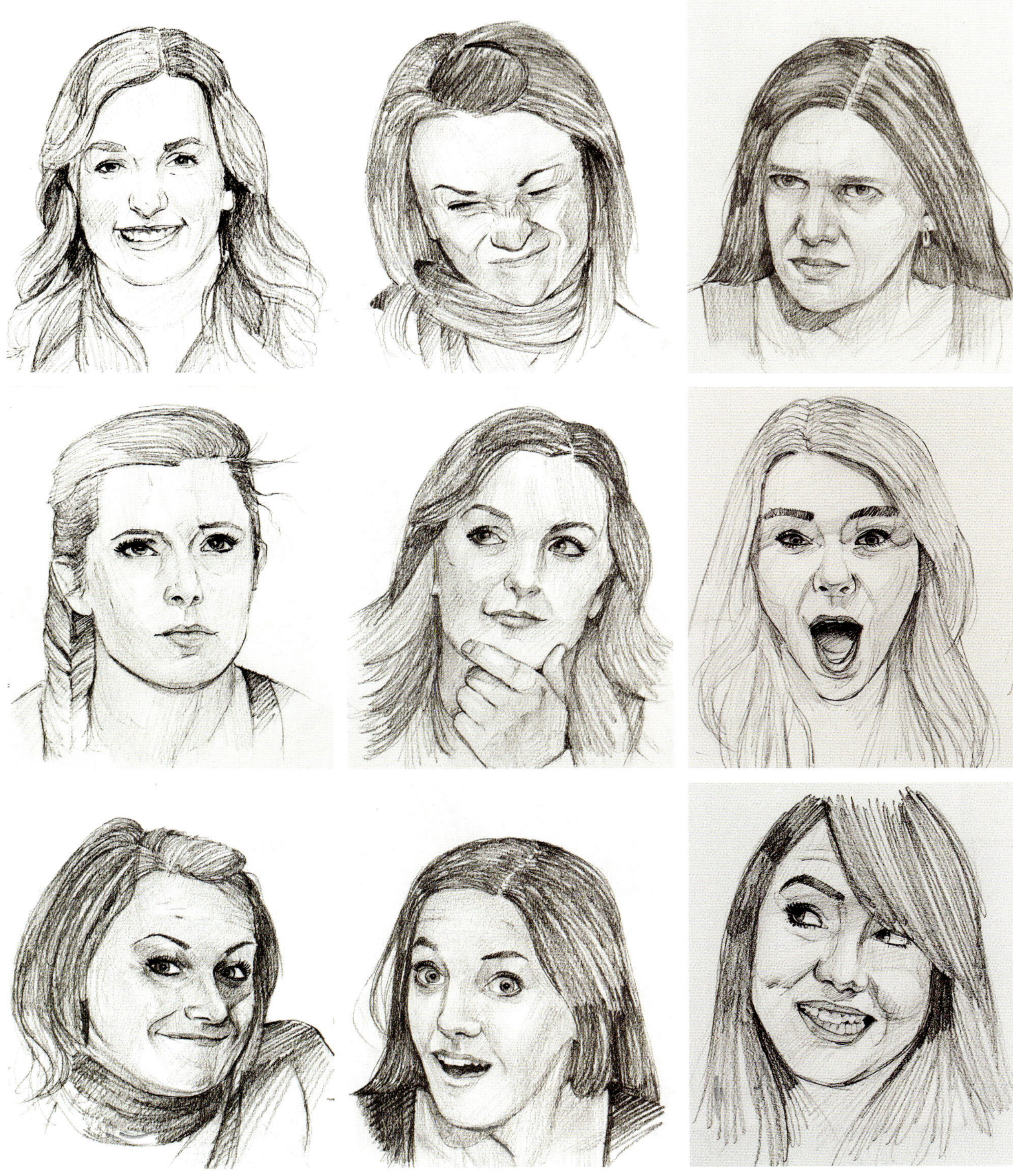

THE EYES

You may be familiar with the saying "the eyes are the windows to the soul." As such, the eyes are one of the most, if not the single most, important feature in any standard portrait. They are usually what the viewer notices first.

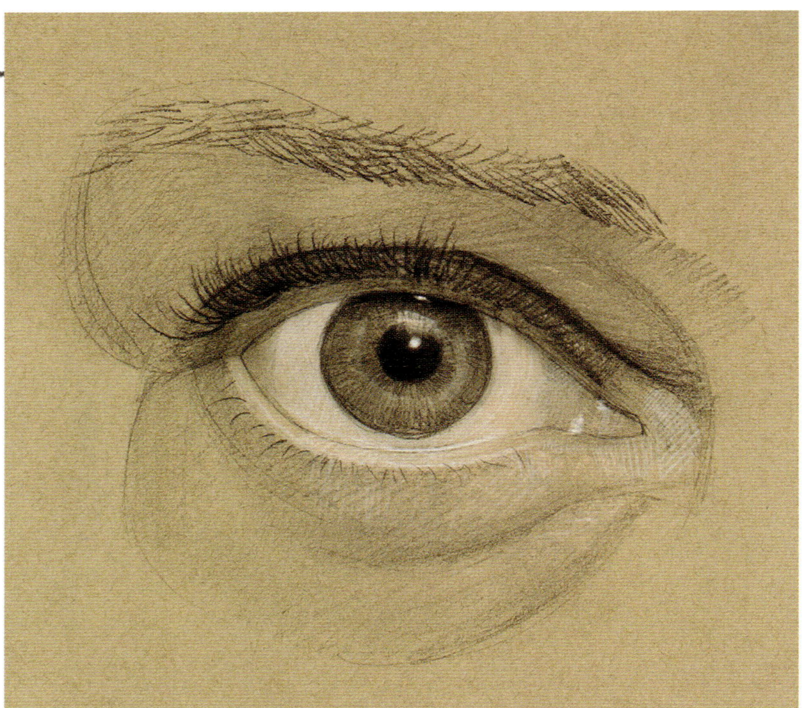

Basic Eye Structure

It is important to understand the basic structure of the eye, which is essentially a sphere covered on all sides with skin. As important as the eyes are, some of the most common mistakes in portraiture are made when rendering the eyes. Here are two things to keep in mind to avoid these pitfalls:

- The eye is like any other object in nature: it has form, it is subject to shadows (from the eyelid) and it needs to be rendered with volume.
- The eyeball almost never appears totally white. It's typically closer to a 10 to 20 percent gray (depending upon lighting). Revisit our discussion on value and highlights in chapter 1. The actual highlight on the eyeball—often only a hint of pure white—will be the most effective and dramatic.

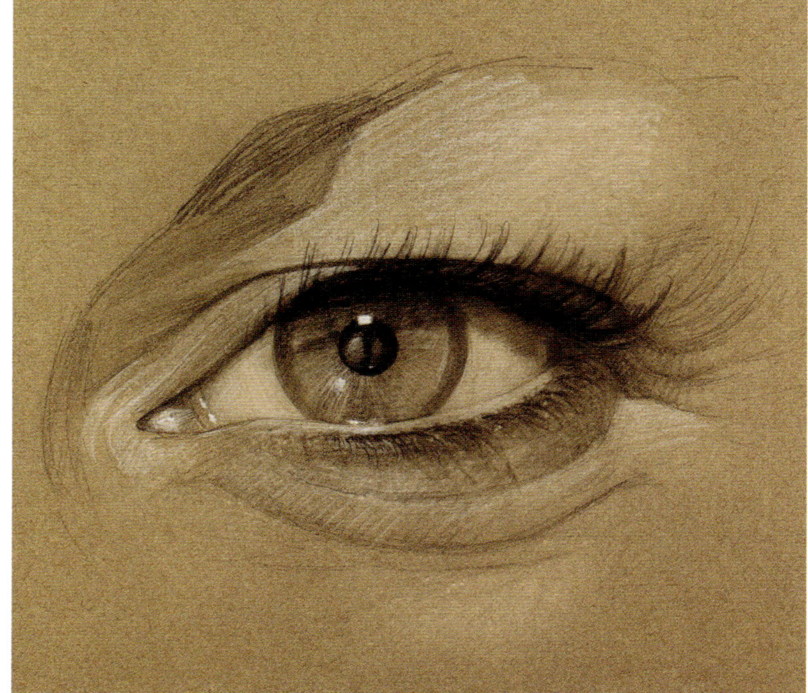

Importance of Eyelashes

Remember that eyelashes are important, too. We spend a lot of time shaping and darkening our eyelashes to make our eyes pop, so as artists we want to apply that same principle to our drawings. Pay special attention to the form of the eyelashes. They are almost never straight, and they taper as they extend.

DRAW AN EYE

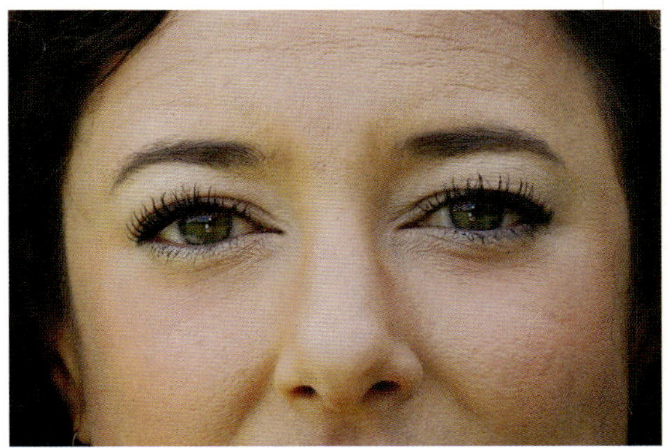

Reference Photo

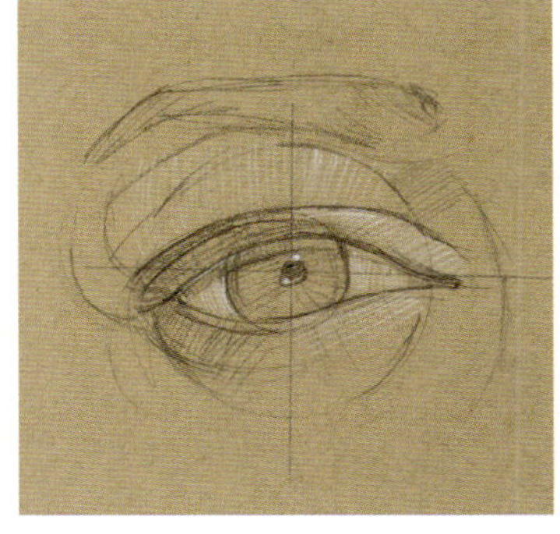

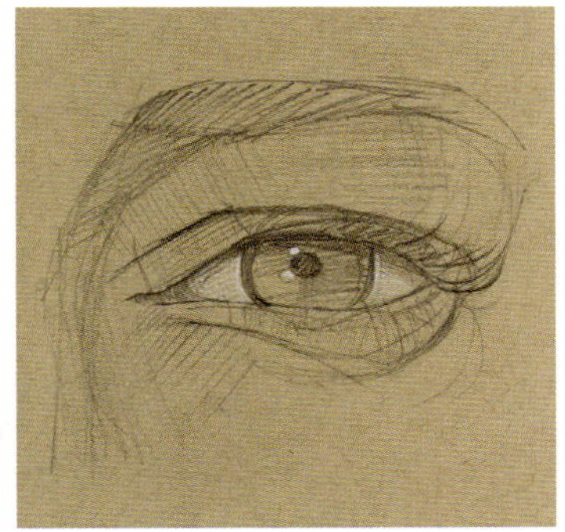

Thumbnail Sketches

Consider the eyeball before the skin (eyelids) drapes over it. We know an eyeball is almost spherical. So how does that affect the shadows, the shapes of the skin folds and creases? It helps to understand the contours and basic elements of the eye before attempting to draw them. Really study the shapes, don't just draw what you remember.

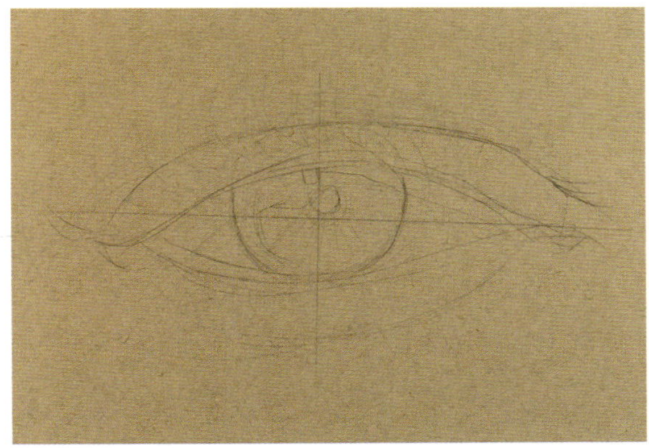

1 ***DEFINE THE SHAPES***

Begin with two perpendicular lines that a circle can be built off of. Very lightly indicate the pointed shape of the eyelid and the crease above it. It is important to work lightly because some of these lines will be erased. Indicate the pupil, noticing where it actually is and not where you *think* it should be.

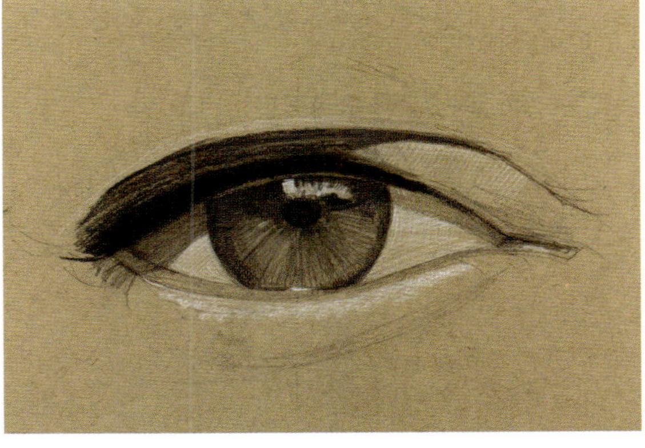

2 ***ADD THE VALUES***

Introduce tone and contrast. Remember that the eyeball itself has form. There will be shadow cast from the eyelid onto the sphere and there will be volume to the eyeball itself.

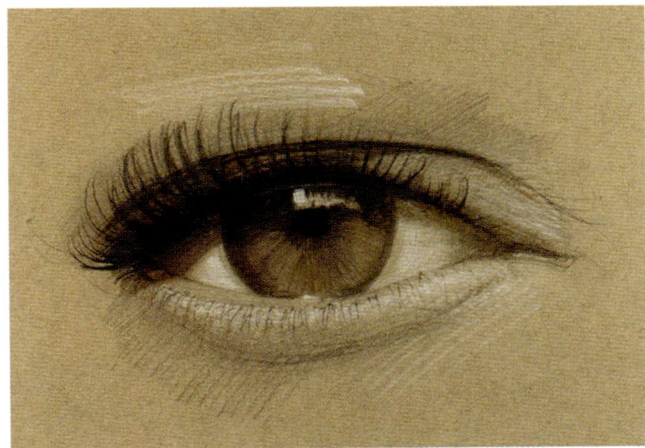

3 ***REFINE AND ADD DETAILS***

Add the finishing touches: eyelashes, more shadows and highlights (there is often a highlight right where the iris meets the lower eyelid).

Remember to refer back to your reference. One classic error when drawing the eye is to stop looking at the reference and draw what we think we know. Notice that the eyelashes have volume—they curve—and the iris is lighter and darker in areas based on how much light hits it.

THE NOSE

The nose is one of the most interesting parts of the face. It can be challenging, as it is made up of a series of planes that are mostly curved. For this reason, it's important to pay attention to the volume of the nose as you draw it.

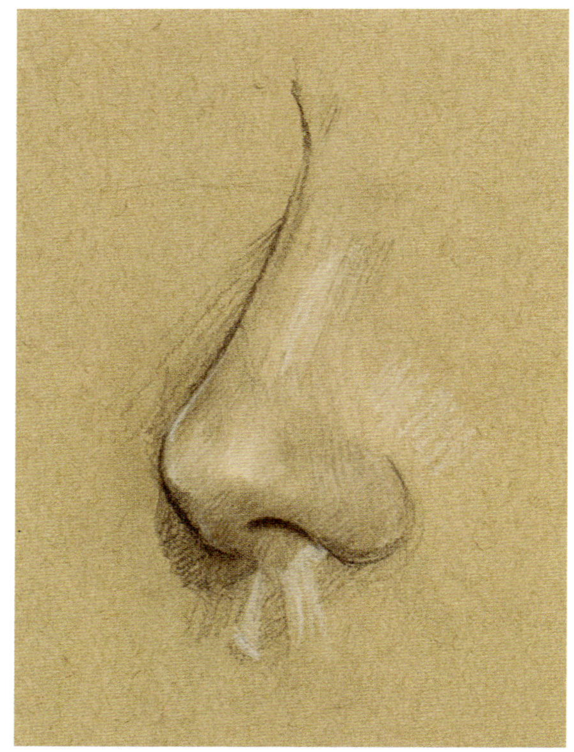

Basic Nose Structure

You will notice that many portraits feature a slightly turned head rather than head-on. This makes it easier to show volume in the nose, often creating a more visually interesting portrait.

A common mistake is to make the highlights too prominent or obvious. In this illustration, note the effectiveness of the subtle highlights and soft transitions.

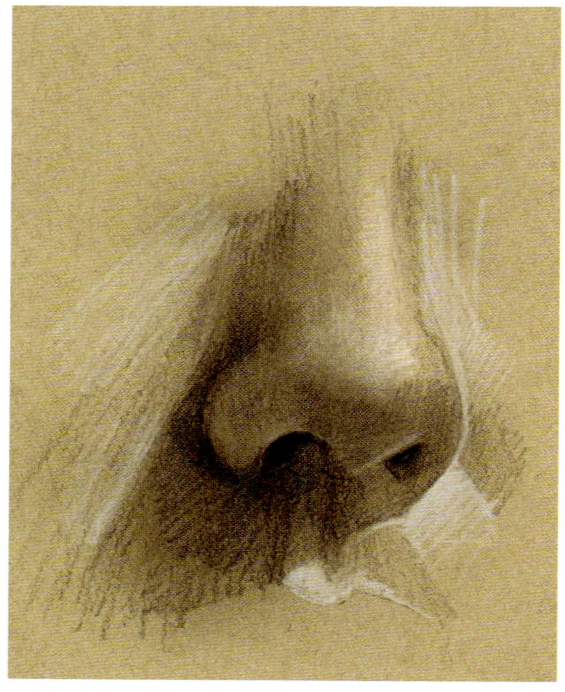

Importance of Nose Shadows

Here is a nose from the front. Shadows help to define volume, but you also have to pay special attention to the values (especially in the nostrils). Check your reference against your grayscale finder. You'll see that areas you think are very dark are in fact only 70 or 80 percent gray.

Also keep in mind that because it sticks out farther than any other feature on the face, the nose usually throws a bigger shadow than any other part of the face.

DRAW A NOSE

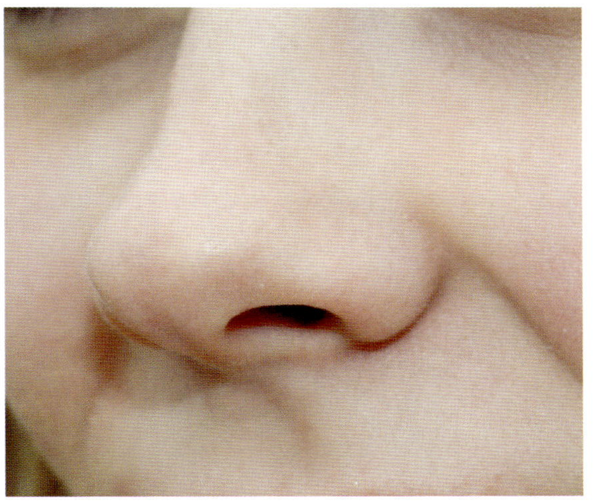

Reference Photo

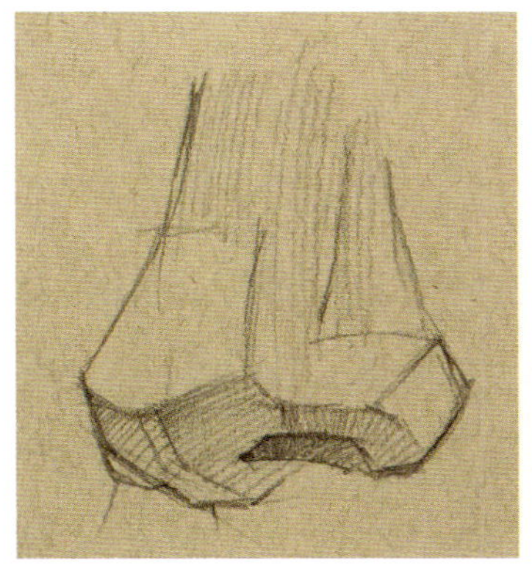

Thumbnail Sketches

To understand the nose, it helps to break it down into a series of planes and shapes. Notice how the nose renders equally well with angles and lines as it does with circles and rounded shapes.

1 ***INDICATE THE FEATURES***

Lightly indicate a series of simple geometric lines. The nose is almost never straight, but when you place your first indication lines it's fine to draw them straight. As you work, adjust and find the right lines and shapes by deviating from these straight lines.

2 ***ADD THE VALUES***

Begin to indicate lights and darks. The underside of the nose will be the darkest part, while the top of the nose will be the lightest. Where these two areas join (at the front of the nose) is often the most interesting part of the whole portrait. Pay special attention to it.

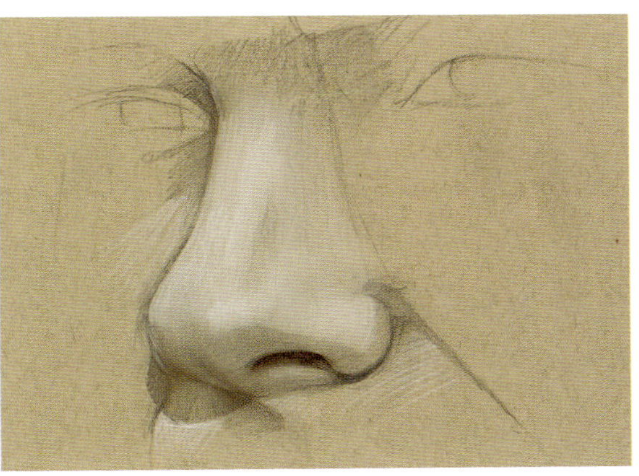

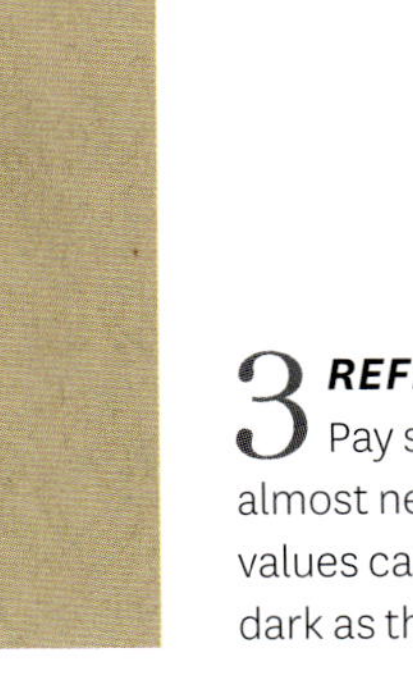

3 ***REFINE AND ADD DETAILS***

Pay special attention to the nostrils—they are almost never as dark as you think they should be and values can vary a lot (much of the nostril is only half as dark as the darkest part).

THE MOUTH

The mouth is the most unusual feature on the face (especially the lips) and one of the most difficult for artists to get right (especially the teeth). At first glance, what we see mostly of the mouth are the lips.

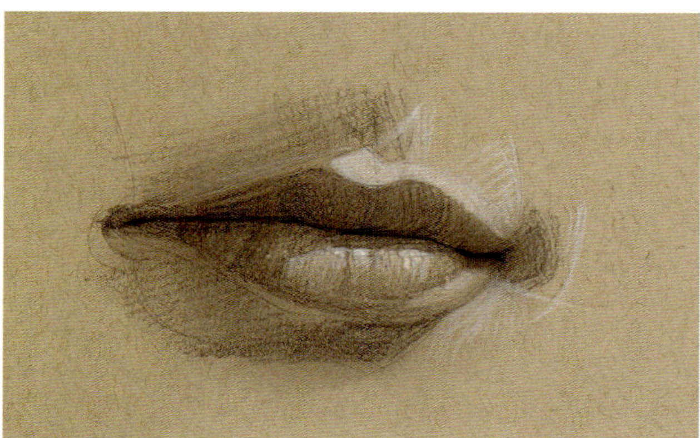

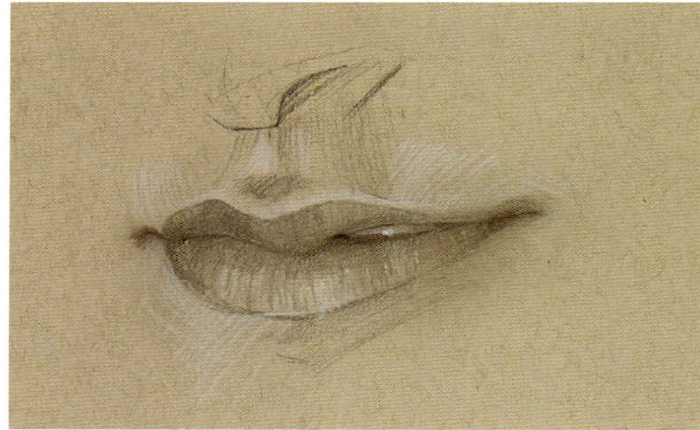

Basic Lip Structure

The lips move freely, are flexible and soft. What makes the lips so unusual in structure compared with other facial features is that they are essentially the transition between the interior of our face (the mouth) and our exterior skin. This is especially apparent in the corners of the mouth, where the division between the lips and the skin becomes increasingly hard to find.

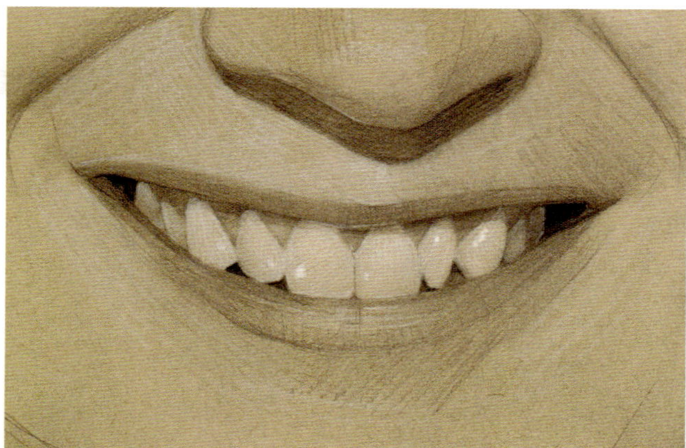

Avoid Too Much White

The teeth, much like the eyes, are often given too much white and therefore look forced. "Less is more," is a very useful saying to bear in mind when it comes to teeth.

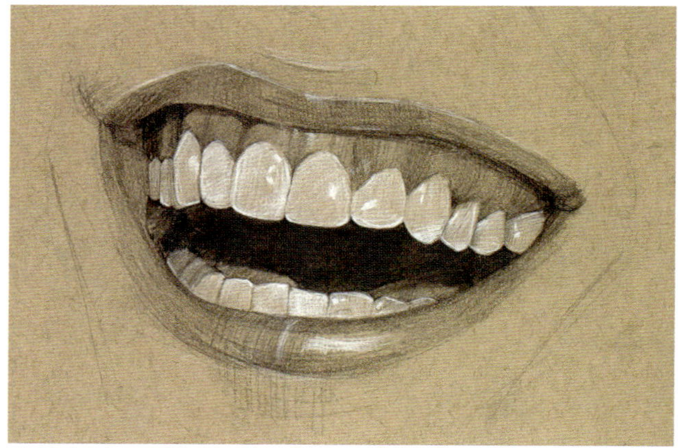

Don't Outline the Teeth

When we look at someone who is smiling we do not see each individual tooth. We actually see the teeth as one large light mass. So it is important not to overemphasize the divisions between teeth.

DRAW A MOUTH

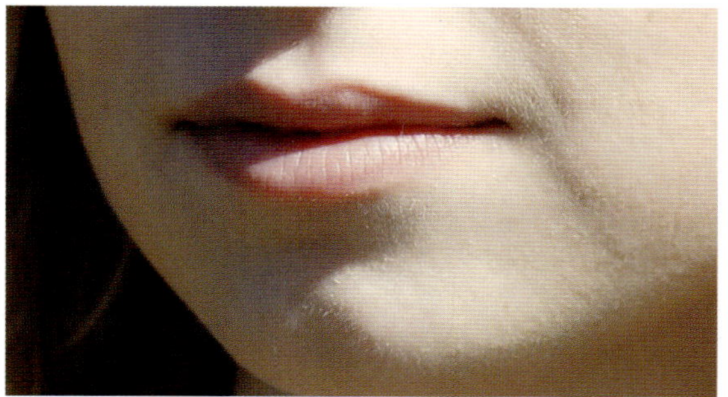

Reference Photo

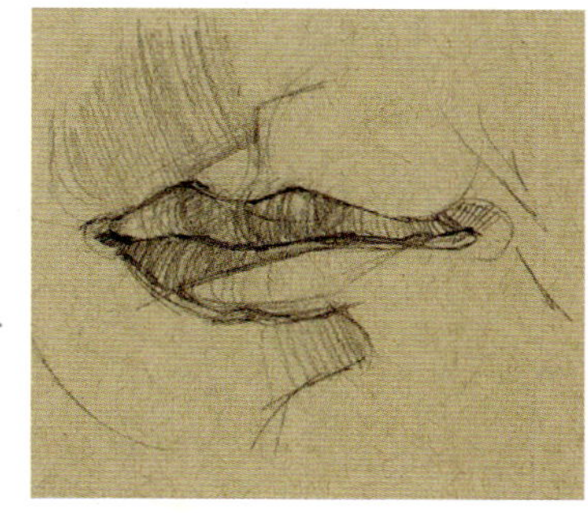

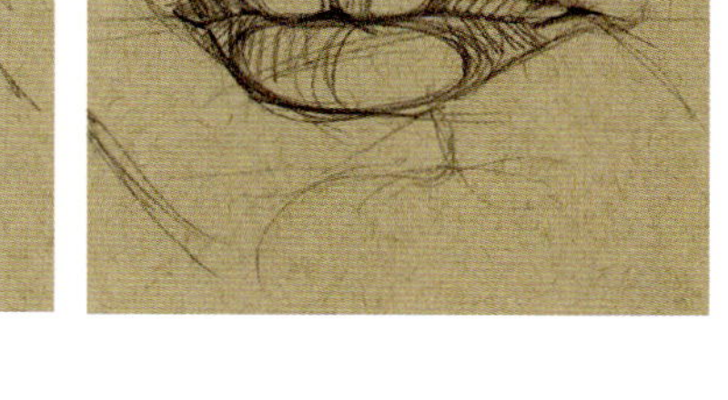

Thumbnail Sketches

The closed mouth is best thought of as a series of ovals laying horizontally. Notice how the shapes cast shadows—these shadows are crucial for correctly indicating the volume of the lips.

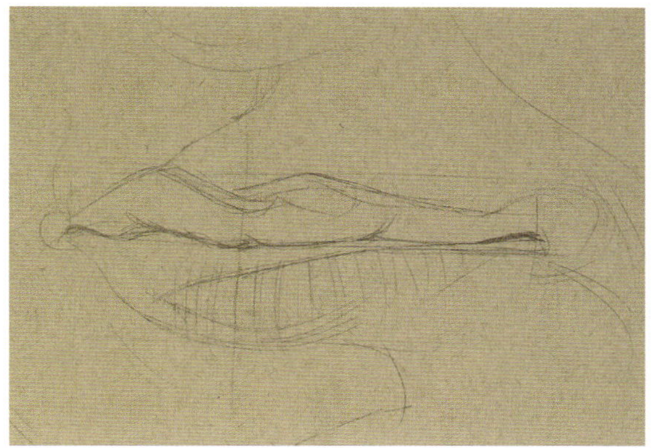

1 *DEFINE THE SHAPES*

Indicate the basic shapes of the mouth. They will usually fit within a horizontal rectangle. Look at the shadows and highlights as shapes, not as elements on top of the features. This will help you get the proportions right.

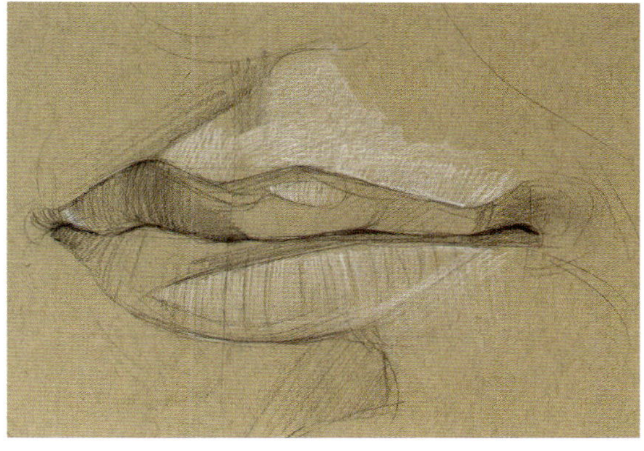

2 *ADD THE SHADOWS*

More than any other feature, shadows define the mouth and give it volume. The upper lip faces slightly down so it almost always is in shadow while the lower lip usually has a strong amount of highlights. Define the line between the two lips, but notice that it is never a solid thickness throughout. Vary the line width and pressure.

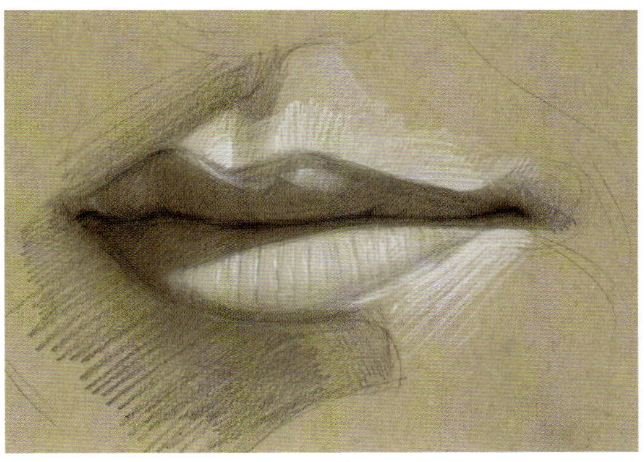

3 *ADD HIGHLIGHTS AND DETAILS*

Add more highlights and refine the shadows. The corners of the lips are often the key to a successful, lifelike portrait. Look at the *Mona Lisa*—her mystery lies in those lip corners. The lips often have pronounced lines and ridges; make sure your pencil strokes follow that pattern.

THE EARS

Ears get a bad rap. We don't pay much attention to them in everyday life, and when drawing a portrait they are often an afterthought or even an oversight. (I once presented a finished portrait to a client only to notice at the last minute I had forgotten to render the ear!) But it is important to understand how to draw ears, even if they don't fit prominently into a portrait.

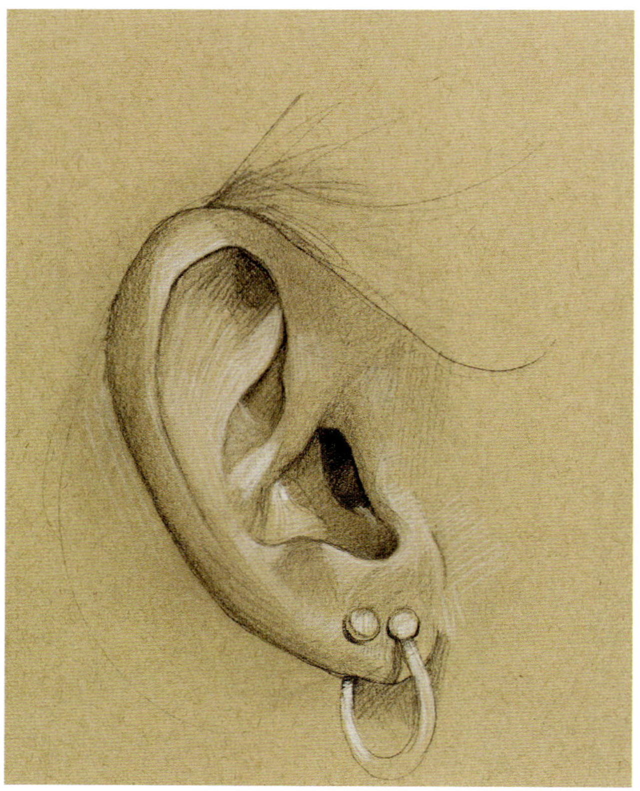

Basic Ear Structure

The ear, when you really look at it, is a pretty odd thing. I have heard other artists compare an ear to a seashell—and you can see why. Exotic curves, chambers, hard and soft edges. The ear is a very small part of the body and a difficult one to render.

The ear's primary purpose (aside from holding up your glasses) is to get sound into the inner ear. So it makes sense that it is shaped in a way that bounces sound waves into the hearing canal. Your job as an artist is to simplify those shapes so they make sense in order to see the underlying shapes.

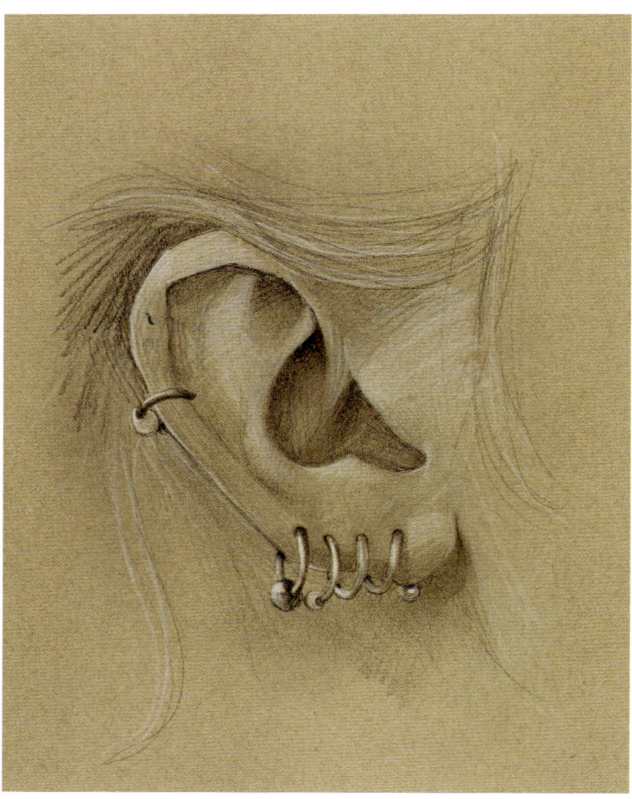

Earrings

Ears are the most commonly adorned part of the face. Many people have earrings, far more than lip rings or nose or eyebrow piercings. Depending upon how complex you intend to make your portrait, you may wish to include a model's earrings—or not—and you may even decide to add earrings that are not in your reference if they add some visual interest to your portrait.

DRAW AN EAR

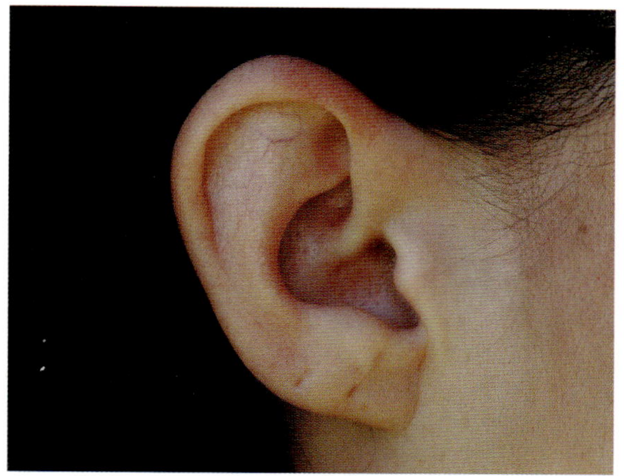

Reference Photo

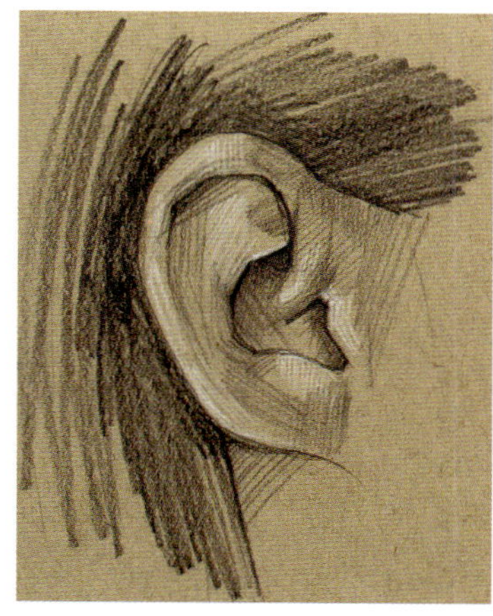

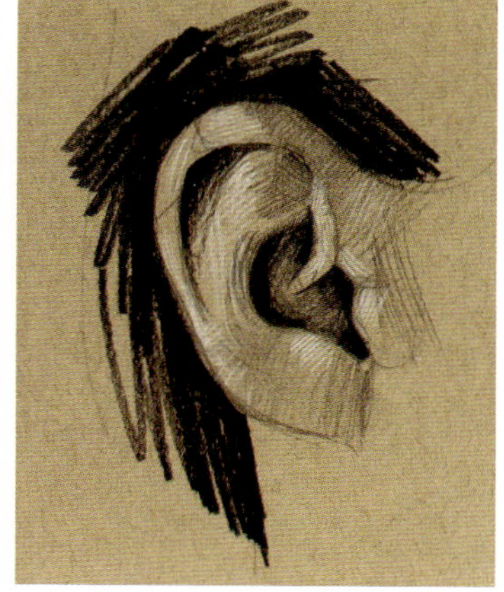

Thumbnail Sketches

When you study the ear, you see that there are a series of ovals and linear shapes within various planes. This gives us a lot of highlights and shadows. Be sure to observe them carefully. Draw what you see!

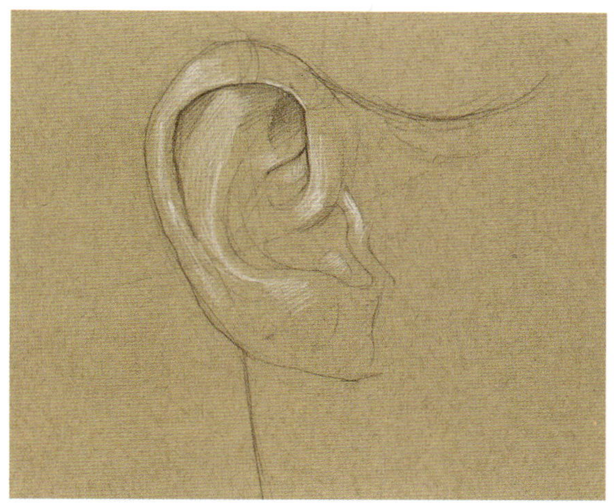

1 ***DEFINE THE SHAPES***

Draw the shape of the ear, then add highlights and shadows. Note that as you get deeper in the ear, each section is farther away and therefore more in shadow.

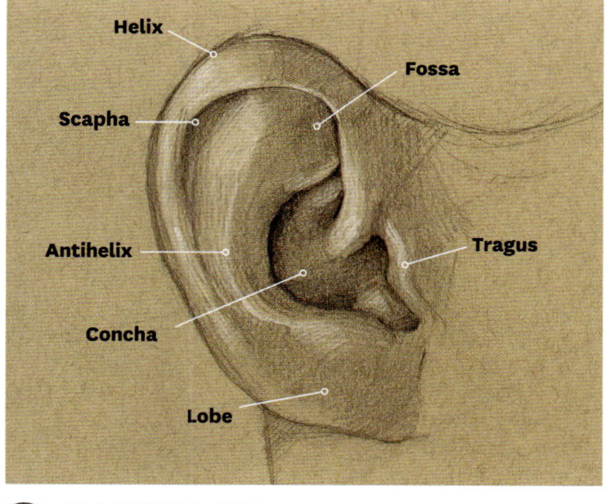

2 ***ADD THE VALUES***

Begin to define the darkest areas. The concha—the entrance to the ear canal—is often nearly black. Pay attention to the different planes. Notice where the highlights are on the lobe, helix, etc.

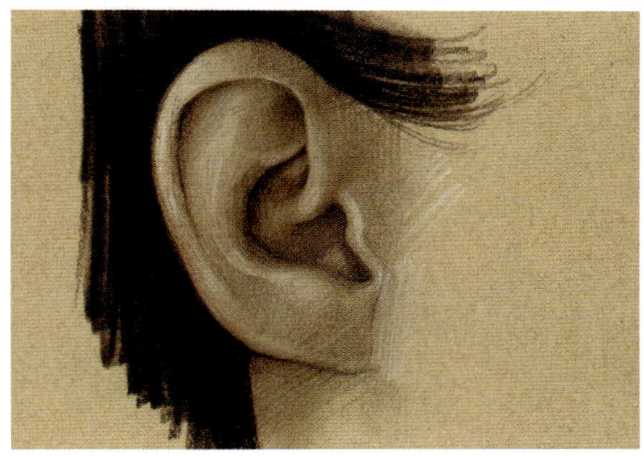

3 ***FINALIZE THE DETAILS***

When rendering the hair behind the ear, be sure the darkest dark of the ear relates to the darkest part of the hair. Define the shapes of the ear with pencil strokes that mimic the form of each part.

CLOTHING AND ACCESSORIES

Most of the portraits in this book are what is commonly referred to as "head and shoulders," thus accessories are somewhat limited. For these types of drawings, hats, glasses and jewelry are the main types of accessories you would be likely to include. As the artist, it is always your choice whether or not to include them.

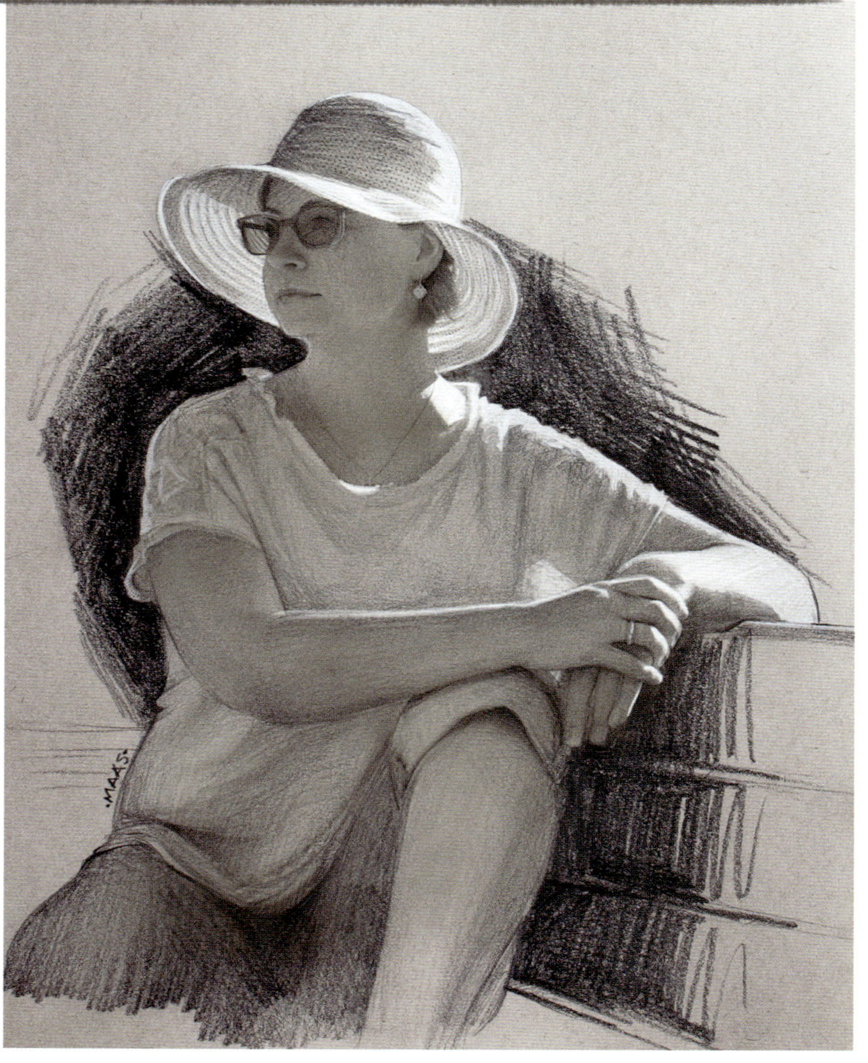

Hats

If you place your model in a hat, be sure to control where the light is so you can get interesting effects on and around the hat. In this drawing you can see how I have paid attention to the soft light through the model's hat as well as the harsher light directly hitting the back of her neck. I also have allowed filtered light to show through the back of her shirt under her arm.

Chelie
Graphite and white charcoal on toned paper
14" × 11" (36cm × 28cm)

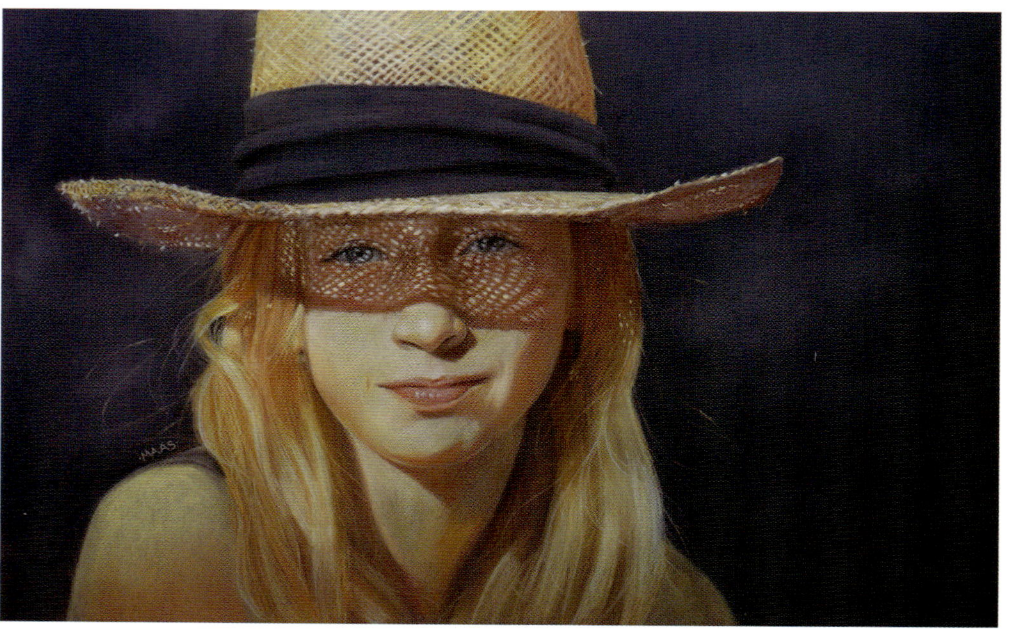

Accessories as Focal Points

Here I made the accessory the star of the show. The filtered light that comes though the straw hat and the texture of the hat itself are key focal points in this pastel drawing.

Gypsy Eyes
Pastel on paper
14" × 24" (36cm × 61cm)

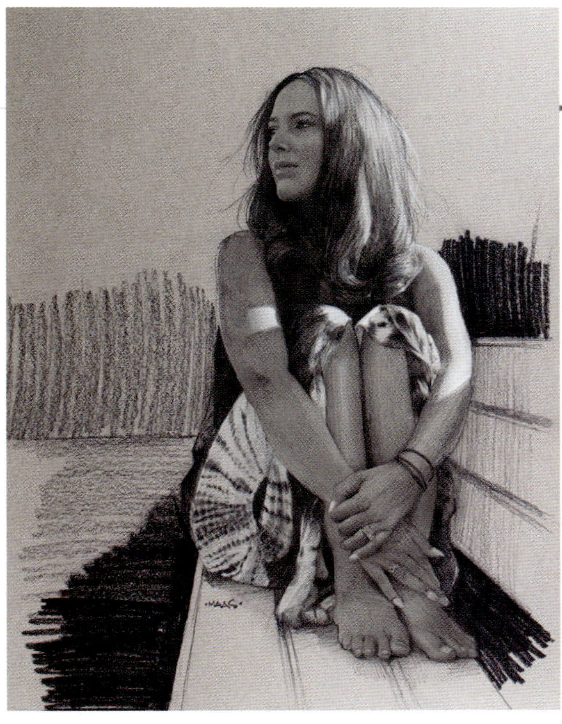

Emphasize Patterns for Volume

In full-body portraits, clothing and accessories become more important. In this pose, the body is so compact that we only really see the skirt because I chose to emphasize the tie-dye pattern. It helps to give volume to that part of the drawing. If I had drawn it as a dark skirt, for example, it would have made the whole pose feel more flat.

Alli
Graphite and white charcoal on toned paper
14" × 14" (36cm × 36m)

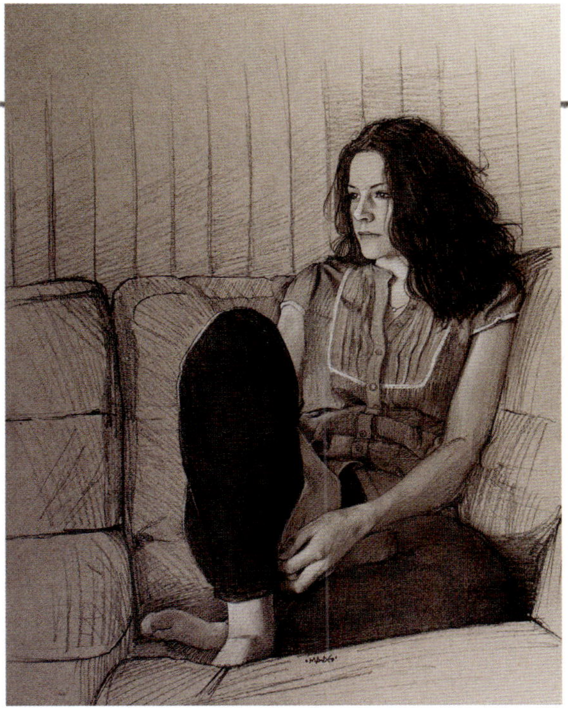

Choose a Simple Detail

The clothes are simple in this drawing but the frilly lace and pattern on the shirt help tie all the less detailed areas together.

Rhiannon
Graphite and white charcoal on toned paper
14" × 11" (36cm × 28cm)

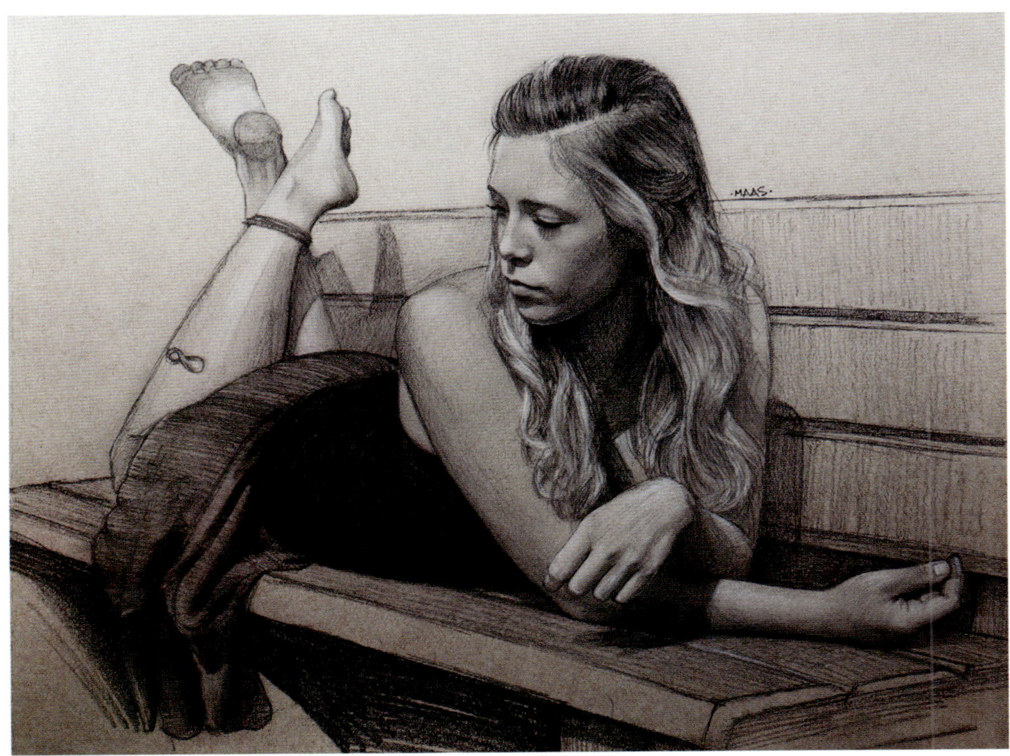

Create Parallels Between Clothing and Features

Here the flowing skirt is a complement and mirror of her hair. I purposely made the shirt darker so that I could draw parallels between those two areas.

Tovah No. 3
Graphite and white charcoal on toned paper
11" × 14" (28cm × 36cm)

HAIR

Depending upon your model, the hair may be the largest single element in the portrait.

Hair should be the easiest area to render, since it is fairly forgiving. You can get hair mostly right and no one will notice. Yet, it is a part of the portrait that artists struggle with the most. This usually has to do with trying to include too much detail.

Think of hair in terms of broad mass, and then, once you have the bulk of the shape and form rendered, look at individual strands.

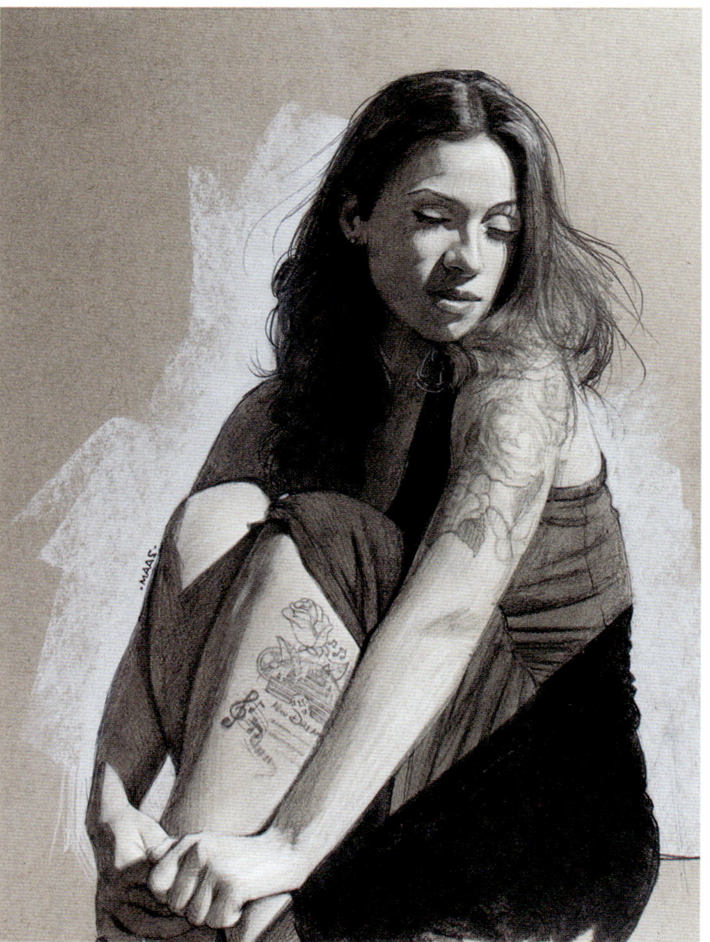

Simple Forms
The hair in this drawing is rendered very simply: form, highlights and some random strands.

Alisa No. 4
Graphite and white charcoal on toned paper
14" × 11" (36cm × 28cm)

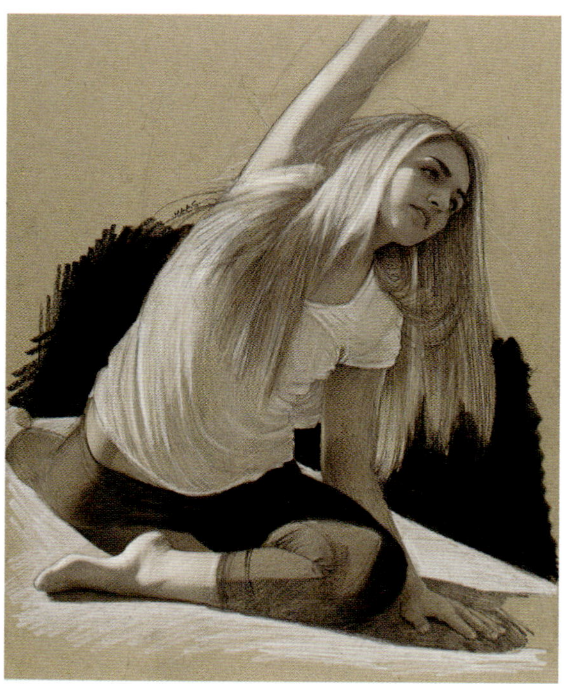

Strong Highlights
Here the hair helps explain the light as it hits the model. We see a strong shot of color on her cheek, while most of her face remains in shadow. The hair has been rendered as a large mass, with highlights and shadows across the whole surface. Only once this is done are details like individual hairs added.

Chelsea Dance Series No. 4
Graphite and white charcoal on toned paper
14" × 11" (36cm × 28cm)

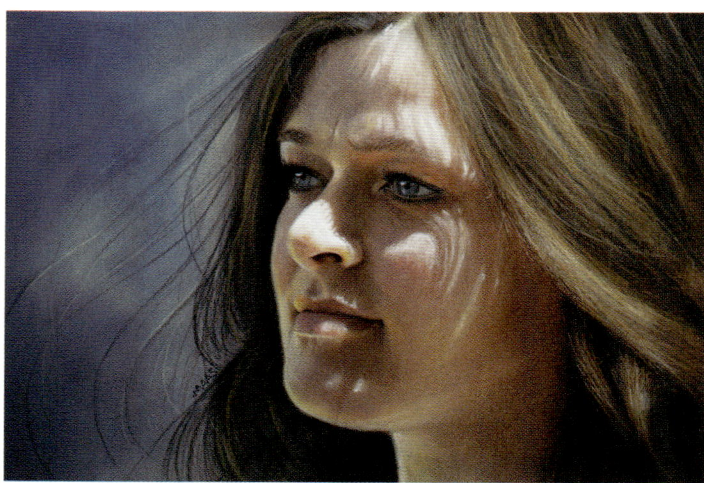

Add Individual Strands Last
In this pastel drawing I focused on many individual strands of hair, but this was only after I rendered the sections of hair.

Chantelle
Pastel on sanded paper
12" × 16" (30cm × 41cm)

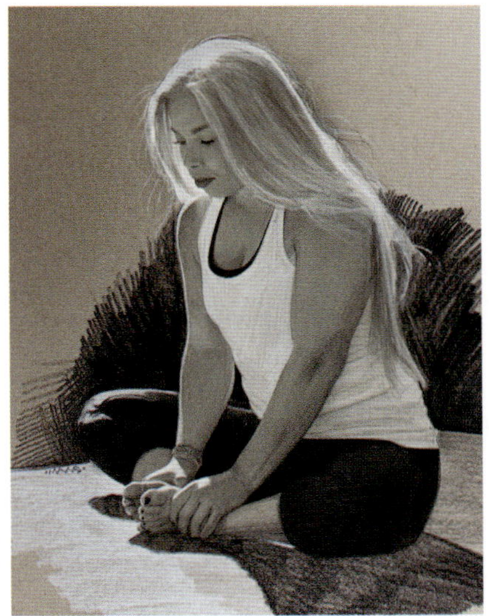

Elise Dance Series No. 2
Graphite and white charcoal on toned paper
14" × 11" (36cm × 28cm)

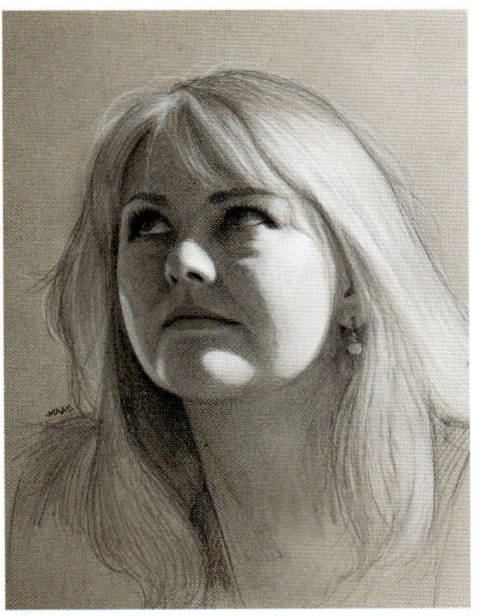

Mandy
Graphite and white charcoal on toned paper
14" × 11" (36cm × 28cm)

Light, Blonde or Backlit Hair

Light hair can give artists a tough time, especially backlit hair like this. The key is to keep the pressure light and work from general to specific. Don't attack individual strands until you block in the main areas of volume. Note here that the strong highlights are probably close to 0 to 10 percent gray, while the bulk of the hair not in highlight is mostly in the 40 to 60 percent gray. Too much dark here would overpower the drawing.

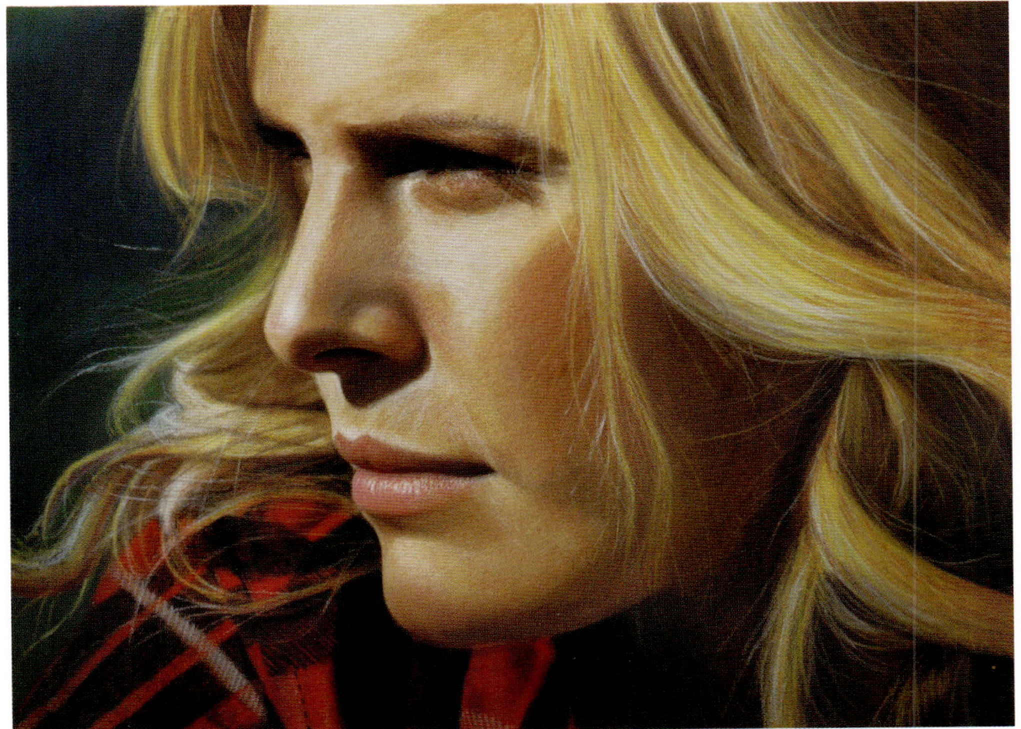

Simplify Hair in Close-Ups

Here's an example of a close-up portrait where the hair is a crucial part of the piece. And yet in pure real estate (the amount of the page is uses up) we don't see that much hair. Without the context of the face you may think the hair was simply a series of abstract shapes. Had I spent too much time or added too much detail to the hair, it would have taken away from the main focal point (her face).

Don't Give Up
Pastel on sanded paper
12" × 16" (30cm × 41cm)

TIPS FOR RENDERING HAIR

From a technical standpoint, hair can be difficult to render. Here are a few simple principles to keep in mind.

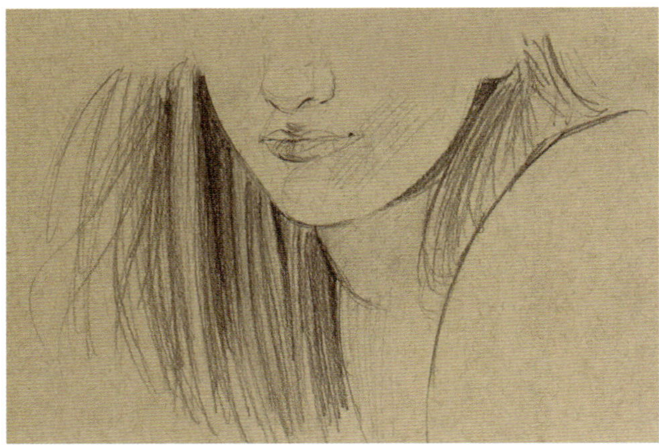

General to Specific

Rendering hair is a lot like painting a forest. You want to look at the overall mass of the trees before considering the details. In this drawing the rendering is very rough and very quick, but you can see how it's immediately obvious what you're looking at.

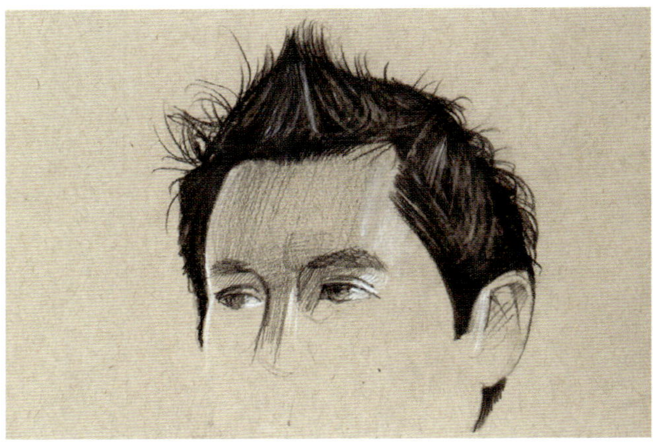

Draw with the Eraser

One of the problems with drawing hair is that there are many areas of lights and darks within the hair masses. In other mediums (oil, acrylic, pastel), it is possible to layer lighter areas and highlights over the darks of the hair, but with pencil that isn't the case. However, your eraser offers an opportunity to do just that—whereby you essentially draw by lifting with your eraser.

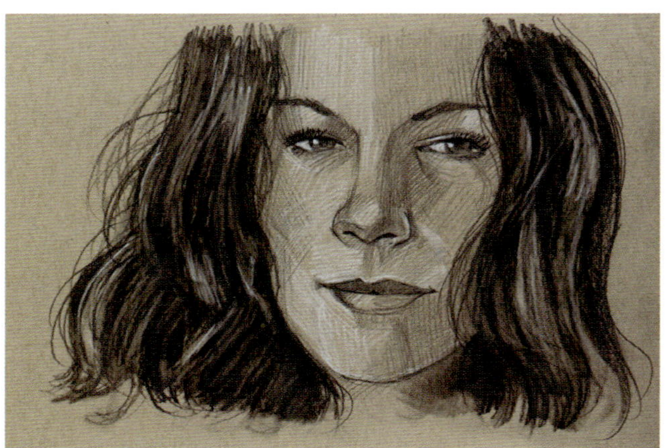

Strive for Flowing Strokes

It is crucial to make your strokes flow with the hair. When we look at hair, we see a mass, but we also see individual strands. These are caught in shadows and highlights, and even though each strand of hair is the same thickness, they often appear to get thinner or thicker depending upon how the light hits them. Carefully and deliberately apply your strokes in the direction and shapes in which they fall.

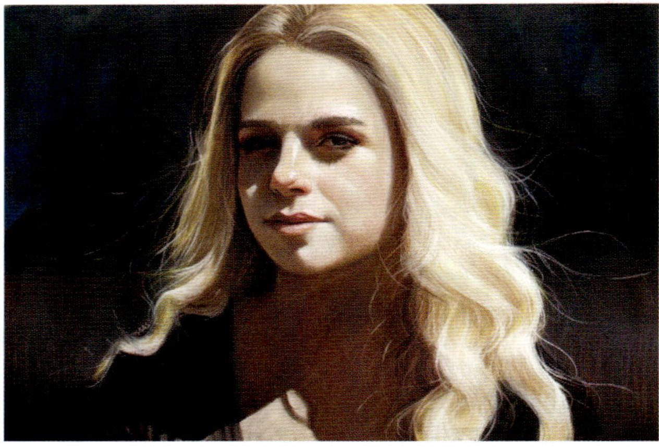

Vary Your Lines

In this example, the hair spirals and sways. The strokes are applied in varying thickness, intensity and darkness—but always in the correct direction—creating organic-looking hair.

DRAW LONG HAIR

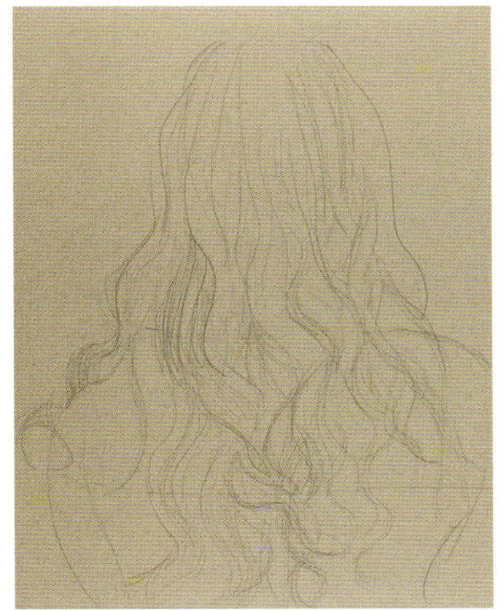

1 *LOOSE BLOCK IN*
Block in the basic head and shoulders, then lightly and loosely lay down the overall shapes and forms of the hair. As you draw, turn your page often to help the hair cascade around the head shape.

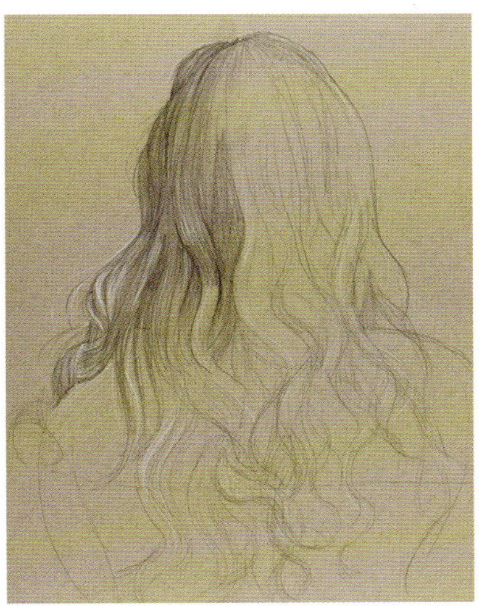

2 *ESTABLISH VALUES*
Establish some of your mid-tones. Start looking at overall shapes of the hair—not individual strands.

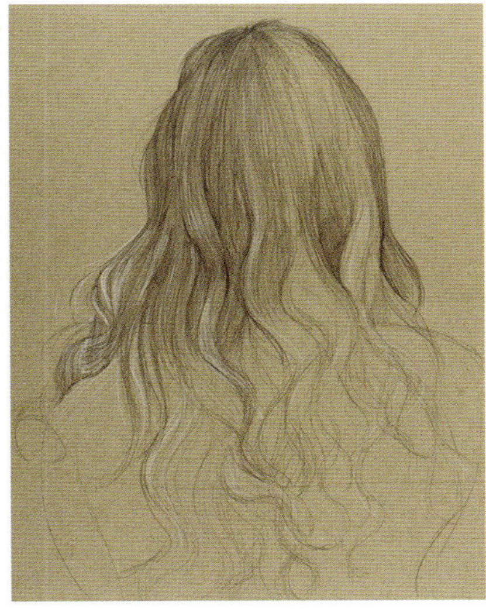

3 *BUILD UP FORM*
As you begin to build up forms and shapes of the hair, darken the areas that recede. Add some highlights by lifting them out with your kneaded eraser.

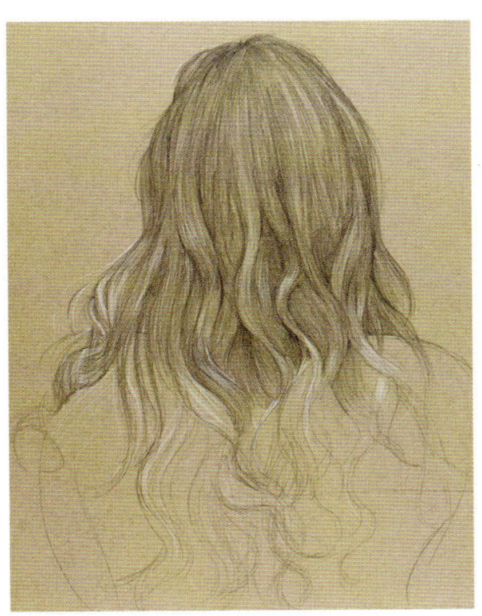

4 *CREATE HIGHLIGHTS*
Keeping everything organic and flowing, lift out more highlights with your eraser and add in more darks with your darker (softer) pencils.

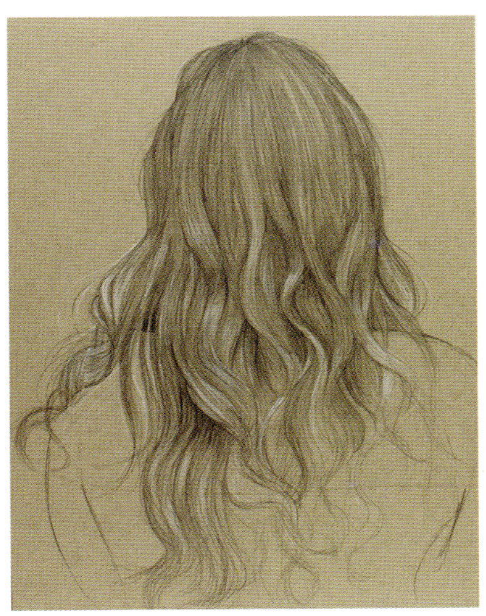

5 *BRIGHTEN THE HIGHLIGHTS*
As you darken and lighten the shapes, begin adding some lighter highlights with white charcoal. Make sure to vary your pressure and line thickness.

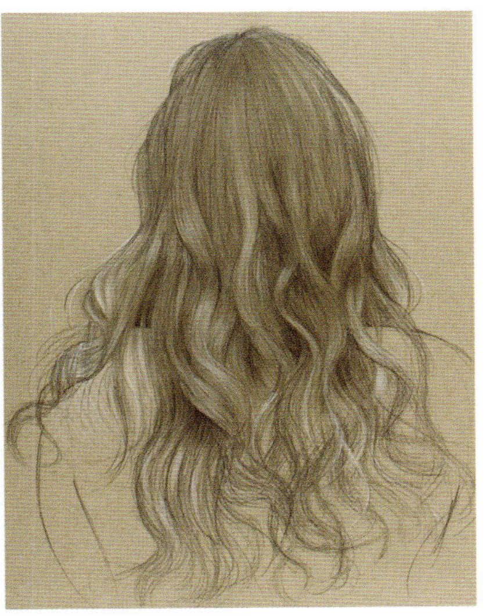

6 *FINISH THE DRAWING*
In the finished drawing, you can see that some parts are barely more than a few simple lines. This gives an energy to the drawing that would be lost if you were to finish each square inch.

HIGHLIGHTS ON HAIR

Like other parts of the human form, hair is subject to highlights. Unlike other parts, the highlights can take on forms and shapes that can be quite unusual. Hair protrudes, it recedes, it sticks straight up! As artists, we need to capture what we see, but we also need to simplify it so it makes sense to the viewer.

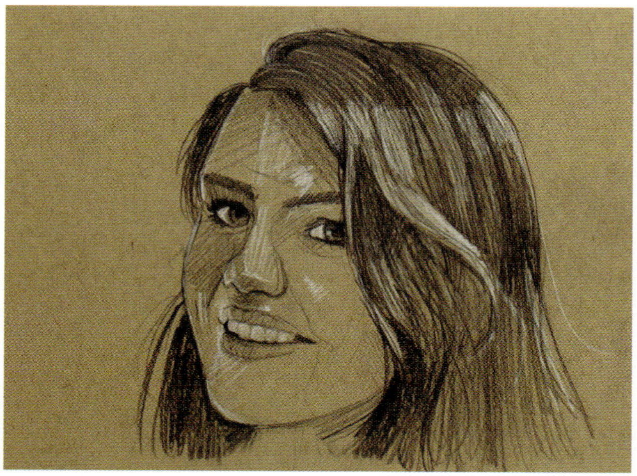

Protruding Section of Hair

This quick sketch shows how highlights can take on a shape of their own when one section of the hair sticks out. Notice the solid bar of light that goes across the top of her head. It's actually the small section of hair that sticks out just below this area that takes on a strong highlight. This is because the hair that protrudes catches more light than the hair that sits flatter on her head.

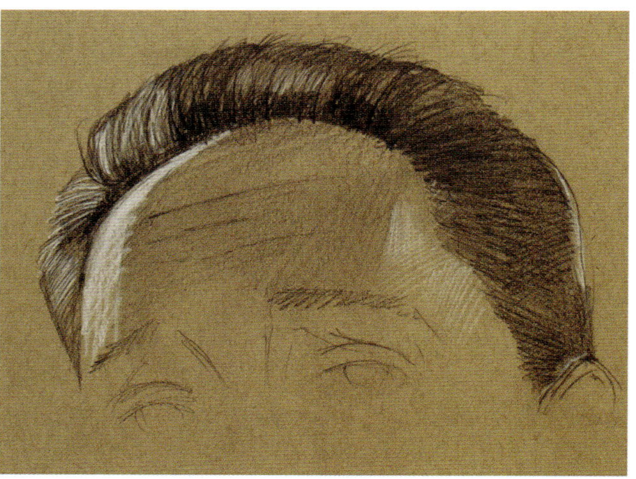

Short Hair

Even short hair is subject to highlights. The highlights are, of course, much smaller areas but visible nonetheless. Here I have blocked in the whole form of the hair, then pulled out small highlights of individual strands.

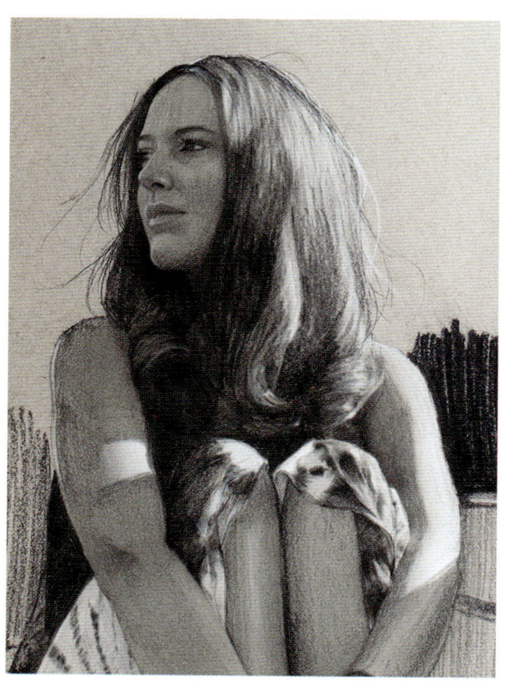

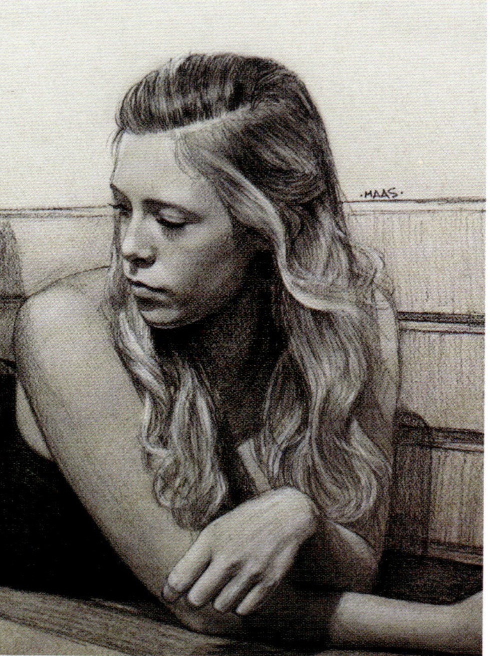

Simplify the Hair in Full-Body Portraits

Both of these portraits are full-body drawings (view them in full on the Clothing and Accessories page), so the hair is rendered in a simple way. Notice the value ranges in the hair, and also the individual strands and wisps that can give a simple rendering so much life.

DRAW HAIR WISPS

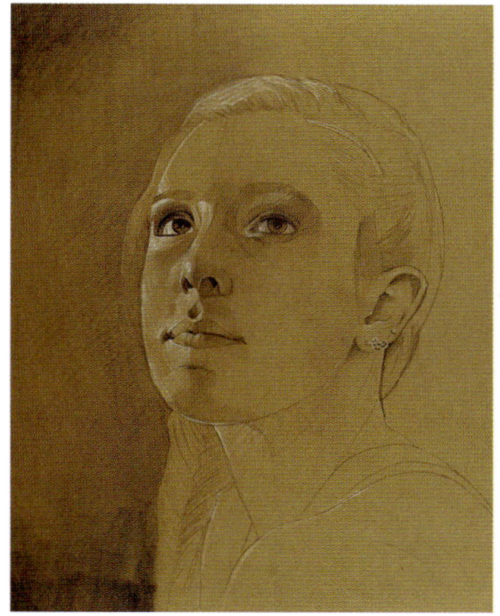

1 *LOOSE BLOCK IN*
Block in the drawing and lightly establish where the wisps will be. Don't put too much detail into this stage; we simply want to understand where we will end up putting in those flyaway hairs.

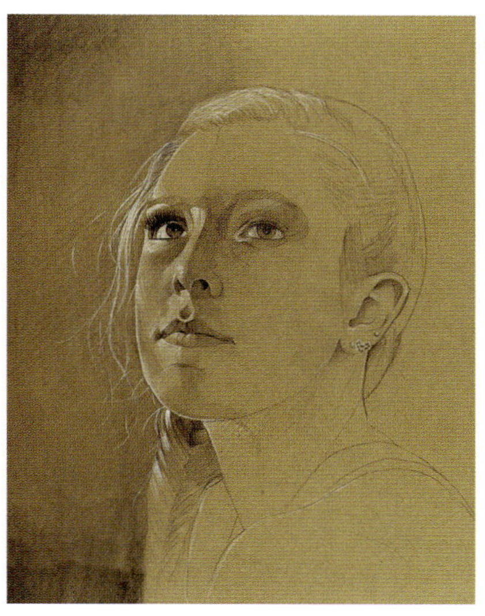

2 *ESTABLISH VALUES*
Establish the overall values, leaving areas for the wisp highlights. Thin and fine hair is subject to highlights and shadows just like every other solid object. Vary the thickness and intensity as you develop the wisps.

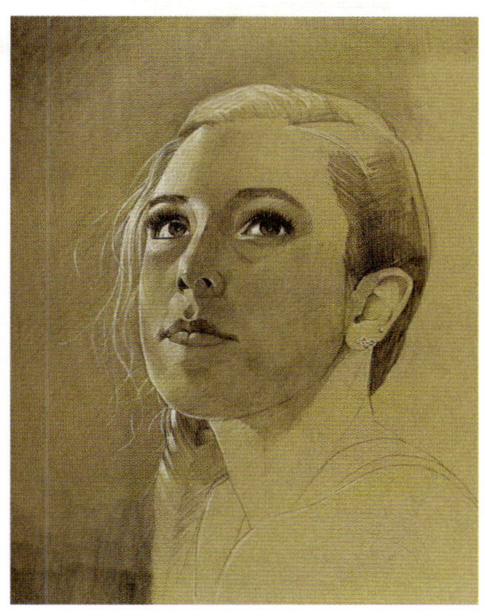

3 *STRENGTHEN THE WISPS*
Intensify some of the highlights in the wisps and add some of the darker areas of the hair on the other side of the head (viewer's right).

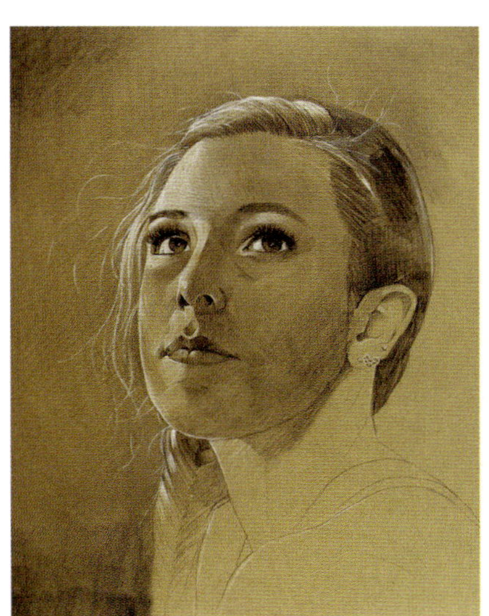

4 *BUILD UP TONE*
Avoid the temptation to work too much on individual strands. Work through values and tone so you know how strong (or soft) to make the wisps.

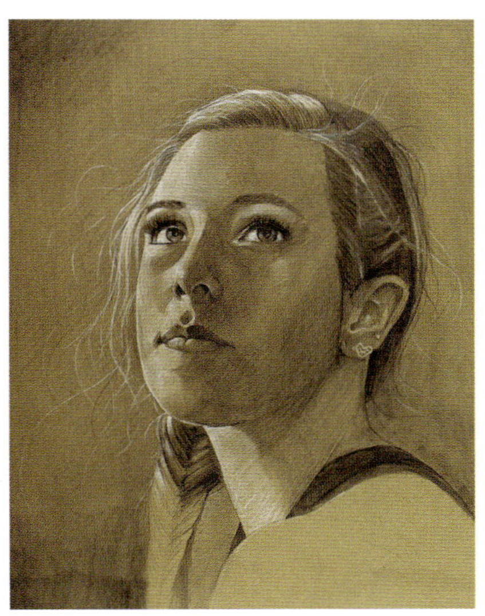

5 *ADD HIGHLIGHTS AND SHADOWS*
By adding highlights and shadows here we can see just how much impact our wisps will have. We can also better understand how many wisps we can add without them overtaking the drawing or looking forced.

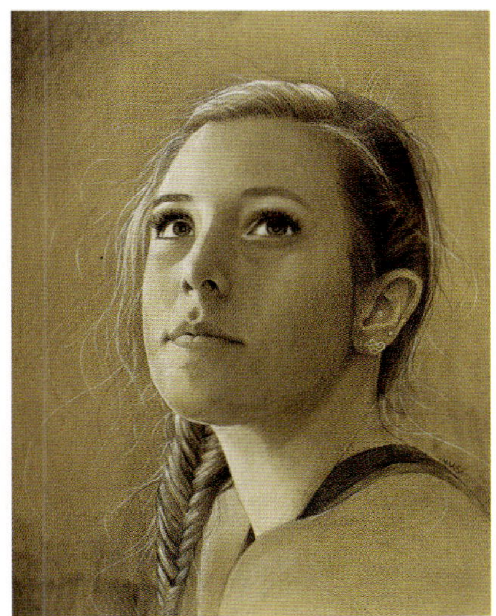

6 *FINISH THE DRAWING*
I like how the contrast of the tight, sharp edges of the ponytail help the wisps fade in and out of focus. The highlights on the face, the top of the head and the right side hairline are also important to establishing a value map for this drawing.

FACIAL HAIR

Though it may be tempting to treat facial hair as simply normal hair on the face, it is usually coarser, less dense and more well-kept than hair on someone's head. Therefore, it requires a different rendering.

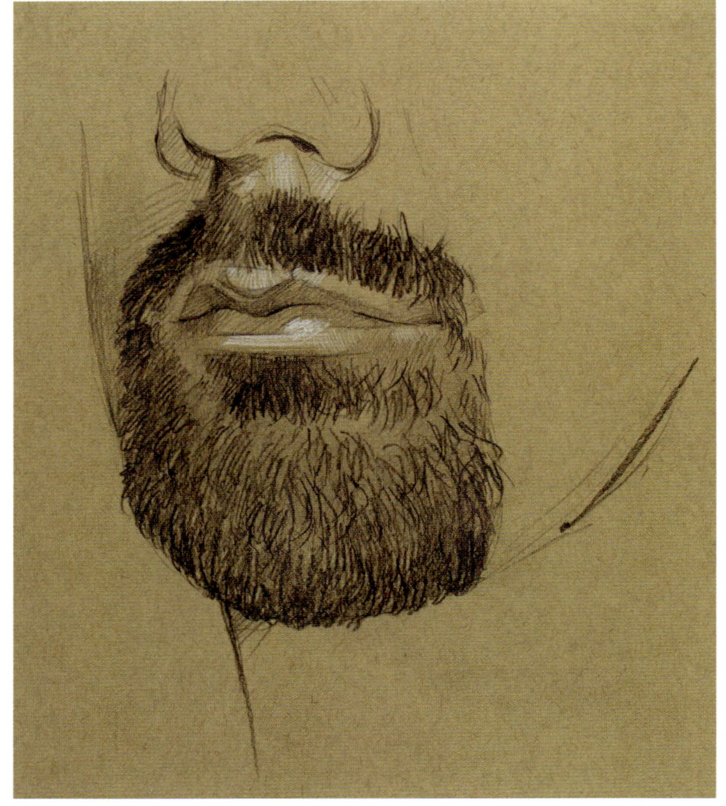

Do Render Individual Facial Hairs

Unlike hair on your head, facial hair is often best rendered in individual strands. This is because most people with facial hair keep it trimmed. Even big bushy beards have nowhere near the number of actual hair strands as what we see on someone's head. The best rule for drawing facial hair is to make sure your strokes go in the direction and style as the facial hair. Keep them short, quick and varying.

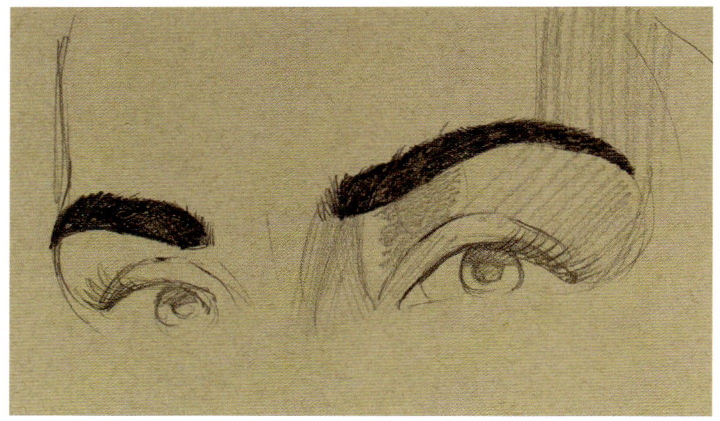

Eyebrows

When we think of facial hair we usually think moustaches, beards, goatees or Van Dykes, but really any hair on the face is facial hair, including eyebrows. Eyebrows vary a lot so be sure to closely study those of your subjects—they may have bushy brows or nearly invisible ones. This is important in creating an accurate portrait as eyebrows are one of the more important parts of the face in terms of establishing likeness.

DRAW FACIAL HAIR

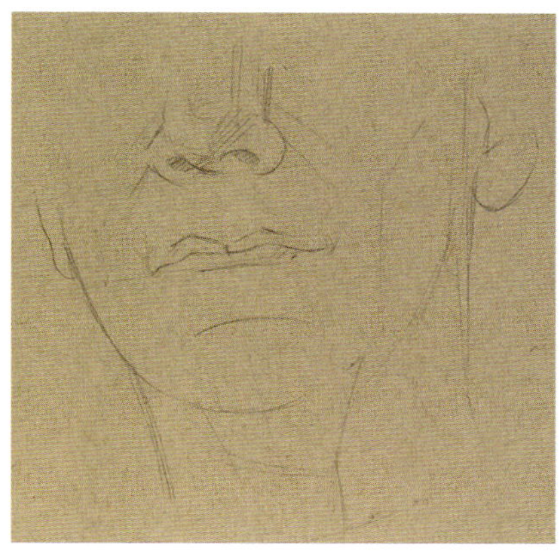

1 **LOOSE BLOCK IN**
Define the face without the facial hair to begin. This is important so that accurate proportions can be achieved.

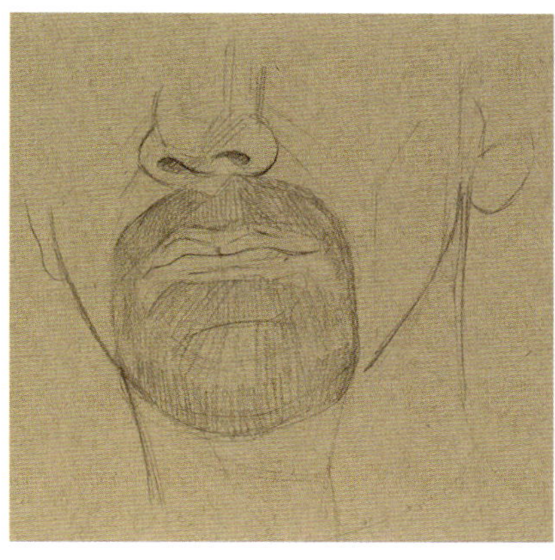

2 **DEFINE THE FACIAL HAIR AREA**
Because facial hair has volume, it will actually go beyond the lines of the face.

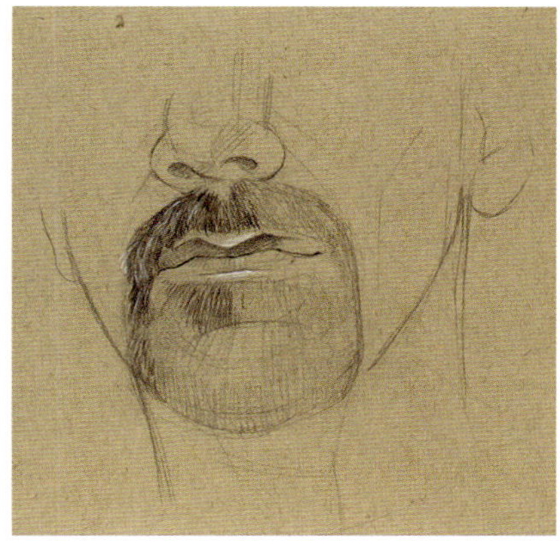

3 **RENDER THE OVERALL SHAPES OF THE HAIR**
Block in the whole area of facial hair, paying attention to the shadows and highlights. Though made up of individual hairs, facial hair is still just one mass. Much as we do with a forest made up of individual trees, we view it as a single shape from a distance.

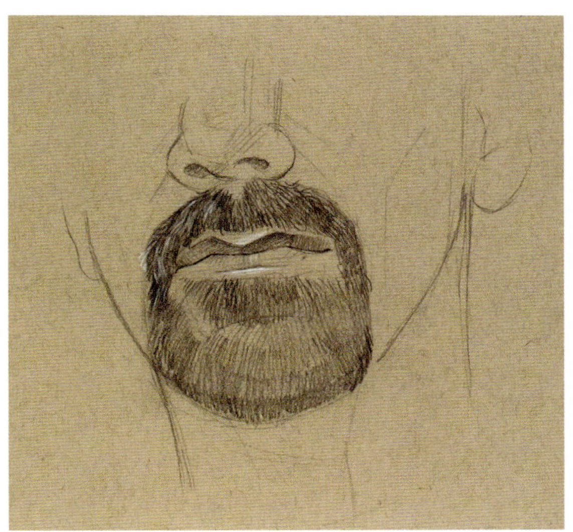

4 **LIFT OUT SOME HAIRS**
Use an eraser (kneaded or click) to lift out some hairs. Facial hair is almost never all the same shade—unless someone has dyed it. By lifting out certain sections, you are essentially drawing with your eraser and adding an element of depth.

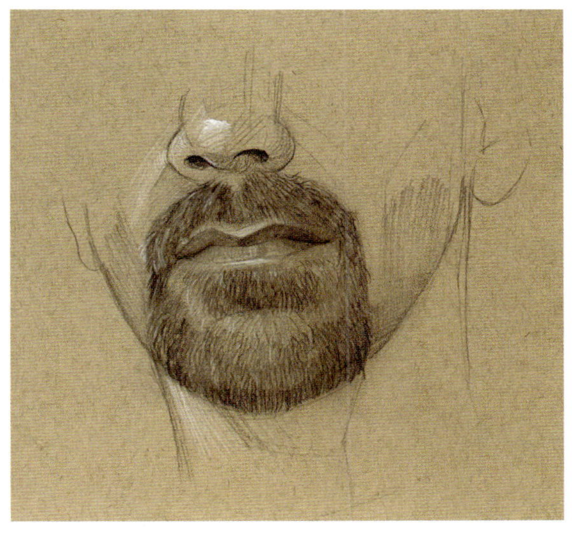

5 **ADD THE DETAILS**
Using a very soft pencil (6B or 8B), draw individual hairs. Be careful to add them selectively in relation to the shapes and shadows of the facial hair. This is crucial to ensure that the facial hair looks accurate.

SKIN TONE

Skin tones and color vary considerably from person to person and even from season to season with the same person. As someone ages, the skin will change, too. Since most of the drawings in this book are monochromatic, we look mostly at skin tones as values, meaning the skin tone will not vary as drastically from portrait to portrait.

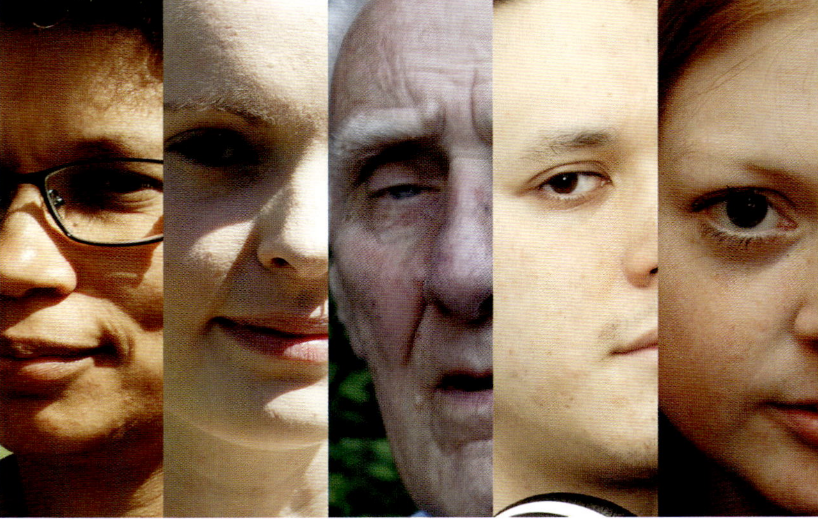

Color Photo Reference
Here are five different people. When we study the color photographs, there is a wide variation among their skintones.

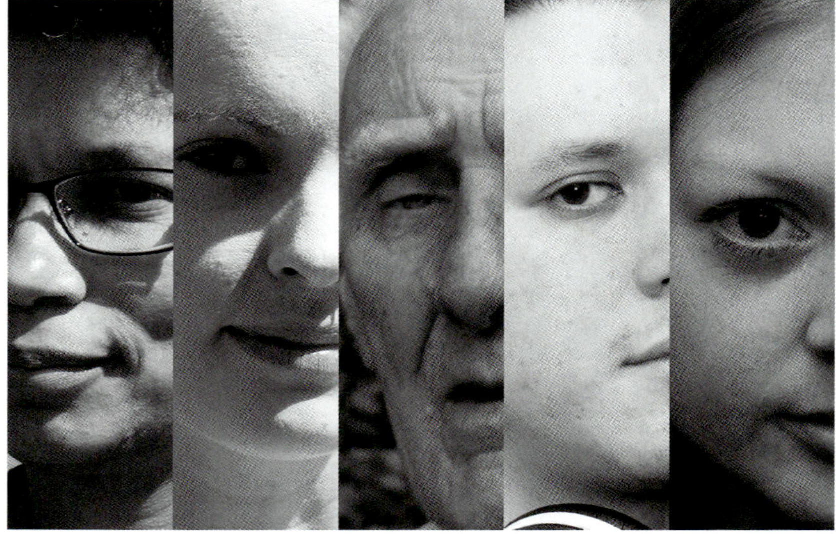

Grayscale Photo Reference
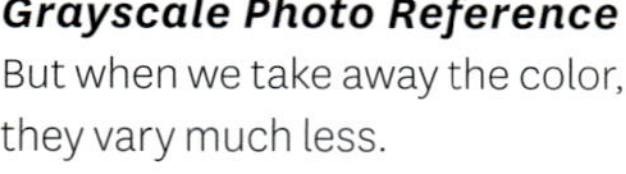
But when we take away the color, they vary much less.

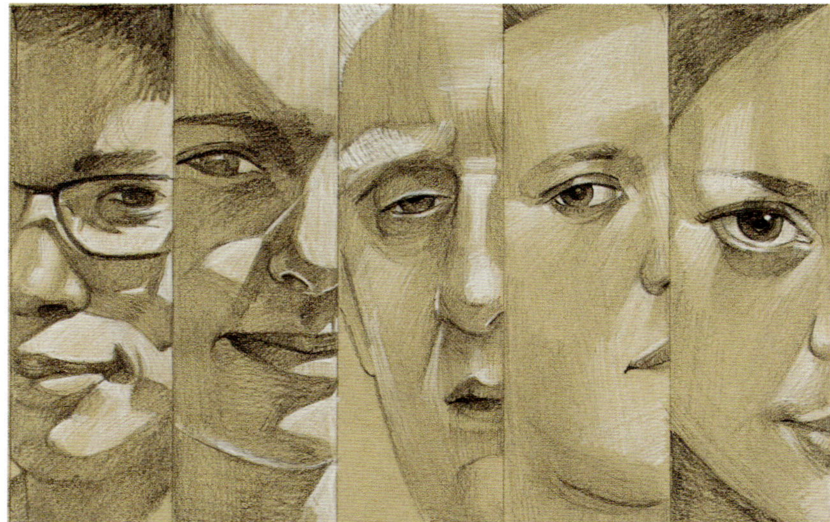

Graphite Drawing
Skintone is even less pronounced in graphite. Tone and value are all that we see. Individual color is quite difficult to distinguish in a monochromatic drawing.

HANDS AND FEET

Most of the drawings in this book are what we call "head and shoulders" portraits, meaning they show the face, the hair and the tops of the shoulders. However, some of the most interesting portraits are full-length or full-body. Full-body drawings can often tell as much if not more about the sitter than a head and shoulders portrait, even though it means there are fewer details in the face.

When attempting a full-body portrait, it is important to accurately render the hands and feet. Hands and feet are difficult to draw, but are also incredibly helpful for establishing secondary and tertiary focal points.

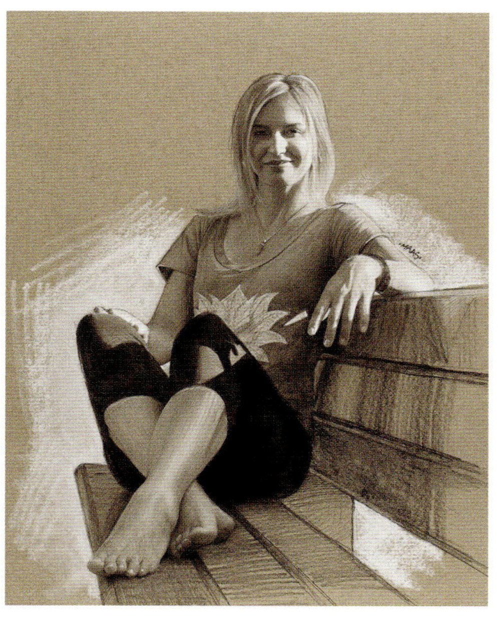

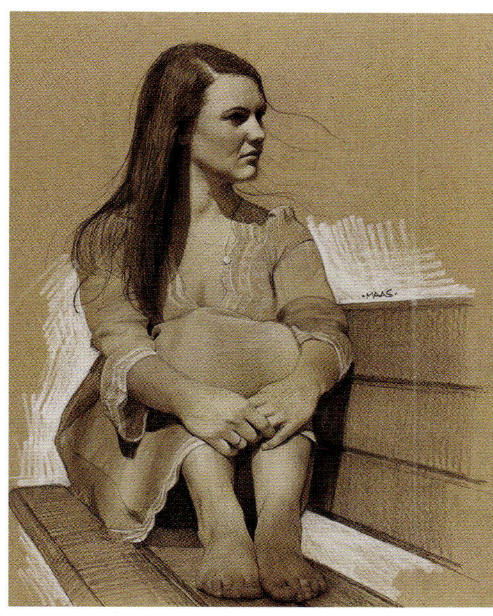

Ground the Composition with Hands and Feet
In these portraits, the hands and feet are as important as the heads and faces. They bring the whole drawing to life and give weight and grounding to the composition.

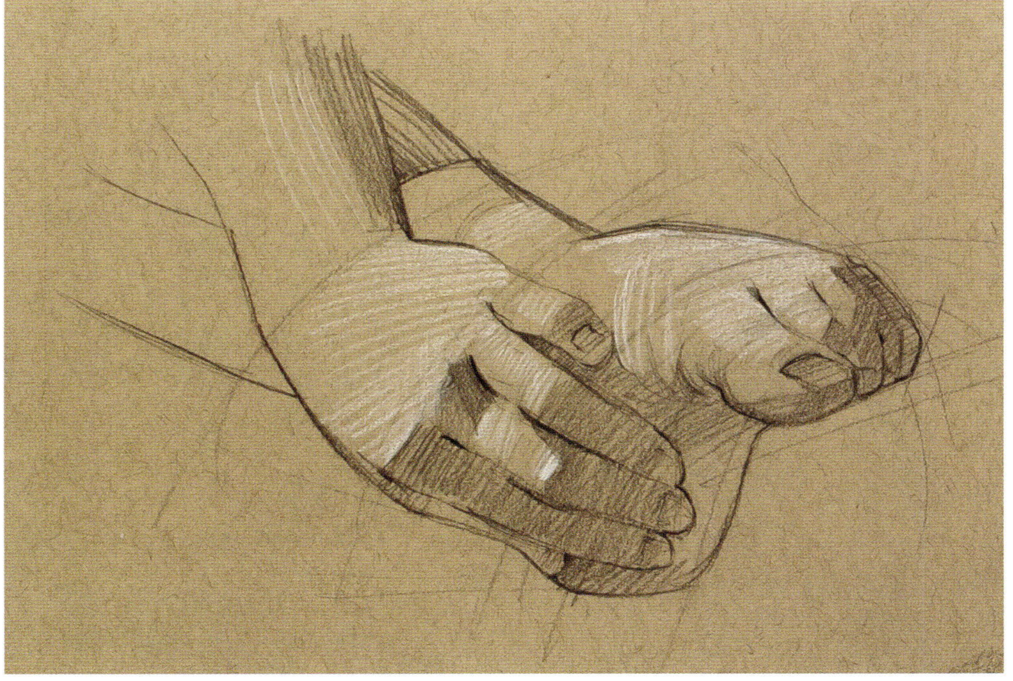

Accurate Proportion Is Key
You don't always have to have a lot of detail in the hands or feet. Simply blocking in the shapes accurately and proportionately can be enough.

Notice here how I only partially indicate fingers or toes. Try drawing them as shapes—observe the whole hand or the whole foot—and then slowly refine them with enough detail to get the point across. You want the viewer to think that you left details out on purpose, not because you forgot or didn't know how to draw them.

4 THE BLOCK IN

In the simplest terms, a portrait is done in two stages: the block in (the initial line drawing) and the rendering. To nonartists, the rendering is the more impressive portion. It is where shading, tone, value and contrast are all implemented. From a time-based standpoint, the rendering is often 80 to 90 percent of the time spent on the work.

To artists, however, the block in is often where the magic happens. I would theorize that with enough interest, anyone could learn to render in a matter of years or possibly even months. The block in, however, can take years, if not decades to perfect.

The block in is the foundation of your work. No amount of rendering can fix a poor foundation, so this stage is crucial to set yourself up for success. There are several methods you can use to get your block in right and start enjoying drawing right away. We will tackle four of them: the grid method, tracing, freehand and the Maas method.

How you chose to block in your drawing is a personal choice. Whether you choose to use a grid, to trace, to use the Maas method or to draw freehand, just understand the limitations and advantages of each method.

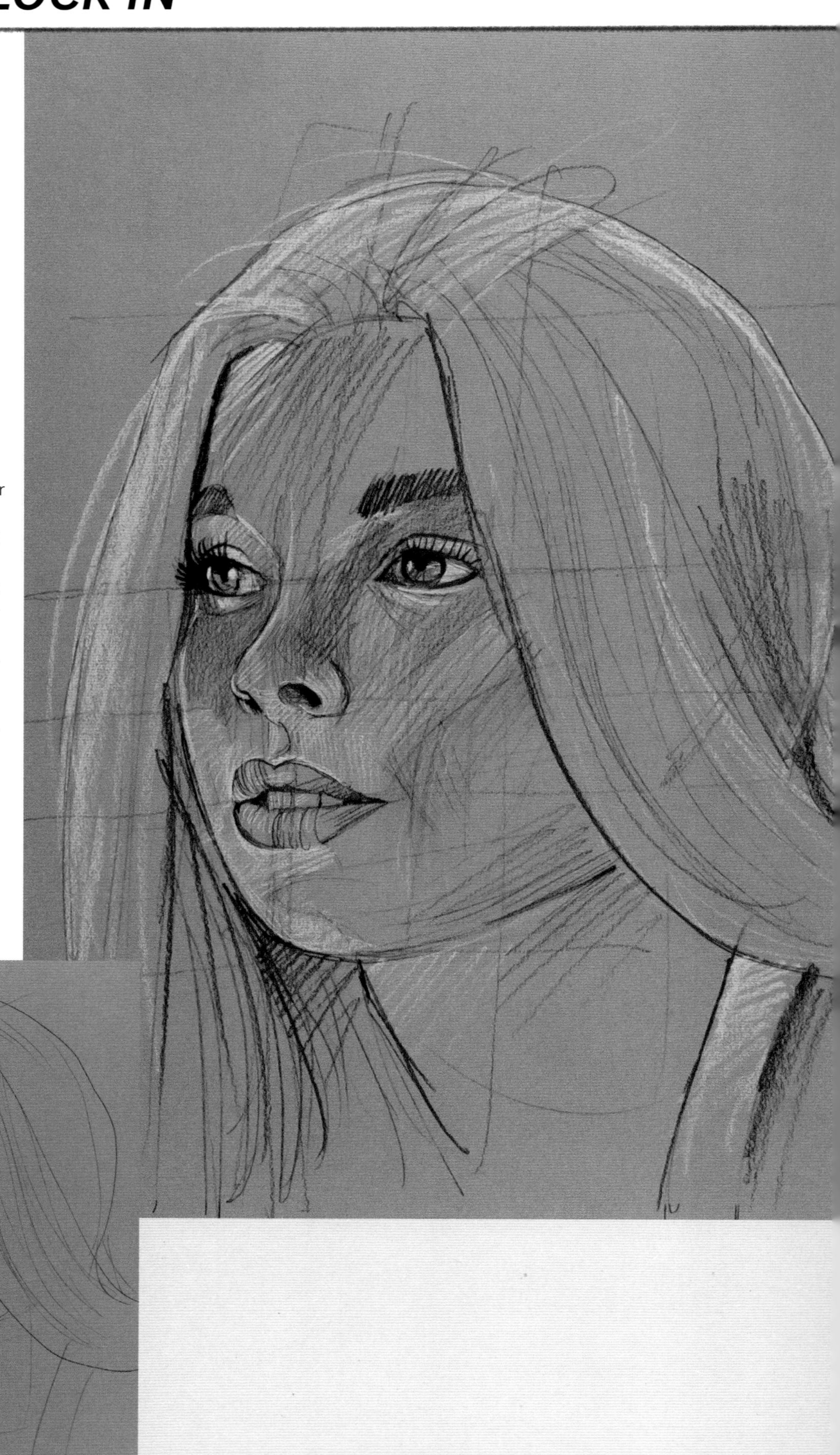

Block In of Elise
Graphite on toned paper
14" × 11" (36cm × 28cm)

THE GRID METHOD

The grid method was developed centuries ago (some say as far back as the Egyptians) but became popular in the Italian Renaissance. The technique is simple: Place a grid over your reference photo, draw a grid on your paper and draw in individual blocks.

It is often taught as an alternative to tracing. Since you are using a scalable grid and marking in your own lines, it is considered purer than tracing, but just like tracing, some rely on it as a crutch.

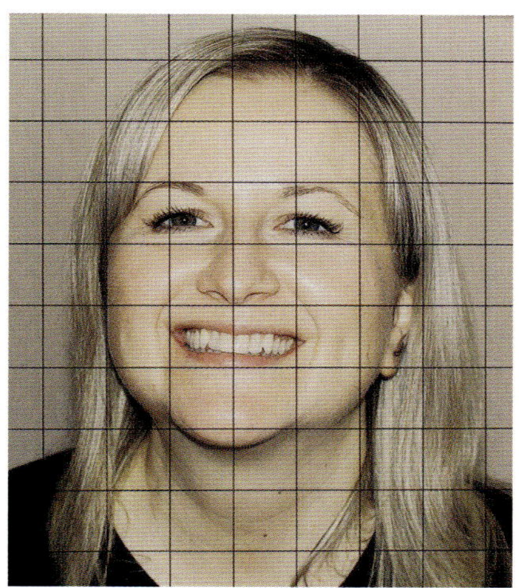

1 **GRID OVER REFERENCE**
Draw a grid over your actual reference photo, or do it digitally on your device or computer screen.

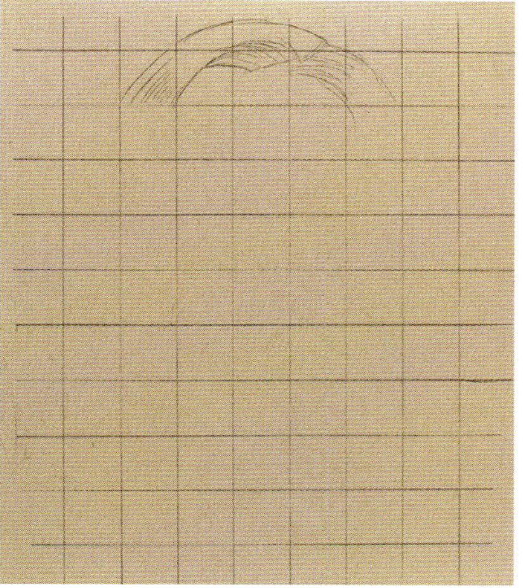

2 **FRESH GRID**
Draw a grid on your blank paper the same scale as your reference. The squares can be any size, but make sure they are evenly spaced. Begin drawing what you see in each individual square of your reference into the corresponding square on the blank paper.

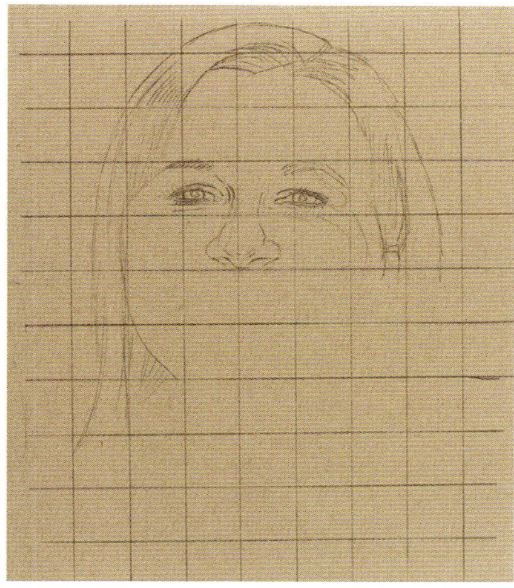

3 **BUILD UP THE DRAWING**
As you build up your drawing, erase the gridlines in completed squares. Be careful not to erase any of the drawing lines you've just laid down.

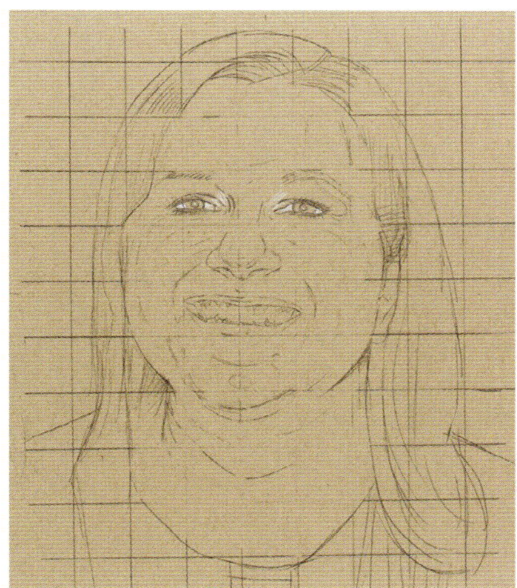

4 **CONTINUE DEVELOPING THE DRAWING**
Continue to develop your drawing, erasing gridlines as you go. You may start to add highlights to begin building form.

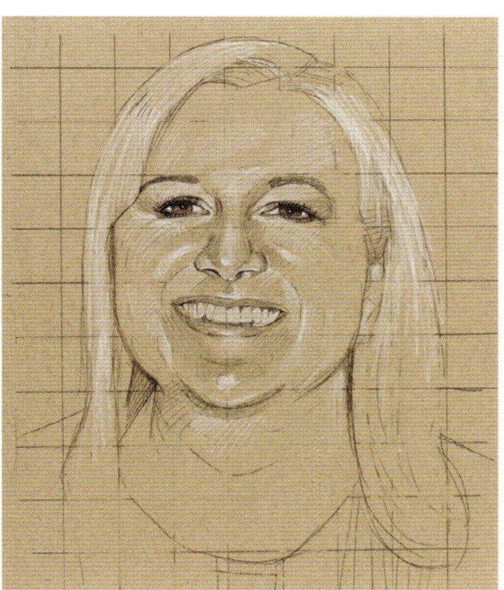

5 **ADD HIGHLIGHTS**
Erase the grid lines within the face and freehand the highlights and shadows. Or, leave some grid lines and apply highlights by referencing the grid. Be careful; if you apply white directly over a graphite grid line, it will show through, and you'll have to erase the whole area to remove it.

GRID METHOD PROS AND CONS

The advantage to the grid method over other methods is that you are actually drawing, not tracing your lines. The grid method can be far less intimidating than drawing freehand. You can also take a reference of any size and make a grid of any size, as long as it is proportional.

The disadvantage to this method is that you can become reliant on grids. It will become increasingly difficult to draw from life if you depend on the grid too much, as it does not give you a solid foundation. You also mark up your paper with a grid that either needs to be drawn over completely or erased.

TRACING

Let me get this out of the way: Tracing is not a dirty word. It's not cheating, it's not against the rules and ultimately it's nobody's business but yours. You would be surprised how many great artists use some form of tracing or transfer. As far back as Leonardo da Vinci, we know that artists used *camera obscura*: a method of using light and mirrors as an early form of projector. Many commercial artists and illustrators trace or project in order to save precious time on deadlines.

World-renowned artists are not asked what block-in method they used when they submit their paintings and drawings to shows and galleries. Tracing, like any other method, is simply one way to complete the journey. Is it right for you? Only you can answer that.

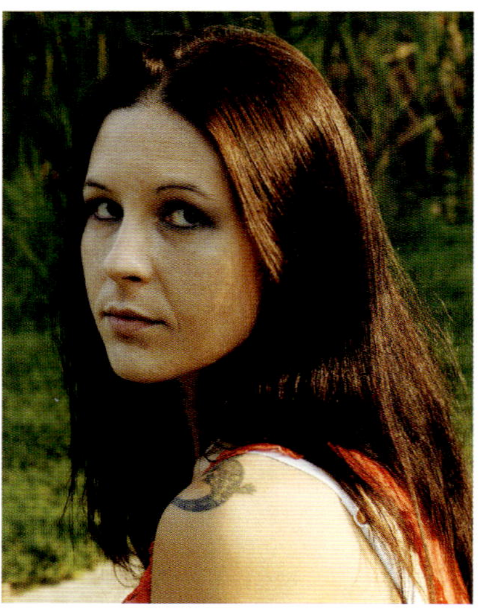

Reference Photo

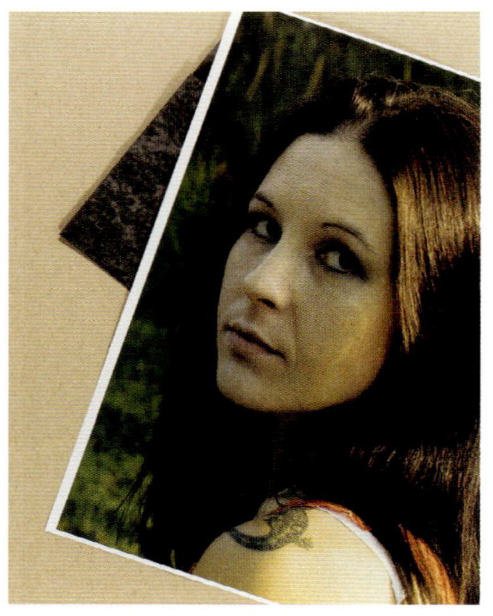

1 *PLACE THE TRACING PAPER*
Begin by taping your photograph (I am using a color printout) to your paper. Then simply slide the transfer paper under the print and draw on top of it.

To illustrate the principles of tracing, I am using transfer paper. You could also use a light board or a projector. I use the word "tracing" interchangeably with using a projector or transfer paper because they are essentially the same practice.

2 *BEGIN TRACING THE IMAGE*
Even though you are tracing the image on to the page, continue to look at things like line quality and variation when transferring the contour.

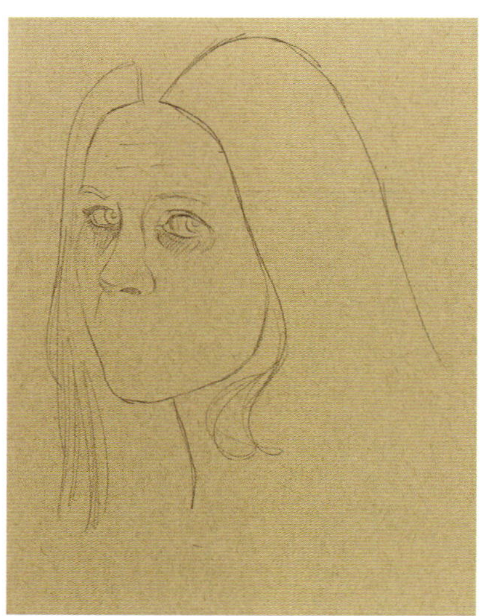

3 *ESTABLISH FORM*
Establish and develop form as you proceed with the rendering.

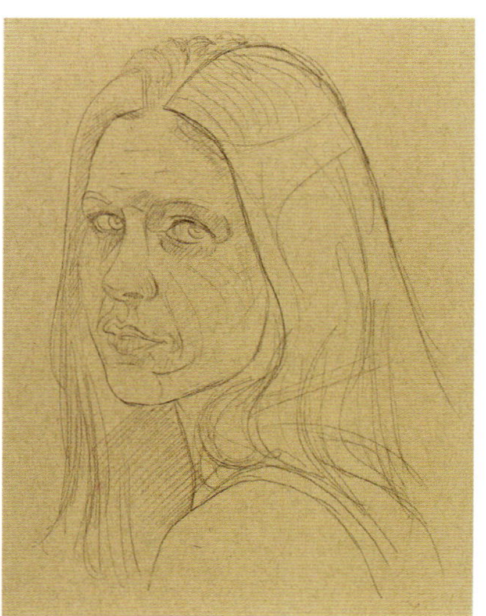

4 *EVALUATE THE LINES*
Look closely at how you have transferred the lines along with the direction of the form. See how the lines that follow the form of her cheek or the curve above her eyes are deliberately drawn in.

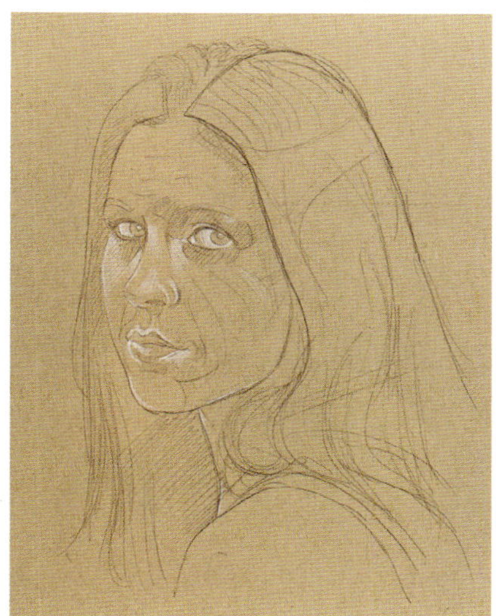

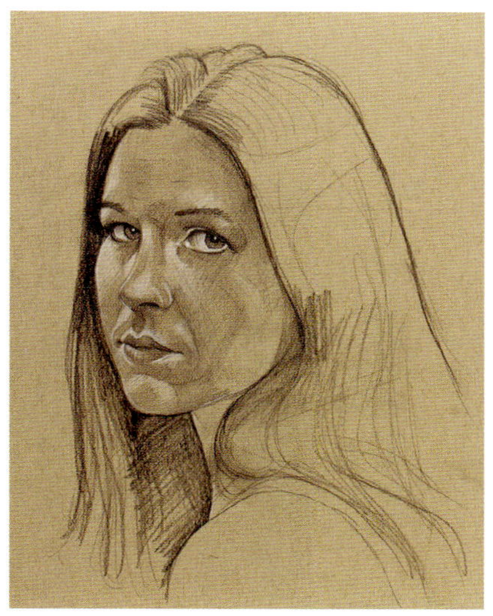

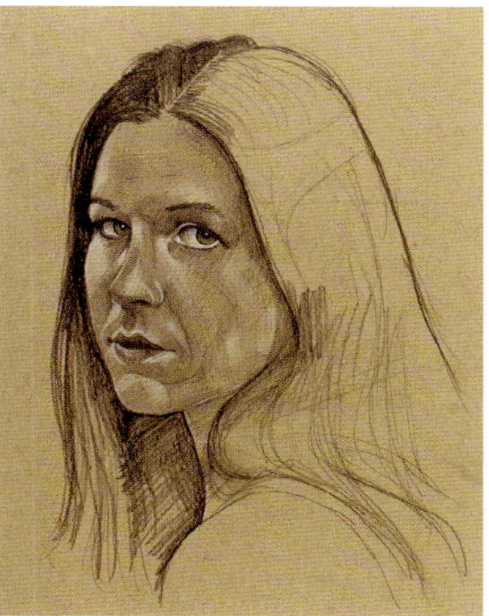

5 **CONTINUE RENDERING**
Once the block in has been traced or transferred to your paper, continue to render until your drawing is complete.

6 **CONTINUE BUILDING FORM AND VALUE**
Pay attention to the forms and values of the subject as you gradually build them up. By doing this, you are learning to draw. The process is simply slower than other methods.

7 **EVALUATE AND FINISH**
For this drawing, I removed the taped reference at an early stage and continued to finish it on my own, but you may continue to refer back to your photo for as long as you wish.

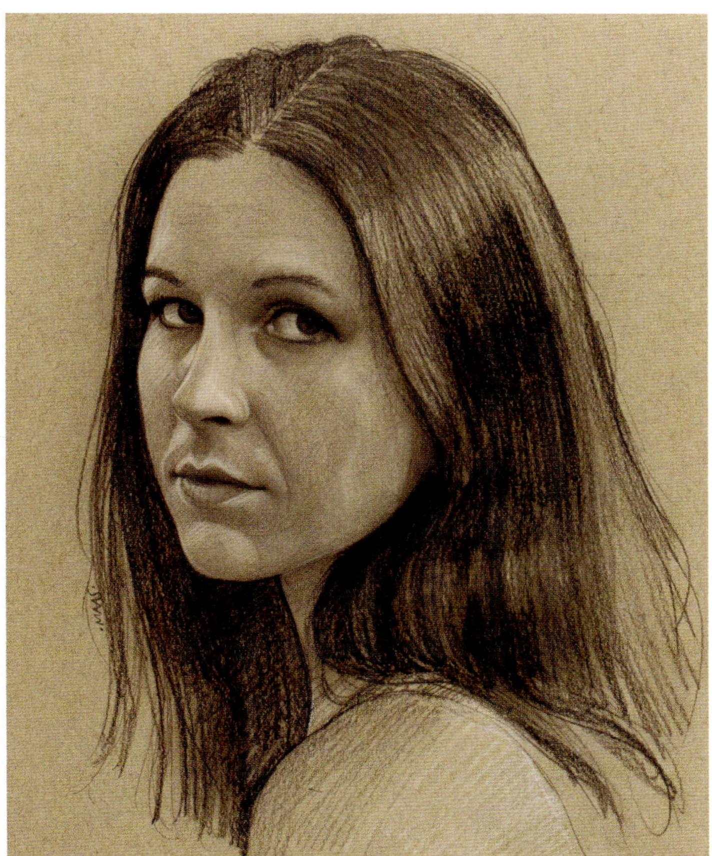

TRACING METHOD PROS AND CONS

The advantages of tracing are clear: you get the right information on the page and can begin with a "perfect" foundation. You can figure out exactly how your piece will end up on the page (no awkward crops). If you are drawing on expensive papers, you can also lay down your block in without damaging your page from overwork or erasing.

The big disadvantage to tracing, however, is if you trace all the time, you become reliant it. Skills are not built as readily with this method.

Trish
Graphite and white charcoal on toned paper
12" × 9" (30cm × 23cm)

FREEHAND

In a perfect world everyone would draw freehand. Freehand drawing is just what it sounds like: you draw without aids or encumbrances. You typically will draw general to specific with no guides other than those you lay down as you go.

Freehand drawing is the end goal for most of us. It is not just that it signifies the most lofty accomplishment in drawing, it also opens up every possibility for an artist because you can literally draw anything, at any time. You are no longer bound by gridlines or projectors or even working from photos.

Freehand is the most pure form of drawing, but it is incredibly intimidating for many artists. It can be frustrating and may take years if not decades to become wholly proficient at it.

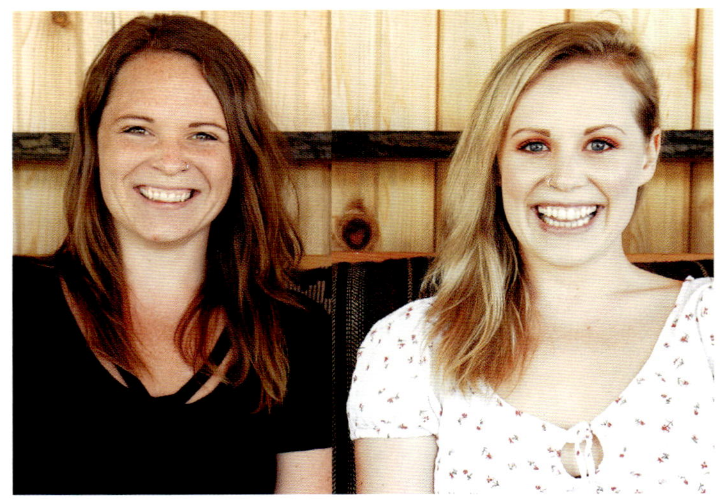

Reference Photo

1 ***THUMBNAIL SKETCHES***

In these preliminary thumbnail sketches, I have applied both measurements (left) and shape breakdowns (right) to work out the initial feature placement and proportions. In addition to getting the measurements correct, the breakdown of shapes is important for freehanding because it allows us to see how each feature relates to the last and how each shape fits within a larger one. In both sketches, keep the lines very light in order to later draw details over the top.

To further illustrate, when we draw a nose, we may be consciously drawing a nose, but in reality we are drawing shapes. These two sketching steps are just two parts of the puzzle, but use them together and you are well on your way to effectively drawing freehand.

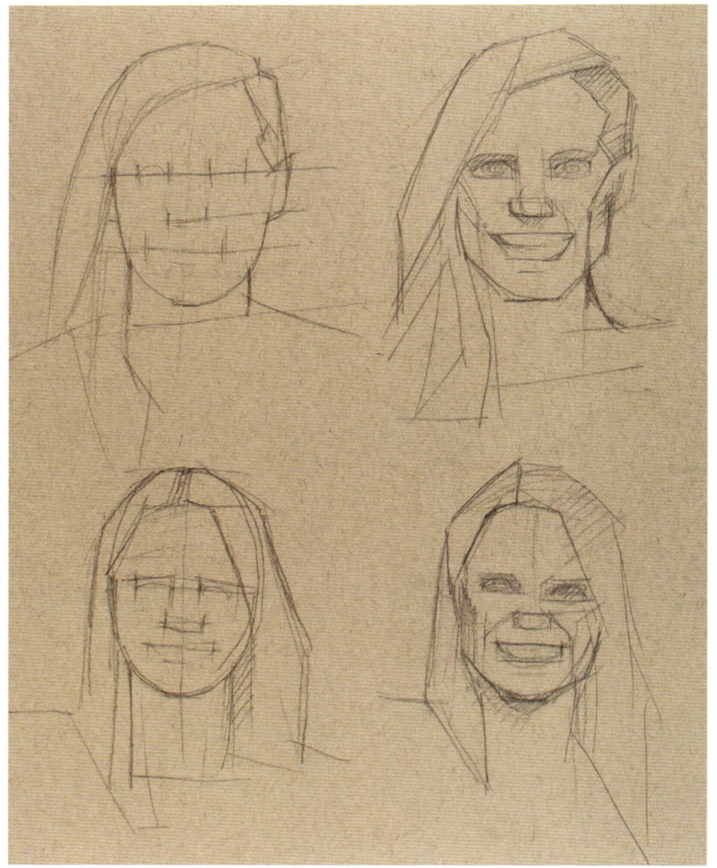

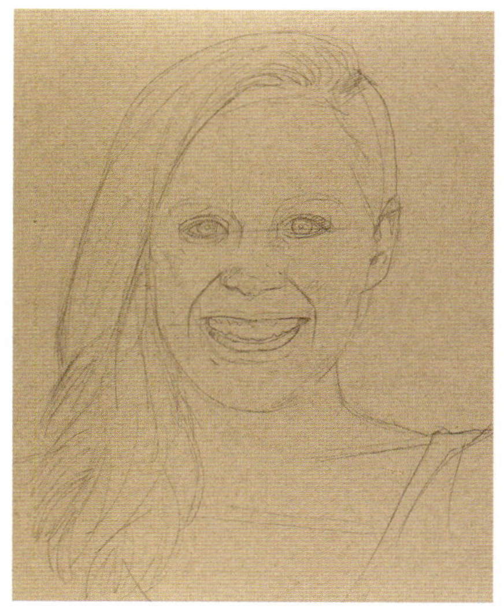

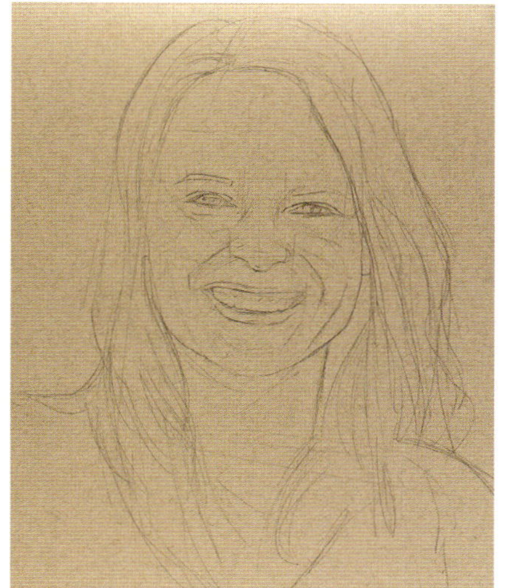

2 *MEASURE LINES AND ADD SHAPES*

After you have completed your two types of thumbnail sketches, measure out the lines. Here I am drawing sisters. They have similar features but are also quite different in their overall look. Add in the shapes and define the areas—not just the outer limits of the eyes, but also the shapes that the eyes fit within, not just the outer most edges of the nose, but what spaces the noses fit within.

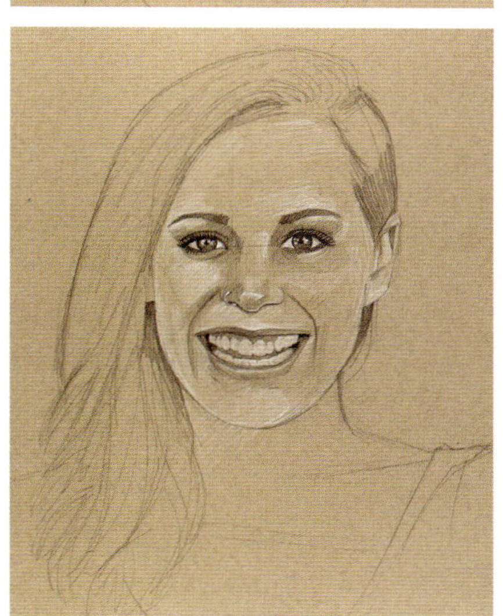

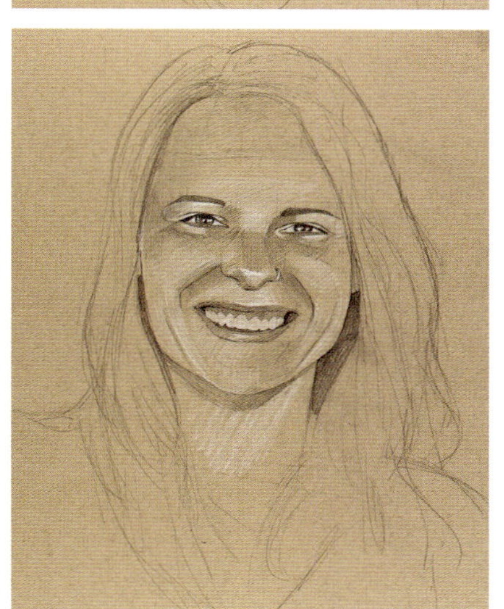

3 *ADD TONE AND VALUE*

Now that you have things in the right places, you can begin to show form. Remember that likeness is only as good as the form that you indicate. This can be done with line only, but is usually more successful with line and tone.

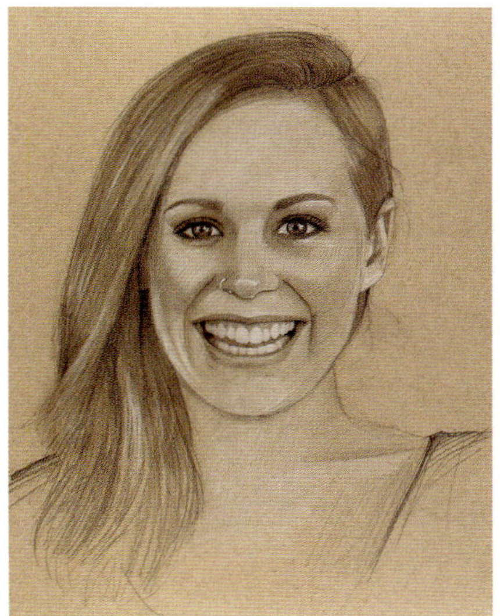

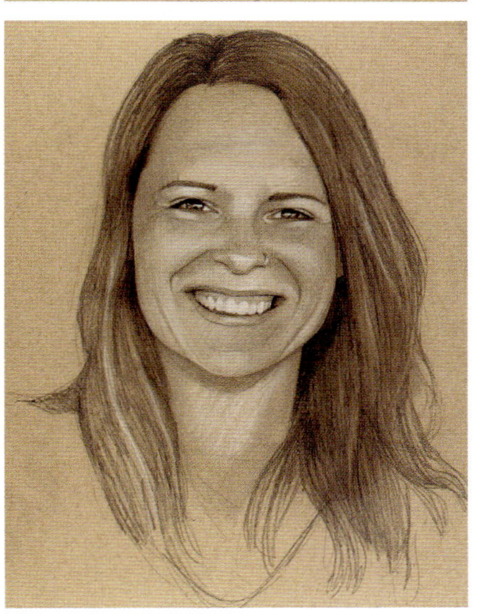

4 *DEFINE THE FEATURES*

Refer back to the What Makes a Likeness page in chapter 3. Only once you have blocked in the shapes to determine where the features go can you define the features themselves.

THE MAAS METHOD

In addition to the grid, tracing and freehand methods, I have created a fourth method to help my students with the block in stage. With this method—called the Maas method—I have taken the best of the freehand and grid methods and combined them with the age-old tradition of sight-size.

Only you can choose the right method for you, but as you work through the demonstrations in chapter 5, I hope that you try the Maas method at least once. It's an approach you can translate to working from photos or from life. You can tailor it to suit your own needs and, hopefully, it will give you the confidence to draw more. Unlike methods such as grid or tracing, you will learn to build on this method so that one day, you will simply draw freehand.

The Maas method sets up a simple framework on which to create your freehand drawing. Think of it like training wheels that disintegrate when your bike gets up to speed. The method gives you the feeling of security that the grid method might, but without the actual crutch of the grid. Best of all, you can use it under virtually any circumstance.

As I mentioned, the basis for the Maas method is something called sight-size. Sight-size, simply put, is lining up your subject with your paper so that the size of the model is the same size as the paper. In the end, your drawing will be life-size.

Like many techniques in the art world, it's hard to pinpoint where sight-size began. Some say as early as the 1400s, citing references to da Vinci and others using the method. But it wasn't until Scottish artist Sir Henry Raeburn explained the method that we had a definitive version.

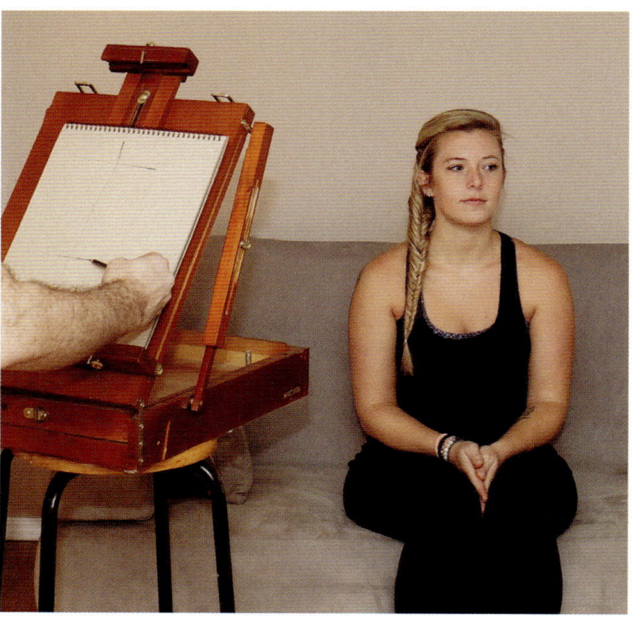

Easel at Casual Distance
Here we see the artist drawing his model at a casual distance.

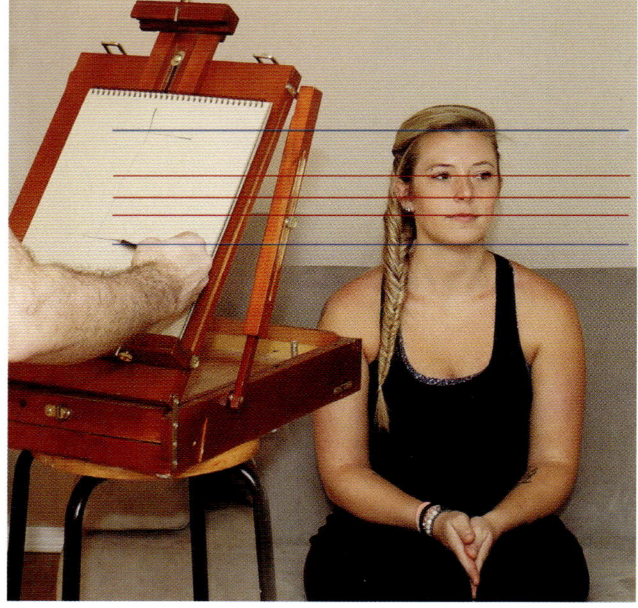

Easel at Sight-Size Distance
If the artist moves his easel so that it is in exactly the right position, the guidelines of the model's face will line up exactly with the lines on the paper.

Make a line on your paper indicating the top of the head and another mark indicating the bottom of the chin. These marks can be made at any distance from the model; their purpose is to allow you to decide what size you want the head to be on your page.

After the marks are made, move the easel closer or farther away from the model until the top of the head and the base of the chin line up with the marks on your paper. Once everything is lined up, sketch the remaining horizontal lines for the eyes, the nose, the mouth—all at an accurate height based on a sight-size relationship with the model.

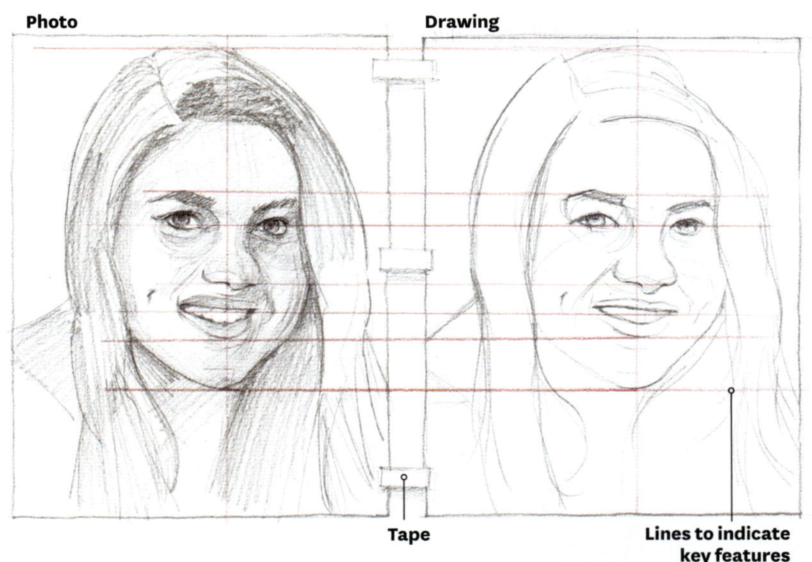

Sight-Size Method from a Photo

By applying the sight-size method to a photograph, we can measure out lines to indicate key features. This allows us to make sure that we have a foundation, or a starting point, to begin an accurate drawing. Note, however, that with this method, the photograph you use must be the same size as your intended finished drawing in order to provide an accurate reference.

As with sight-size life drawing, line up your reference photo with your drawing paper and mark guidelines for the head, chin and major features before you begin. These marks will assist you in creating an accurate drawing.

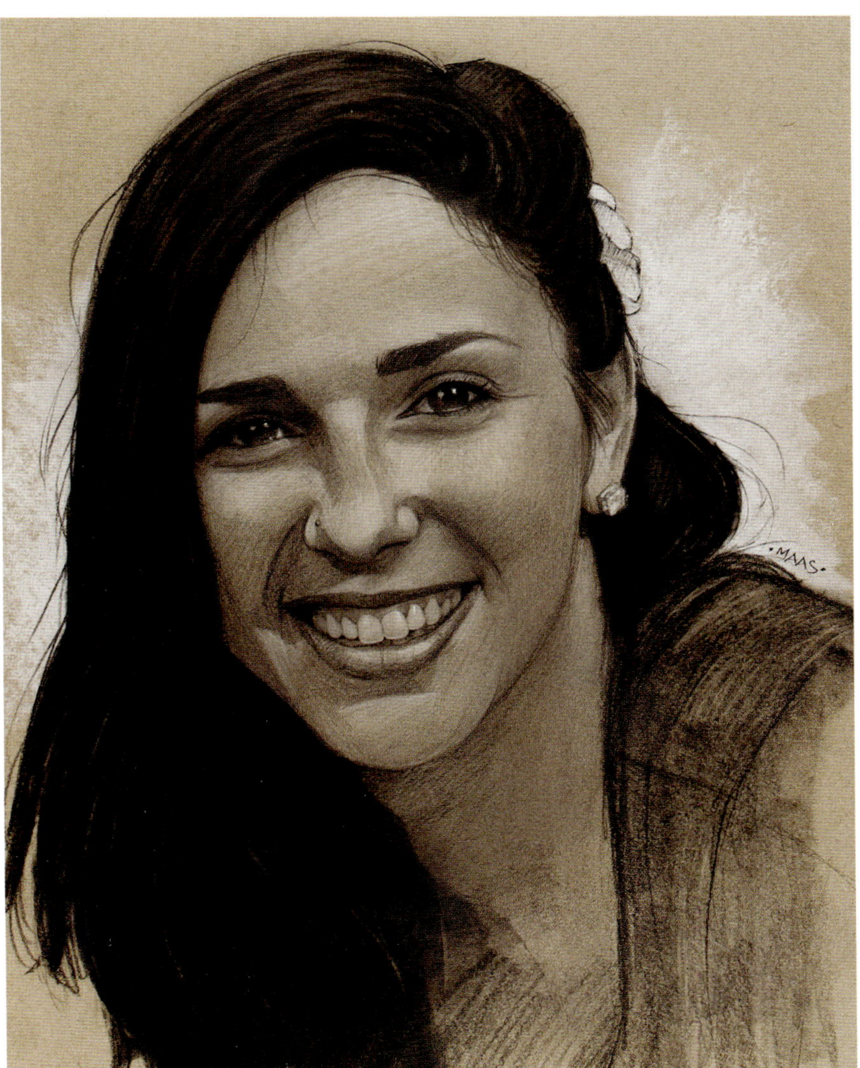

MAAS METHOD PROS AND CONS

Unlike the grid and tracing methods, the Maas method is the closest to freehand drawing when it comes to helping you learn to draw without the need for tricks or encumbrances. With this method, you are simply learning the foundations for measuring, and as you become more comfortable with it, you will be able to translate those methods into pure freehand drawing.

Emilie
Graphite and white charcoal on toned paper
14" × 11" (36cm × 28cm)

THE MAAS METHOD

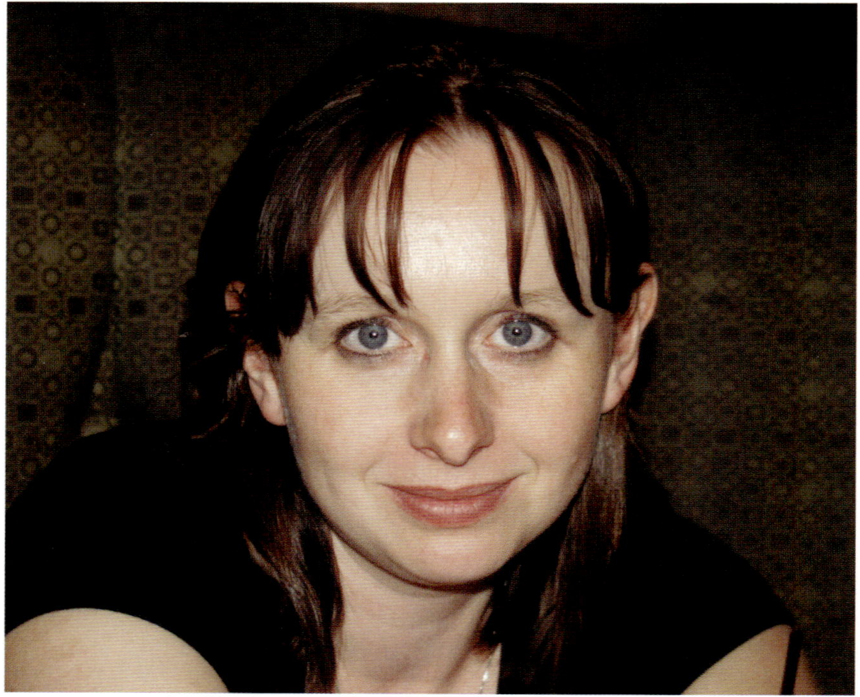

Reference photo

1 MARK THE HORIZONTAL LINES
Tape your reference directly next to your drawing paper and lightly draw horizontal lines across from the reference onto the paper indicating the top of the head, bottom of the chin, eyes, ears, nose and mouth.

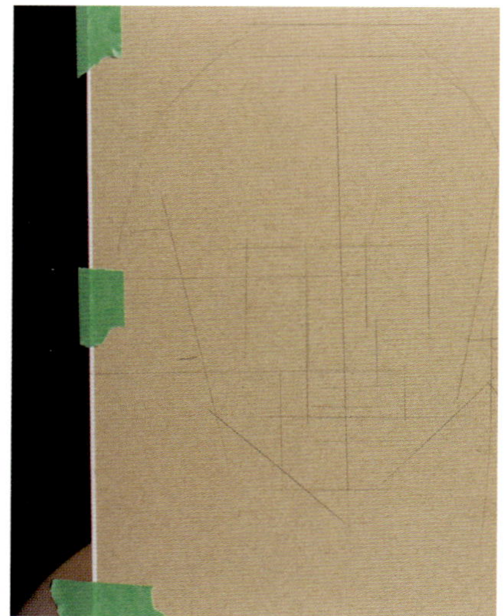

2 MARK THE VERTICAL LINES
Tape the reference to the top of the paper and do the same as step 1, but with the vertical lines including the center of the face, sides of the head, chin, and sides of the eyes, mouth and nose.

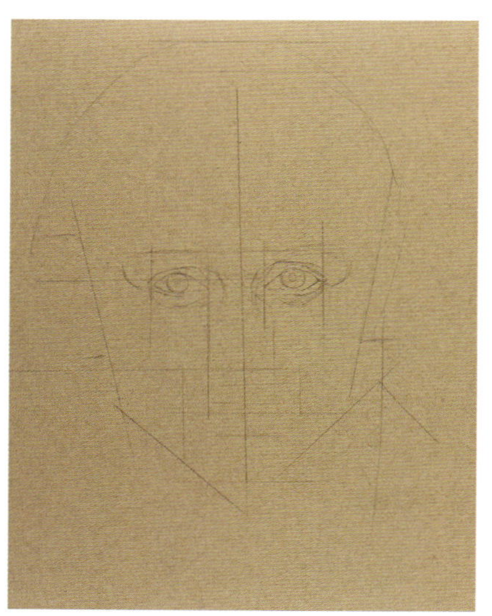

3 RENDER THE MOST PROMINENT FEATURES
Start with whatever features are the most obvious or prominent. In this case, render the eyes. Keep your reference taped next to your drawing while you block in the features.

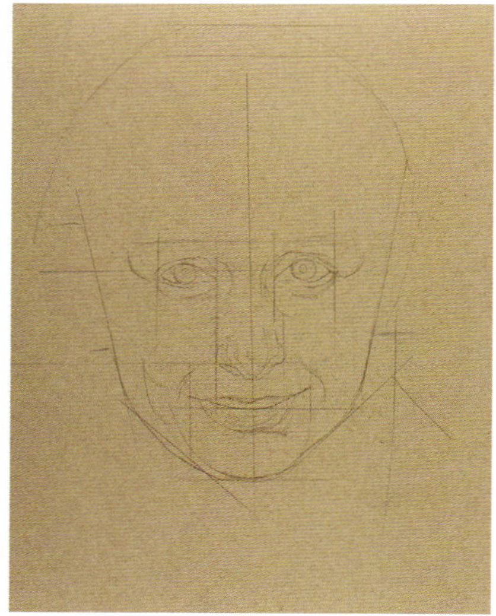

4 ADD OTHER FEATURES
Some, like the eyes and nose, are totally laid out by connecting the vertical and horizontal lines added in steps 1 and 2. Others, such as the smile lines, are laid in based on the relationship to the other features and elements.

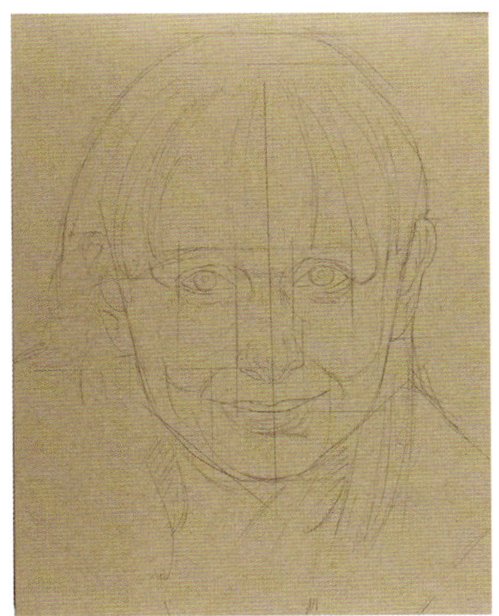

5 *FINALIZE THE FEATURES*
Double-check the lines against your reference that is still taped next to your drawing. Going forward, the rest of the drawing can be completed freehand if you wish.

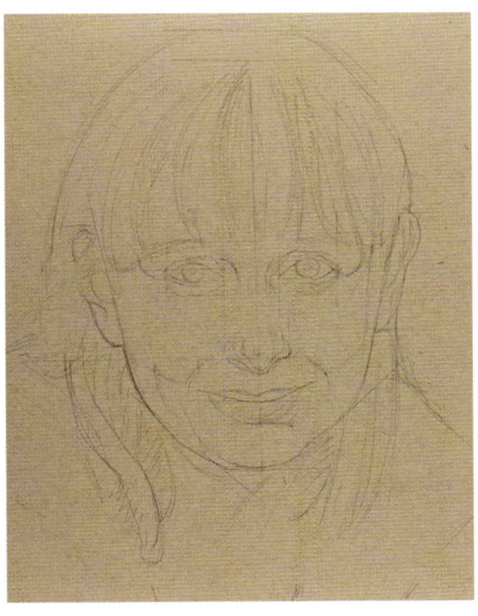

6 *ERASE THE LINES*
Even though your initial lines are quite light, erase them especially if white charcoal will be going over the top of those areas.

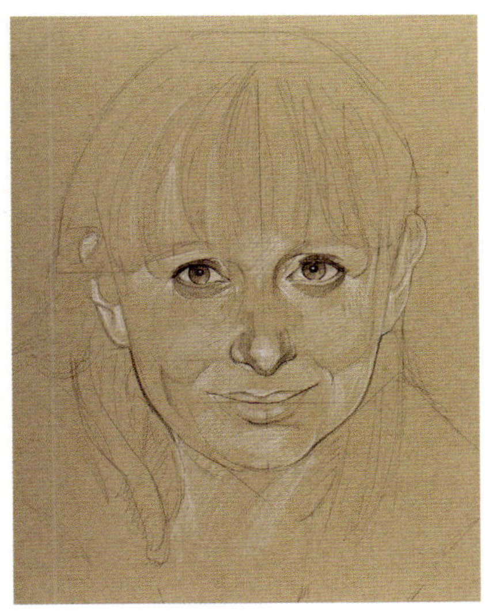

7 *START ADDING TONE*
Here, lights and darks are added simultaneously because the drawing is on toned paper. Begin adding white charcoal and graphite to block in the initial values.

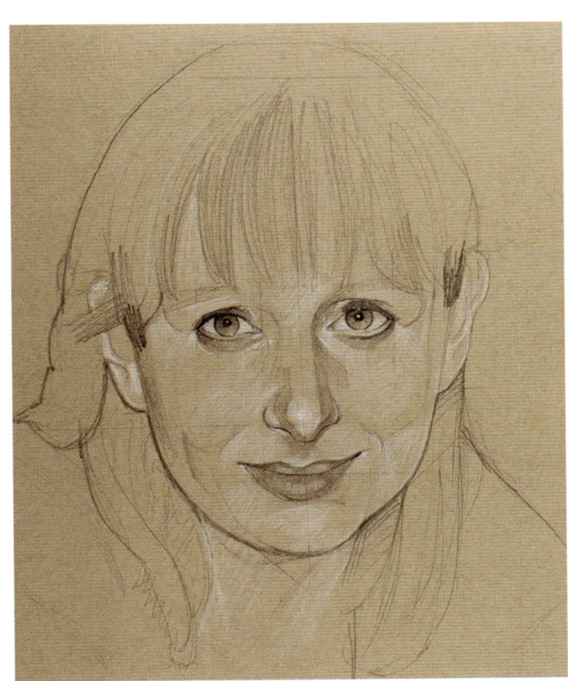

8 *ESTABLISH THE EXTREME LIGHTS, DARKS AND MIDTONES*
Define edges and use shapes to indicate form. Establish the darkest darks and lightest lights so the midtones will be easier to define in the next few stages.

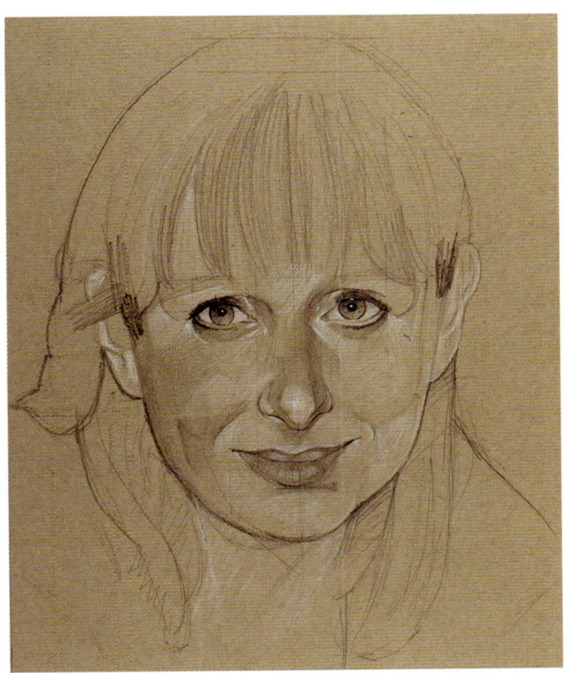

9 *DEFINE THE CHEEKS AND NOSE*
Begin to define the form of the cheeks and nose to establish a likeness.

10 ***ADD THE HAIR*** Block in the darkest sections of hair so the rest of the values can be compared to it. Compare the drawing now to previous stages and notice how different the darker areas look in comparison.

11 ***COMPLETE THE VALUES*** As the drawing gets closer to completion, refine each area so it relates to all of the other parts. Refine the details and consider all edges (hard and soft).

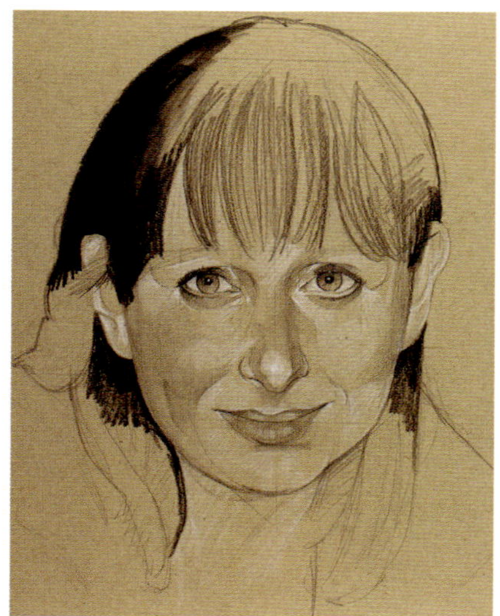

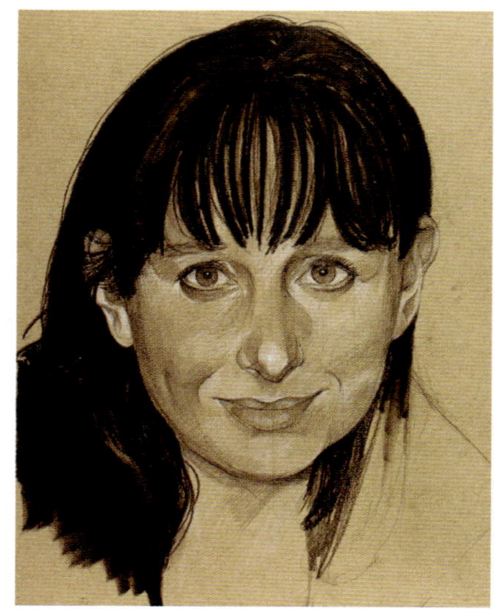

HARD VS. SOFT EDGES

You may have heard artists refer to edges as either soft or hard, but what does that mean? Simply put, a hard edge is wherever an edge is well defined or definite—you can tell where the object ends. A soft edge, on the other hand, disappears or fades into the edges around it. Look at the example of Madison. Most of the edges of her shirt are hard, but her hair fades into the background in some places. Her pant legs also fade into each other and the seat below her. This use of hard and soft edges allows the artist to guide the viewer's eyes around the image.

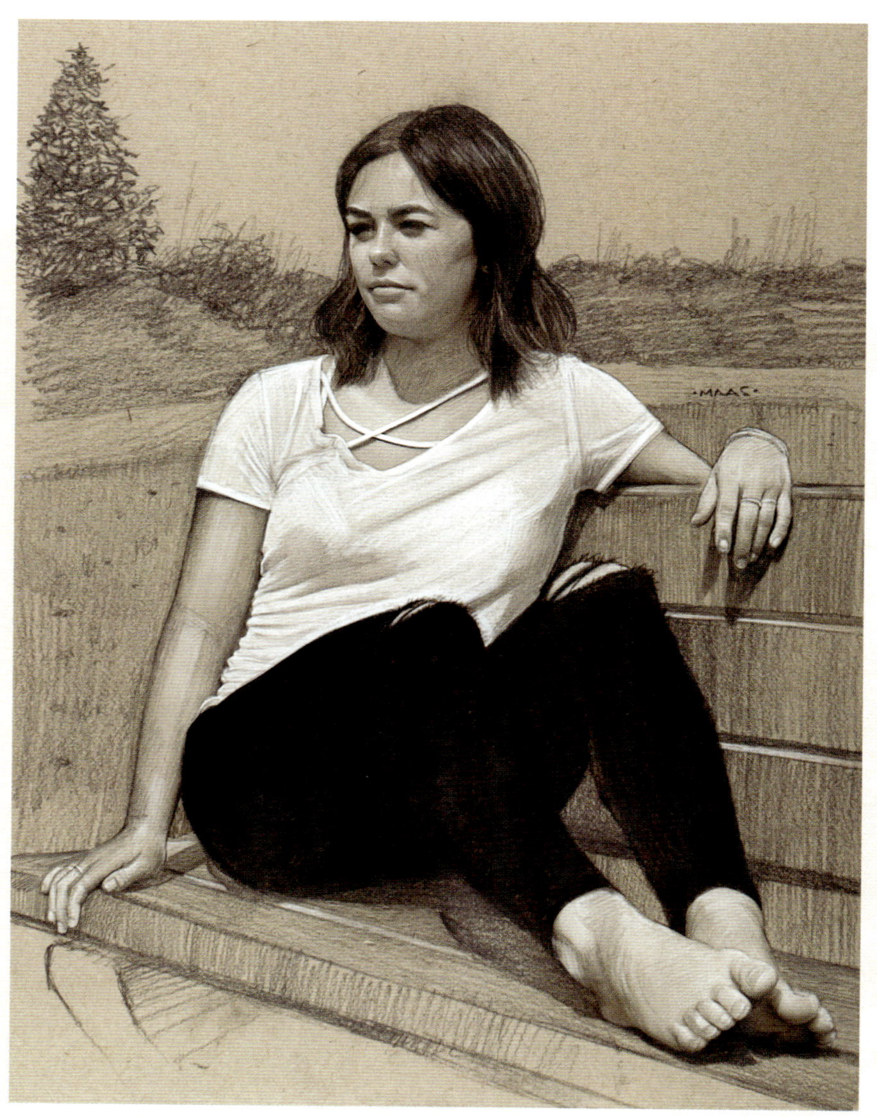

Madison 2
Graphite and white charcoal on toned paper
14" × 11" (36cm × 28cm)

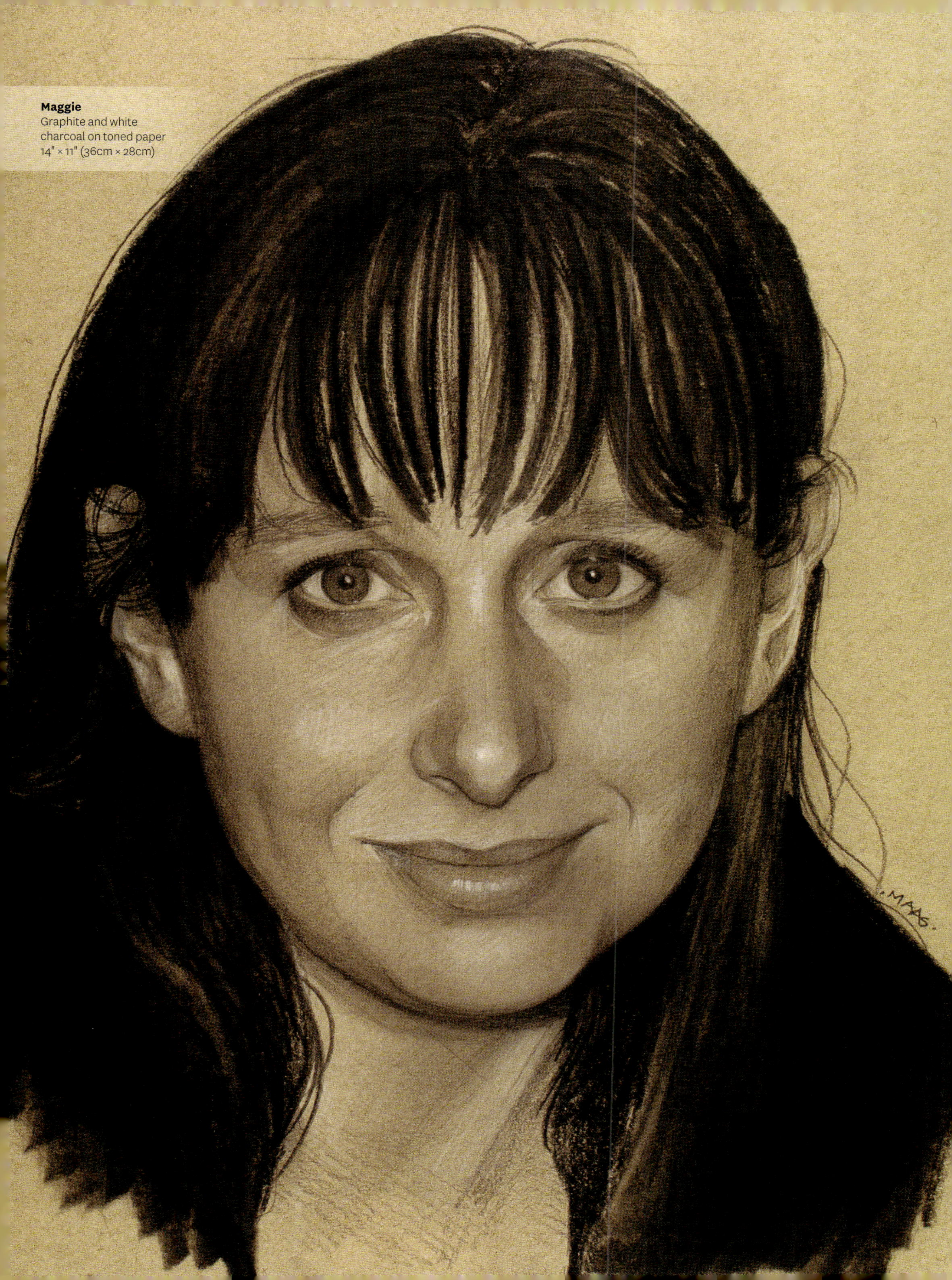

Maggie
Graphite and white charcoal on toned paper
14" × 11" (36cm × 28cm)

5 PORTRAIT DEMONSTRATIONS

You now have all the tools necessary to start drawing your own portraits. In the next half of the book, we will concentrate exclusively on complete step-by-step demonstrations.

Each demonstration lists the materials used as well as the block-in method (Maas method, freehand or tracing). The vast majority of the portraits are on toned paper (Strathmore toned tan or Stonehenge Kraft), but there are a few on white as well as a full-color demonstration in pastel. Experiment with the materials and different block-in methods, and most importantly, have fun!

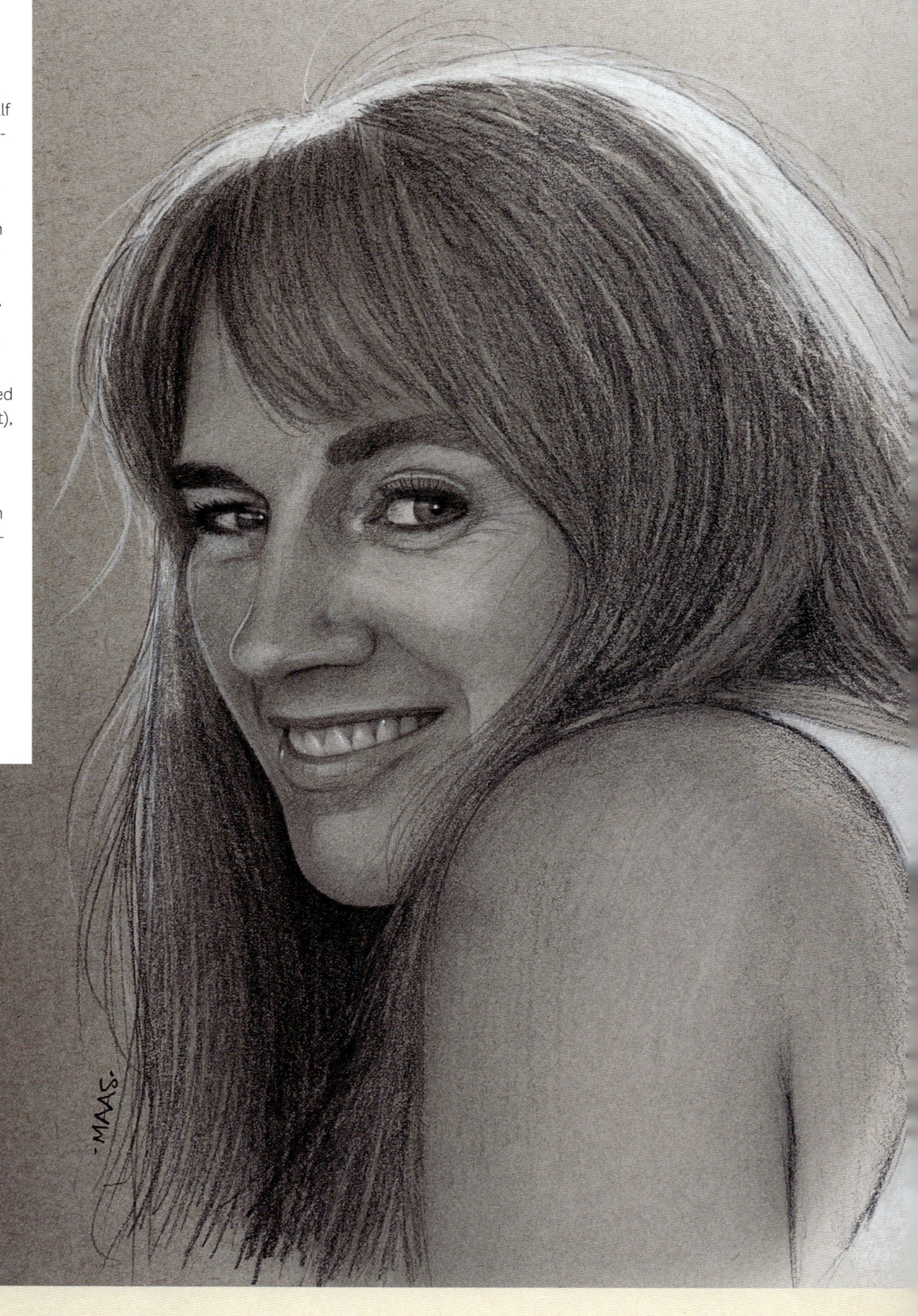

Debbie
Graphite and white charcoal on toned paper
14"× 11" (36cm × 28cm)

THINGS TO CONSIDER

Here are a few things to consider before you set out to complete the demonstrations in this chapter.

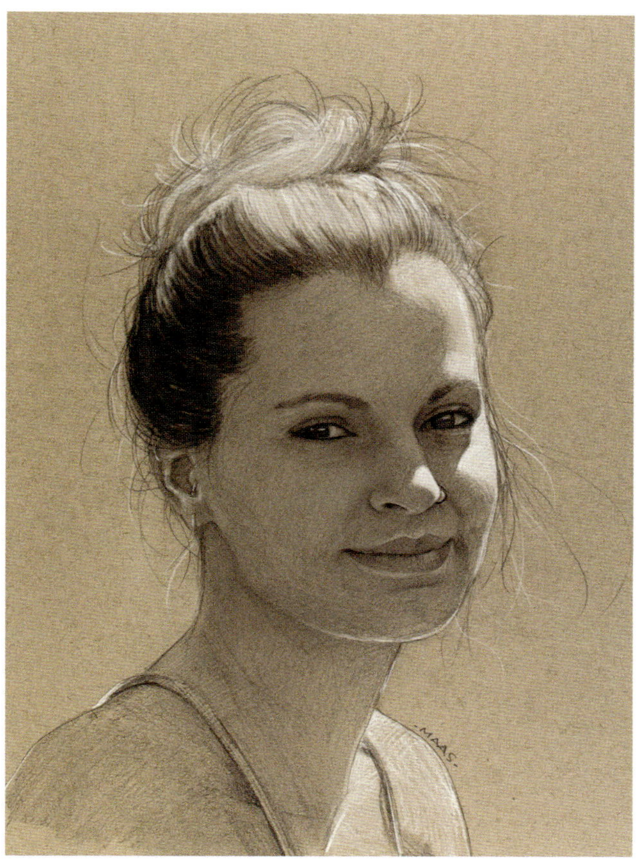

How Big Should You Draw?

Everyone has a size that works best for them. For me it always comes down to how big will the head be? My preference is to work in a way that from the top of the head to the base of the chin the face will measure 7 to 9 inches (18 to 23 centimeters). For this reason most of my portraits are done on 14" × 11" (36cm × 28cm) paper. If I am working in pastel I usually prefer a slightly larger head, around 8 to 11 inches (20 to 28 centimeters) in height, so using a paper that is 16 " × 12" (41cm × 30cm) gives me a little more room to work.

Lynnsey
Graphite and white charcoal on toned paper
14" × 11" (36cm × 28cm)

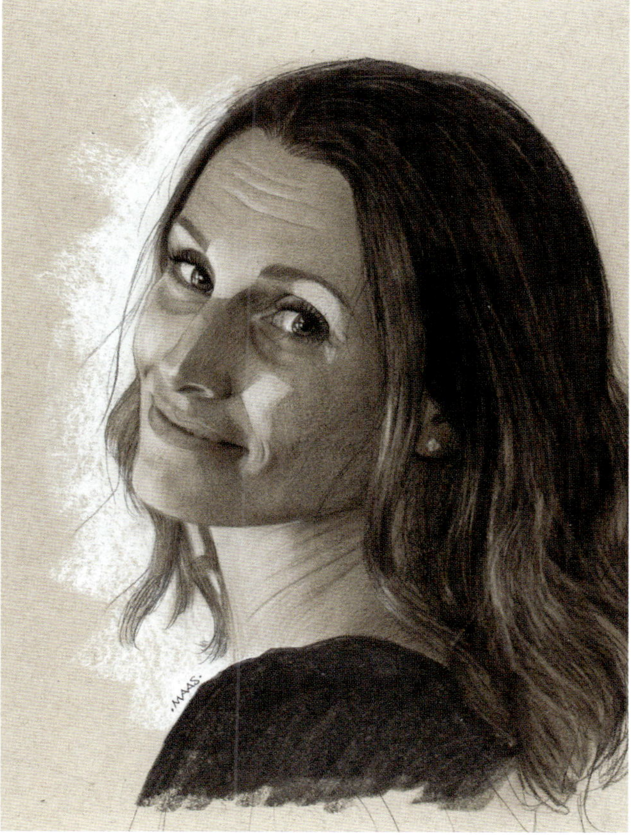

Work in the Direction of Your Dominant Hand

I am right-handed, so most of the time I try to work from left to right. If you are left-handed, you may have better results following the demos by working right to left. This way you won't smudge your work surface as much as you work. If you do find yourself smudging, place a piece of paper under your hand to stop or hinder the amount of damage.

Carrie
Graphite and white charcoal on toned paper
14" × 11" (36cm × 28cm)

DEMONSTRATION

ALISA

Alisa is a natural beauty. Her hair has streaks so the color ranges from quite dark to light blonde. This poses an interesting challenge when rendering. I liked my reference photograph but decided the portrait would be better vertical, so I cropped down the image to just head and shoulders.

Materials

DRAWING METHOD

Maas

TOOLS

14" × 11" (36cm × 28cm) Strathmore 400 toned tan sketch paper

ebony pencil

HB, 2B, 4B, 8B woodless graphite pencils

kneaded eraser

white charcoal pencil

white Conté stick

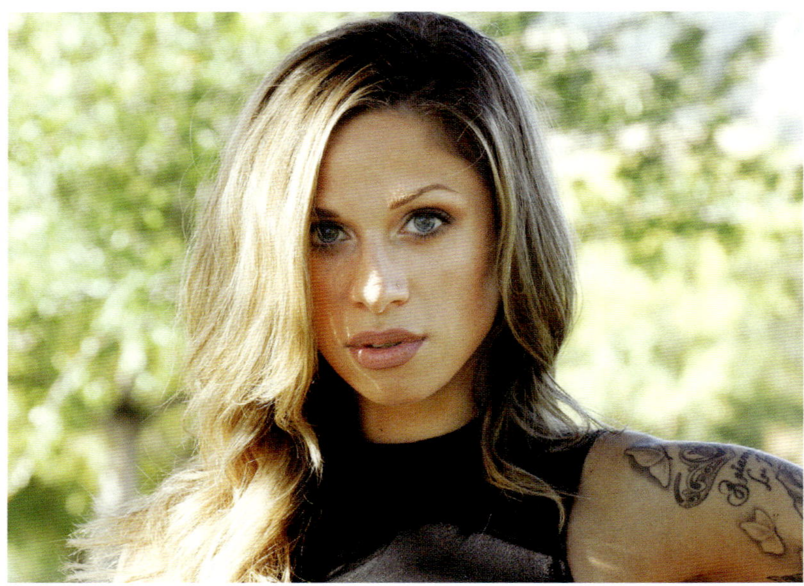

Reference Photo

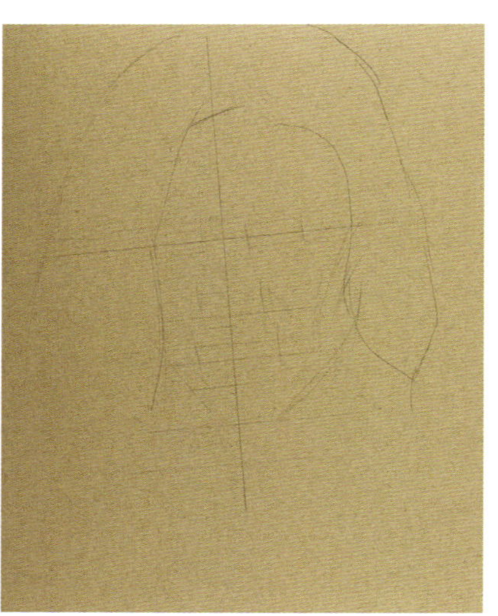

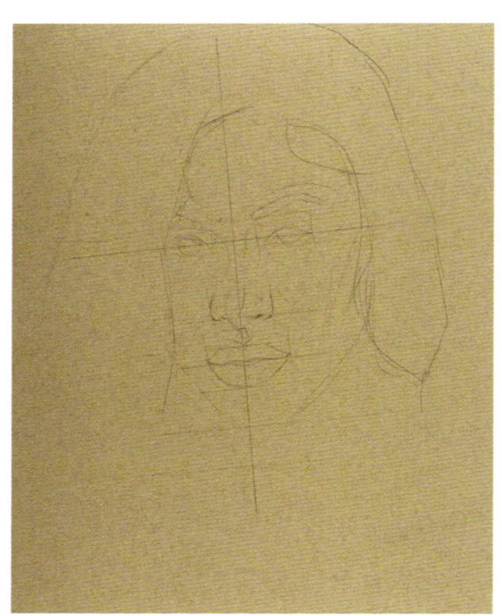

1 *BLOCK IN THE INITIAL LINES*
Using an HB or 2B pencil, lay down the center vertical line that bisects the face and a rough measurements of overall head size. Keep it light!

2 *MARK THE VERTICAL LINES*
Using the Maas method, tape your reference above your drawing and lay down the vertical lines according to the reference.

3 *INDICATE THE FEATURES*
Render the initial features such as the eyes, mouth and nose. Work lightly and don't be afraid to erase some of the working lines if they become too dark.

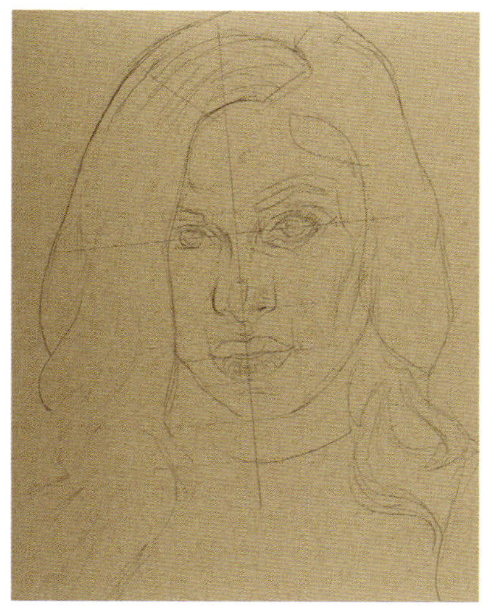

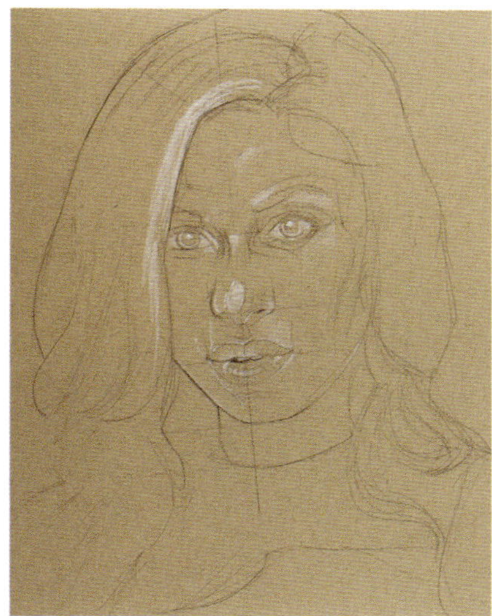

4 *FINISH ADDING THE FEATURES*
Finish laying in the lines for the hair and features. At this point the drawing is a complete line drawing. No form or tone has been addressed but the basic features should be in the correct places because of the guidelines.

5 *BEGIN THE HIGHLIGHTS*
Since we are working on toned paper, add the highlights using the white charcoal pencil. (This will be later in the process if you are working on white paper.) Vary the pressure of the white charcoal as you would with graphite—more pressure for the very bright areas and less pressure for the slighter highlights.

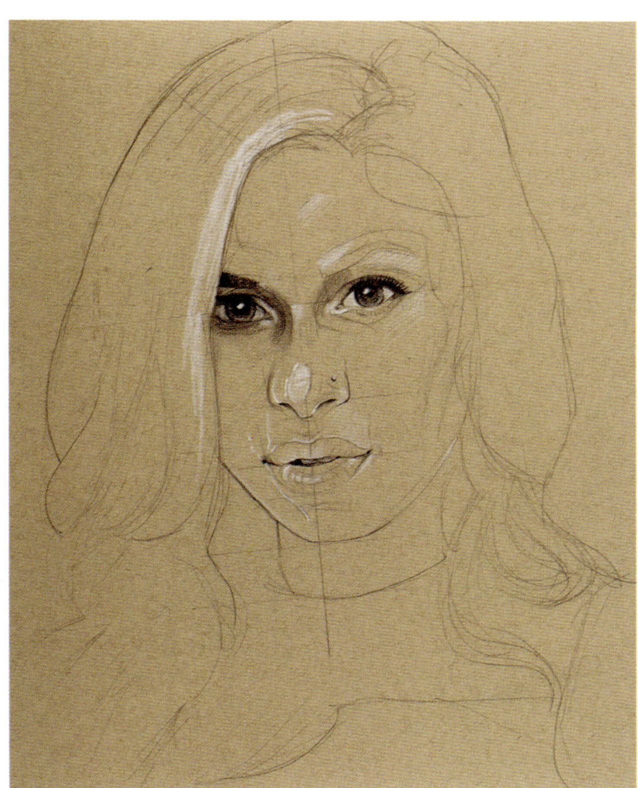

6 *BEGIN THE DARKS*
Using a 4B pencil, begin rendering the eyes. They are typically the darkest part (and the main focal point) of most portraits. This is also a good time to double-check the overall structure and features.

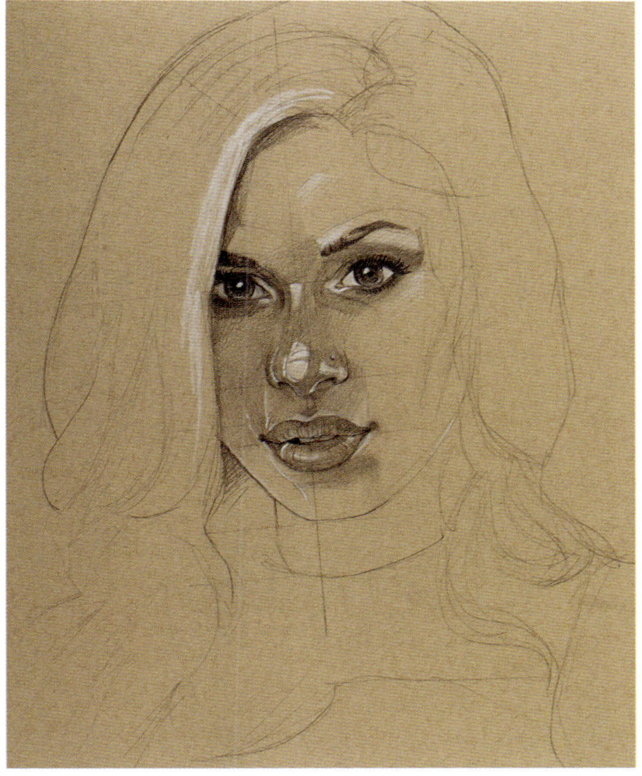

7 *ADD MIDTONES*
Once the light of the highlights and the dark of the eyes, nostrils and mouth have been established, add the midtones with an ebony pencil.

8 ***CONTINUE THE HIGHLIGHTS*** Continue developing the hair and face highlights with white charcoal, paying attention to how you vary your edges.

9 ***ESTABLISH THE HAIR MIDTONES*** The strong light of the reference photo presents an interesting challenge: the face is largely in shadows while the left side of the hair is very bright. A woodless pencil (2B or 4B) is ideal for this as it has a wider point of contact.

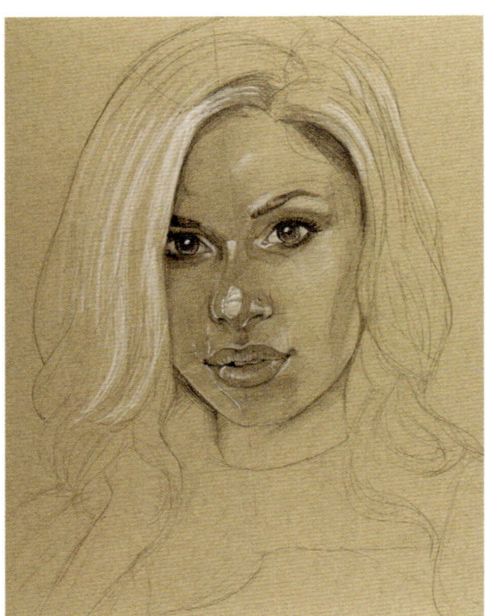

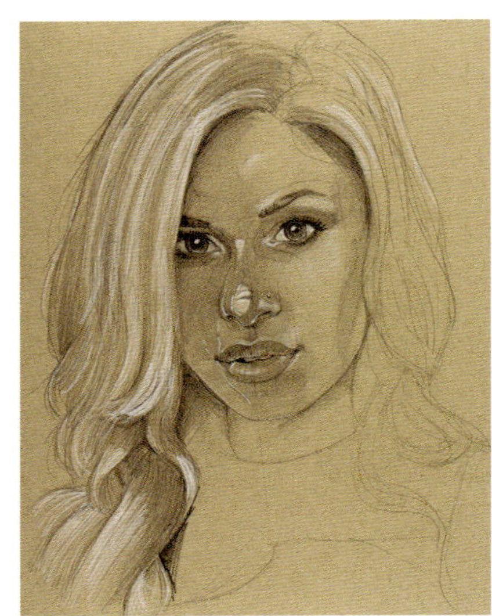

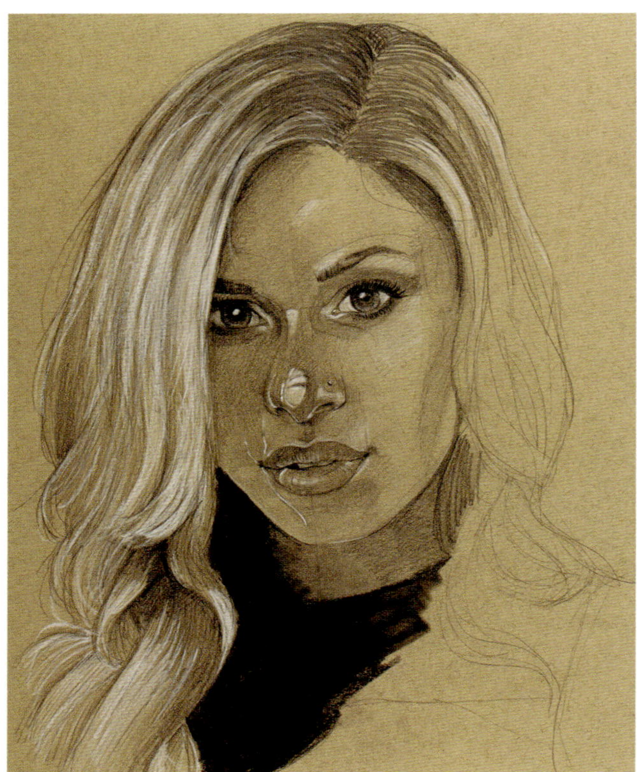

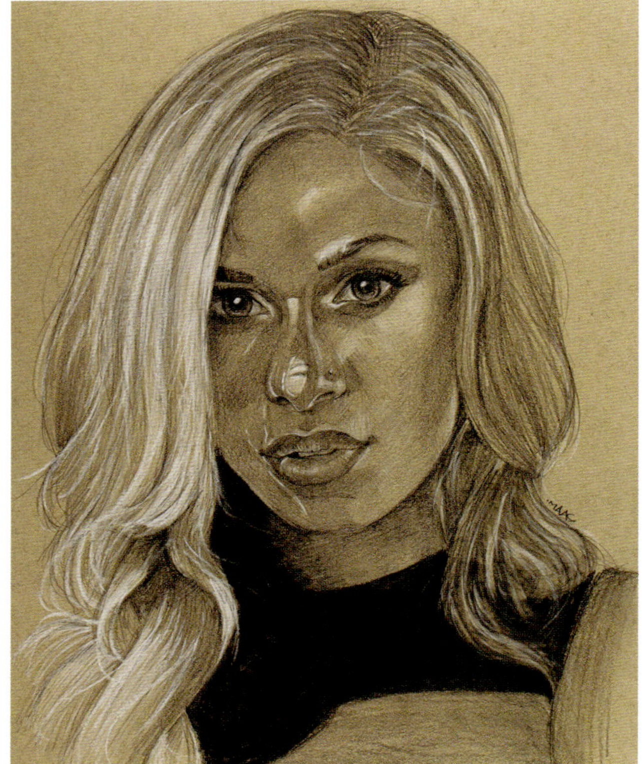

10 ***CREATE MASSES OF HAIR*** Switch between a 4B woodless pencil and a kneaded eraser to establish streaks by drawing and lifting graphite. Remember to make your pencil strokes in the same direction as the hair in order to gradually build up the hair mass. Add the dark area of the shirt using an 8B pencil (I find General's woodless pencil to be the absolute darkest available) to help establish the darkest darks. This may require adding more midtones to the face in relation to the dark values added in the clothing.

11 ***EVALUATE AND FINISH THE DRAWING*** Continue to build up the tone and contrast while paying attention to hard and soft edges. Introduce hair wisps with a sharp graphite pencil—4B or 8B—and some white conté. It's at this stage that areas that seemed dark enough before may need to be darkened further. Look at the whole drawing as once piece even though it's been developed in parts up until now.

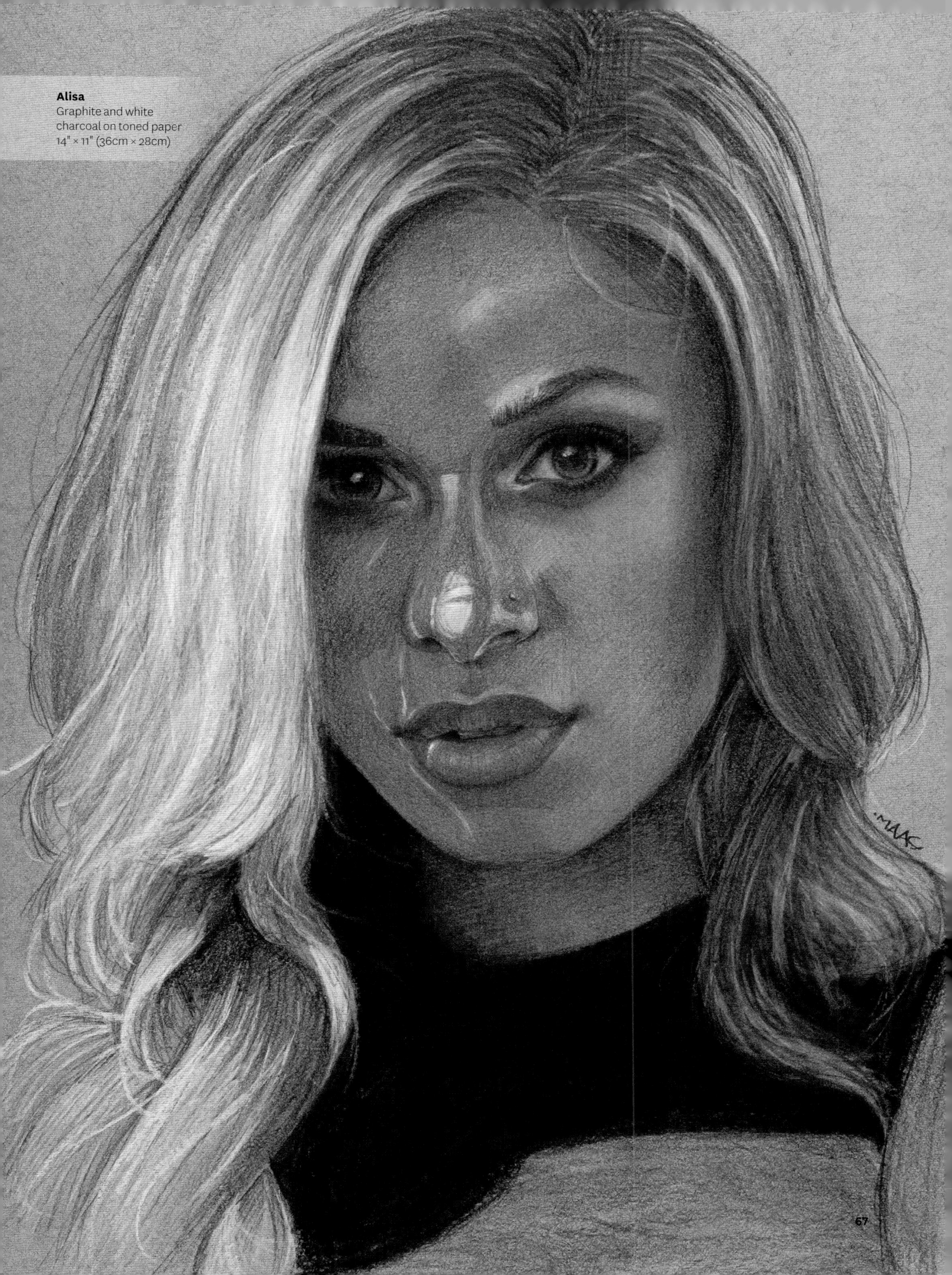

Alisa
Graphite and white charcoal on toned paper
14" × 11" (36cm × 28cm)

DEMONSTRATION

LEO

Leo is a talented musician and deejay. When posing Leo, I chose to include his headphones in the drawing because they are such an integral part of who he is. I liked the strong lighting in the reference shot although I decided to soften some of the darkness on the left side so that I could make the whole portrait a little more balanced. Don't ever feel like you have to draw exactly what you see in the photo.

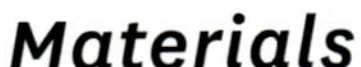

Materials

DRAWING METHOD

Tracing

TOOLS

14" × 11" (36cm × 28cm) Bienfang Bristol white paper

2B, 4B, 6B and 8B graphite pencils

kneaded eraser

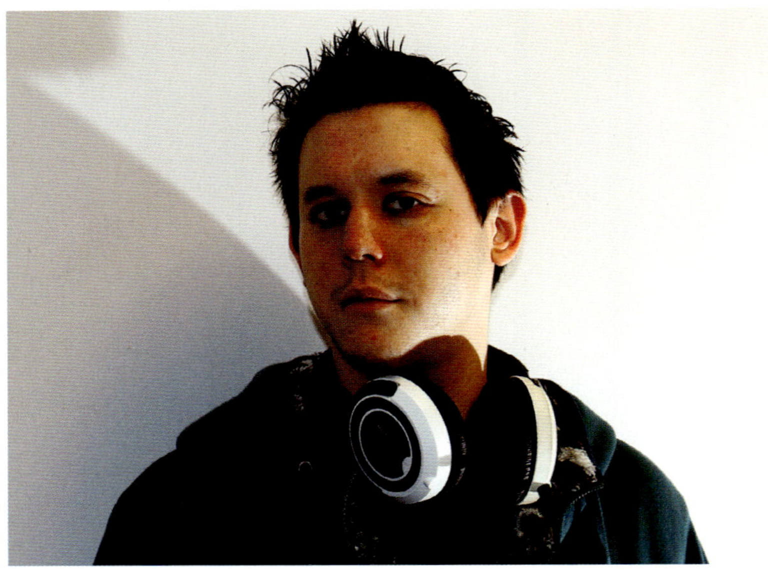

Reference Photo

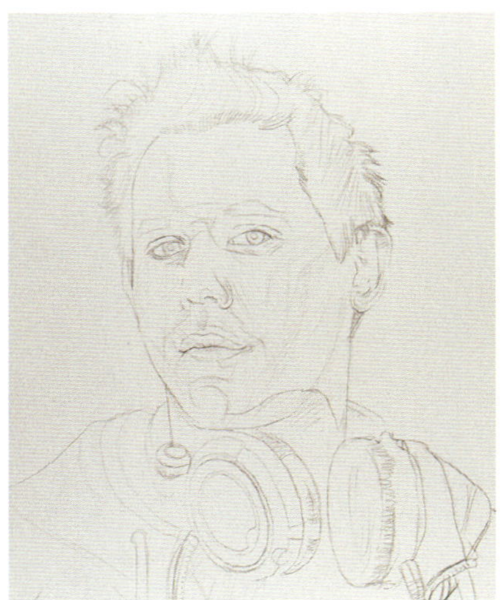

1 *TRACE THE DRAWING*
Begin by tracing your reference using a 2B pencil and a lightbox, projector or transfer paper. It is important to make sure all elements (shapes, not just features) are included. Trace the form not just the outline.

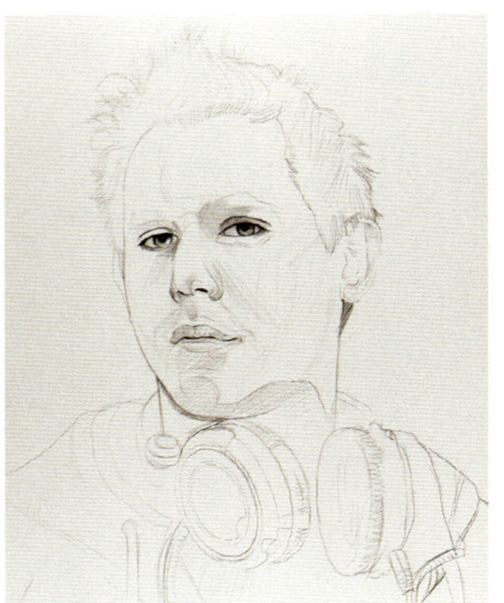

2 *ESTABLISH THE DARKEST DARKS*
Some artists prefer to build up all areas slowly, but by starting with a few key dark areas rendered with a 6B pencil, midtones will be established more easily (and more accurately) later. Eyebrows, and some areas of light tone, are added.

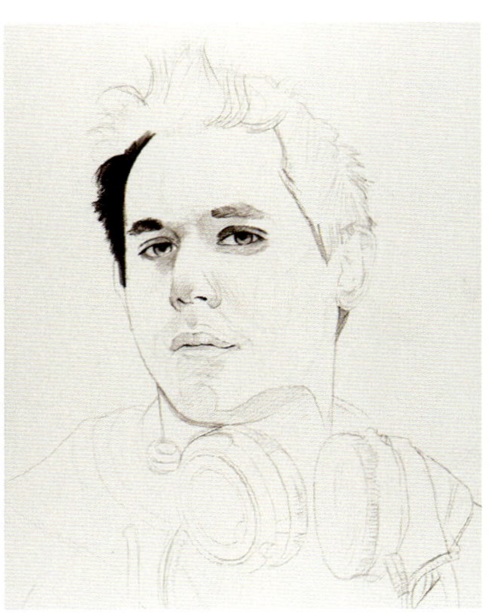

3 *BEGIN THE HAIR*
Because the subject's hair is so dark, render it early with an 8B pencil to help you determine the correct values for the face. Lightly indicate other areas such as the shadow cast by the headphones.

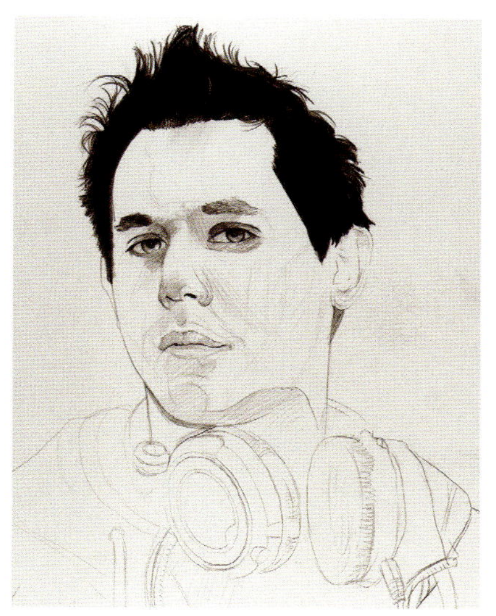

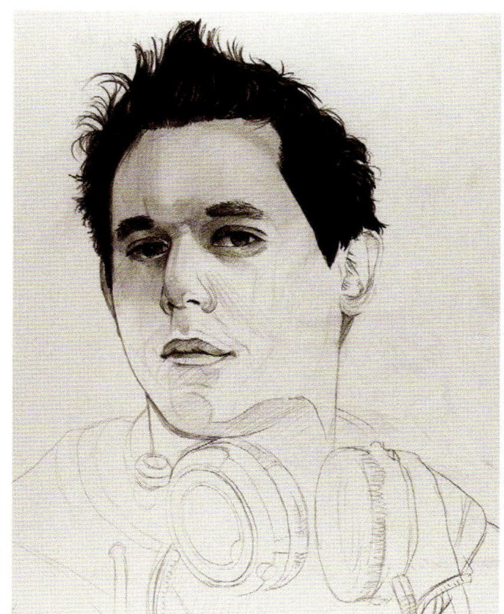

4 ***FINISH THE HAIR***
Finish the main mass of the hair using a 6B pencil, then add the sharp edges and spiky wisps. It is important to treat each flyaway hair thoughtfully. Do not just scribble them in—deliberately draw each spike of hair following the direction and curve as the hair would. Vary the pressure so that each hair looks organic.

5 ***ADD MIDTONES TO THE FACE***
Working down from the hair, add midtones to the forehead, eye areas and cheeks. Lift highlights from the midtones using a kneaded eraser. Use the white of the paper for the whitest whites.

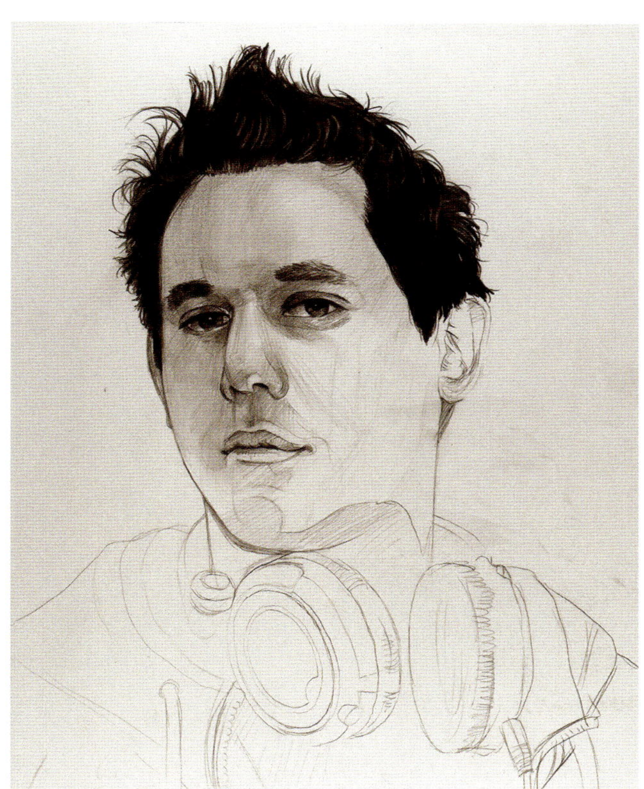

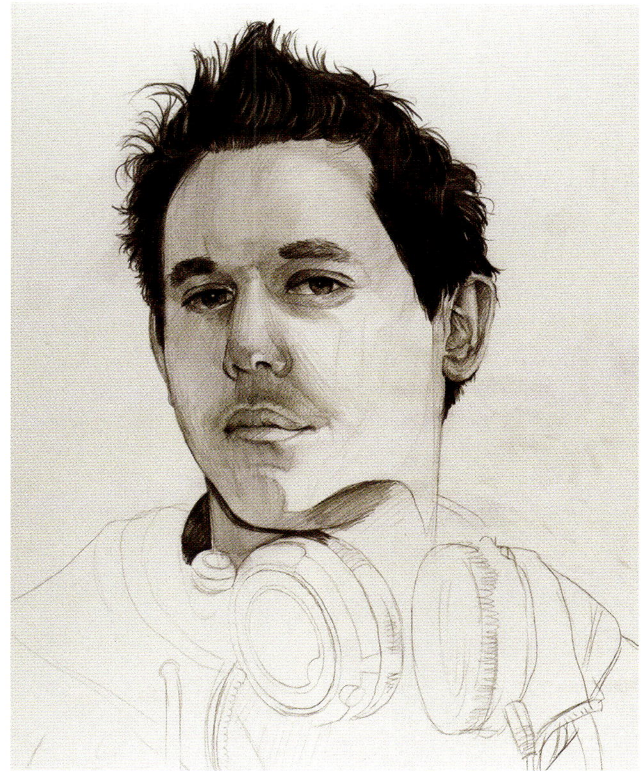

6 ***STUDY THE EYES***
Because they usually provide the strongest area of contrast, the eyes are one of the most significant parts of a portrait, so pay special attention to them. Look closely at the reference. Are the highlights accurate? Is there volume on the eyeball itself? Are there shadows? Make sure to include sharp edges to create a strong focal point.

7 ***BUILD UP THE NOSE AND MOUTH***
Paying special attention to the soft corners of the mouth, build up tones on the lower half of the face. Note that even though Leo is mostly clean shaven, the skin around his mouth is slightly darker from stubble and hair under the surface, as it is with most adult men.

8 ***FINISH THE FACE***
Now that the face is nearing completion, re-evaluate the tones and make adjustments. Add a cast shadow from the headphones on the neck. The line of the shadow is accentuated and makes an interesting secondary focal point (after the eyes).

9 ***RENDER THE CLOTHING***
Because this is a head-and-shoulders portrait, the clothing is not as important, but it does need to be indicated so we don't end up with floating head syndrome. Simple dark tones will help ground the portrait.

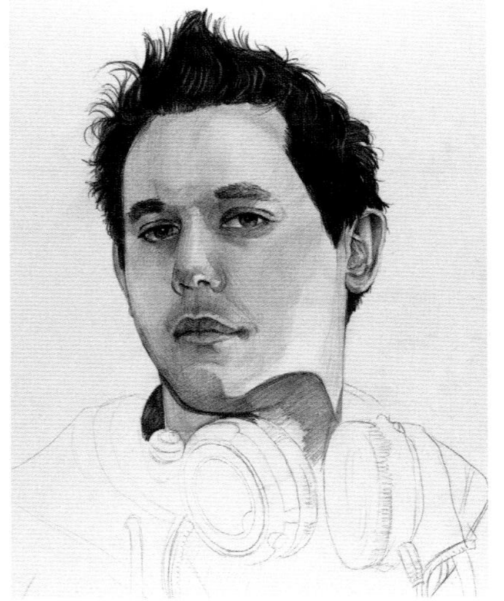

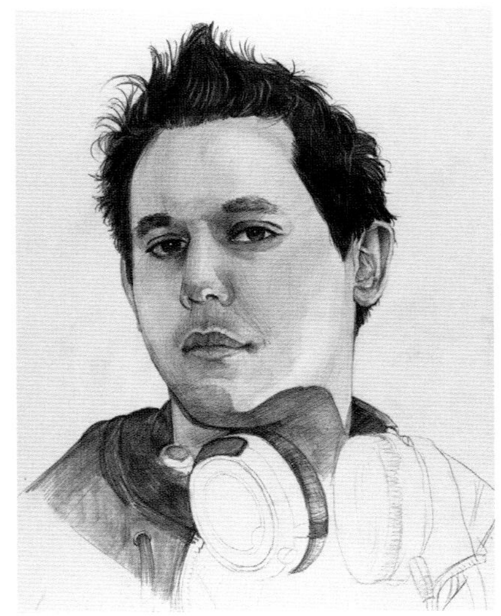

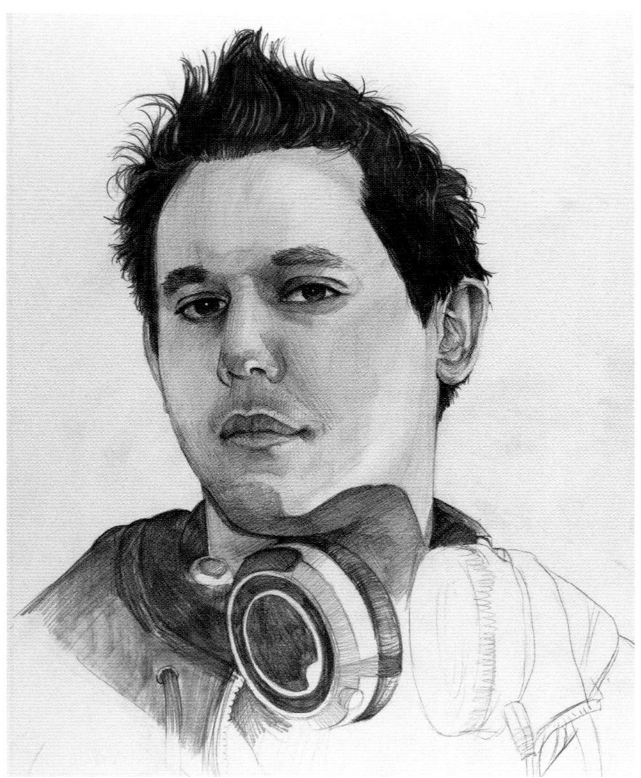

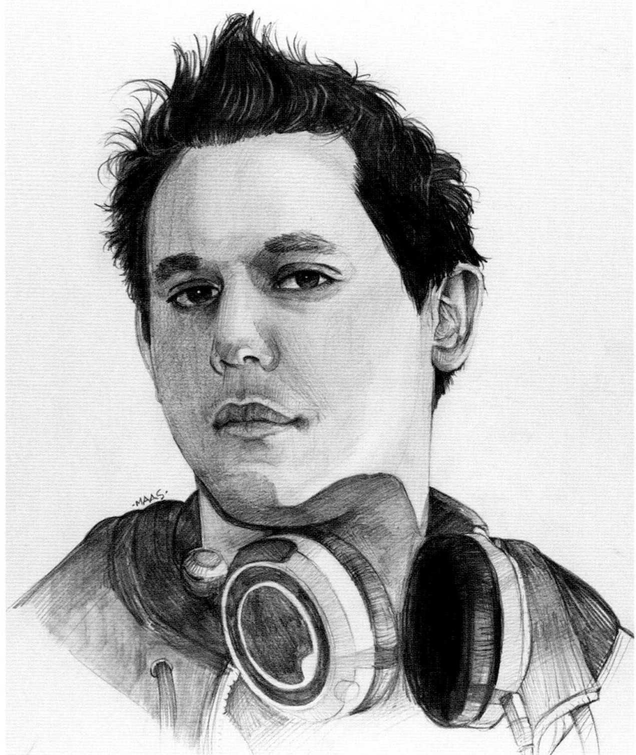

10 ***RENDER THE HEADPHONES***
Add detail to the headphones, clothing and accessories to help tell Leo's story. Notice the interesting shapes, curves and textures in the materials of the earpieces.

11 ***EVALUATE AND FINISH THE DRAWING***
Complete the headphones and clothing, then re-evaluate all the values in the drawing. The dark hair and dark fabric on the headphones make the face look a little washed out, so darkening some areas and shadows in the face bring back energy and focus to the face itself.

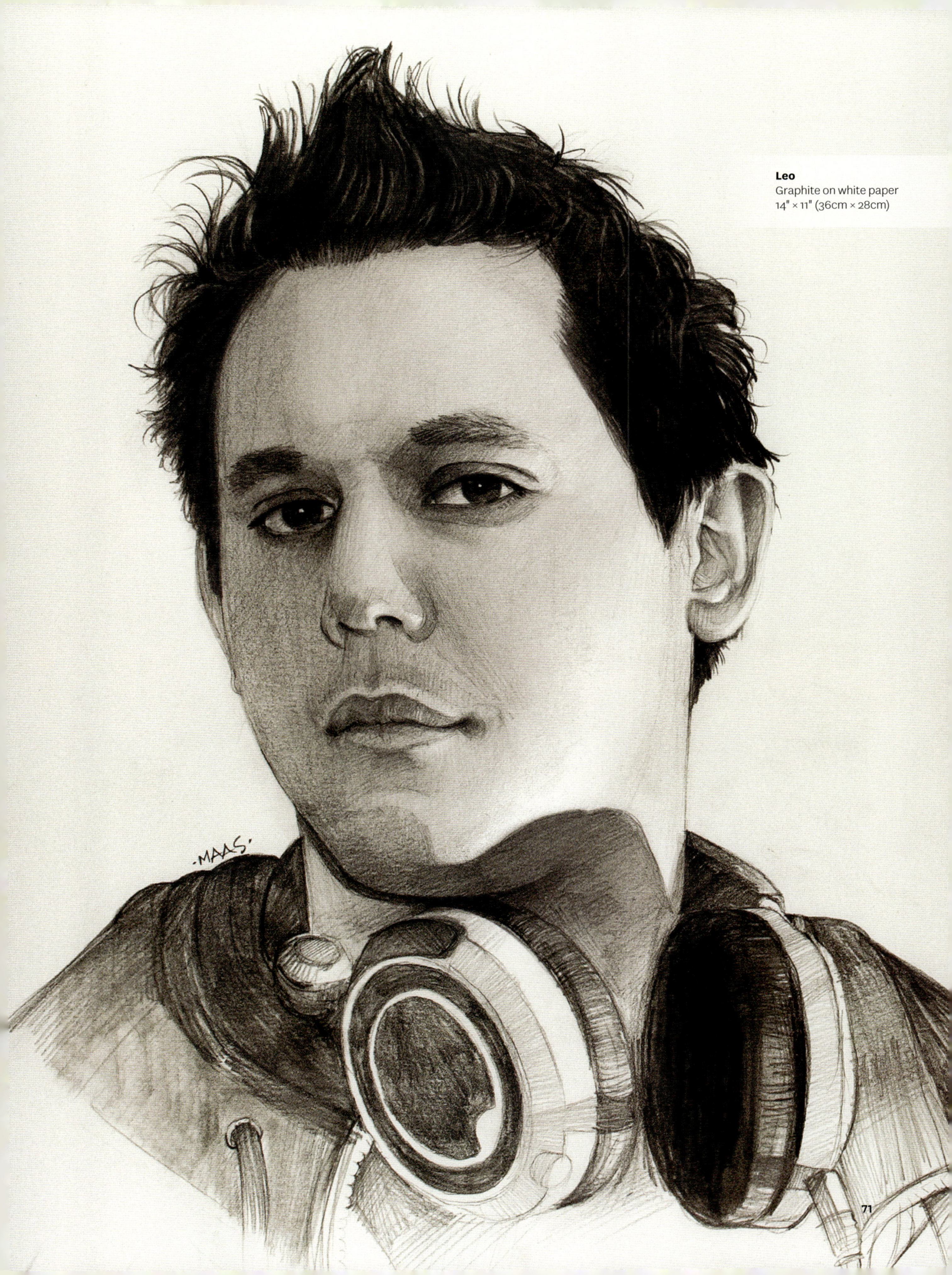

Leo
Graphite on white paper
14" × 11" (36cm × 28cm)

DEMONSTRATION

EMERSON

Emerson was only a few months old when I drew him. Even though he could barely sit on his own, there was an energy in his eyes that I wanted to try to capture. Babies are tricky to draw because they have very soft features. I decided to keep this portrait simple by focusing on his bright, playful eyes.

Materials

DRAWING METHOD

Maas

TOOLS

14" × 11" (36cm × 28cm) Strathmore 400 toned tan sketch paper

ebony pencil

HB, B, 2B and 4B woodless graphite pencils

kneaded eraser

white charcoal pencil

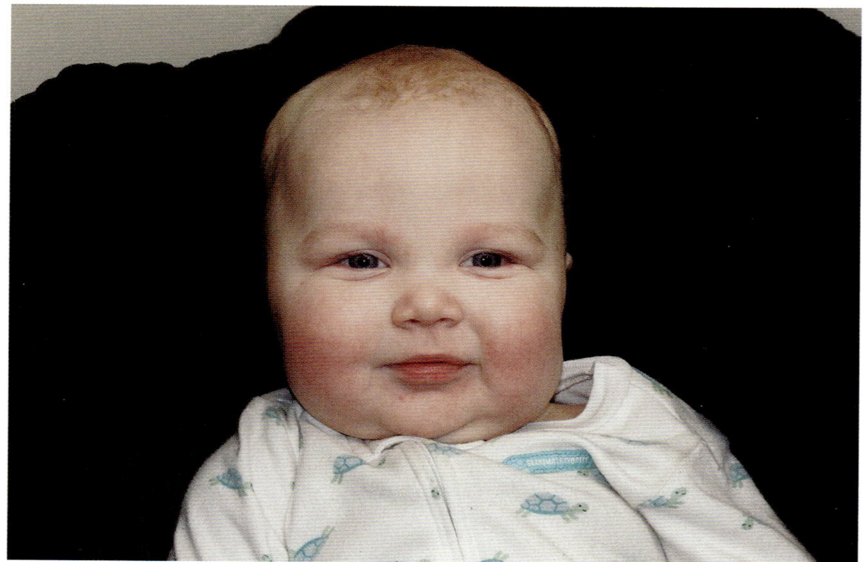

Reference Photo

1 *MARK THE GUIDELINES* Lightly add the key framework lines to indicate the overall shape of the head, the vertical midpoint, and the eyes, nose and mouth.

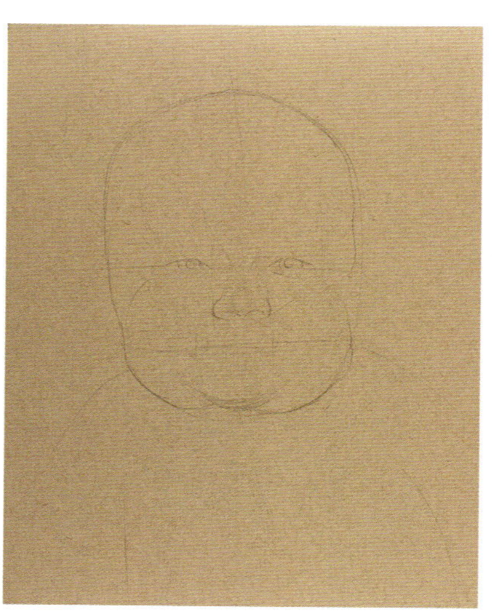

2 *BEGIN TO DEFINE THE FEATURES* Slowly and methodically begin adding features. Use a light touch with an HB or B pencil.

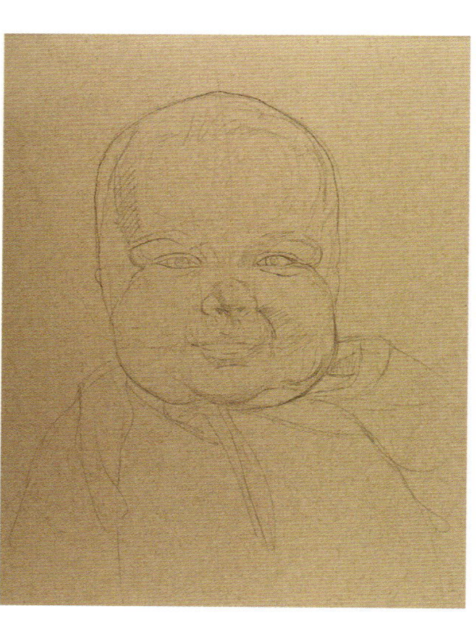

3 *FINISH THE FRAMEWORK* Complete the basic outline of the features (on a baby this usually isn't a lot). Double-check all the proportions. Each line and shape must relate to those that were rendered before them. If something looks wrong in this stage, it will be difficult to correct once the rendering begins.

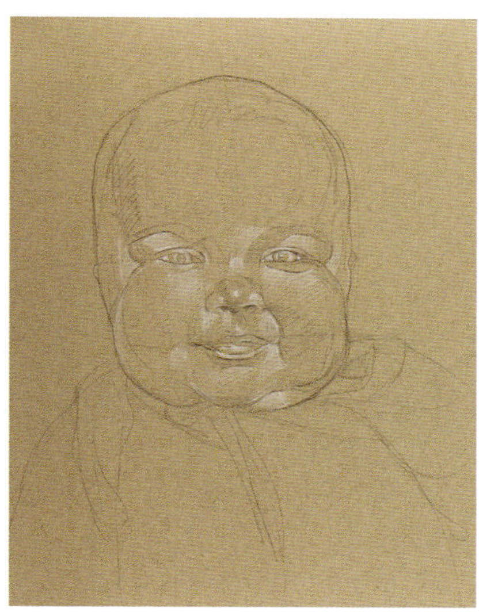

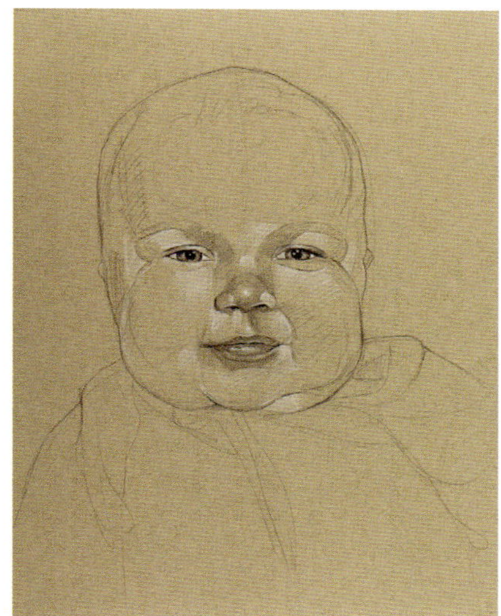

4 ***ADD THE LIGHTS***
Using a white charcoal pencil, establish the lightest lights and some of the mid-bright lights. This may seem counterintuitive if you are used to working on white paper, but on toned paper it is a way of building up lights and darks simultaneously.

5 ***BEGIN THE MIDTONES***
Switch to a 2B pencil and start adding the main features. Don't worry too much about getting all the values right yet—these may change as you add in the rest of the drawing—but be sure to follow the natural form as you lay down strokes.

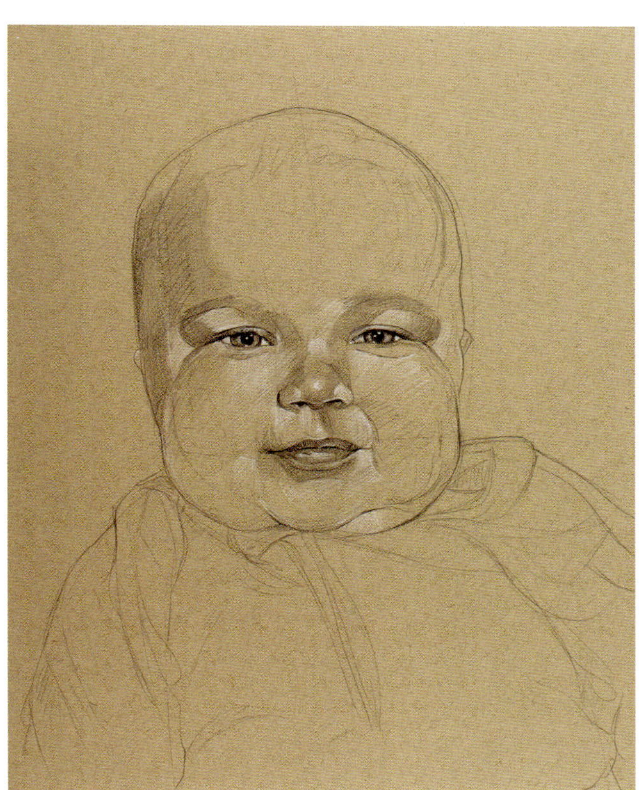

6 ***DEFINE THE SIDE OF THE FACE AND HEAD***
Unlike most adults, babies usually have no hair at all (or very little). This means you'll need to think about the shape of the head in terms of volume and form—how it comes toward you rather than just the side-to-side space. (When a head is covered with hair, there is no need to indicate volume in the top part of the face.) Keep the lines light so they aren't visible through tonal masses.

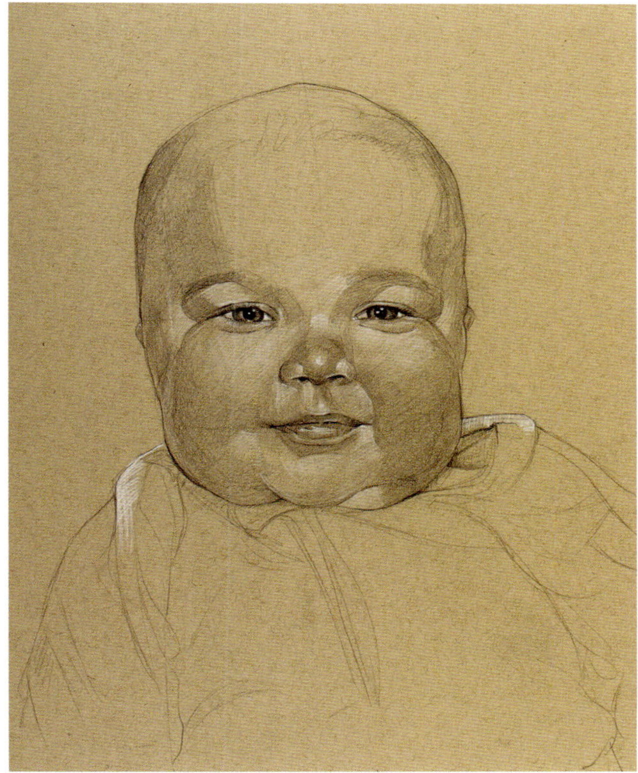

7 ***ADD VOLUME TO THE CHEEKS***
Make those cheeks pinchable! Carefully study the way light and shadow fall on the cheeks. Notice how there are also areas of light within the shadows (around the mouth), showing the various planes on the face.

8 ***RENDER THE TOP OF THE HEAD***
Now that values have been established on the cheeks and face, apply the same tones and value structure to the top of the head.

9 ***ADD VOLUME***
Using a 4B pencil and a light touch, begin adding volume to the head, cheeks and overall face. With a baby, it is particularly important to keep the value changes subtle. If the midtones get too dark, try to lift some tone off with a kneaded eraser.

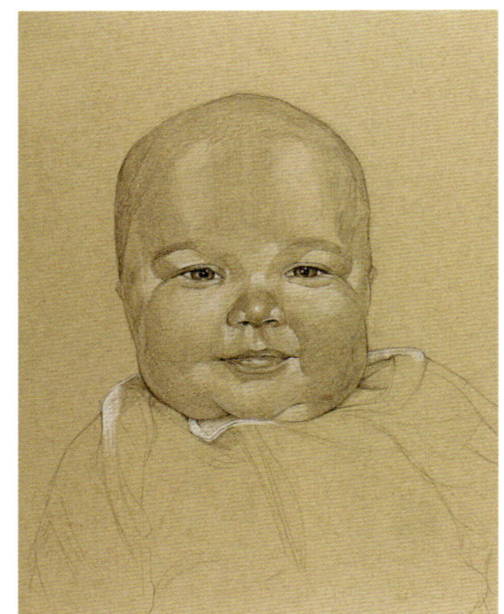

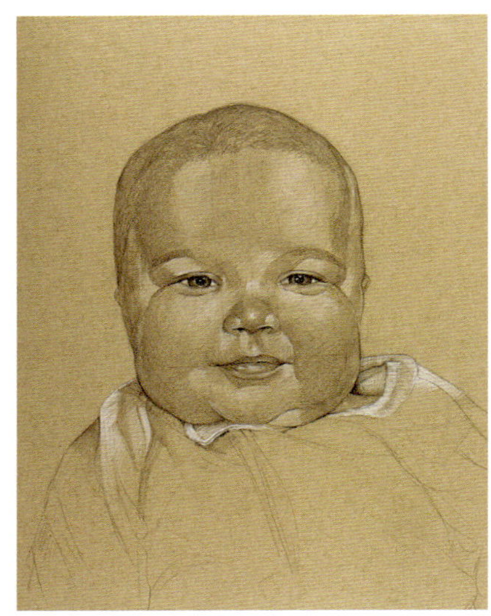

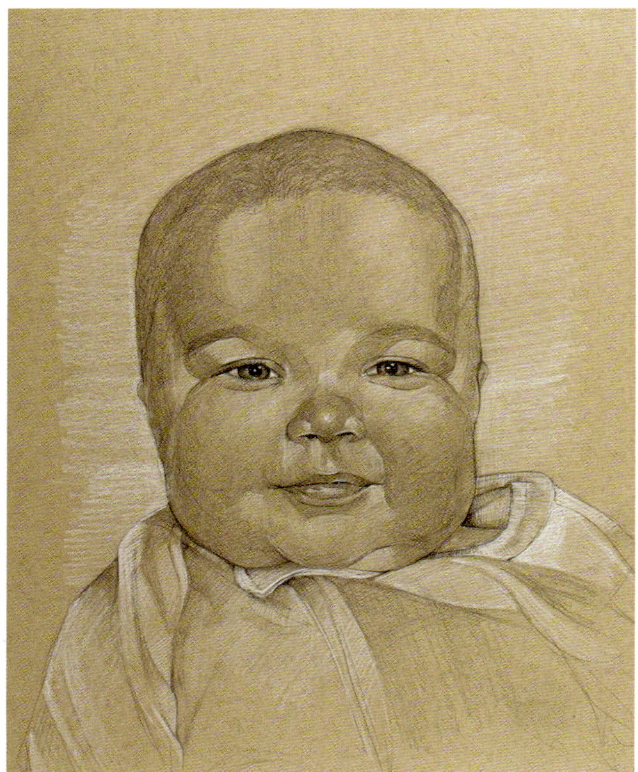

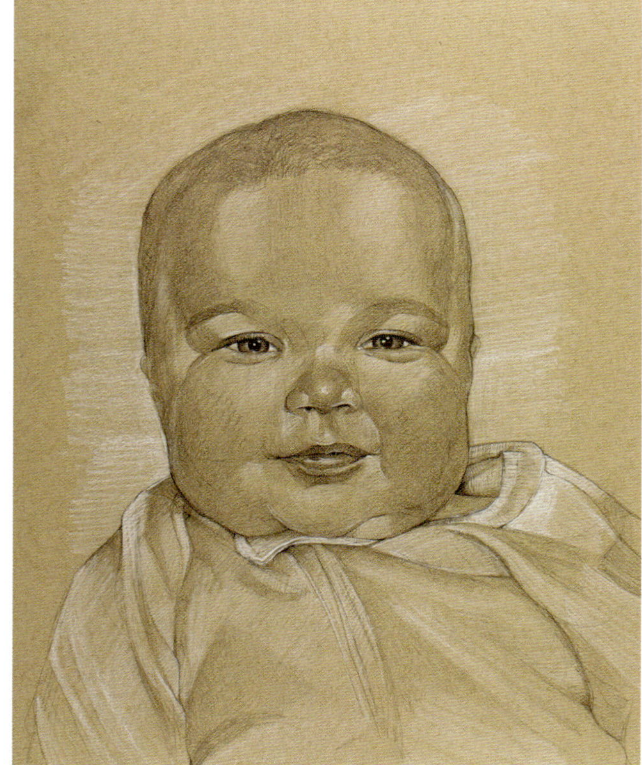

10 ***BEGIN THE BACKGROUND***
Lightly add more lines with a white charcoal pencil to separate the subject from the background. This develops just enough of a tint to help the face come forward, without being too distracting and taking away from his soft features.

11 ***EVALUATE AND FINISH THE DRAWING***
Decide just how much detail to add to the clothing. Often this is minimal, so as to not take away from the face. Continue to darken and develop the features in the face. Make sure the most important areas (eyes, nose, mouth) feature the sharpest, darkest details.

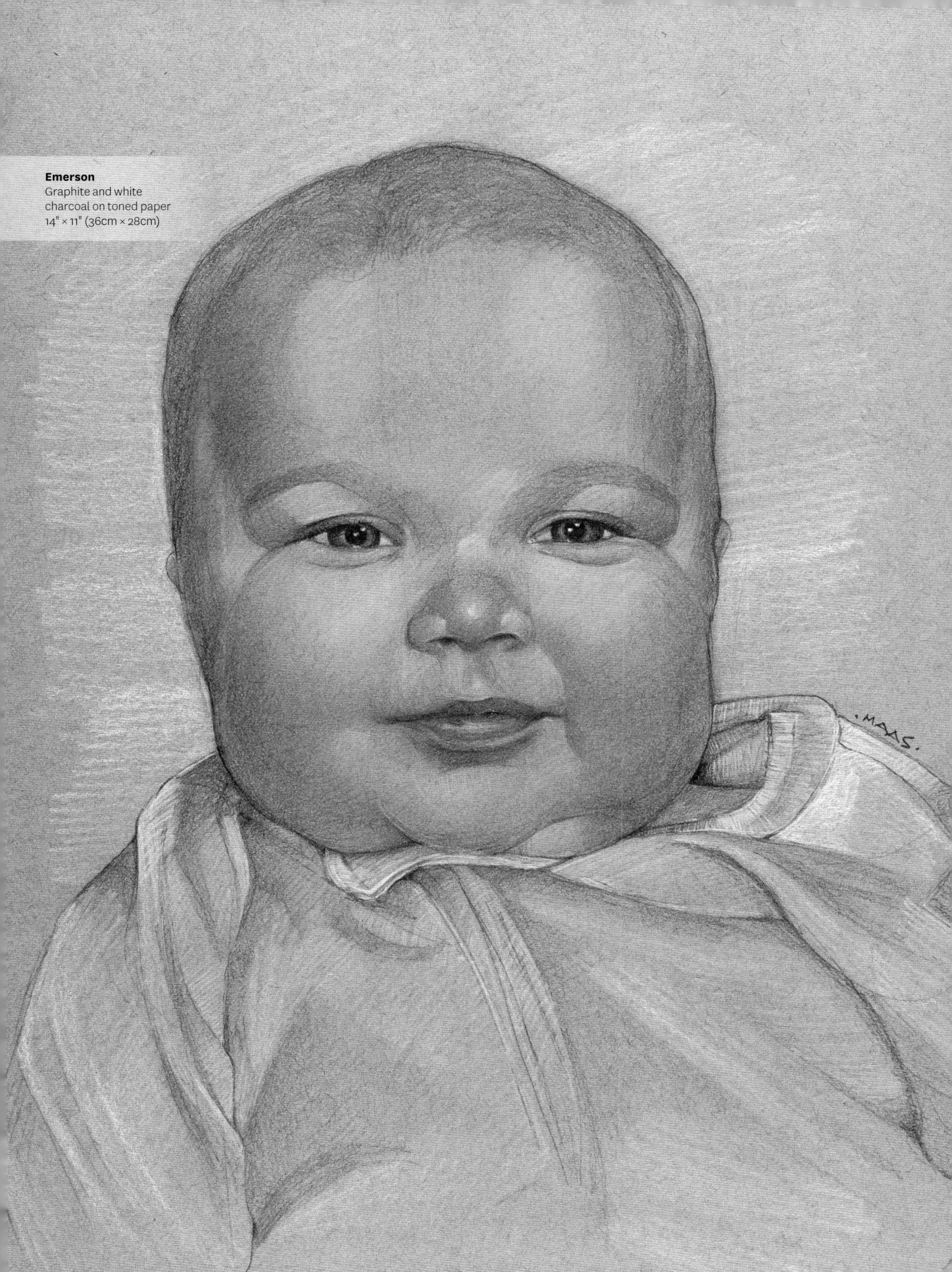

Emerson
Graphite and white
charcoal on toned paper
14" × 11" (36cm × 28cm)

DEMONSTRATION

ARLENA

Arlena is a bright, vibrant young lady. She has such a whimsical charm about her. My goal was to capture her youthful enthusiasm with just a hint of playful mischief. Rather than doing a straight-on portrait, I decided to draw her looking up. I worked from four photos instead of one, and thus used the freehand method, since I had no single reference photo to use for the other methods.

Materials

DRAWING METHOD

Freehand

TOOLS

14" × 11" (36cm × 28cm) Strathmore 400 toned tan sketch paper

ebony pencil

2B, 4B, 6B and 8B woodless graphite pencils

kneaded eraser

white charcoal pencil

white Conté stick

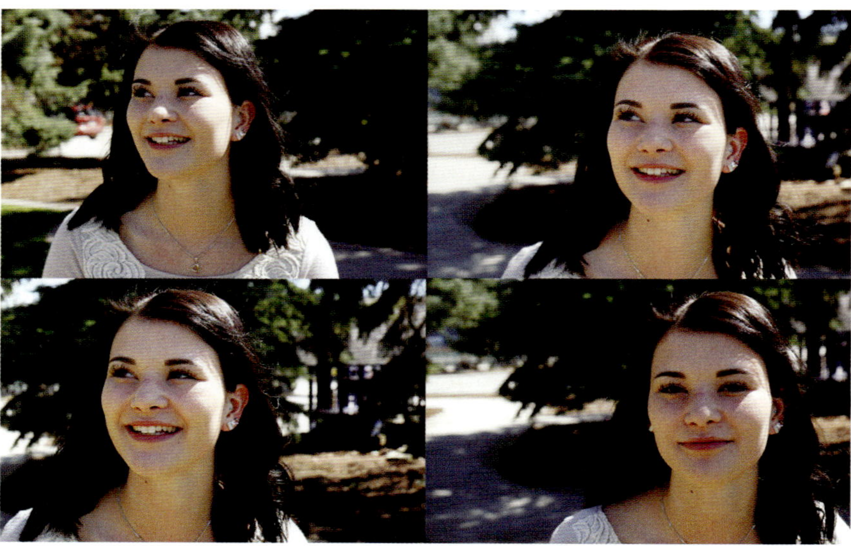

Reference Photos

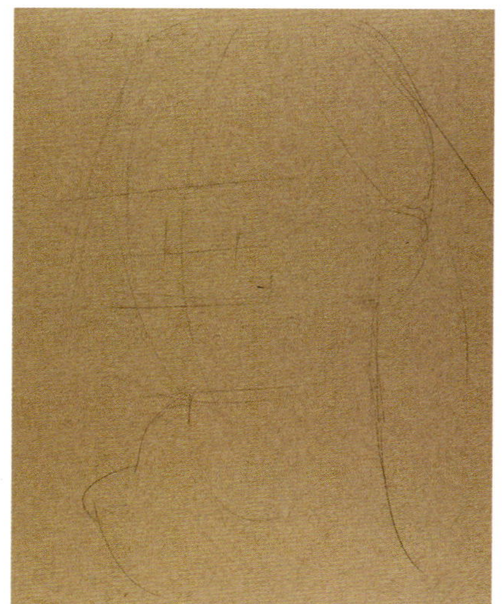

1 *BLOCK IN THE GUIDELINES*
Lay down the structural foundation lines using a 2B pencil. Because this is an amalgamation of several photos, pay special attention to the distances between features.

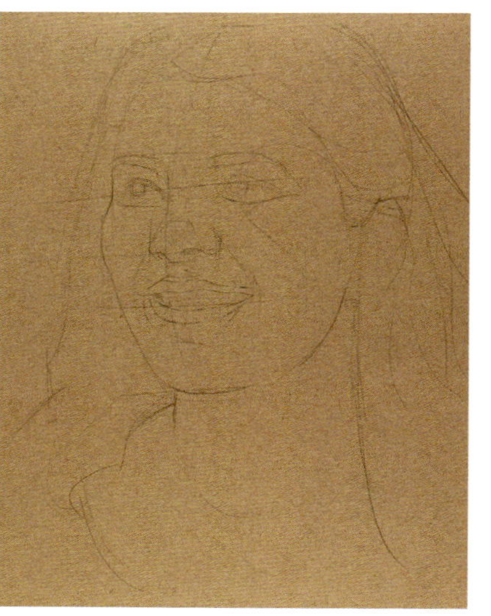

2 *REFINE THE FEATURES*
Using a 2B pencil, lightly indicate the features. Drawing from more than one photo at a time is similar to working from a live model; the goal is to translate the overall forms instead of transcribing each feature and shape.

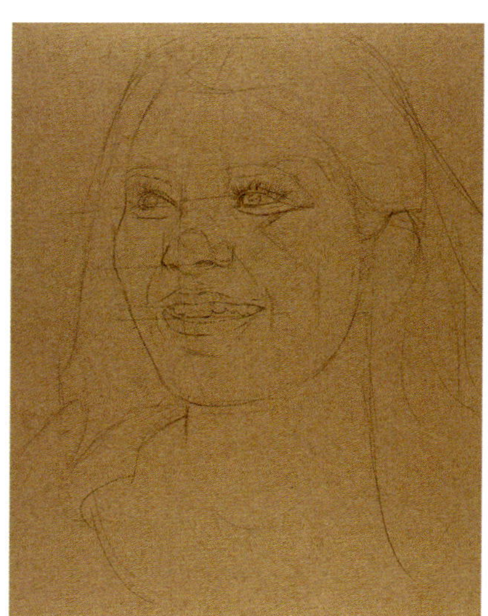

3 *FINALIZE THE FEATURES*
Do a final check of each feature and shape as it relates to the others. This is the time to ensure all features are accurately rendered. Once you add the darker areas and white charcoal, it will be more difficult to adjust the portrait.

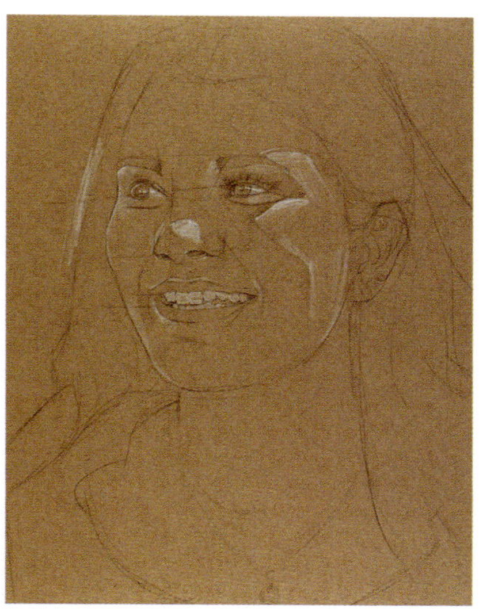

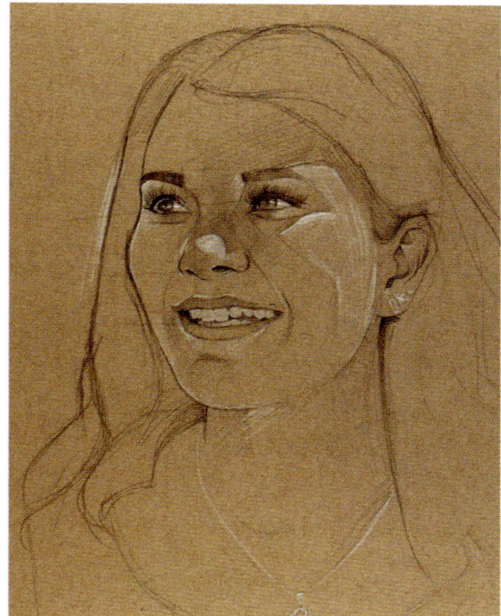

4 ADD THE HIGHLIGHTS
Using white charcoal, define the areas that are the brightest whites. Areas that are slightly lighter should be laid in with a very soft touch. Charcoal, just like graphite, can be more or less intense depending upon the pressure applied.

5 BEGIN THE DARKER TONES
Using an ebony pencil (roughly equivalent to a 3B or 4B), begin adding in some midtones. The key features (eyes, nose, mouth) as well as the hair outline can be addressed. At this stage, it is apparent whether the features are correct or not and whether likeness has been achieved.

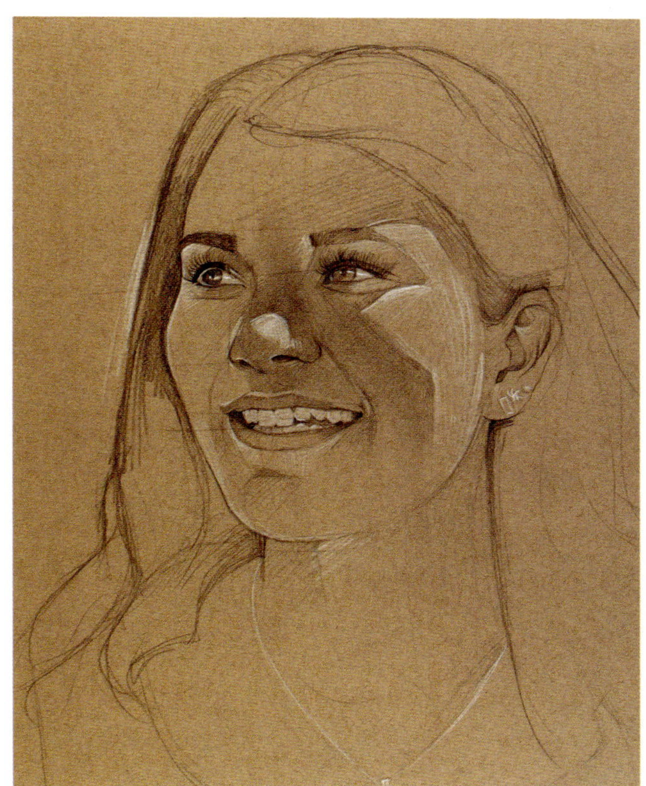

6 DEVELOP FORM IN THE FACE
Adding tone in the cheeks helps define the values of the piece and the form of the face. By adding some key darks with an ebony pencil (the hair at left and the teeth), it's possible to build up values throughout the piece, and not have to go back to darken as many areas.

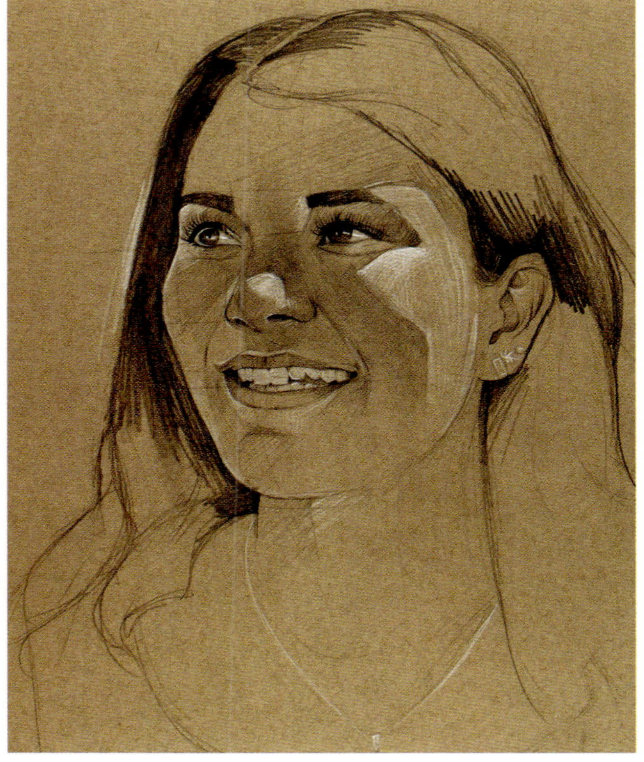

7 DARKEN AND DEFINE THE HAIR
The hair makes up about one-third of this portrait, but because it is so dark, it's important to make sure the values in the face relate to the intensity of the hair. If the midtones begin to look too dark, don't erase them all. Simply use a kneaded eraser to lift some of the pigment from the graphite. It can be done subtly; just soften the value a little at a time.

8 DARKEN THE HAIR AND FACE

Using 6B and 8B woodless pencils, continue to darken the hair and also add values to the face. As one area is darkened, the values on the rest are affected. Start to add some wisps to the hairline.

9 RENDER THE JAWLINE

The rest of the face is beginning to be defined nicely, so adding in the jawline helps finish off the form. The lips and cheeks are darkened, too, and a sharper edge is defined on her left (the drawing's right) cheek highlight.

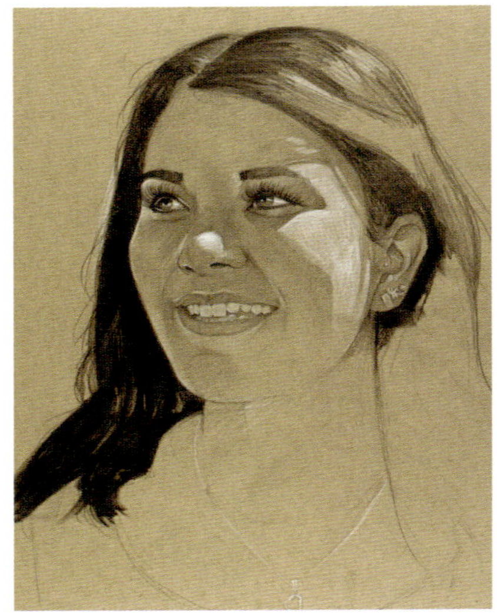

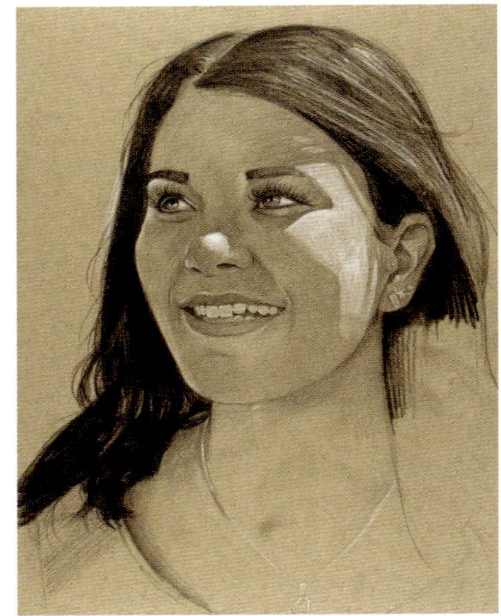

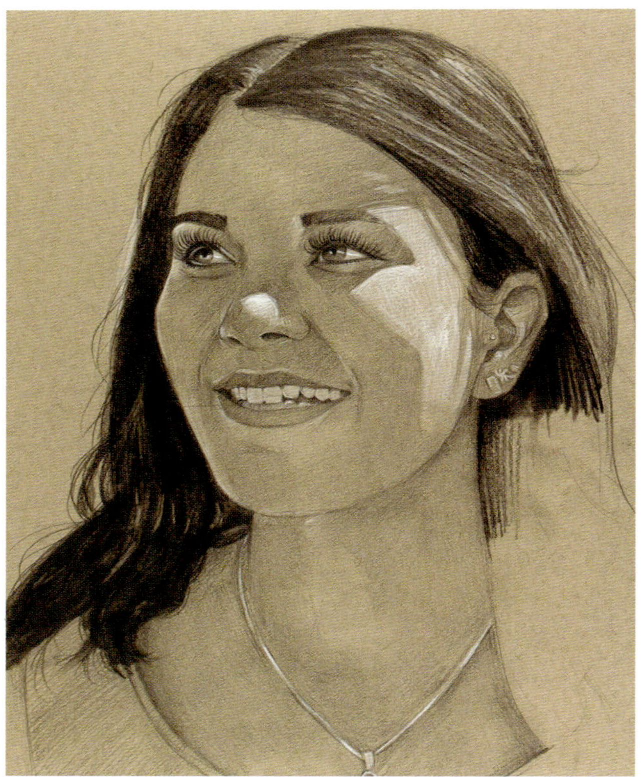

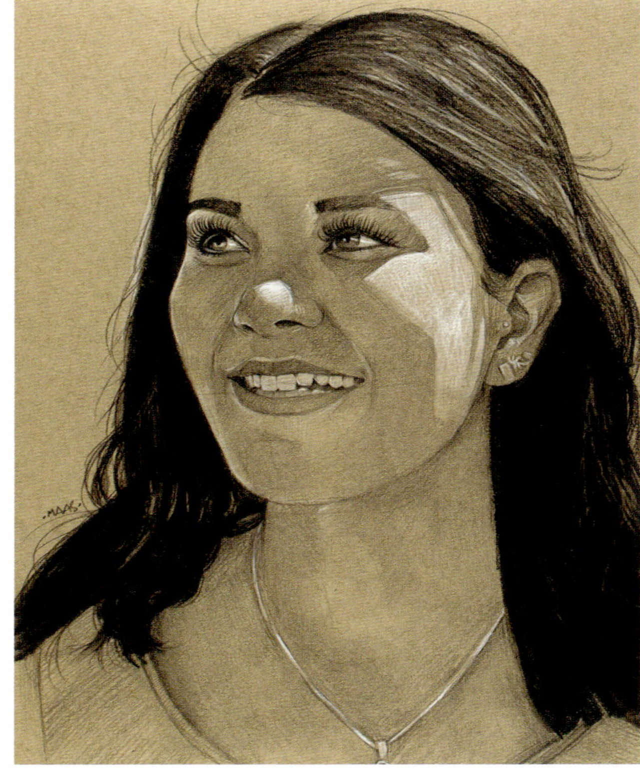

10 ADD DETAILS

Highlights help refine the hair and necklace. It's up to you to decide to include jewelry in your portraits, but in this case it helps define the large area of her neck in shadow.

11 EVALUATE AND FINISH THE DRAWING

Refine and darken the hair. Strengthen the darks around the eyes, nose and teeth. Refine the highlights and add just a touch of detail to the shirt. Add white Conté to the background to separate the portrait from the paper.

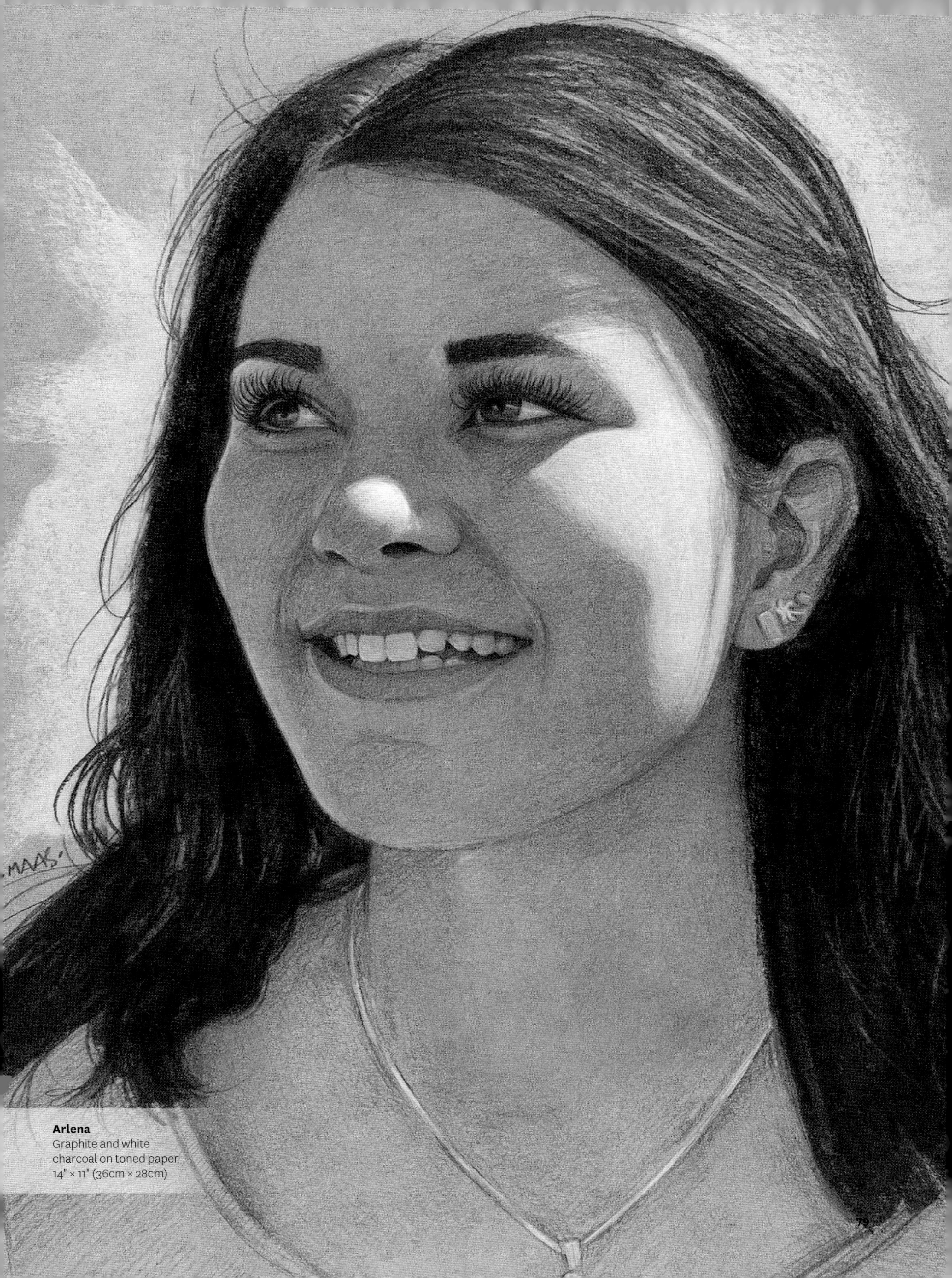

Arlena
Graphite and white charcoal on toned paper
14" × 11" (36cm × 28cm)

DEMONSTRATION

ARIANA

Ariana is a bundle of energy and has a beautiful smile. I posed her indoors using the natural light from a window to give warmth to her face and highlight that huge grin of hers.

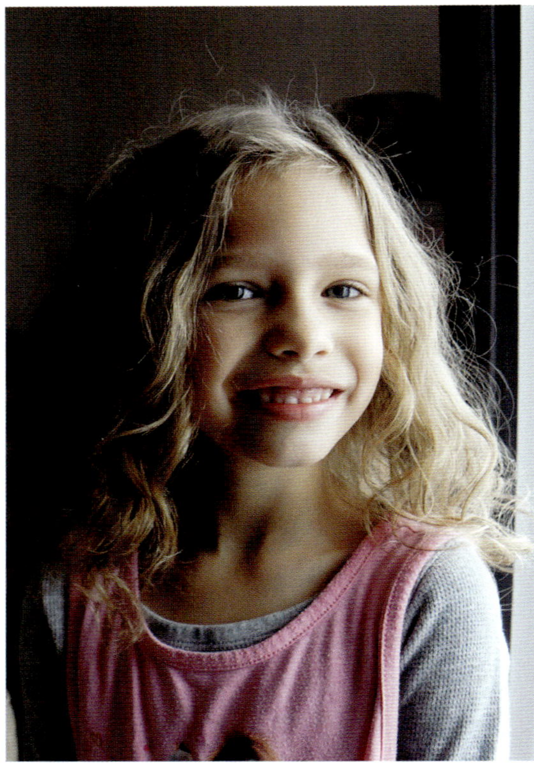

Reference Photo

Materials

DRAWING METHOD

Maas

TOOLS

- 14" × 11" (36cm × 28cm) Strathmore 400 toned tan sketch paper
- ebony pencil
- 2B, 4B and 8B woodless graphite pencils
- kneaded eraser
- white charcoal pencil
- white Conté stick

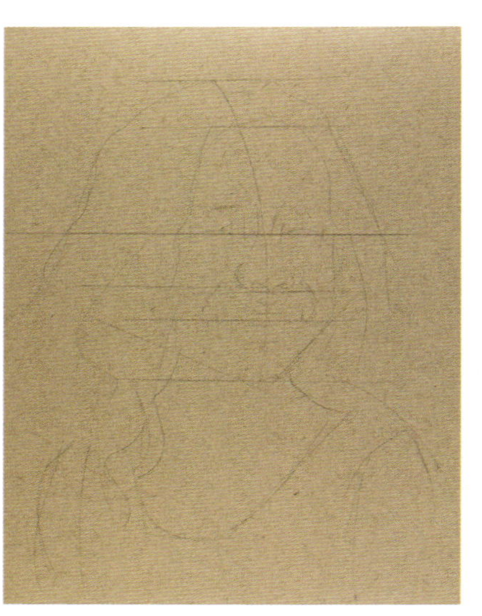

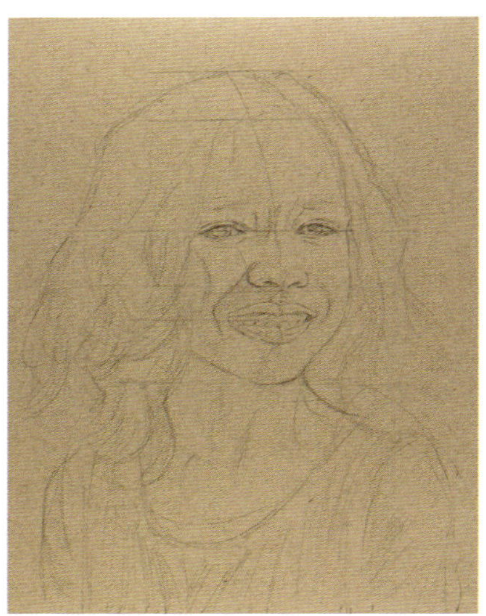

1 *MARK THE GUIDELINES* Using the Maas method and a 2B pencil, define the main horizontal lines for the eyes, nose, mouth and chin.

2 *ADD THE KEY FEATURES* Lightly freehand the overall shape of the face. Use the sight lines from step 1 to help you define the distance between features and shapes.

3 *DOUBLE-CHECK THE FEATURES* This is the key last stage of the block in. Finalize the features and make sure all elements and proportions are accurate. Switching to an ebony pencil at this stage may help you define and separate features from the guidelines.

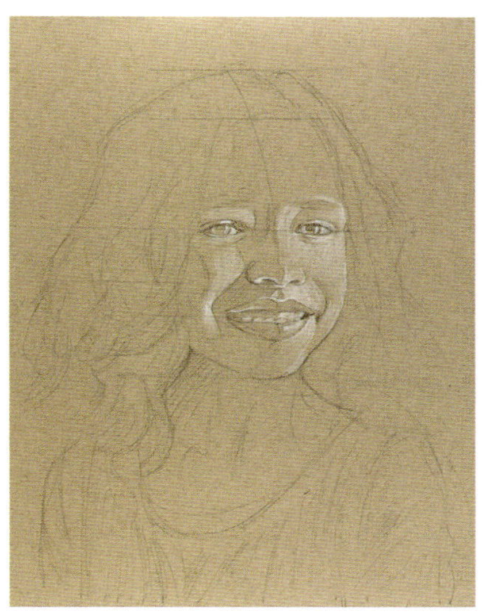

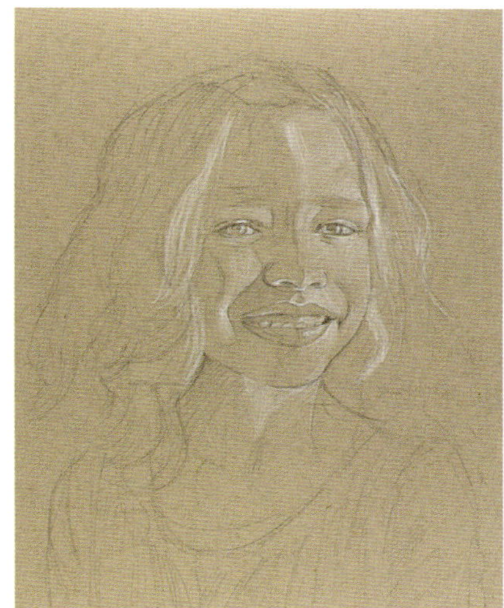

4 *ADD THE WHITES*
Using a white charcoal pencil, add the highlights and bright midtones to the face. Pay close attention to the teeth; keep it subtle—most parts of the teeth will not be bright white. Use a light touch to keep the teeth softer and only press hard with your pencil where there are really strong highlights.

5 *ADD HIGHLIGHTS TO THE HAIR*
Because the hair is quite light, it is important to keep the highlights soft.

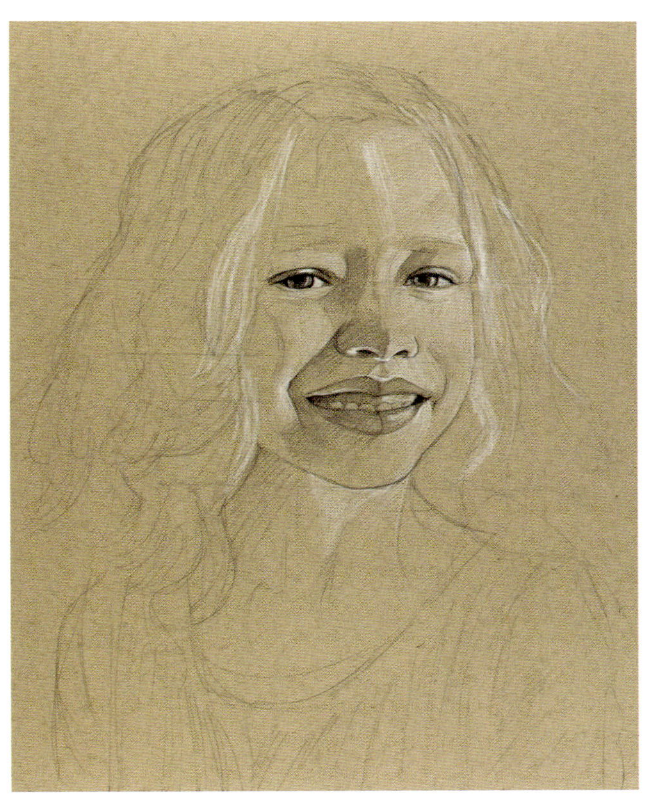

6 *ADD MIDTONES*
Switch to an ebony pencil and add midtones in the eyes, nose and mouth. An 8B pencil may be used (sparingly) to add very dark darks to the irises and the corners of the mouth. Lightly define the teeth and make the areas within the open mouth darker.

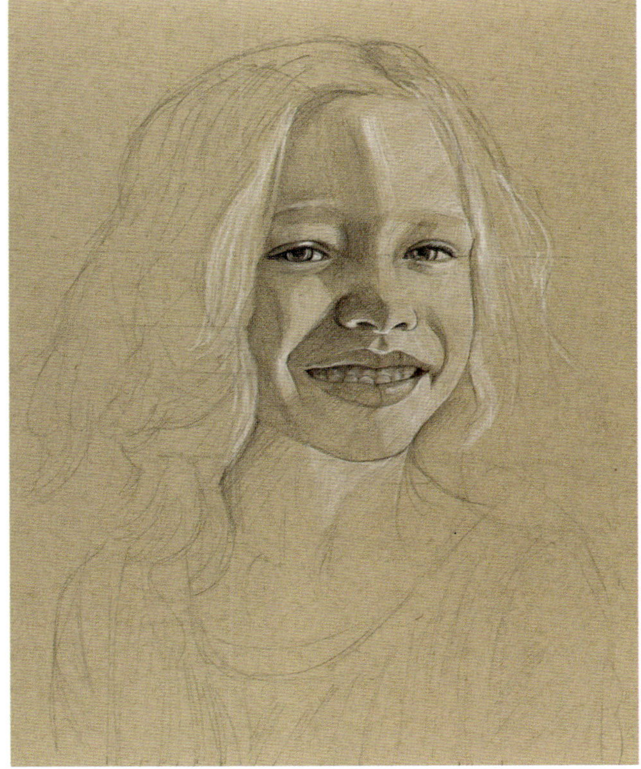

7 *BEGIN BUILDING TONE*
Build tone throughout the face and hair using an ebony or 4B pencil. Watch the values as they relate to the highlights and shadows. The midtones in the drawing are crucial as they create a transition between those areas of high contrast.

8 STRENGTHEN THE AREAS OF CONTRAST

Using a 4B pencil, start to add darker areas and transition the darks to the lights. Add form to the cheeks and neck.

9 DEFINE THE HAIR

Remember that hair, while made of individual strands, should be drawn as a mass. Block in the shapes you see within the hair.

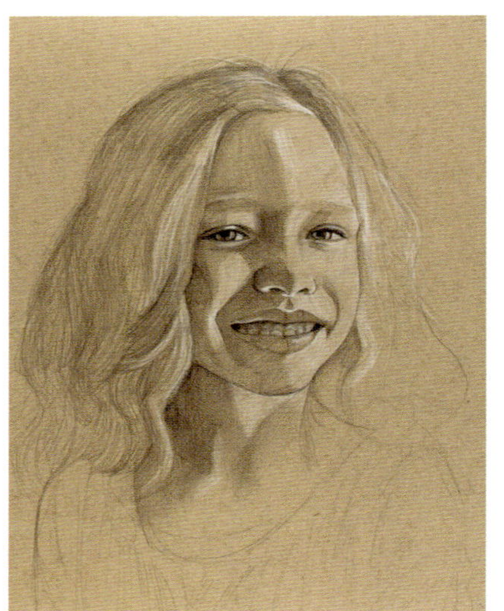

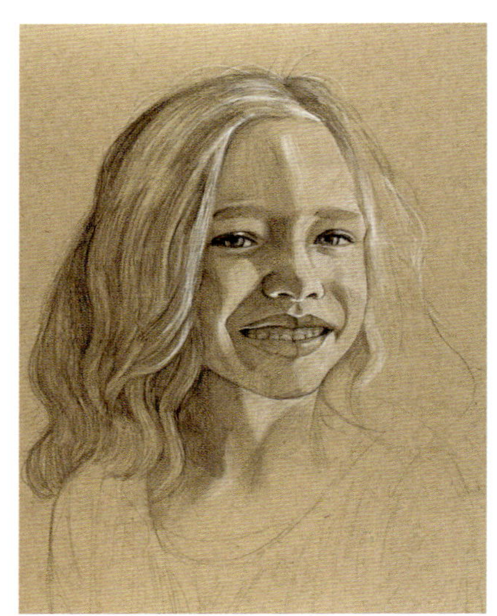

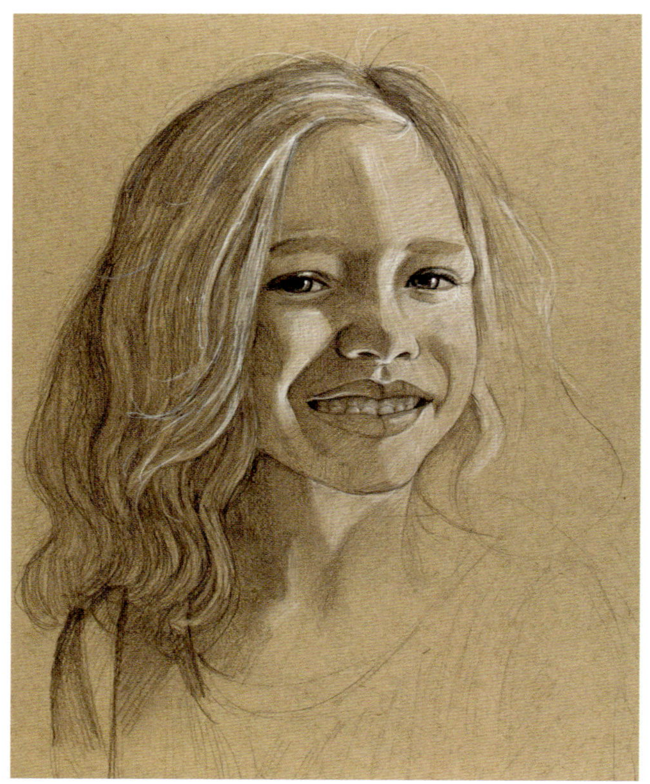

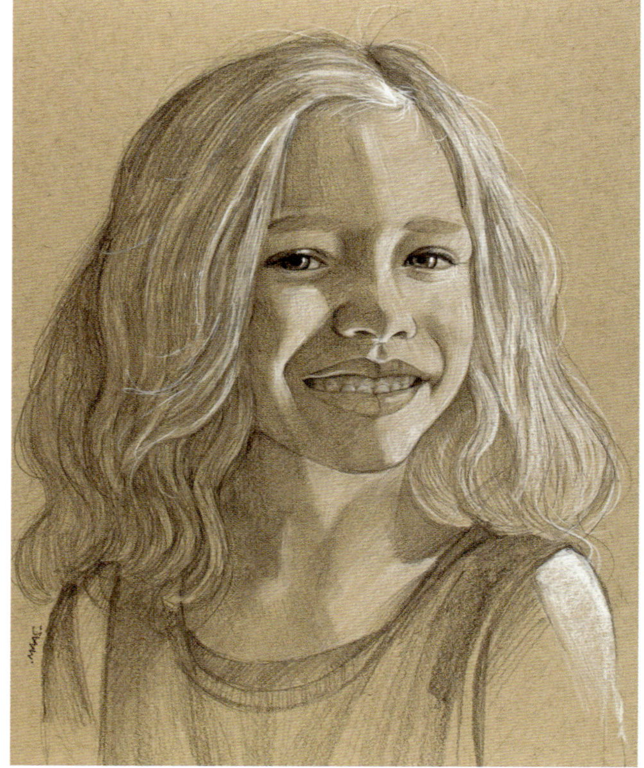

10 ADD HIGHLIGHTS

Using a combination of lifting with a kneaded eraser and light strokes of white charcoal, try to mimic the direction and movement of hair. Vary the pressure with each stroke—within the same stroke even—to emulate the flow of hair.

11 EVALUATE AND FINISH THE DRAWING

Define the rest of the hair, lightly add details on the shirt and refine areas of light and dark to tie all the values together. For a finishing touch, add wisps of hair with the edge of a white Conté stick.

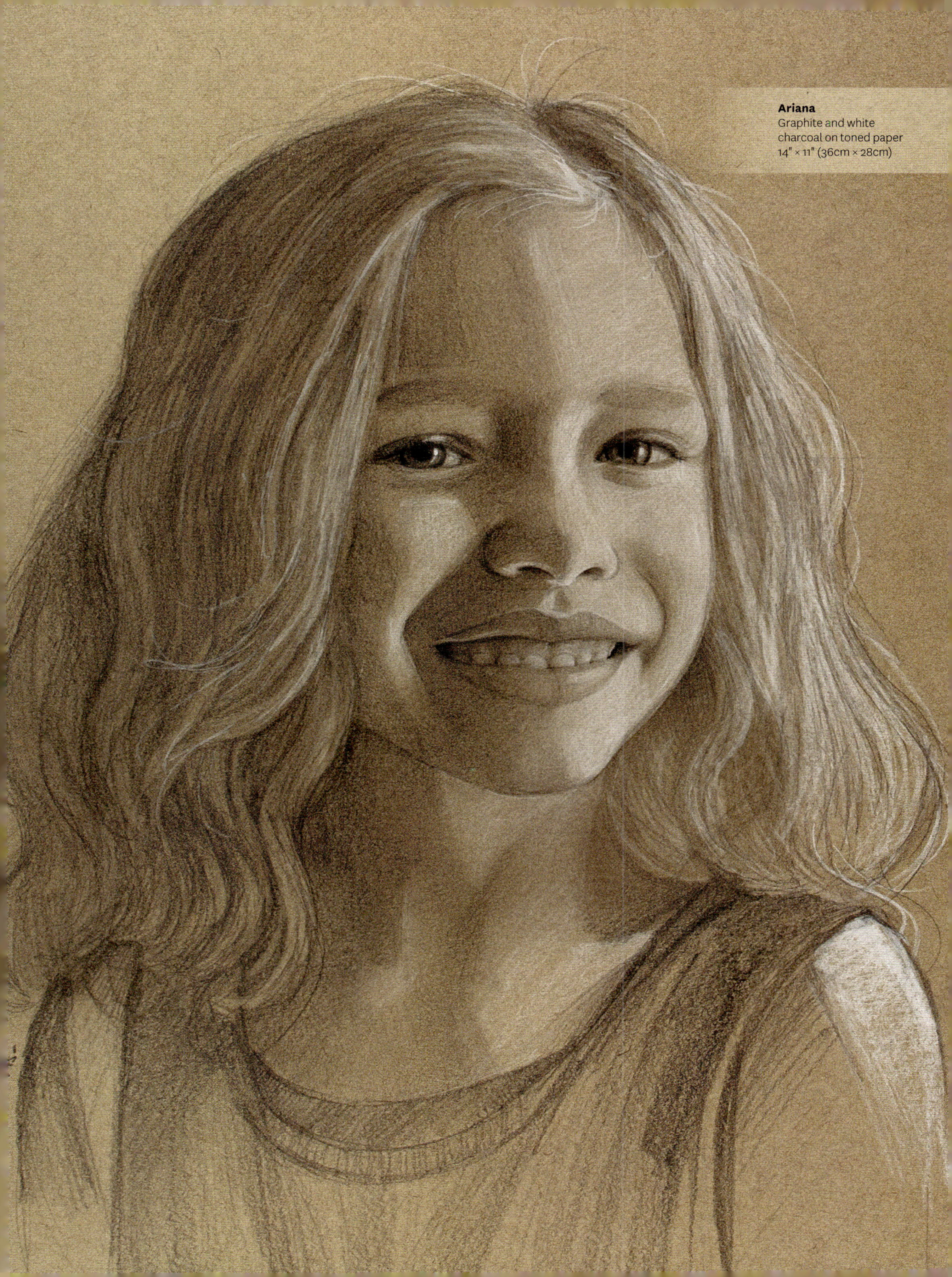

Ariana
Graphite and white charcoal on toned paper
14" × 11" (36cm × 28cm)

DEMONSTRATION

MARINA

Marina is an avid snowboarder and a natural beauty. I wanted to show off her amazing smile and this pose helped me illustrate how she smiles with not only her teeth but her eyes, too.

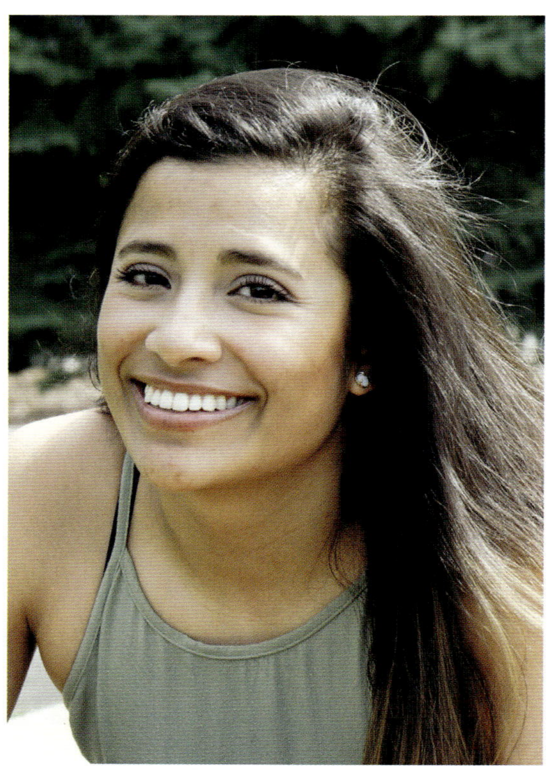

Reference Photo

Materials

DRAWING METHOD

Maas

TOOLS

14" × 11" (36cm × 28cm) Bienfang Bristol white paper

ebony pencil

2B, 4B and 8B woodless graphite pencils

click eraser

kneaded eraser

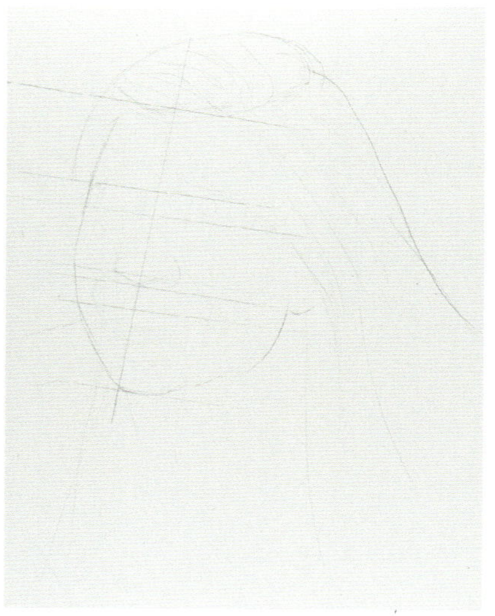

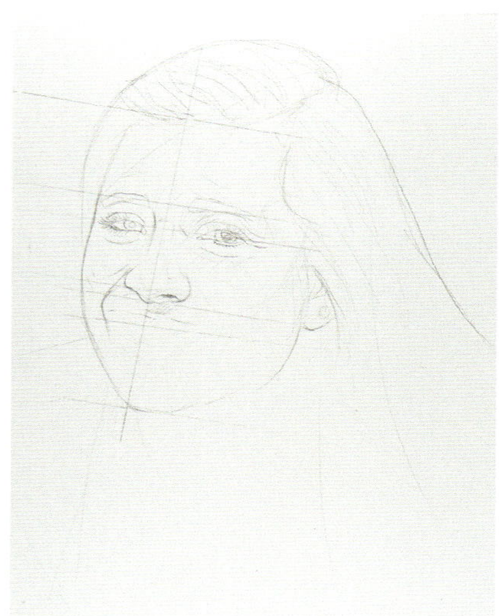

1 ***BLOCK IN THE HORIZONTAL LINES*** Using the Maas method, block in lines with a 2B pencil to indicate the placement of the nose, mouth, eyes and other features. Because the reference is not completely vertical, tape your reference photo at an angle so that a line that bisects the face vertically would be perpendicular to the same line on the drawing.

2 ***DEFINE THE FACE AND HEAD*** Using a light touch, continue adding other elements such as the overall shape of the face and head, and the hairline.

3 ***BEGIN DRAWING IN FEATURES*** Now that the basic framework is laid out, the features can be drawn in with accuracy. A light touch is still important at this stage, so continue using a 2B pencil in case some lines are not quite where they should be.

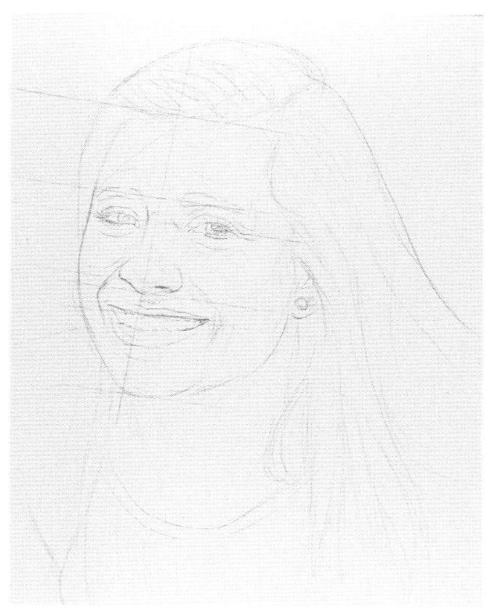

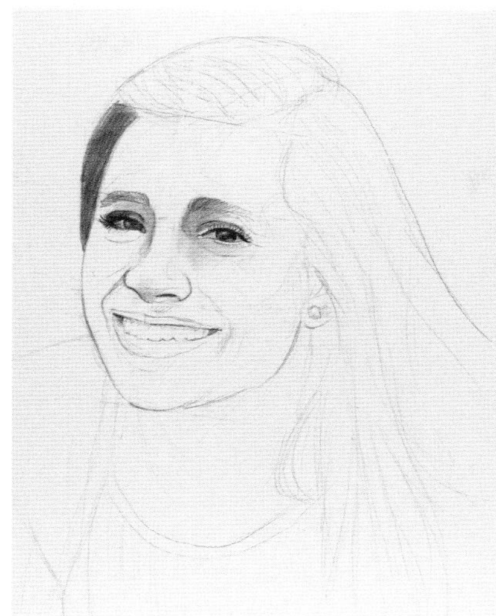

4 *FINALIZE THE BLOCK IN*

Double-check the placement of all the features against the initial block-in lines. If everything looks good, it is time to move on to rendering. If there are some concerns with proportions or placement of features, now is the time to fix them.

5 *ESTABLISH YOUR VALUES*

Begin establishing values with a 4B pencil in key areas like the eyes and part of the hair. This establishes the dark points, which will help show you where to place the highlights and midtones.

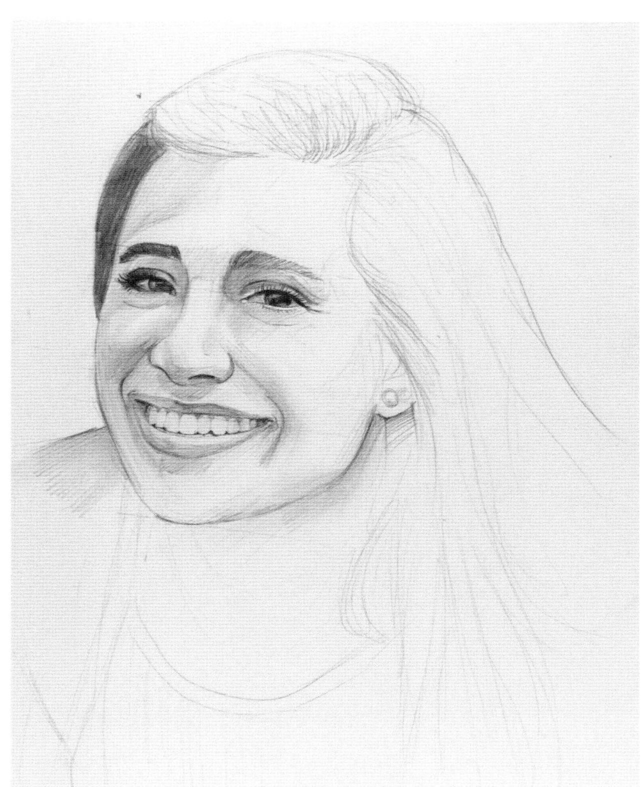

6 *LAY DOWN OVERALL VALUES*

Establish the middle values and define the form. Define the basic form of the nose, eyes and cheeks, and keep it light on the teeth.

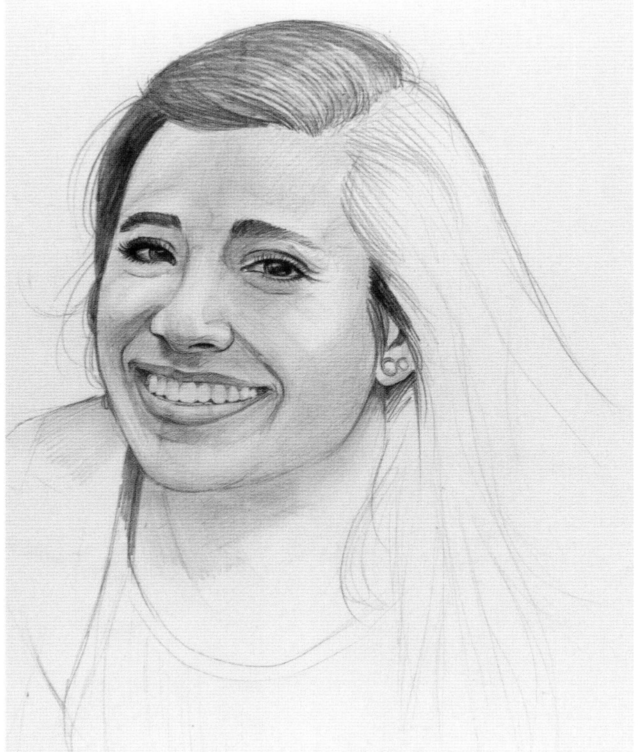

7 *ESTABLISH MORE DEFINED VALUES*

The hair is laid in softly—not too dark—with an ebony or 4B pencil while the rest of the tones are built up. Define the form of the cheeks and lips with shadows and darker values.

8 *CONCENTRATE ON DETAILS*
As the form starts to take shape, add details such as highlights in the hair (lifted out with a click eraser), contrast around the eyes and added values in the neck and shoulder. Lightly render the clothing.

9 *ADD LARGE MASSES OF HAIR*
Since her hair is dark, it's important to add the bulk of it at this stage to ensure that the values in the face are dark enough. There is a strong light from the right, so part of the hair is quite light—define that very softly, and use an eraser to erase hair if the tones get too dark. By using a click eraser, this can be done in strokes that mimic hair strands, giving it an organic, natural feel.

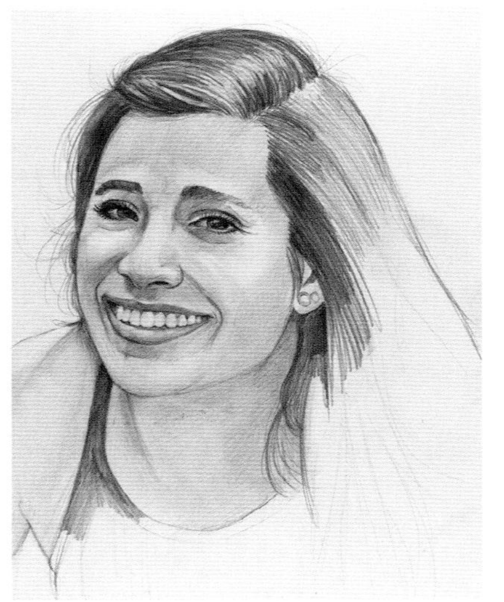

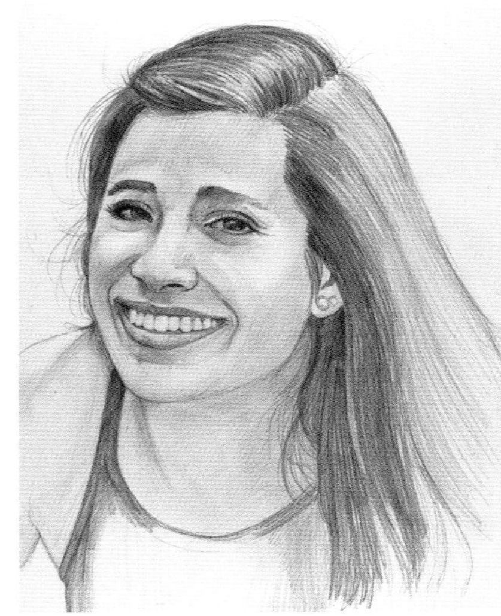

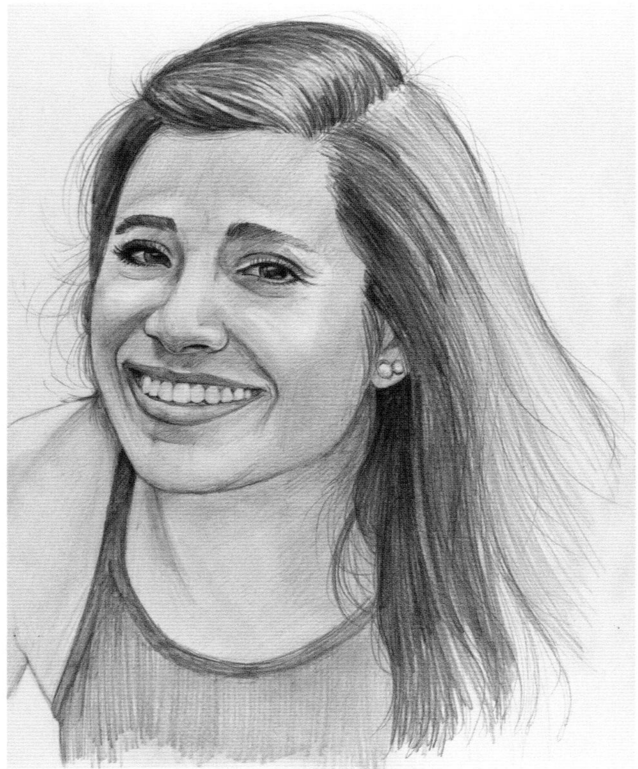

10 *BEGIN TO FINALIZE DETAILS*
Softly render the clothing with a 4B or ebony pencil. Add more stray hairs and sharpen the details in the hair and around the face.

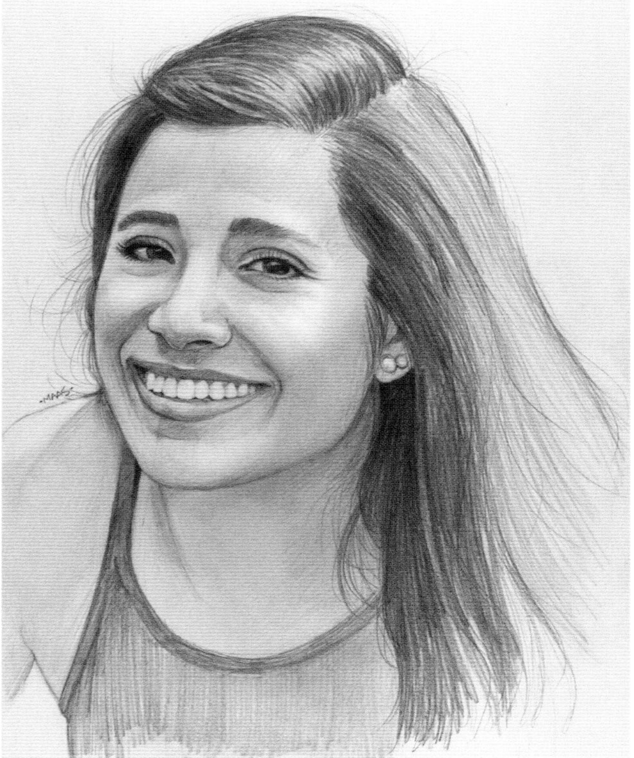

11 *EVALUATE AND FINISH THE DRAWING*
At this stage it's mostly about refining values. The features are done, the form has been rendered. It's all about making sure the darkest darks and lightest lights are established. The darkest darks can be finished with an 8B pencil. The lightest lights should be lifted with a kneaded eraser. Leave the white of the paper for the brightest lights.

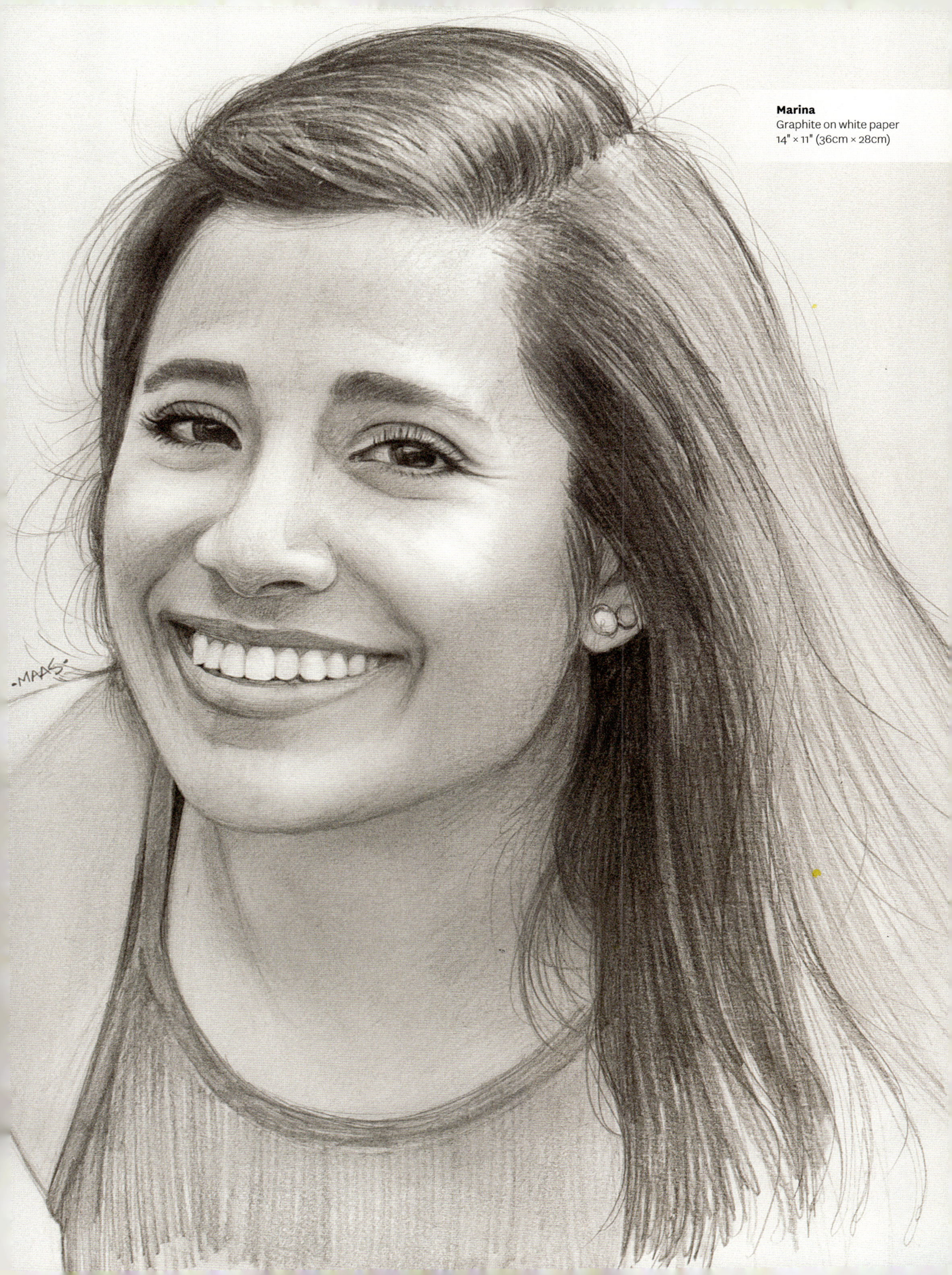

Marina
Graphite on white paper
14" × 11" (36cm × 28cm)

DEMONSTRATION

ARTHUR

Arthur is a typical, energetic kid who loves his dog. Even though his mom is a famous actress (Selma Blair), Arthur is a sweet, down-to-earth boy. What better way to capture him than with his best buddy? This portrait is also interesting because it is a nontraditional pose. Sometimes experimenting with poses that are uncommon for portraits can yield unique results.

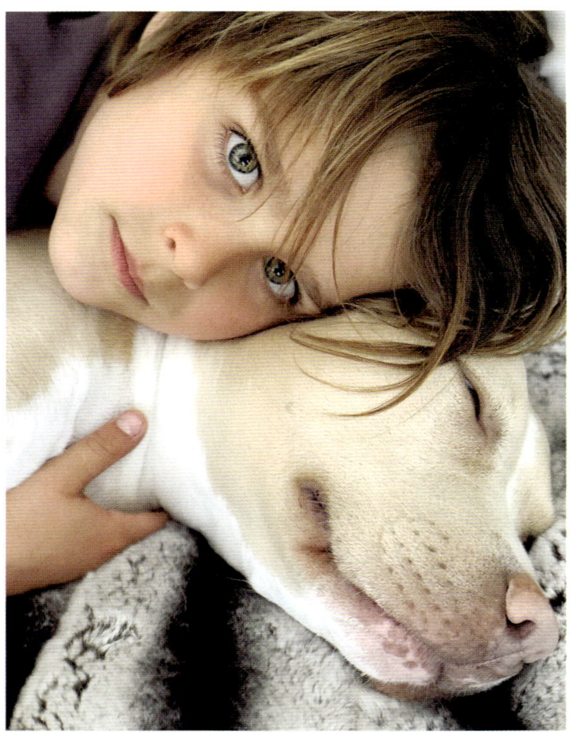

Reference Photo

Materials

DRAWING METHOD

Freehand

TOOLS

14" × 11" (36cm × 28cm) Stonehenge Kraft toned paper

ebony pencil

HB, B, 4B and 8B woodless graphite pencils

click eraser

kneaded eraser

white charcoal pencil

1 LAY DOWN THE GUIDELINES Using an HB or B pencil, lightly establish the first guidelines. Compare each line to the last, as relationships and spacing are crucial at this point.

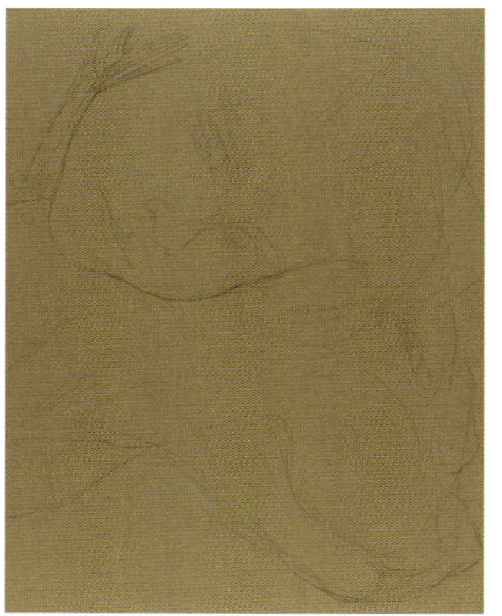

2 ADD THE LARGE SHAPES With the initial lines in place, begin to add the contour lines and large masses such as the hairline, jawline and basic indication of features such as the eyes, nose and mouth.

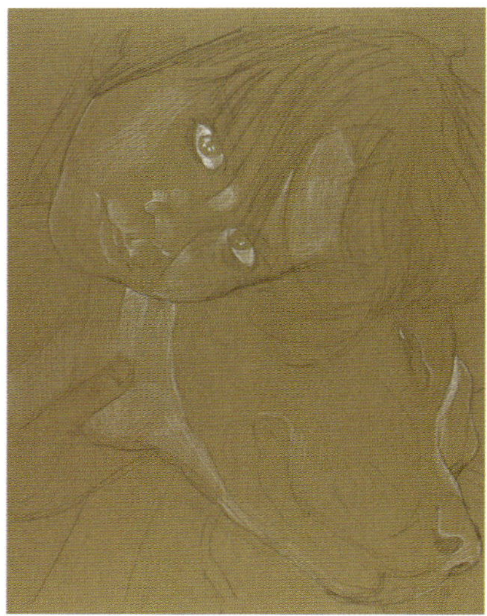

3 ADD HIGHLIGHTS Switch to a white charcoal pencil. Determine the brightest highlights and areas that will be predominantly lighter. On most toned paper, this is the time to layer graphite lightly over the white. The opposite (white over graphite) is not possible.

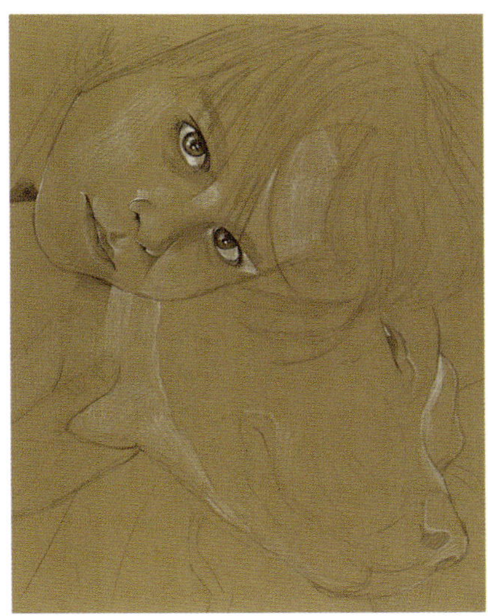

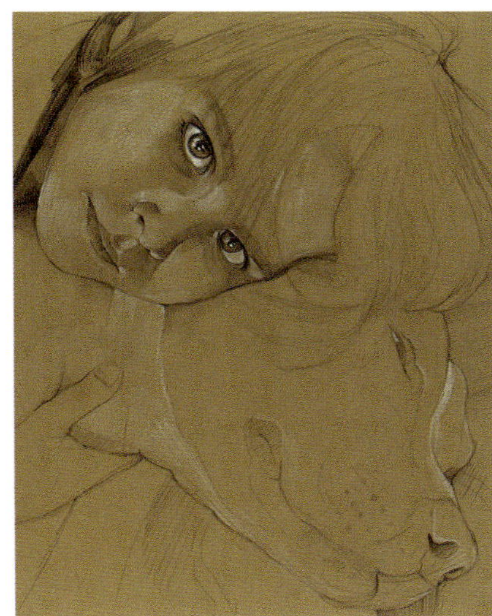

4 MAKE ADJUSTMENTS

At this stage it is important to make sure the proportions and basic lines are correct. Adjusting now means a few extra minutes of corrections. If you begin to render when areas are not complete, it creates a lot of corrective work later.

5 BEGIN ADDING FORM

Using an ebony or 4B pencil, begin to add some of the darks. Darks will be built gradually, not applied all at once, so don't go too dark too quickly. This image is quite complicated with lots of values and levels of shading. It's important to build darks slowly and organically.

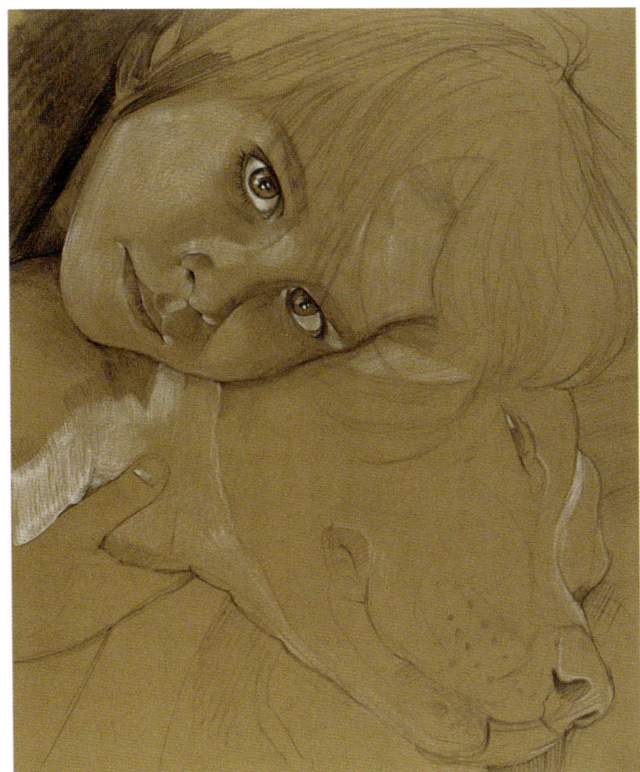

6 ADD THE WHITES OF THE DOG

The highlights from step 3 indicated the brightest whites. The dog, however, has actual white fur. Draw that in at this stage. Pay attention to the direction that the fur grows and also that it is not pure white everywhere. Strokes should vary in pressure (darkness) but not in direction. The direction of your strokes should be consistent.

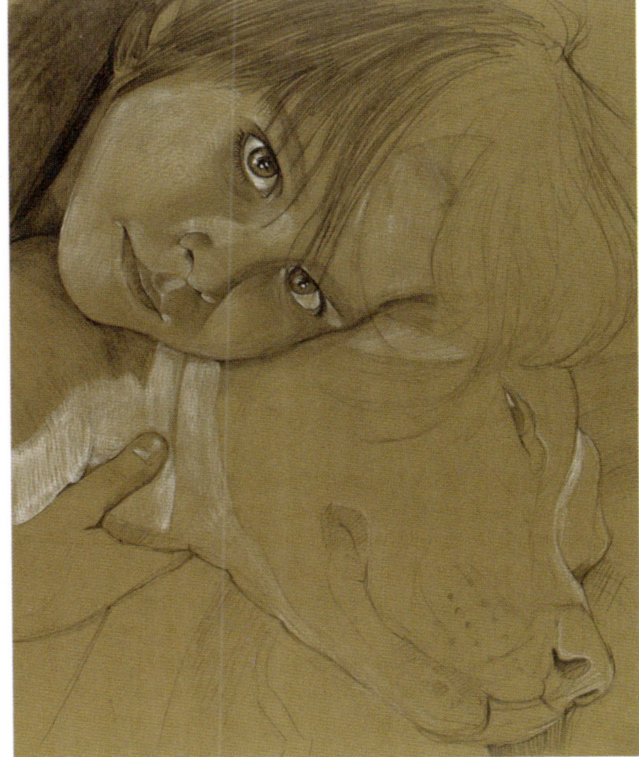

7 BUILD THE TONES IN THE HAIR

Apply the hair as a mass, slowly building form and shape at this stage. Don't focus on individual hairs.

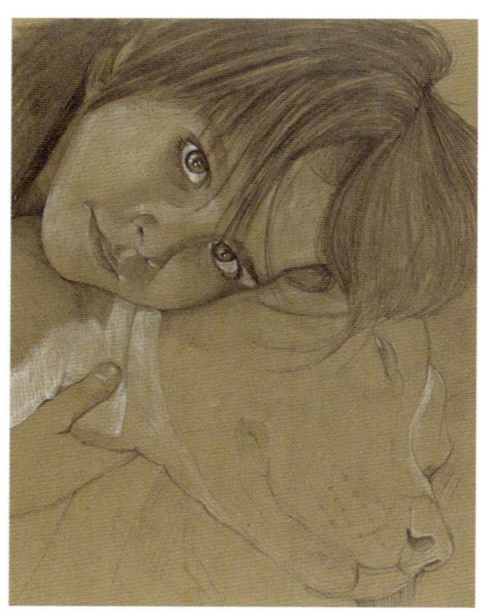

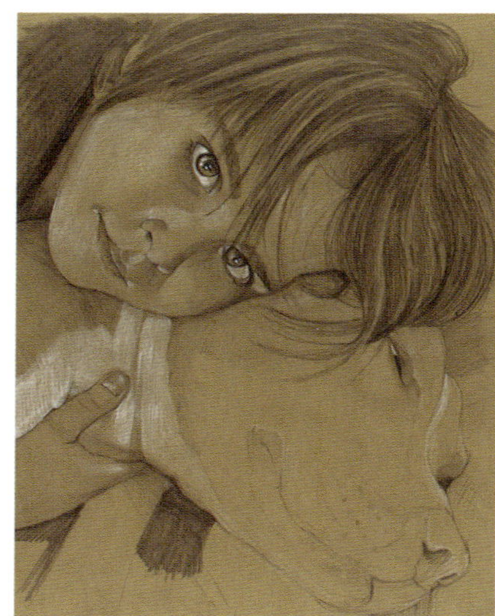

8 *BRING DEPTH TO THE HAIR*

Using an eraser, gently lift out areas to give highlights to the hair. A kneaded eraser should work but a click eraser may help you to work in the direction of the hair and won't gum up as easily. Begin adding individual lines, varying pressure and line darkness to give the hair life.

9 *ADD VOLUME*

Darken the hair and the key features in the portrait with an 8B woodless pencil. Begin to add volume to the dog. It's important at this point to compare values in all parts of the drawing so one area doesn't end up too dark or too light in comparison to the rest.

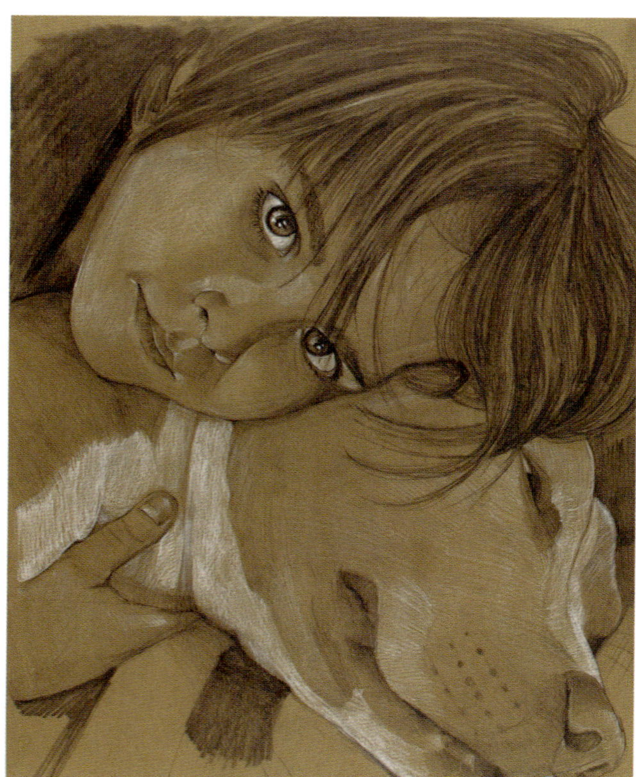

10 *ADD THE FUR*

Using a white charcoal pencil, add the rest of the dog's fur. Also add lines on the face and on areas throughout the drawing that need lightening. This will tie the whole piece together. Keep the pencil very sharp as you work. If the pencil is dull, the white charcoal will mix with the graphite and muddy the area.

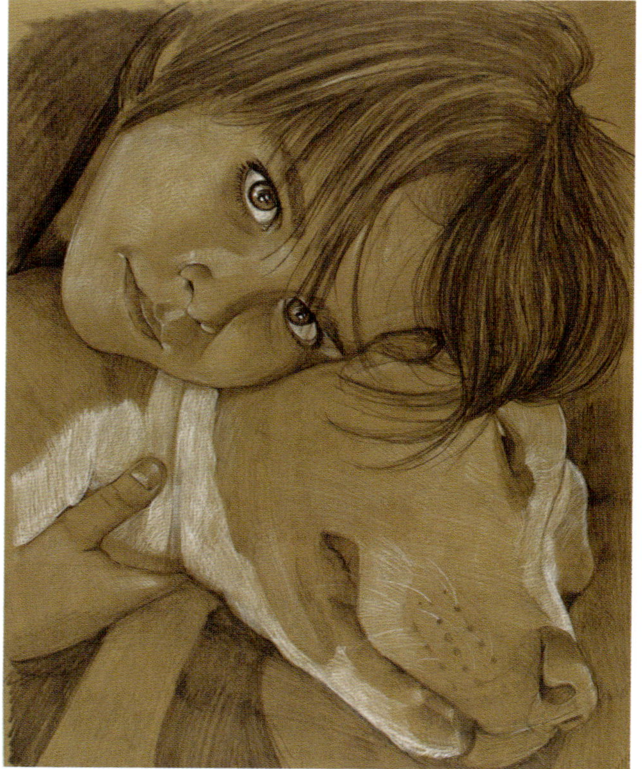

11 *EVALUATE AND FINISH THE DRAWING*

Now that the drawing is nearing completion, hone in on key areas that require development. Darken and sharpen lines near the eyes—this is a key focal point in the piece. Address the background behind and beneath the dog. Darken any areas that seem too light on the value scale.

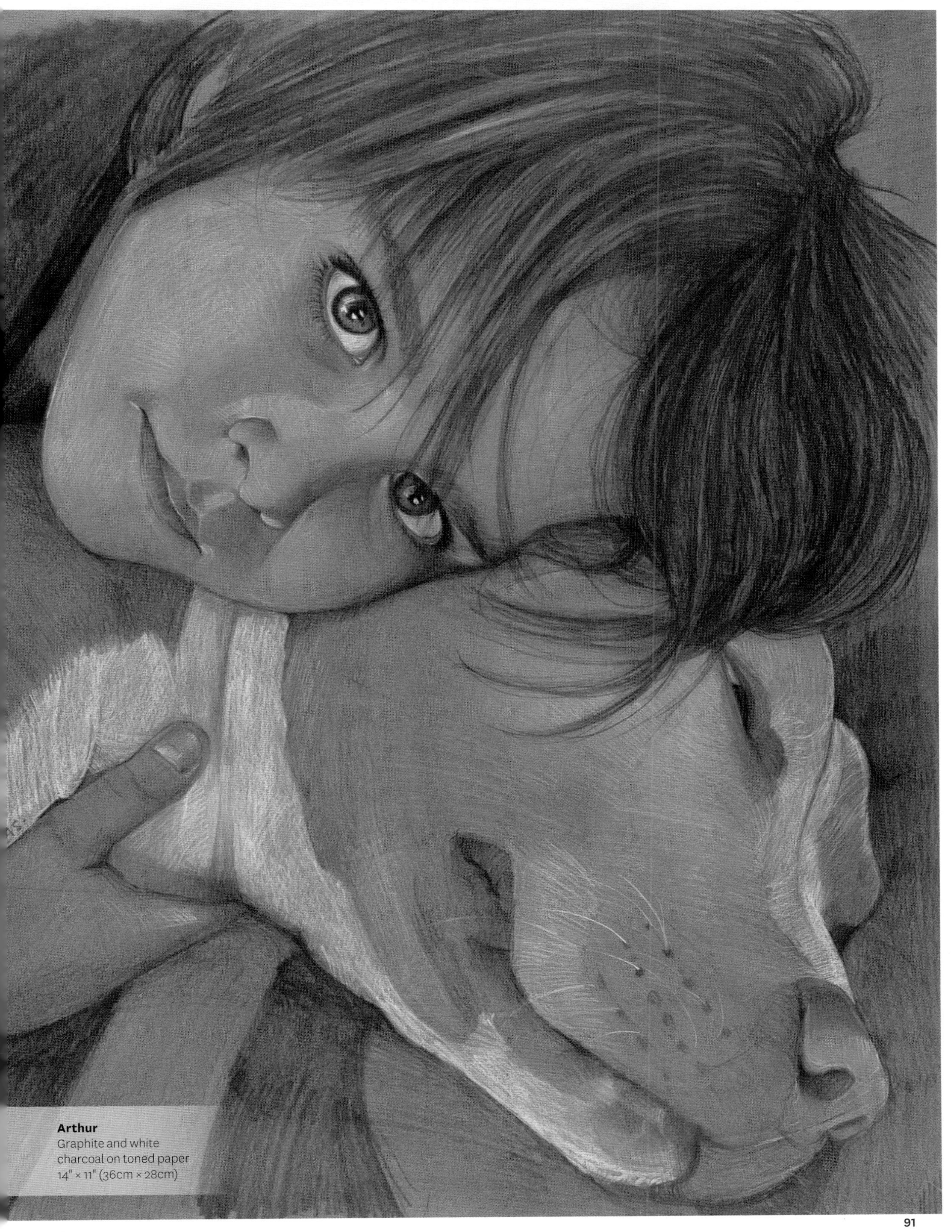

Arthur
Graphite and white charcoal on toned paper
14" × 11" (36cm × 28cm)

DEMONSTRATION

GUNDRUN

Gundrun is a talented jewelry artist. She has a shy confidence and a keen sense of humor, and I wanted to draw her with the slight grin she often has. Her glasses created some interesting highlights and light patterns on her face and made for a great starting point on this portrait.

Materials

DRAWING METHOD

Maas

TOOLS

14" × 11" (36cm × 28cm) Stonehenge Kraft toned paper

ebony pencil

2B, 4B and 8B woodless graphite pencils

click eraser

tortillon

white charcoal pencil

white Conté stick

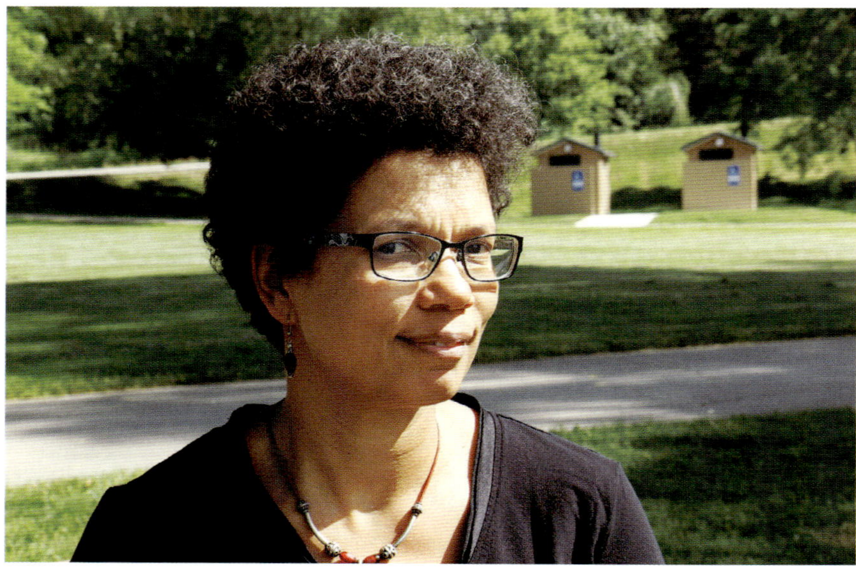

Reference Photo

1 ***PLACE THE HORIZONTAL LINES*** Using the Maas method, lay down the initial lines to build the foundation of the drawing. There is no correct or incorrect number of lines to add—as long as it is clear what line is for what feature.

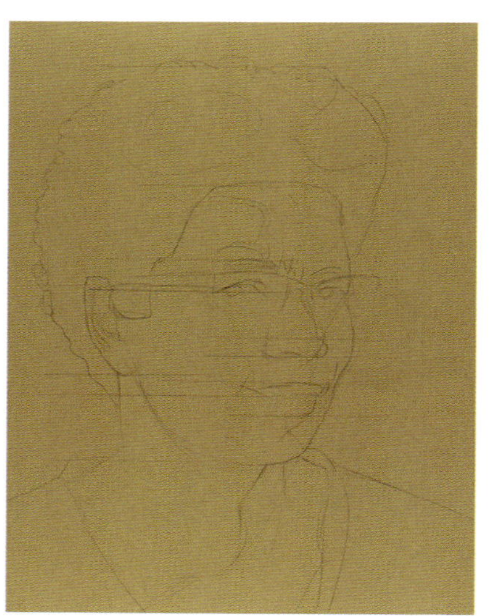

2 ***FREEHAND THE FEATURES*** Using the horizontal lines as a guide, freehand draw the features. Keep it light. A 2B pencil should be perfect.

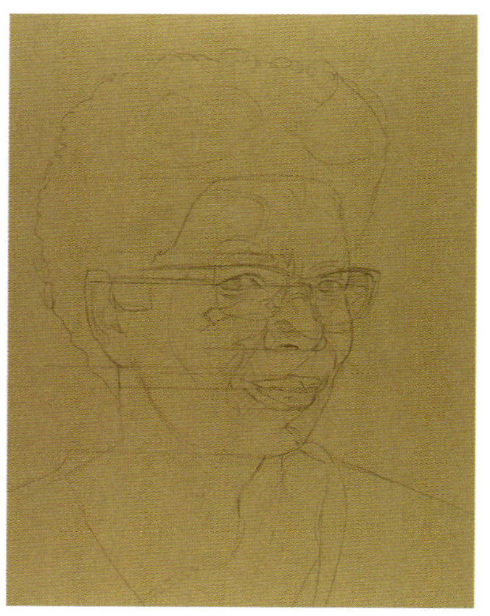

3 ***FINISH OUTLINING ALL SHAPES*** Pay attention to the shapes of the face as well as to the shapes of cast shadows, highlights and other elements. These are just as important on the roadmap to an effective likeness as the facial features themselves.

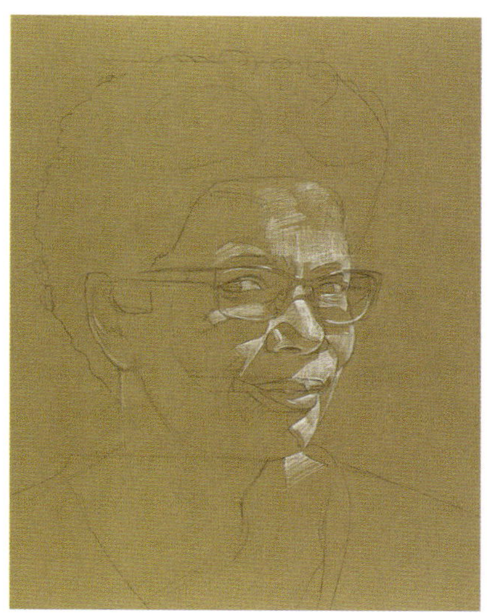

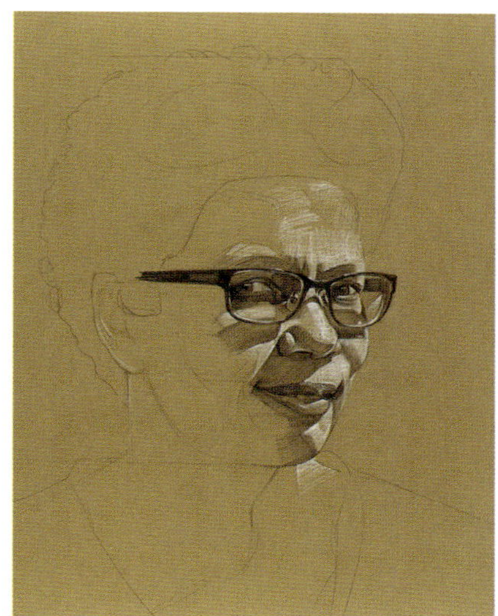

4 ***ADD WHITE***
Switch to a white charcoal pencil and lay down highlights, varying the pressure and intensity. Be sure to add the strokes in the direction of the form of the face.

5 ***ADD MIDTONES AND DARKS***
Using an ebony or 4B graphite pencil, begin adding midtones to the drawing. Be sure to vary the intensity of the values. The darkness of the glasses frames will never be as intense or dark as the cast shadows on the face. Simplify the detail on the glasses. Sometimes you may wish to include all detailing; other times, like here, it may detract from the focal point (the eyes) in the drawing.

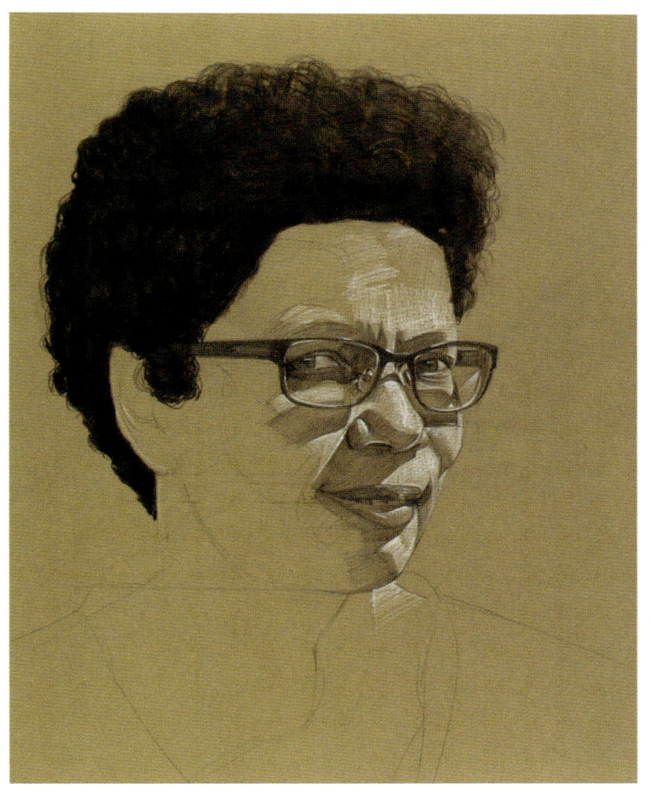

6 ***ADD THE HAIR MASS***
Using an 8B pencil, lay down the large area of the hair. Don't worry too much about the lights and darks in the hair. The goal is to apply the large dark mass. Roughly blend the whole area using a tortillon to get a dark, rich black.

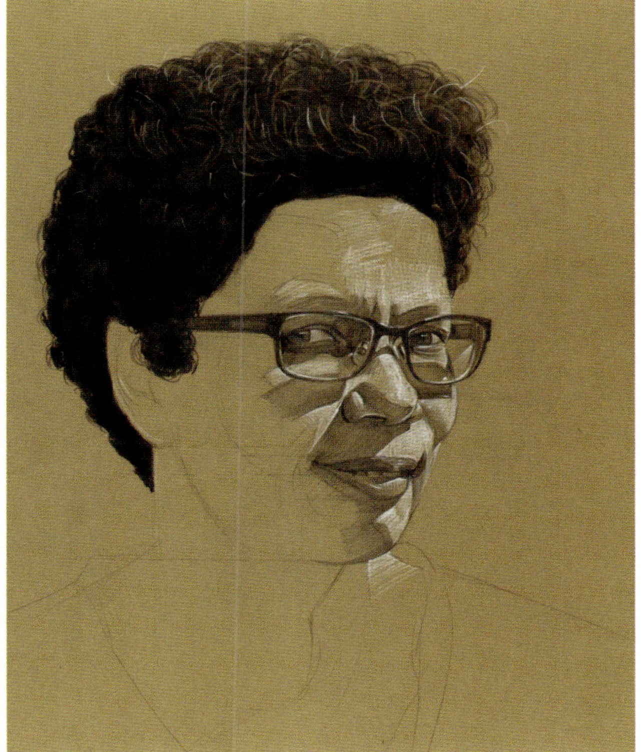

7 ***ADD HIGHLIGHTS TO THE HAIR***
Using a click eraser, begin lifting out highlights. Carefully study the reference. Notice how areas of the hair are lighter and pick away at the hair mass, effectively drawing with the eraser. You can also use white charcoal or the edge of a Conté stick to add a few stray highlights within the hair.

8 ADD MIDTONES TO THE FACE

Now that the large mass of dark has been established in the hair, begin defining midtones in the face.

9 BRING THE VALUES TOGETHER

Continue to work down the drawing, tying in the chin and neck values. By adding a very dark collar, the dark mass of the hair is balanced against the shirt. Compare values throughout the piece.

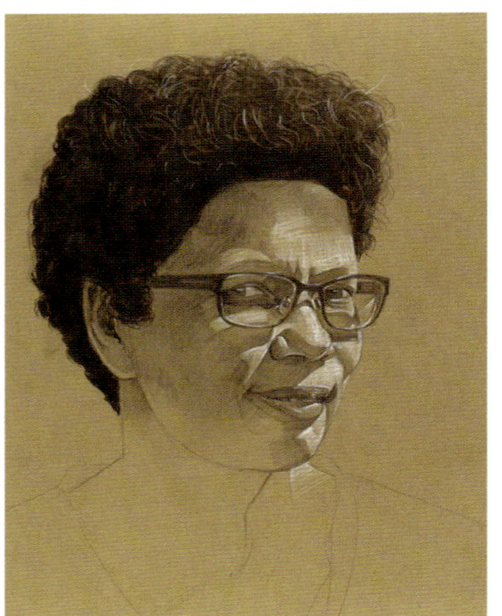

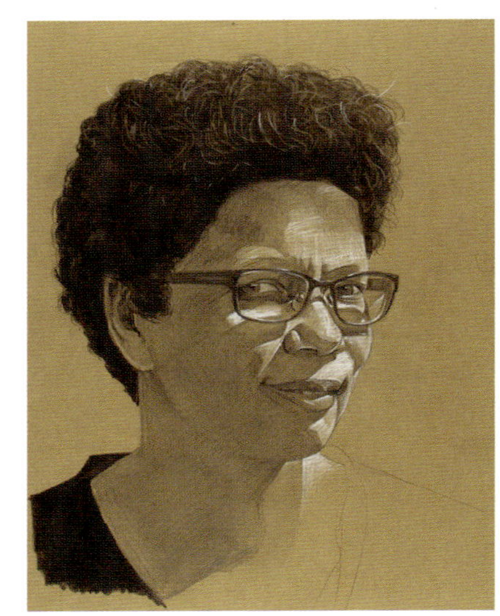

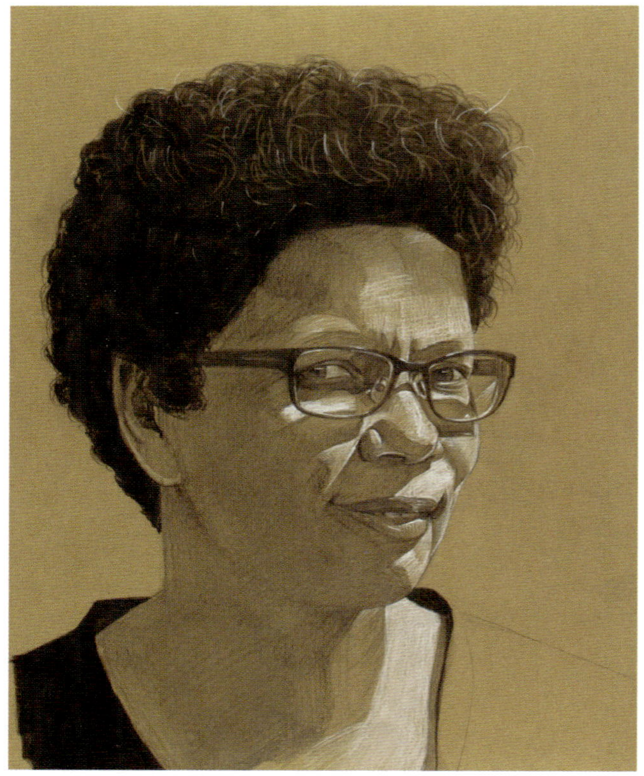

10 STRENGTHEN THE WHITES

Add white charcoal to the neck area and adjust highlights in the face. Check the values of the white charcoal throughout the piece as you would check a graphite drawing on white paper.

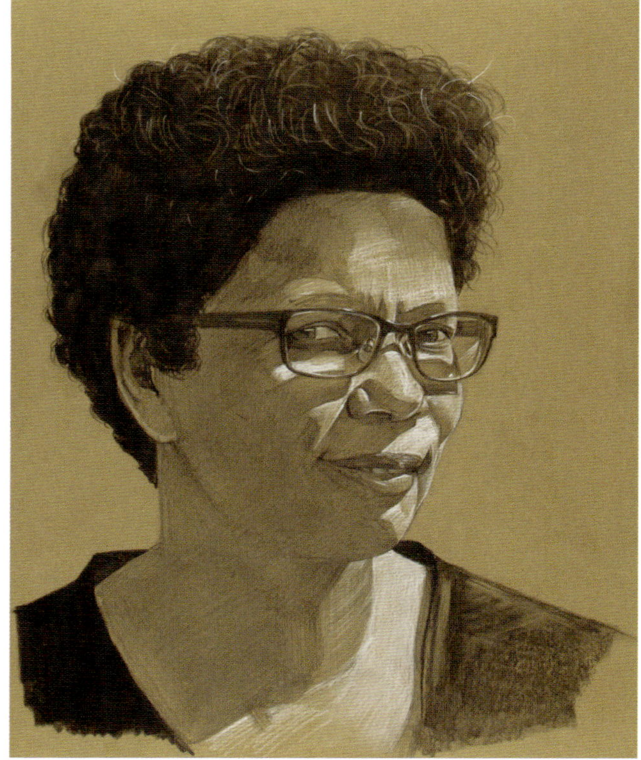

11 EVALUATE AND FINISH THE DRAWING

Add in the shirt on the right and refine the details throughout. Add darker and sharper lines and adjust under-worked areas where some blending is still needed.

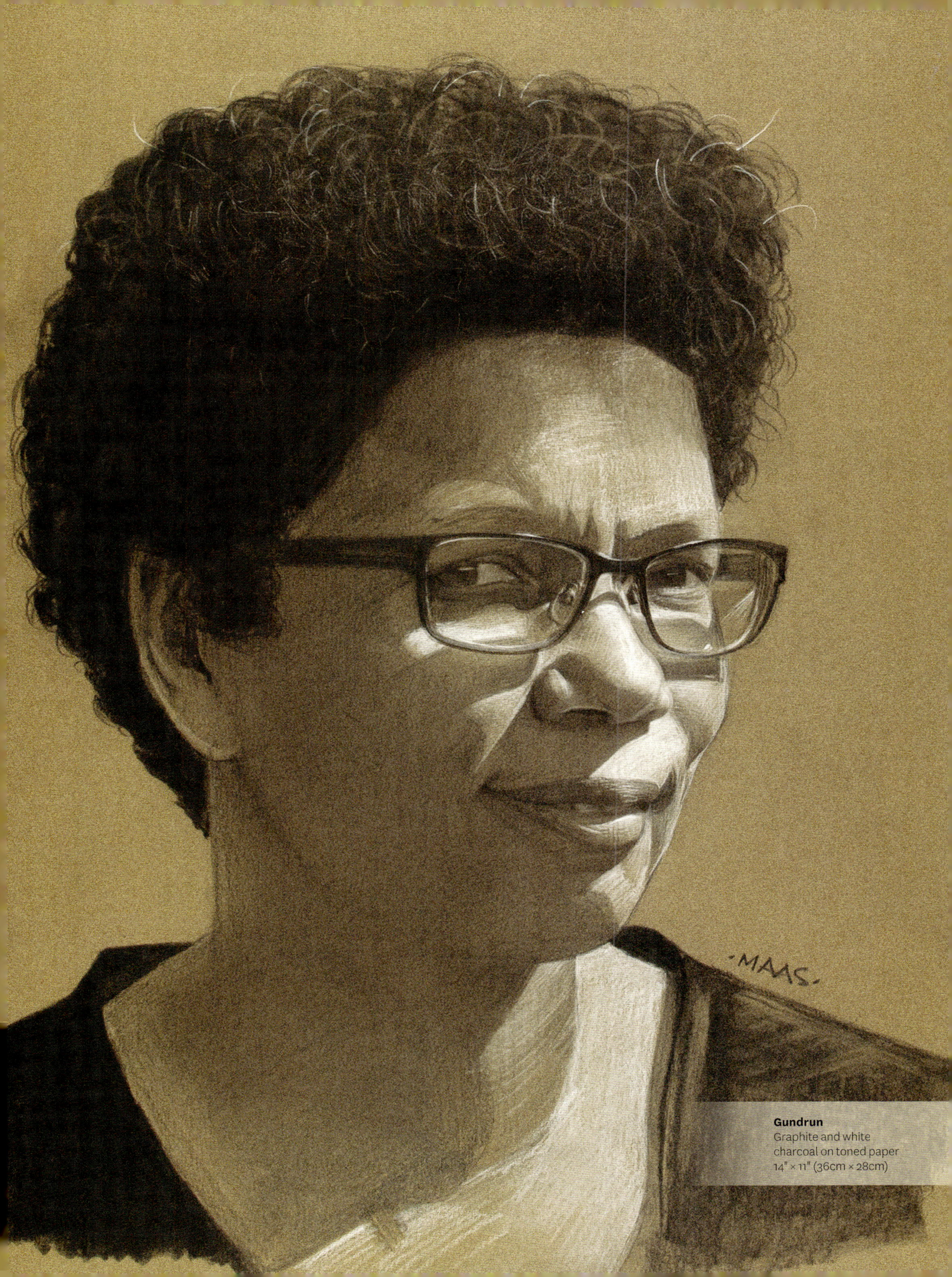

Gundrun
Graphite and white charcoal on toned paper
14" × 11" (36cm × 28cm)

DEMONSTRATION

PAUL

Paul is a retired architect, an avid runner and an octogenarian. He also happens to be my father. Over the years I have drawn my mother many times but only a few times have I drawn my father. I thought this would be a good time to do so and chose a toned paper as the perfect way to illustrate his strong features and thick white hair.

Materials

DRAWING METHOD

Maas

TOOLS

14" × 11" (36cm × 28cm) Strathmore 400 toned tan sketch paper

ebony pencil

2B, 6B and 8B woodless graphite pencils

kneaded eraser

tortillons

white charcoal pencil

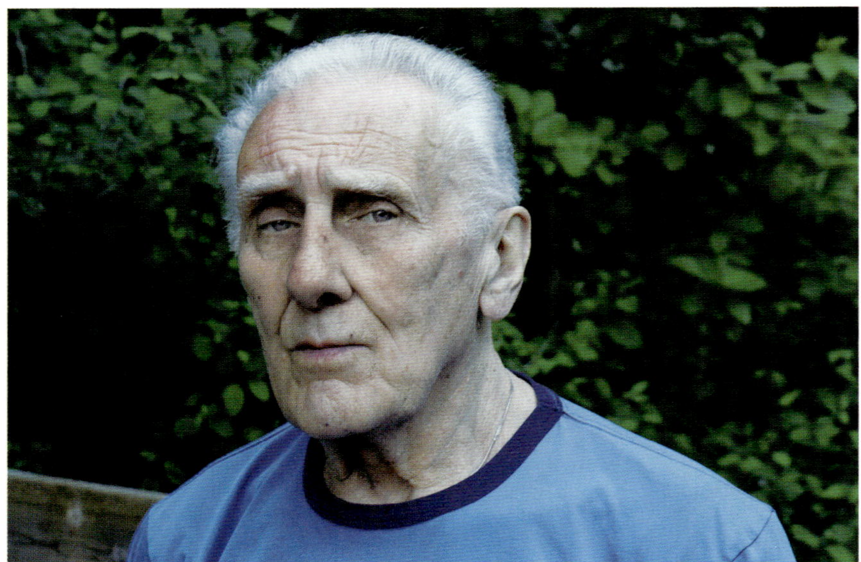

Reference Photo

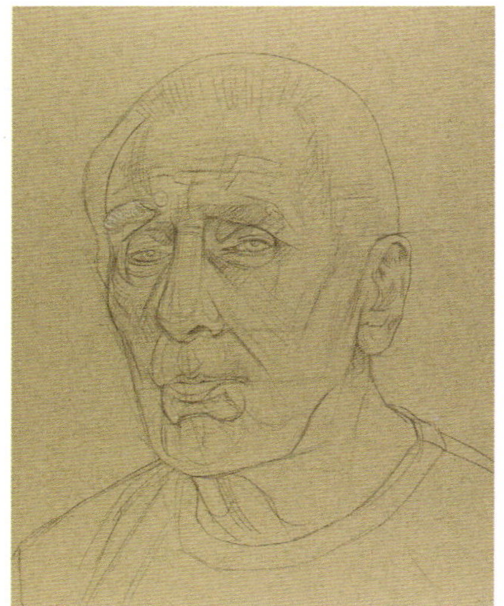

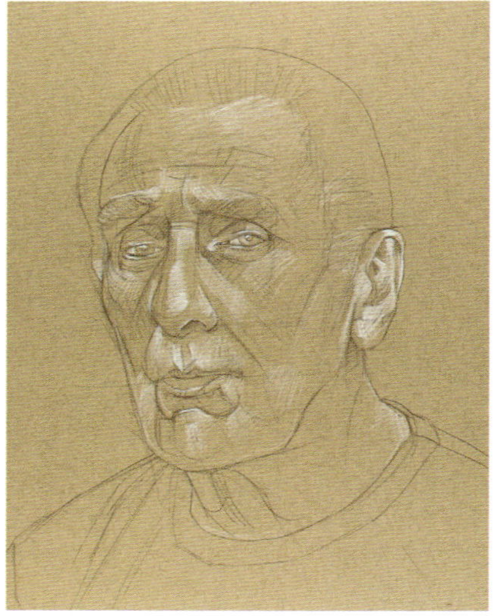

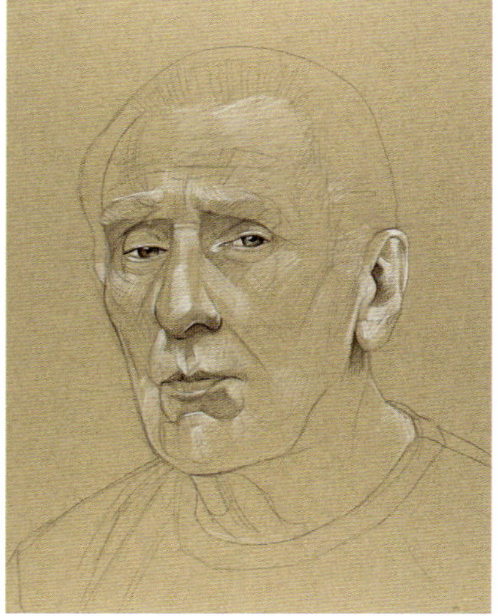

1 ***BLOCK IN THE DRAWING*** Using the Maas method, block in the drawing with a 2B pencil. Because Paul is an older gentleman, there are lots of visually interesting shapes and planes on his face that would not be found on a younger person. Lightly indicate as many of these as possible.

2 ***ADD WHITE CHARCOAL*** Using a white charcoal pencil, lay in the highlights and lighter midtones. Pay attention to the smallest slivers of light, for example, on the hard edge where the nostril sits below the nose edge. Don't worry about adding all the areas of white just yet. Try to get enough in so that midtone values will fit within the whites and the darks.

3 ***ADD THE DARKEST DARKS*** Using an ebony pencil, draw in the darkest darks—the eyes, the nostrils and the mouth shadows. Some of these may need to be darkened (with an 8B pencil) as the drawing is built up, but there is a range of values now (from bright white to dark black), within which the rest of the drawing will fall.

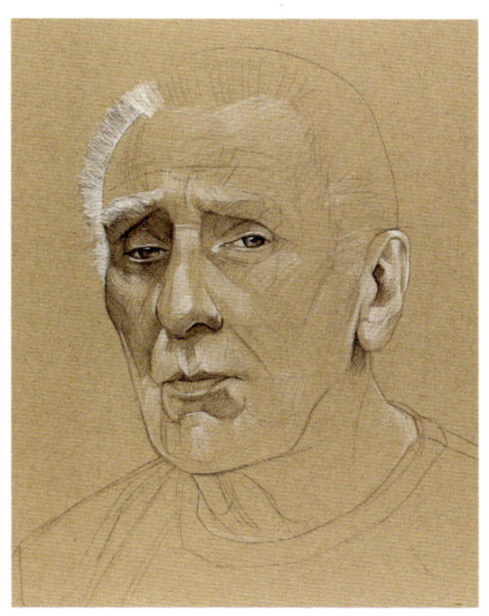

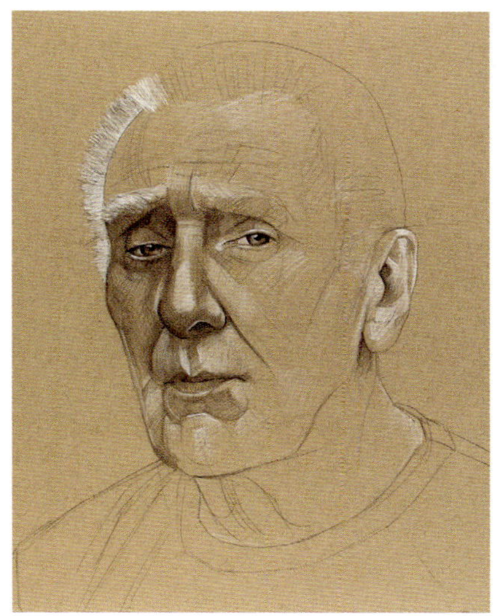

4 BEGIN THE HAIR
Use a white charcoal pencil with a fair amount of pressure to lay in the overall shapes of Paul's white hair. Overlay this with soft lines of 2B graphite to shade certain sections and add depth. Add in some midtones on the left side of the face. Some areas, such as the shadows above and around the eye, will be much darker as they are built up. This is simply a good starting point to establish tone.

5 ADD VOLUME
Using the same 2B pencil (or switching to an even darker pencil such as a 6B or 8B and using a lighter touch), add volume on the left check and nose. Lay down the strokes in relation to the form of the shapes. Curve the lines around each fold of skin and mass.

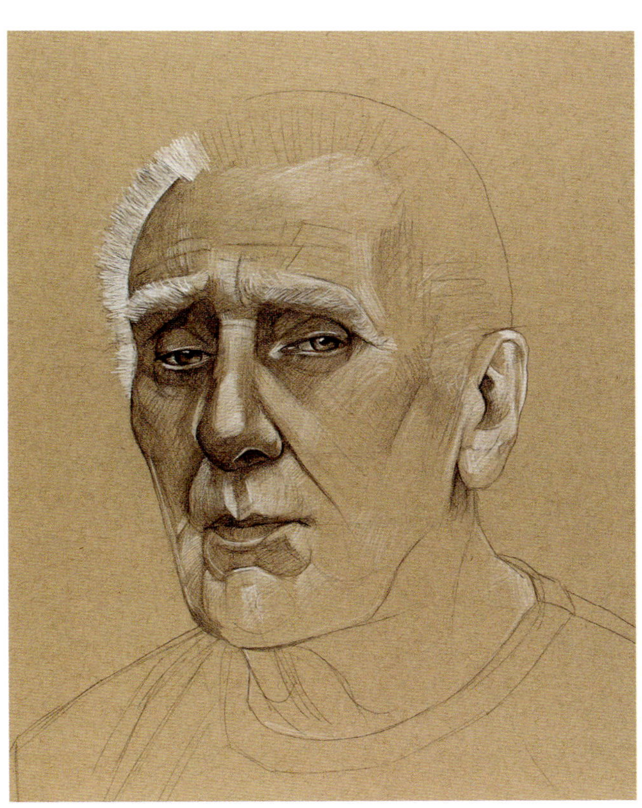

6 RENDER THE RIGHT SIDE OF THE FACE
It is important not to build up the tones on one side only since it will become difficult to create an even value across the piece.

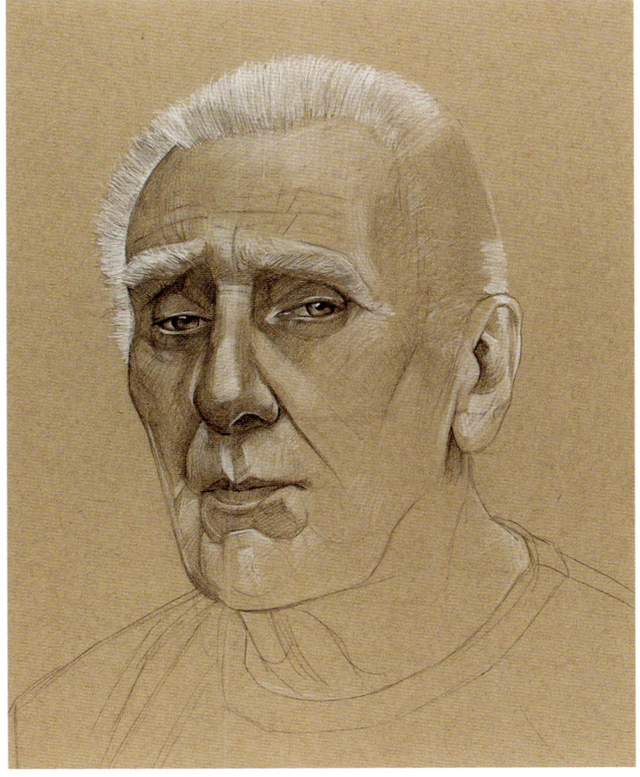

7 ADD MORE HAIR
Begin adding the rest of the hair with a sharp white charcoal pencil. Continue to follow the shape and direction of the hair mass.

8 ADD HIGHLIGHTS AND SHADOW

Despite hair being a mass, it is easy to look at each individual hair. But it's the hair mass itself that has highlights and shadows and takes on its own shape. Carefully use more pressure with the white charcoal where the hair is lighter and less pressure where it is darker. Lightly add graphite (using a very sharp 2B pencil to avoid muddying the paper) in areas to add shading to the hairline.

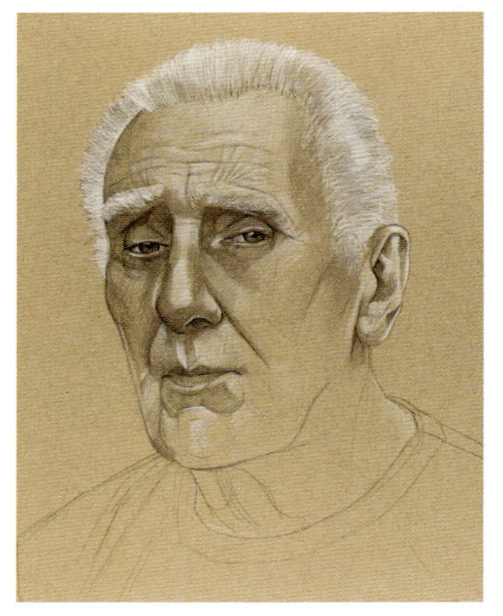

9 ADD A POP OF DARK TO THE BACKGROUND

Since Paul's hair is white, adding an element of dark in the background will help balance the overall contrast in the piece. Apply an even pressure of soft lead such as 8B woodless over the background. Once an area has been laid down, blend the black into a rich dark using a previously-used tortillon. Finish the area with whimsical pencil strokes of a 6B or 8B pencil in an organic fashion.

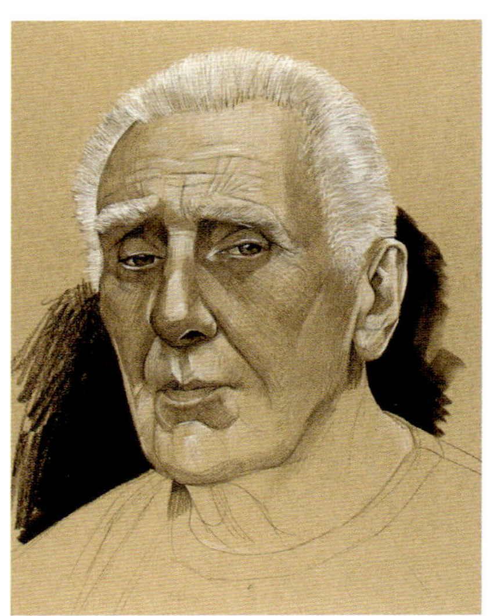

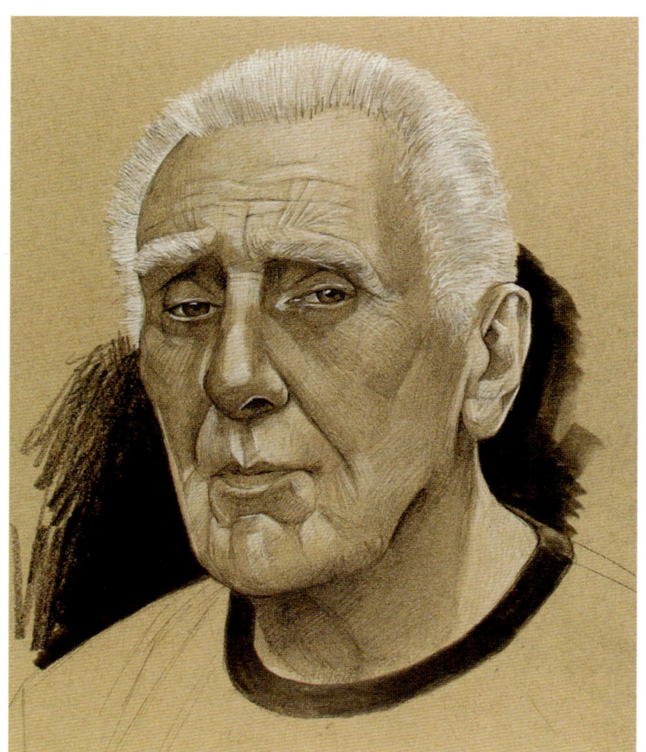

10 WORK THE SECONDARY AREAS

Using the values established in the key areas of the face, render the jawline, neck and collar of the shirt. Choose how much of the clothing to render and how much to leave unfinished.

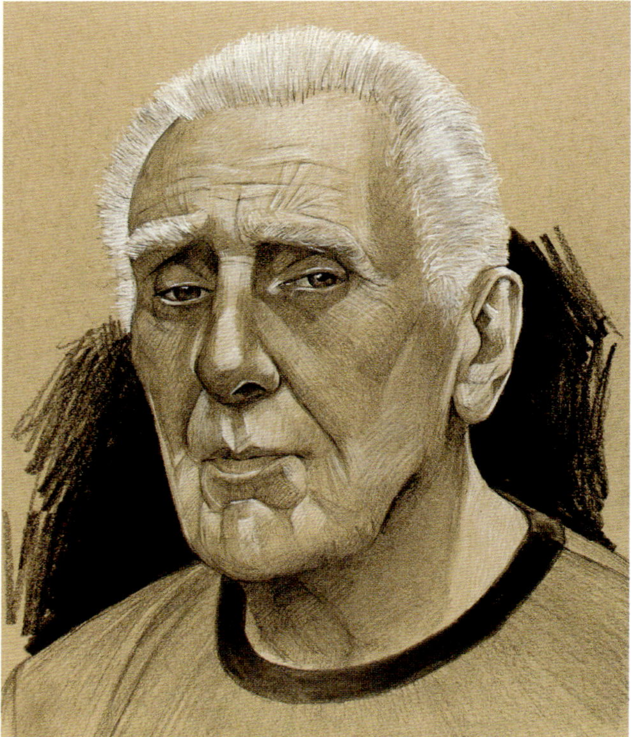

11 EVALUATE AND FINISH THE DRAWING

With the drawing nearly complete, double-check all areas of contrast to ensure the values and tones are correct and will fit with the rest of the piece. This is where parts will be darkened usually, but possibly some areas may be lightened if a highlight needs to be brighter.

Finally, use a clean tortillon to blend out some of the lines. Add more darks and sharpen some of the focal points.

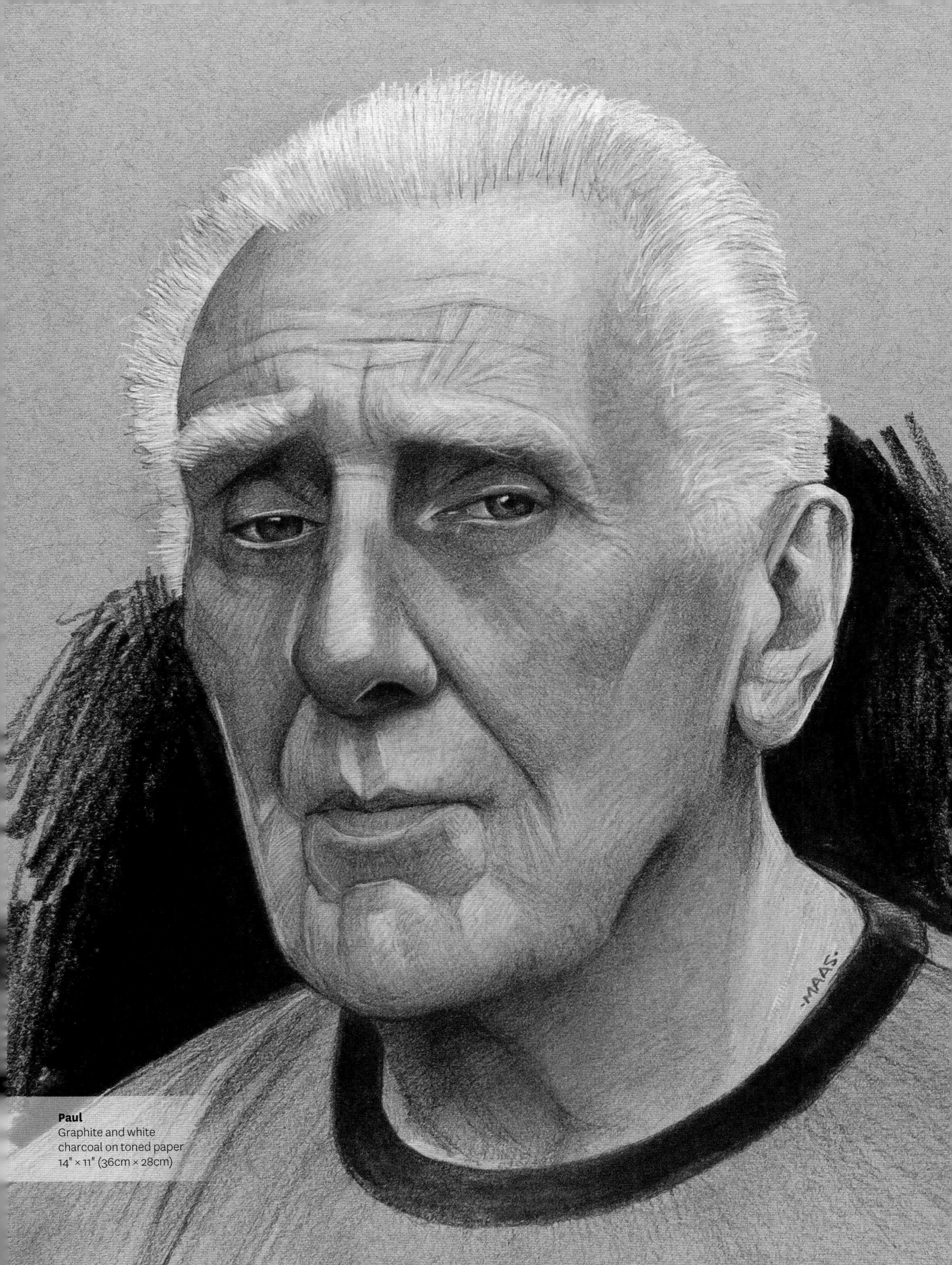

Paul
Graphite and white charcoal on toned paper
14" × 11" (36cm × 28cm)

DEMONSTRATION

KRISTIN

Kristin is an internationally recognized fitness instructor who is often called a trainer to the stars with multiple high-profile celebrity clients. I wanted to include a full-body portrait among the demonstrations and Kristin seemed like the perfect choice.

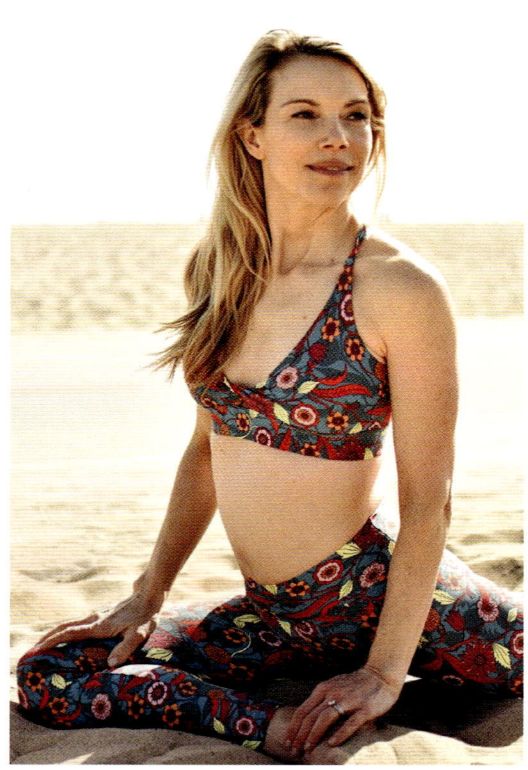

Reference Photo

Materials

DRAWING METHOD

Freehand

TOOLS

14" × 11" (36cm × 28cm) Bienfang Bristol white paper

HB, 2B, 4B, 6B and 8B woodless graphite pencils

kneaded eraser

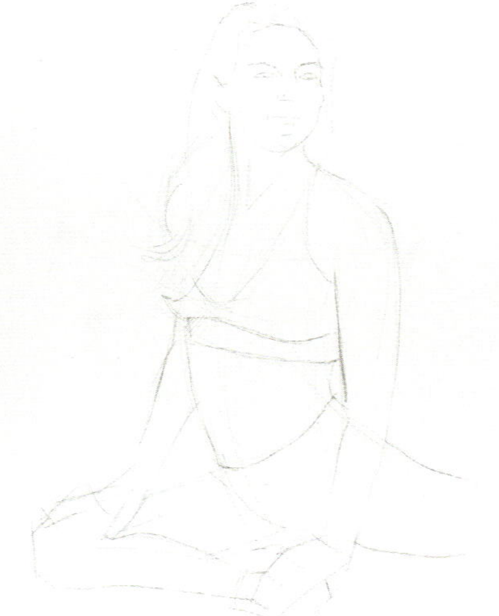

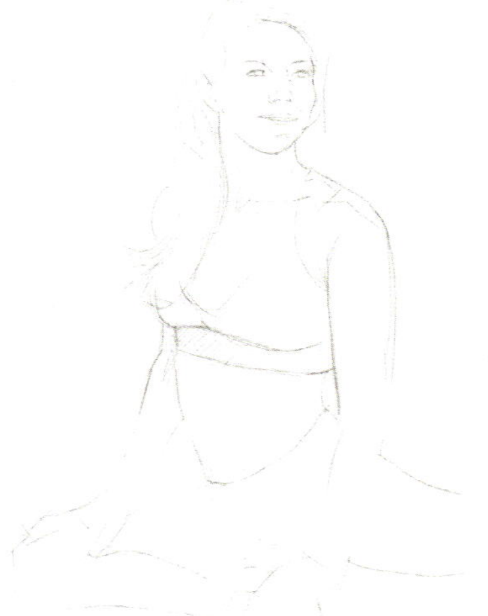

1 ***LAY DOWN INITIAL LINES*** Drawing the full body is not a whole lot different from drawing the face. Using an HB or 2B pencil, begin with a series of foundational lines. Pay attention to the size of the head, the curvature of the spine and other key points, such as shoulder width and leg length, that will serve as a roadmap for the drawing.

2 ***DEFINE THE EDGES*** Very lightly indicate the contours of the body. Notice how the hands are blocked in as simple geometric shapes at this stage. Keep it very light.

3 ***REFINE THE FORM*** Begin darkening the lines using a 2B pencil. Pay attention to correct form and double-check each line in relation to the rest of the drawing. Use the side of the pencil to measure the width of the shoulders, for example, and test them against the length of the leg.

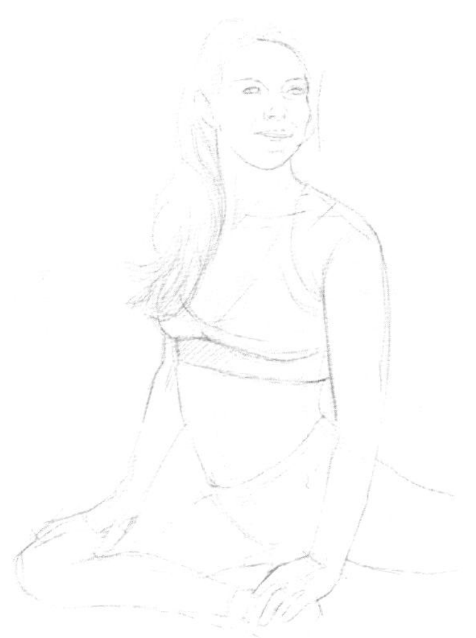

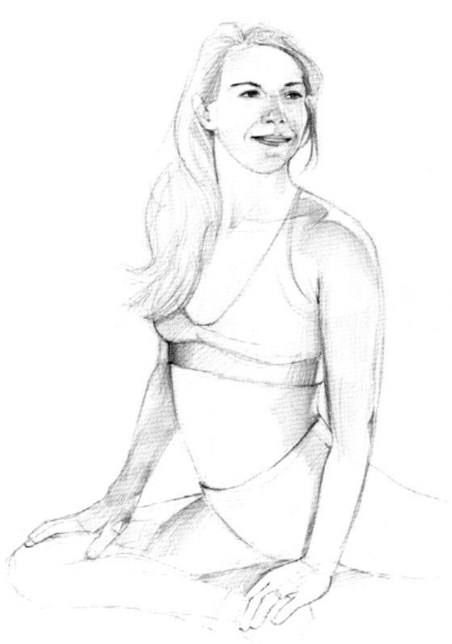

4 FINISH THE BLOCK IN

Render and refine the hair mass, the details on the hands and the clothing. It is time to begin rendering the form.

5 PLAN THE VALUES

Using a 2B pencil, lightly begin to make note of the highlights and shadows. Notice the strip of light on the right shoulder and the area on the torso beside the right arm. These will be secondary focal points because of how the light hits the form.

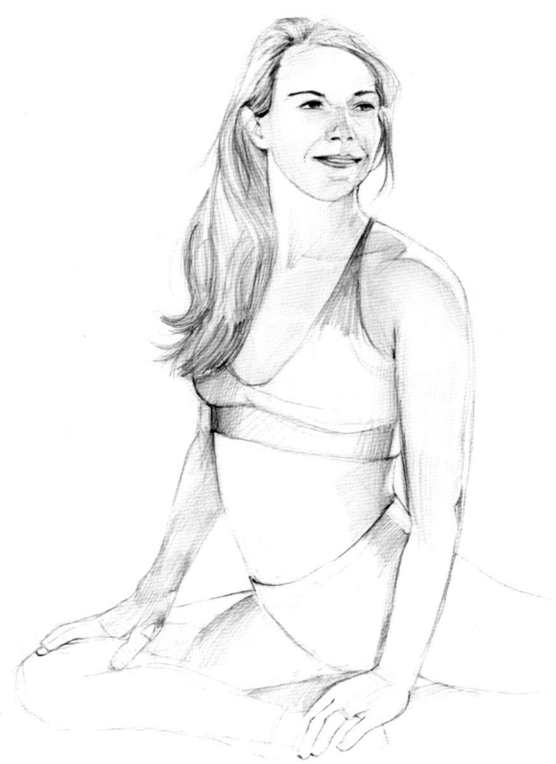

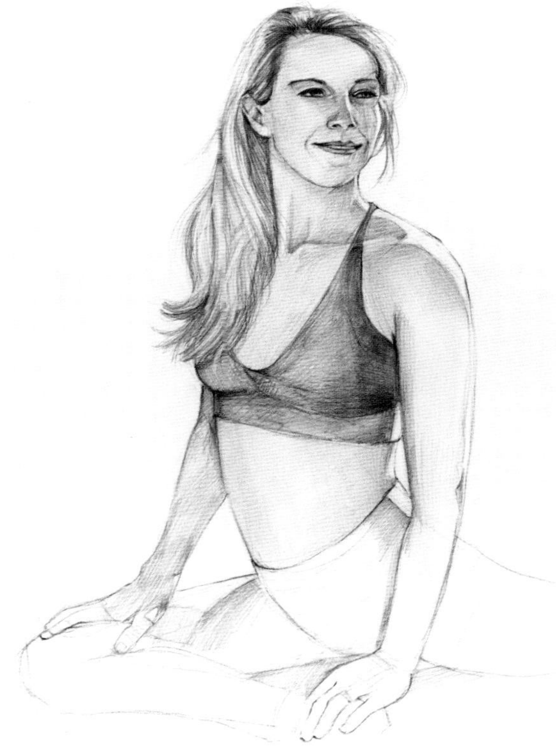

6 BEGIN TO ADD MIDTONES

Switching to a 4B pencil, add form to the hair, keeping the lines organic and in the same direction as the hair itself. Add some darks with either the same pencil (with more pressure) or with an 8B pencil in various parts of the drawing so that values will continue to build evenly across the piece.

7 ESTABLISH THE DARKS

Simplify the pattern on the clothing. While it's a very neat pattern and could lend itself to a rendering, putting too much detail in clothing can sometimes take away focus from the face and the person. Darken the sports bra with a 6B or 8B pencil and start to establish darks in the face and hair.

8 RENDER THE LEFT LEG AND TORSO

Using 4B and 6B pencils, render the form of the leg, the left arm and the torso. Pay attention to the values in the sports bra as they should match the yoga pants. Ignore the patterns on the reference and look for the shadows and highlights on the forms themselves.

9 RENDER THE RIGHT ARM AND RIGHT LEG

Pay special attention to the crest of the shoulder where the highlight hits the crest of the deltoid muscle and near the elbow. It's important, when drawing a full-body portrait, to consider these sorts of areas that add visual interest and secondary focal points.

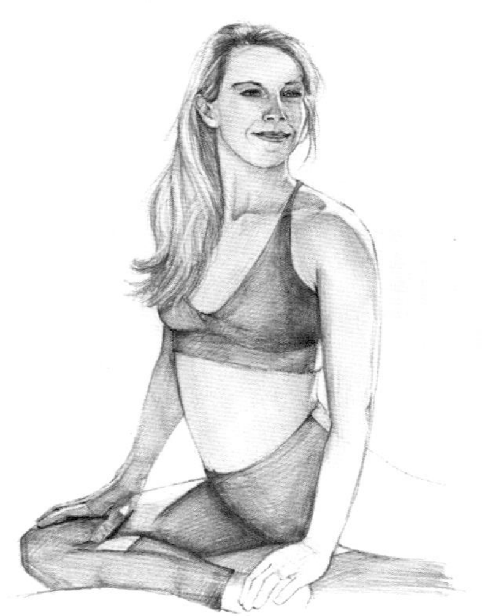

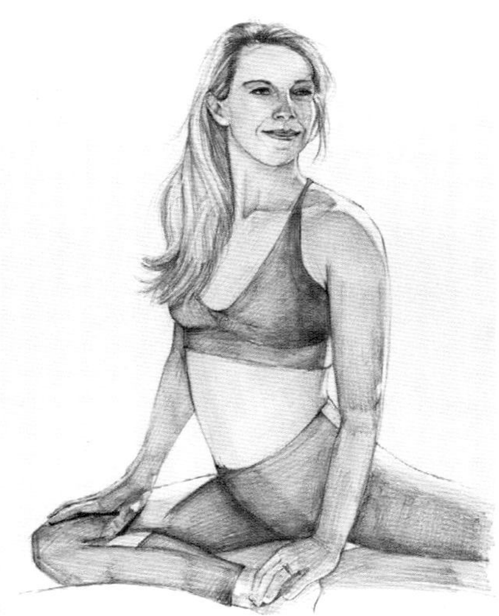

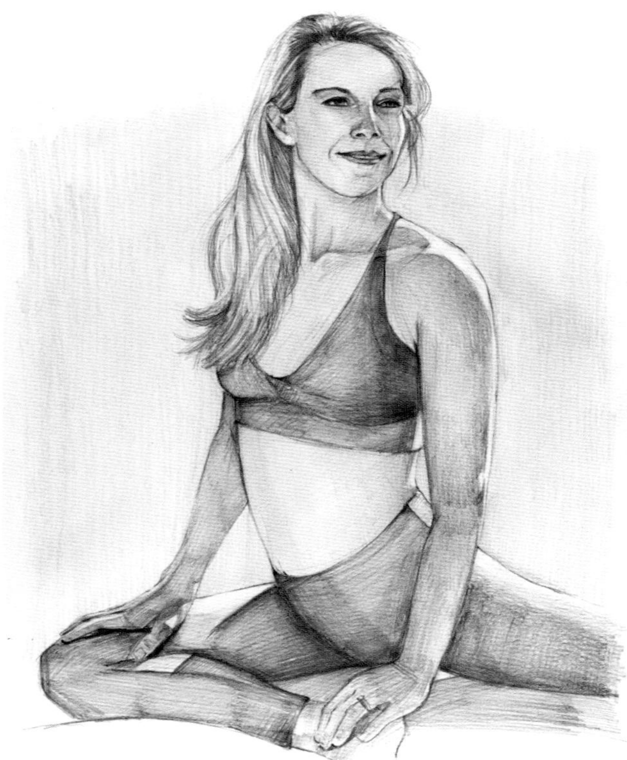

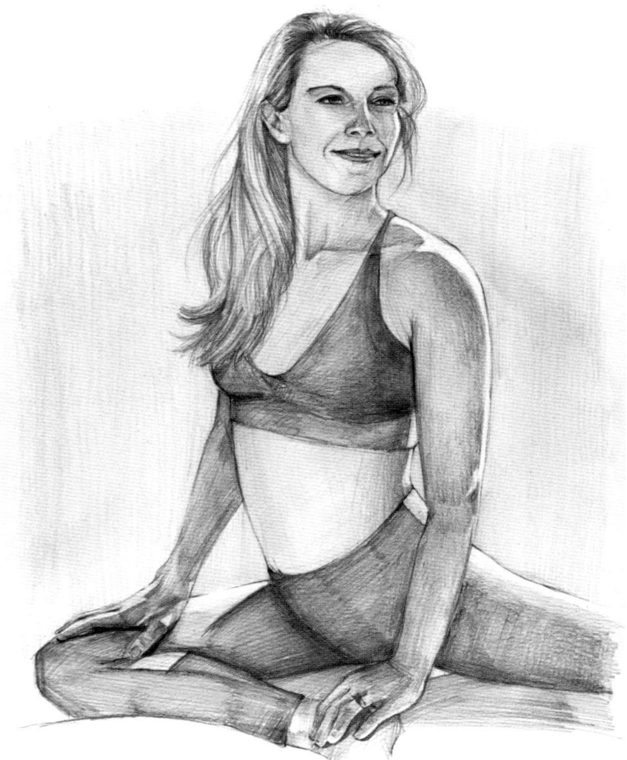

10 ADD A BACKGROUND

This piece is midtone heavy, so it would be a bad idea to leave the paper completely white or to make the background black. Either would make the piece look dull. The compromise is a soft gray background around 10 to 15 percent black on the value scale. Lightly draw this background in with a 2B pencil, keeping the strokes the same direction.

11 EVALUATE AND FINISH THE DRAWING

Using a 6B or 8B pencil, darken the areas that need a little more pop. A kneaded eraser will help bring back highlights that have gotten dirty from secondary graphite dust. Sharpen details on the hands and face.

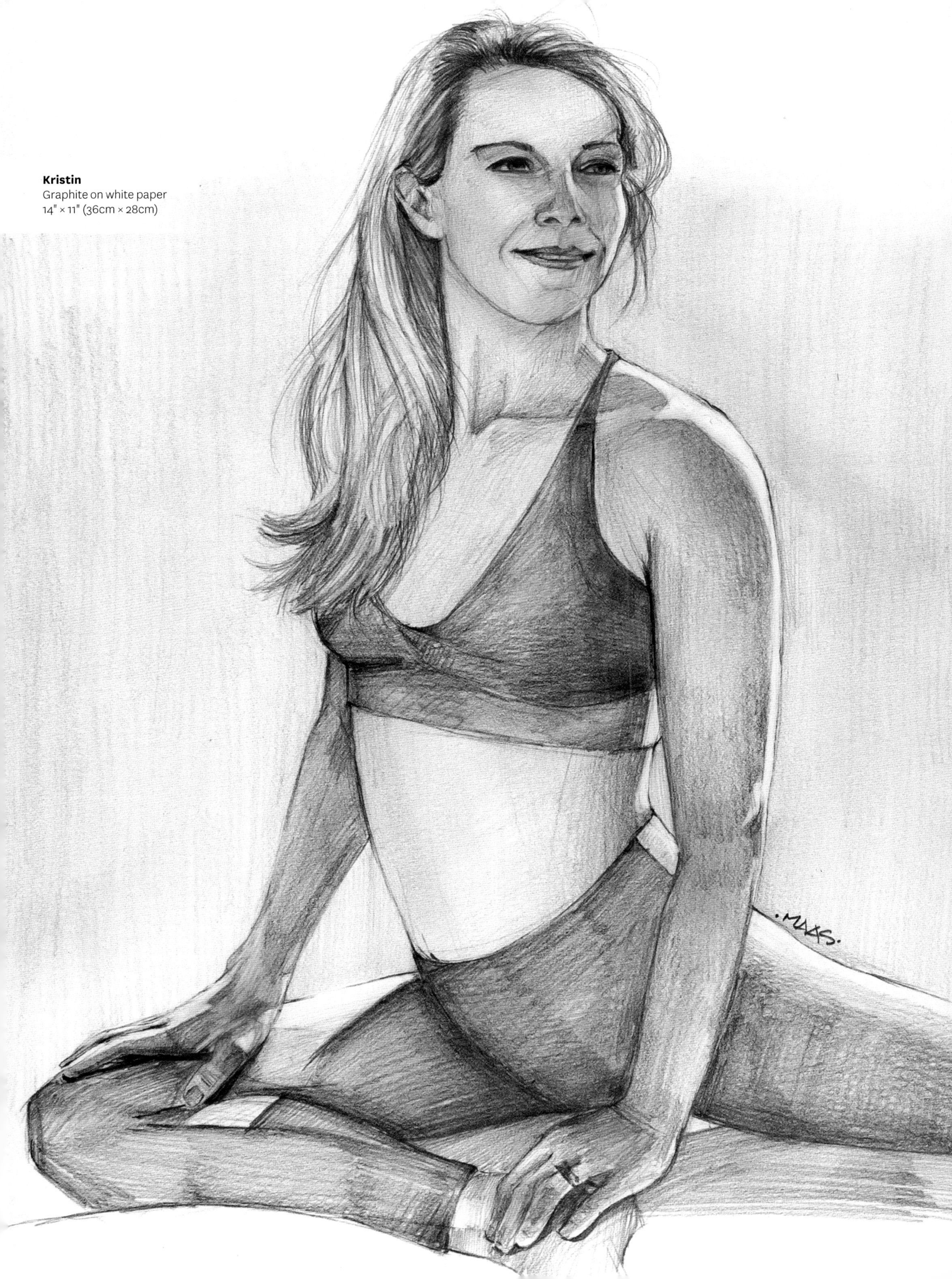

Kristin
Graphite on white paper
14" × 11" (36cm × 28cm)

DEMONSTRATION

CARY

Cary Elwes has been a well-known actor for nearly four decades. His most famous role is as Westley from *The Princess Bride*. His wife, Lisa Marie, sent me this photo that she took of him in Paris. Even though it is somewhat less detailed and lower in contrast than most reference I like to work with, there is a natural and genuine quality to Cary's smile. I wanted to bring out the twinkle in his eyes with this portrait.

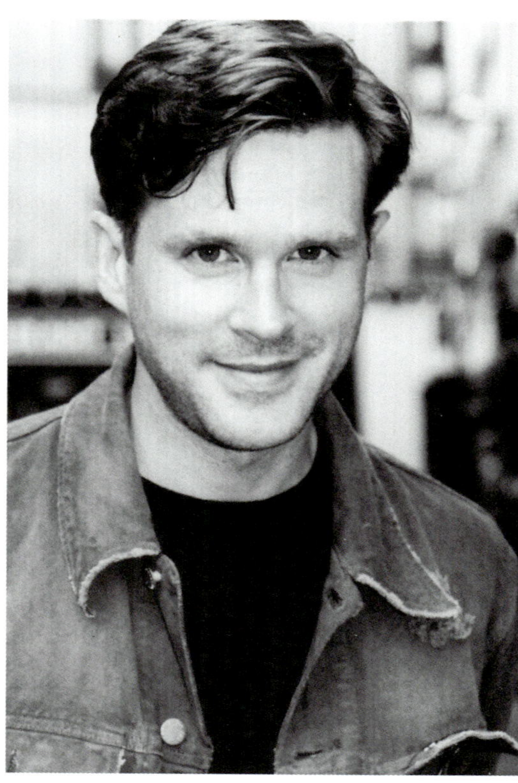

Reference Photo

Materials

DRAWING METHOD

Maas

TOOLS

14" × 11" (36cm × 28cm) Bienfang Bristol white paper

2B, 4B, 6B and 8B woodless graphite pencils

kneaded eraser

tortillon

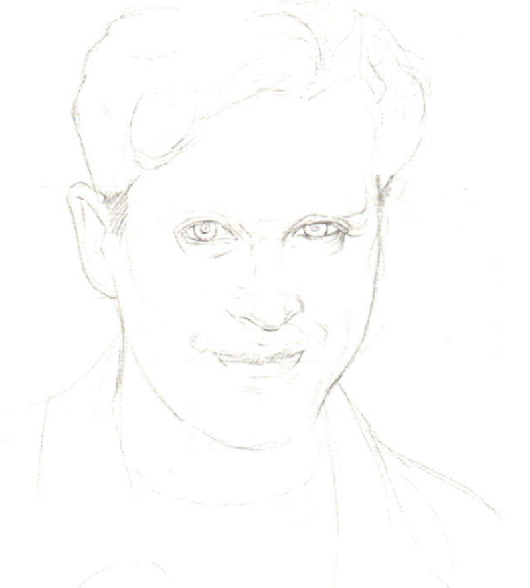

1 *BLOCK IN THE FEATURES*
Using the Maas method, draw horizontal lines across the reference photo to indicate the key features of the face. Add some lines for the sides of the face and the hairline by comparing them to the horizontal lines.

2 *REFINE THE FEATURES*
With the guidelines in place, begin lightly drawing the shapes of each feature. A 2B is ideal for this. If any guidelines are missing from the initial stage, add them now to help determine feature placement.

3 *DOUBLE-CHECK PLACEMENT*
This is a crucial stage. The main features are blocked in, but we must ensure that all elements are in the right place. It's true that you can render or erase areas later, but the more that is correct at this stage, the less work it will be to make fixes later on.

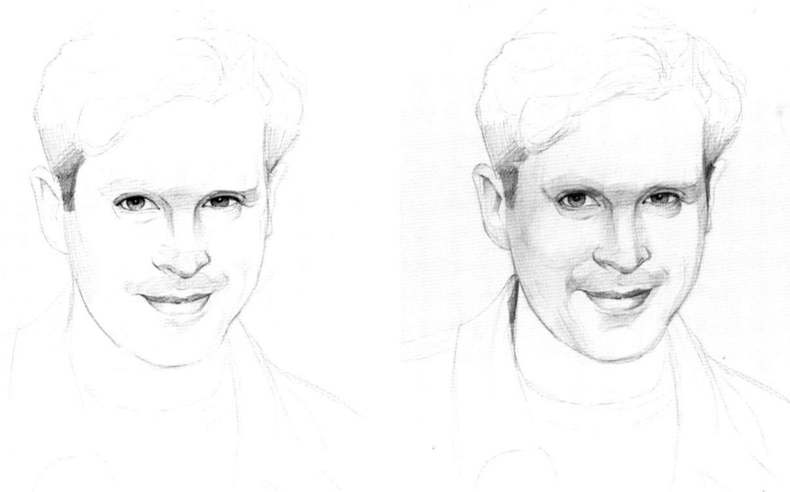

4 ADD THE DARKS

Using a 4B pencil, enter the darkest darks of the portrait. These are the focal points—usually the darkest parts of the eyes, nose and mouth. This helps to define the most important parts of the face but also to establish the value scale.

5 BUILD UP THE TONES

Continuing with a 4B pencil, lightly add tone to the whole face. Build up volume with light, layered strokes, always in the direction of the form. Because we are working on white paper, pay special attention to the transitions from light to dark. The white of the paper will be the brightest highlights.

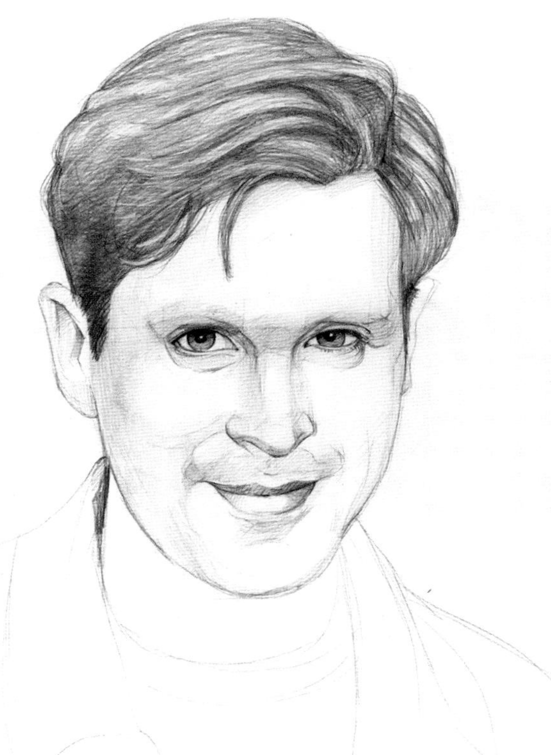

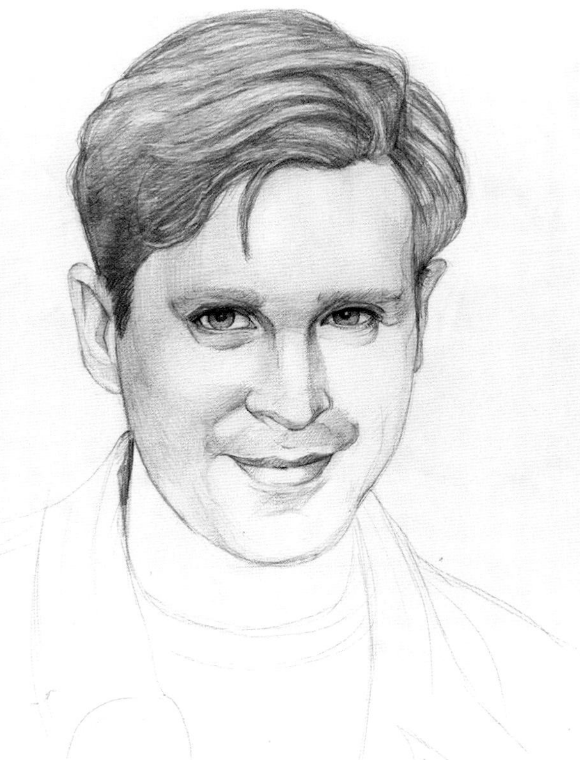

6 RENDER THE HAIR

Using a 6B pencil, render the hair using long rhythmic strokes in the direction of the hair mass. Sometimes it is easier to turn the drawing surface on its side or even upside down to achieve organic strokes. Alternate between rendering with pencil and lifting out highlights with an eraser. Remember, achieving volume in hair mass takes a fair amount of building up.

7 ADD FORM TO THE FACE

Switching back to a 4B pencil, darken the existing form. Now that the hair has a good foundation, it's a good idea to go back and develop the values in the face to match the darkness of the hair. Add form to the face.

8 DEVELOP AND DEFINE FORM

Cary has several recognizable dimples in his face, so it's important to render them in a subtle manner. This can be achieved by a combination of light, layered strokes but also gently picking graphite off with a kneaded eraser. It's a subtle transition, so this may take a few attempts. Erase if necessary.

9 DARKEN THE VALUES AND ADD STUBBLE

Using a 6B pencil and a light touch, continue darkening any areas that need refinement. Cary has some noticeable stubble that adds to the darkness in that part of his face. Gently render it with a dull 4B pencil by applying dots in a random order. Make sure to vary the pressure and pattern of the dots. Be sure not to press too hard or they will be too prominent and stick out.

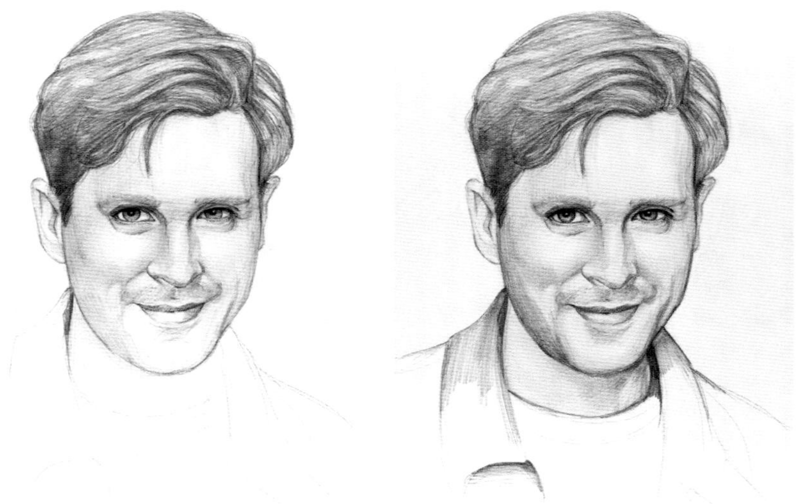

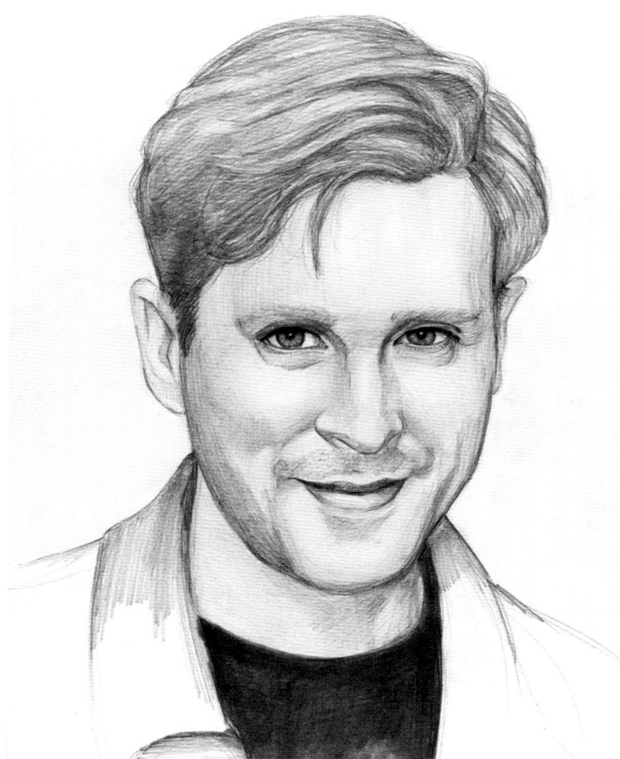

10 ADD THE CLOTHING

Render the clothing in a simple manner with an 8B pencil and blend it gently with a tortillon. Don't make it too dark and don't add too many details. The dark shirt creates a nice balance in the drawing, but it also shows that the values in the rest of the piece need to be darkened a bit.

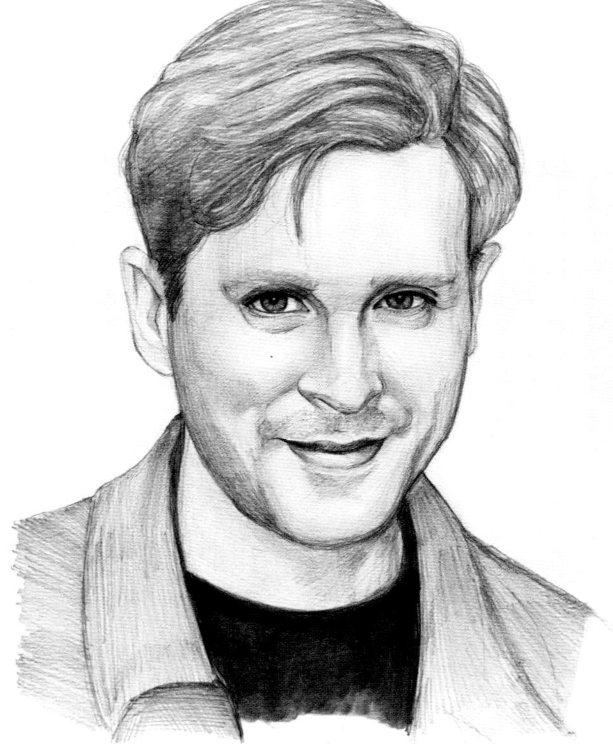

11 EVALUATE AND FINISH THE DRAWING

Finish rendering the clothing and go back and adjust other values to match. Darken the darks with a 6B pencil and bring out highlights with a kneaded eraser. At this stage, it is clear that the reference photo is showing Cary's hair as too dark, so use a kneaded eraser to lift some of the graphite in the hair to make the values lighter.

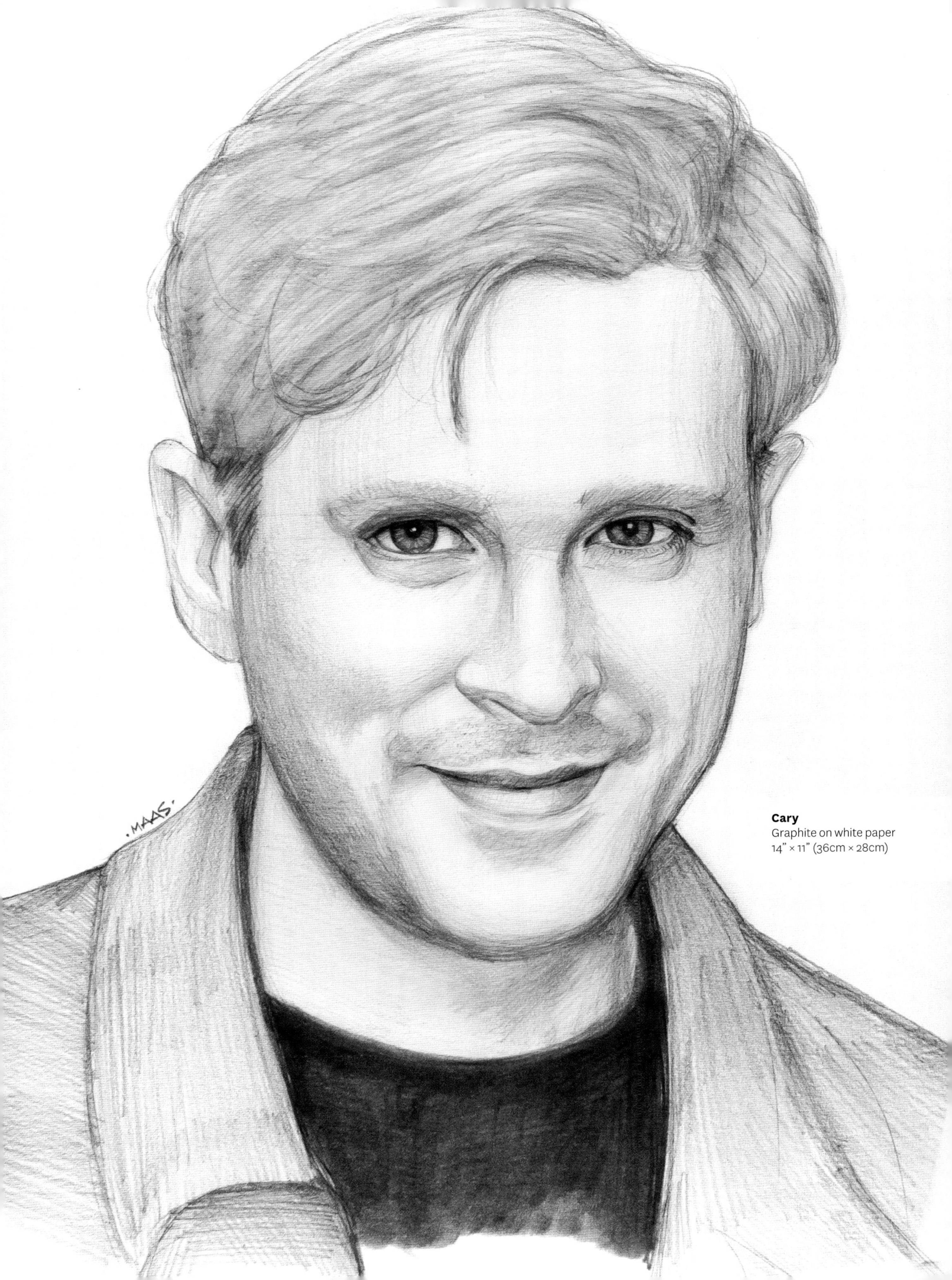

Cary
Graphite on white paper
14" × 11" (36cm × 28cm)

DEMONSTRATION

JANICE

Janice is a surgeon with a wonderful sense of humor. I wanted to showcase her charming smile and keen eyes in this portrait. The straight lines of her glasses balance nicely against the organic feel of her dreadlocks.

Materials

DRAWING METHOD

Maas

TOOLS

- 14" × 11" (36cm × 28cm) Stonehenge Kraft toned paper
- ebony pencil
- 2B, 4B, 6B and 8B woodless graphite pencils
- click eraser
- kneaded eraser
- tortillon
- white charcoal pencil
- white Conté stick

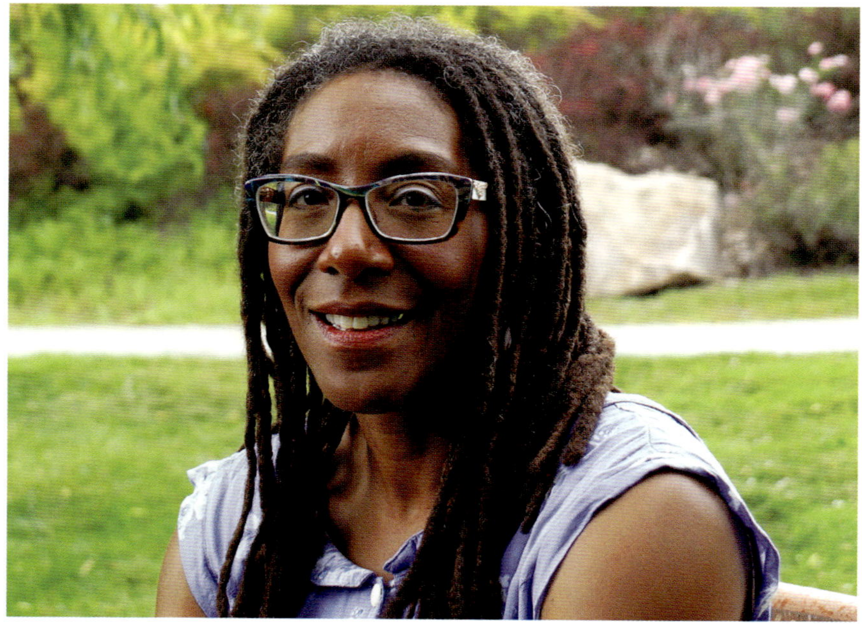

Reference Photo

1 BLOCK IN THE INITIAL LINES
Using the Maas method, draw horizontal lines across from the reference photo to indicate the key features of the face.

2 LIGHTLY ADD THE HORIZONTAL LINES
Indicate the overall shapes by comparing the distance between the horizontal lines to work out the visual measurements for the rest of the face.

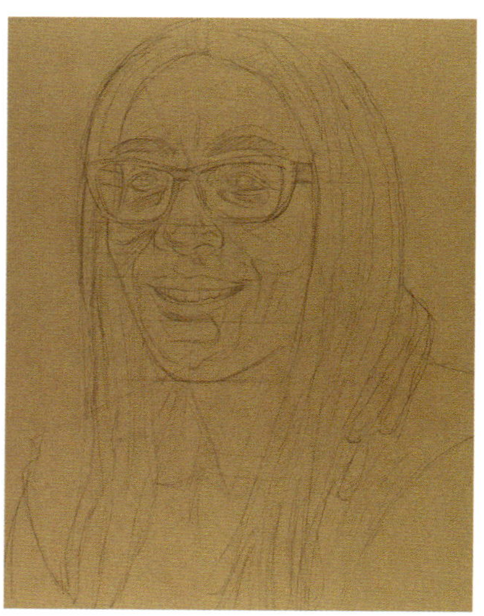

3 REFINE THE FEATURES
Now that the guidelines are in place, use a 2B pencil to lightly draw the shapes of each feature. Remember that shapes from highlights and shadows also help define the likeness, not just the features themselves.

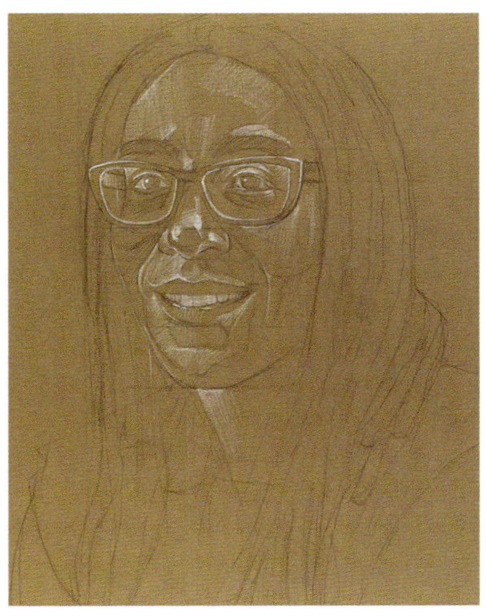

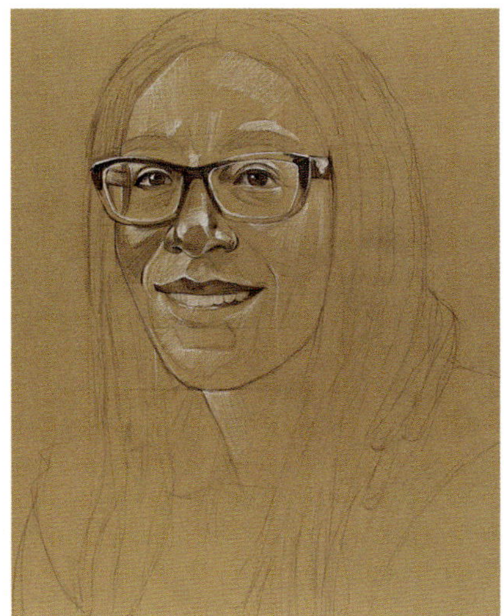

4 *ADD THE WHITE HIGHLIGHTS*

Using a white charcoal pencil, add the largest areas of white to the piece. Vary the pressure of the pencil—the highlight on the tip of the nose, for example, is much more intense than the light below the lips.

5 *ADD THE DARKEST DARKS*

Switching to an ebony pencil, render the key darks. The eyes, some of the dark shadows in the cheeks and the glasses are good places to get a sense of dark values.

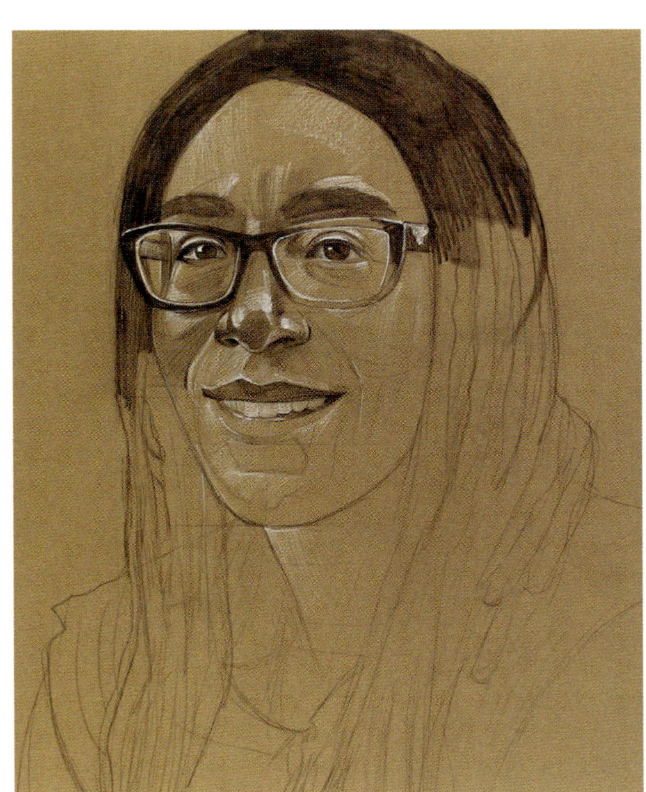

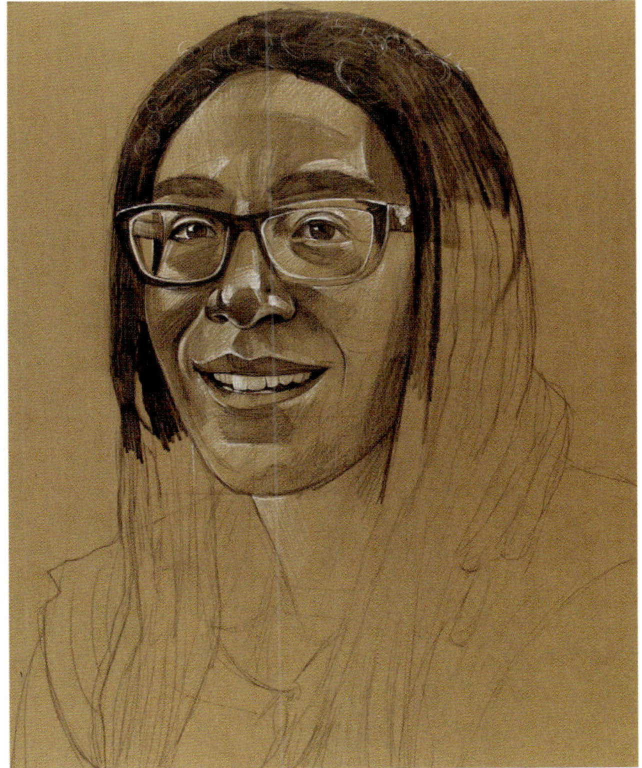

6 *BLOCK IN THE HAIR MASS*

Using a 6B woodless pencil, begin to block in the hair. Do not apply too much pressure as this may burnish the paper. Instead, once some pigment has been laid down, go over it with a tortillon to achieve a darker, richer black.

7 *CONTINUE RENDERING THE HAIR*

Work down the face, adding darks and volume. At the same time, continue to render the hair. Pay attention to how the dreadlocks fall and begin picking out some lights with a click eraser. Don't worry about too much detail in the hair at this point.

WHAT IS NEGATIVE SPACE?

While this sounds like something bad in a science-fiction film, negative space is simply the space around and between the subject of an image. When you look at the image of Janice, you can see how I have chosen to draw her from an angle where both her pose—and the negative space around her pose—are at the most interesting. Pay attention to the shapes in between and around a subject, like the spaces around and through Janice's dreadlocks.

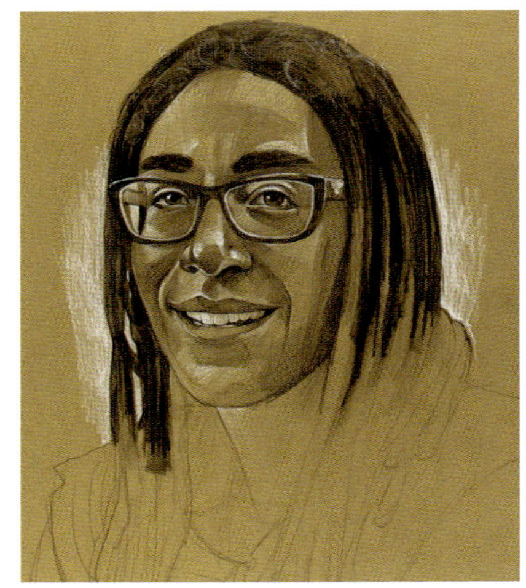

8 ***ADD VISUAL POP*** The dark edges of the dreadlocks will have more impact if you add some white. Using a white charcoal pencil, render light lines being careful to keep them in the same direction. Be sure to render the negative space between parts of the hair strands.

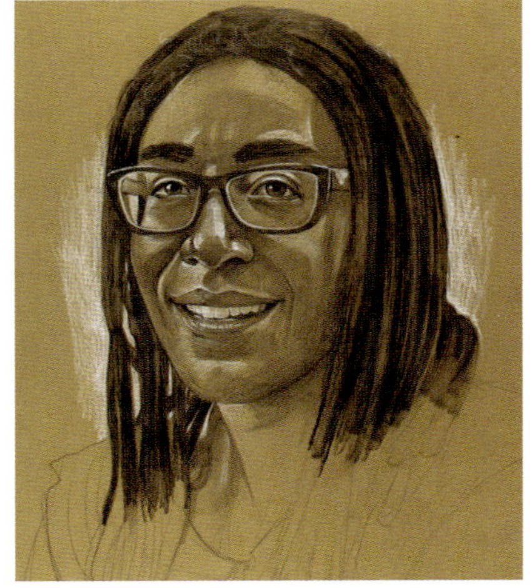

9 ***DEFINE THE FORM IN THE FACE*** Using a 6B pencil for the face and an 8B pencil for the hair, continue to add volume and value. The hair will take time to build up, so be patient as each section is rendered. Use a three-step pattern of drawing with the pencil, blending with a tortillon and lifting out highlights with an eraser.

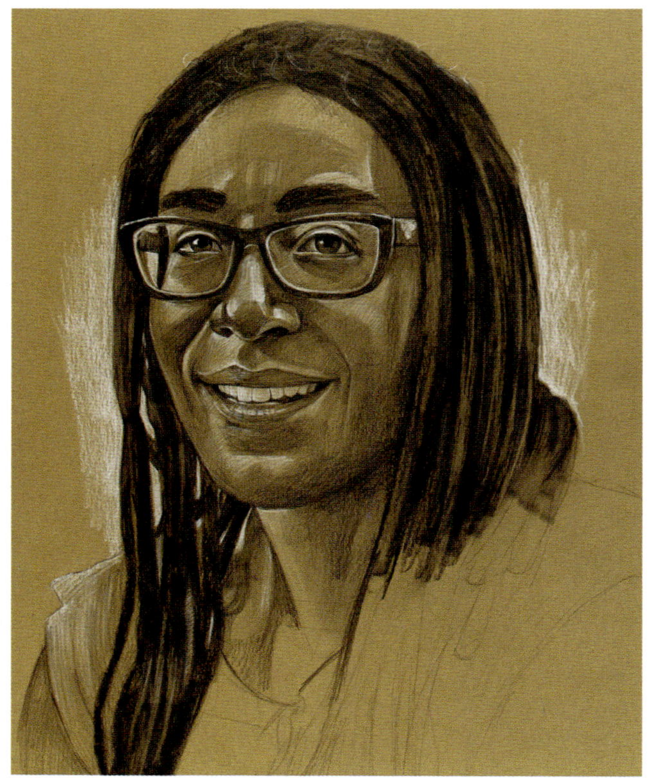

10 ***DEFINE THE CLOTHING AND LEFT SIDE OF THE HAIR***
Begin rendering the clothing using a light touch and a mix between white charcoal and a 2B pencil. The detail should be minimal so the clothing remains secondary compared with the rest of the portrait.

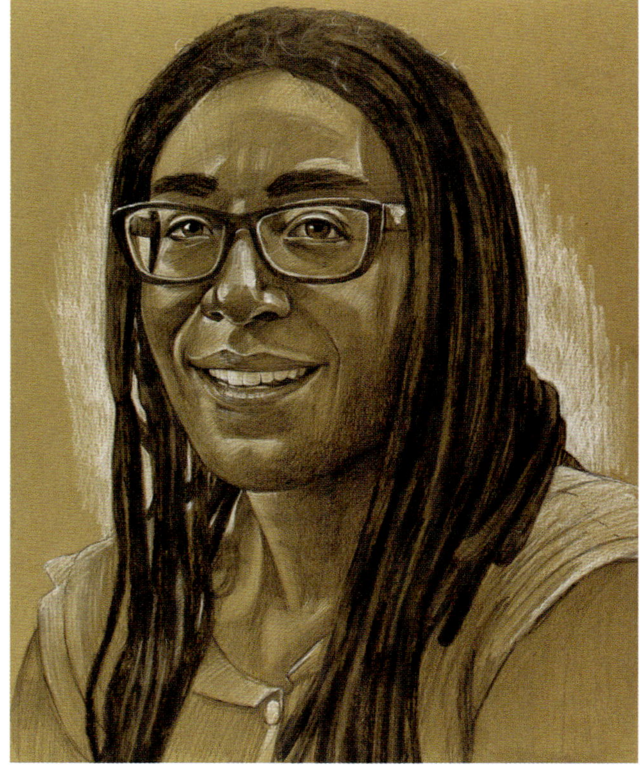

11 ***EVALUATE AND FINISH THE DRAWING*** Complete the clothing and right side of the hair. At this stage the main components are complete, but it's time to refine and add details. Using a click eraser, lift out light areas of hair. Blend the hair mass into the defined shapes of the dreadlocks. Use a white charcoal pencil to add wisps and other individual hairs.

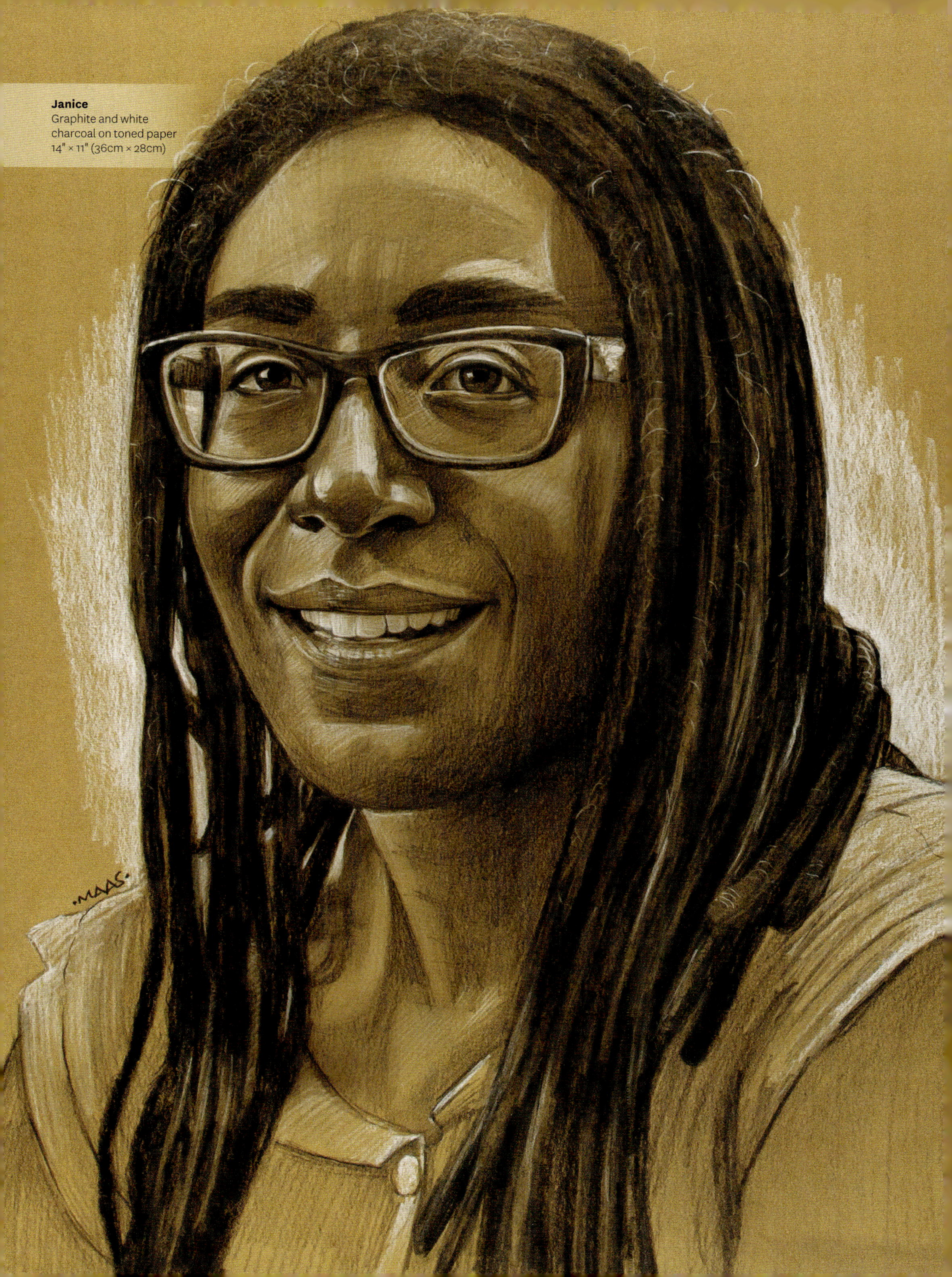

Janice
Graphite and white charcoal on toned paper
14" × 11" (36cm × 28cm)

DEMONSTRATION

LAWRENCE

Lawrence is a quiet fellow with thoughtful eyes. I wanted to capture his gentle nature and reserved confidence. Lawrence keeps his hair tightly buzzed, so that poses a different challenge for us: rendering mostly exposed scalp versus hair.

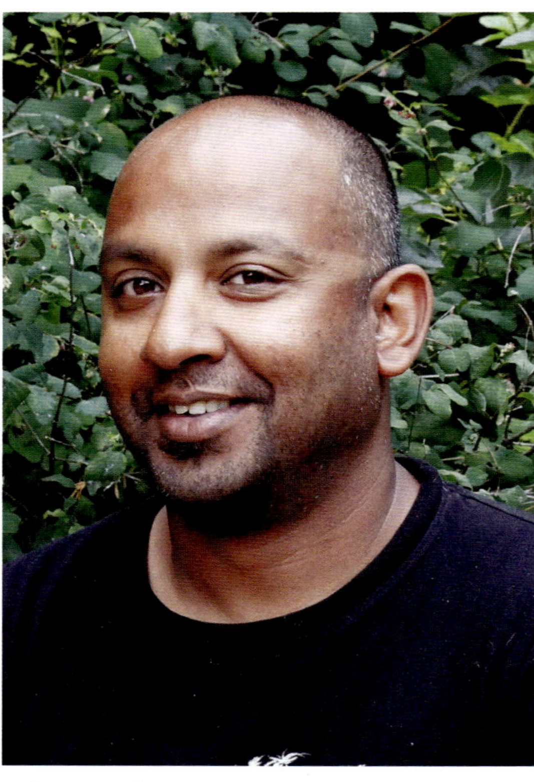

Reference Photo

Materials

DRAWING METHOD

Maas

TOOLS

14" × 11" (36cm × 28cm) Bienfang Bristol white paper

2B, 4B, 6B and 8B woodless graphite pencils

tortillon

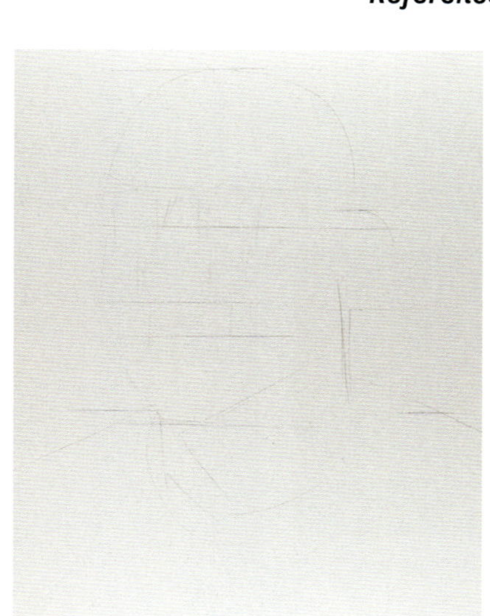

1 ***BLOCK IN THE INITIAL LINES*** Using a 2B pencil and the Maas method, draw horizontal lines across from the reference photo to indicate the key features of the face. Vertical lines can be added either freehand (relating to the horizontal lines) or by taping the reference to the top of the page and using the Maas method a second time.

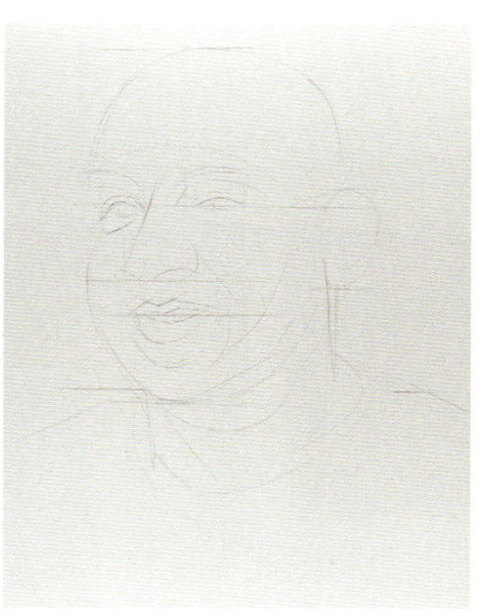

2 ***INDICATE KEY FEATURES*** Place the features according to the guidelines from step 1. Don't worry if they aren't perfect at this stage. Keep the lines light so they can be corrected easily.

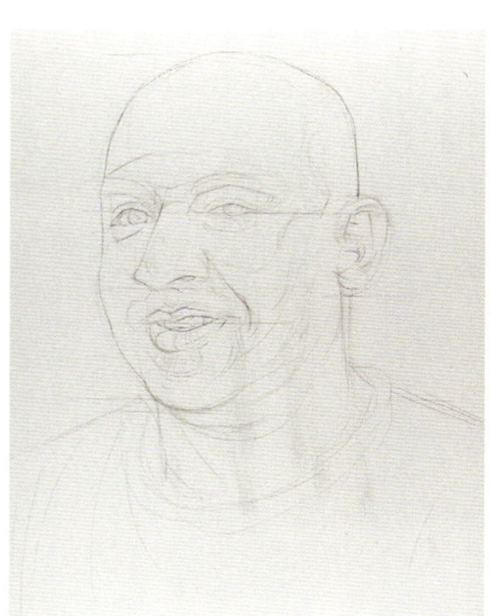

3 ***REFINE THE LINES*** Pay more attention to the details and begin honing in the correct lines. Use the guidelines that represent the highlights and shadow lines to help determine spacing for features. Keep it light.

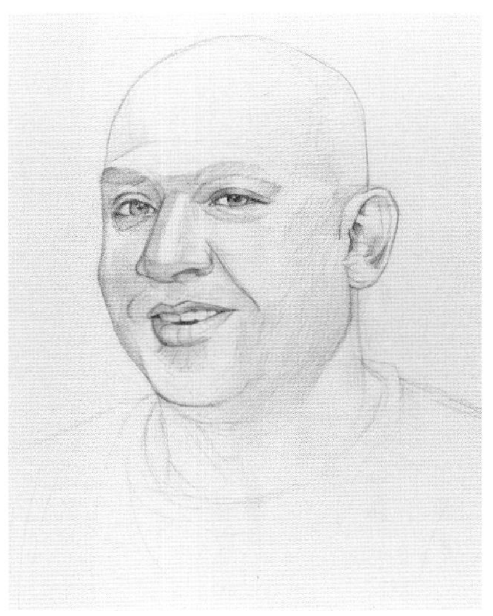

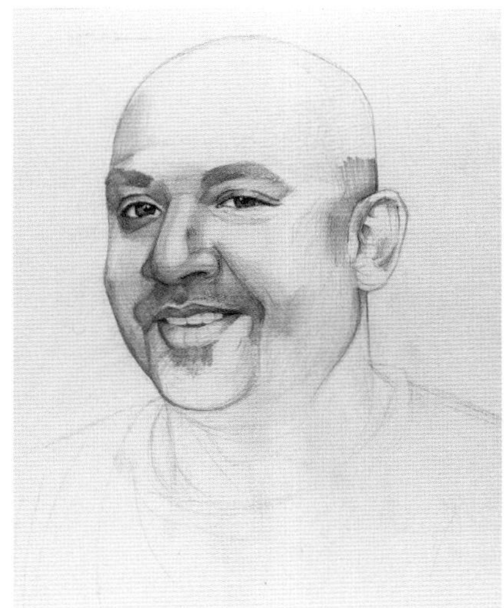

4 ***START TO ADD TONE***
Continue using a 2B pencil, gradually increasing the pressure to draw the lines a little darker. Start to look at the values and build up tone. Lawrence has a rounder face, so volume will be important to get his likeness correct.

5 ***ADD DARKER VALUES***
Switch to a 4B pencil and study the values in the reference. Some areas are quite dark, although the piece will need to be darker still. Begin building up areas of 40, 50 and 60 percent black.

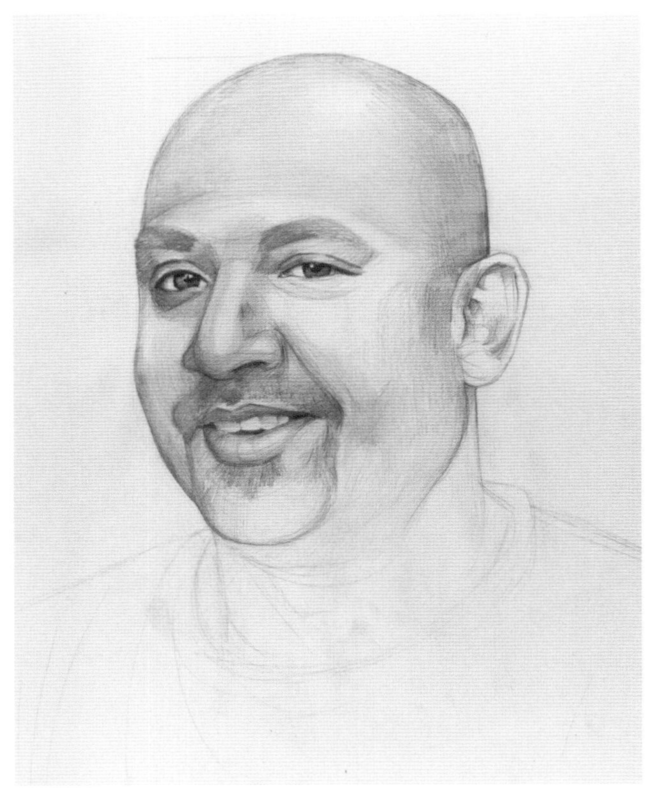

6 ***ADD FORM TO THE TOP OF THE HEAD***
Much like the facial hair mini demonstration in chapter 3, when you draw a head with stubble like Lawrence's, you should first draw it without concern for the hair. Draw the form and add tone and value in this stage as if the model was bald. A 4B should still be sufficient, but a 6B could also be used for the darker values.

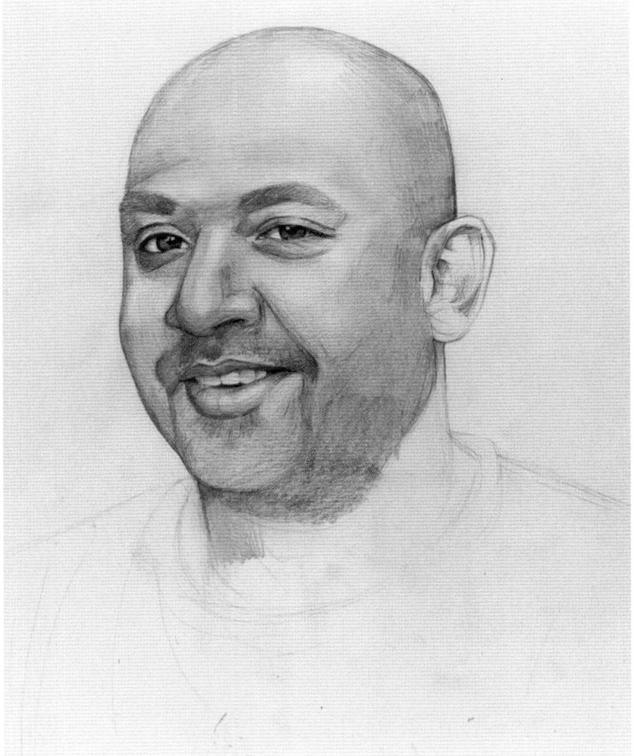

7 ***FINISH THE MIDTONE VALUES***
Work down the face and complete the basic values. Lawrence has quite dark skin, so even the highlights will have a certain amount of tone to them. At this stage we should have established a good deal of the midtone values.

8 ESTABLISH DARK AREAS

Switch to a 6B or 8B pencil. Loosely add in the hair mass for Lawrence's goatee. Begin to build up values around the eyes and complete the ears.

9 ADD SOME STUBBLE

Using a moderately dull 6B pencil, indicate stubble on the top of the head and around the ear. The reason to use a duller pencil is that it will make the hairs a little less abrupt—a sharper pencil would make them stand out too much and draw attention away from the key focal points such as the eyes and smile. Build the values down the whole side of the face.

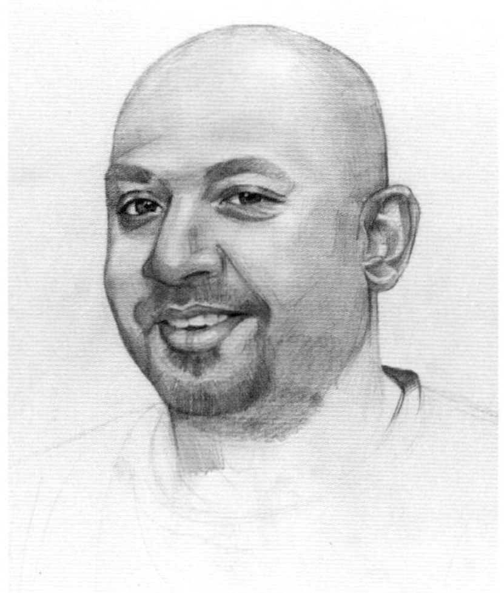

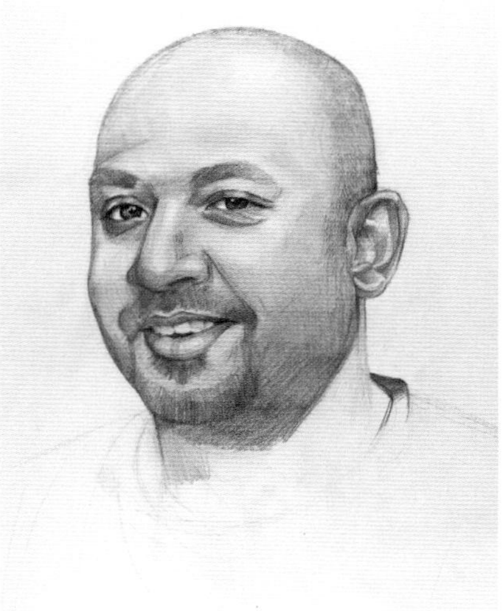

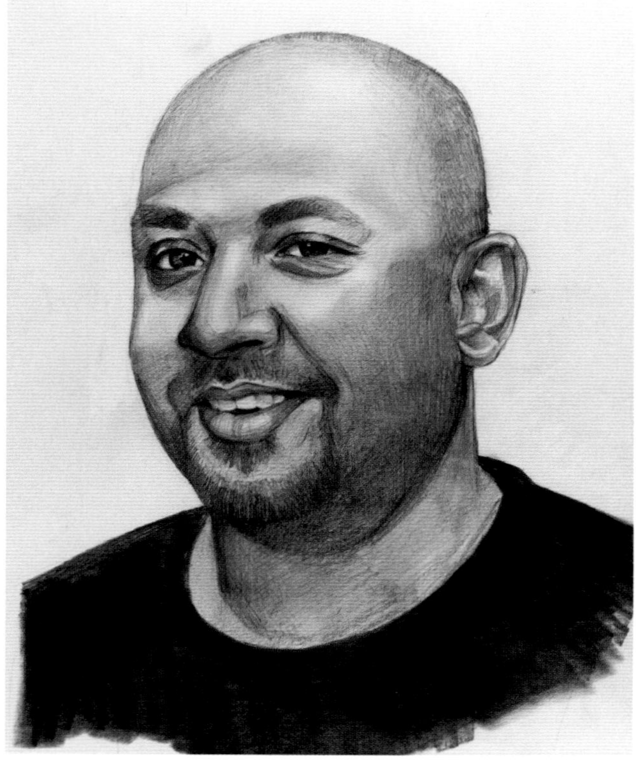

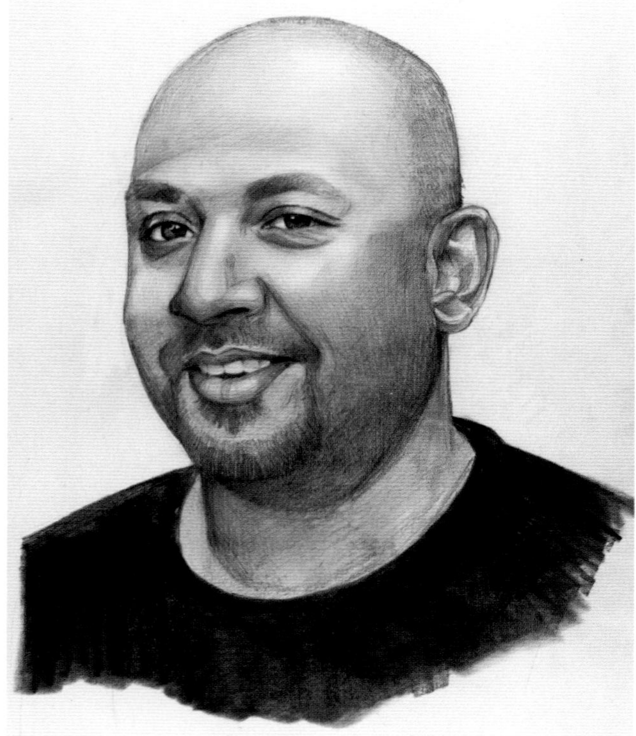

10 RENDER THE SHIRT

Because the shirt is dark and Lawrence has a dark complexion, use a 6B or 8B pencil to lay down a good amount of pigment. Don't press too hard as this can cause graphite shine. Instead, use moderate pressure and when finished, blend with a tortillon—preferably one that has been used before and already has dark graphite pigment on it.

11 EVALUATE AND FINISH THE DRAWING

Using a tortillon, soften some of the abrupt lines. Evaluate all the features, values and form to ensure that his likeness is accurate. Place any remaining final details. The transitions between shadow and highlight are often the areas that need a little more smoothing or blending.

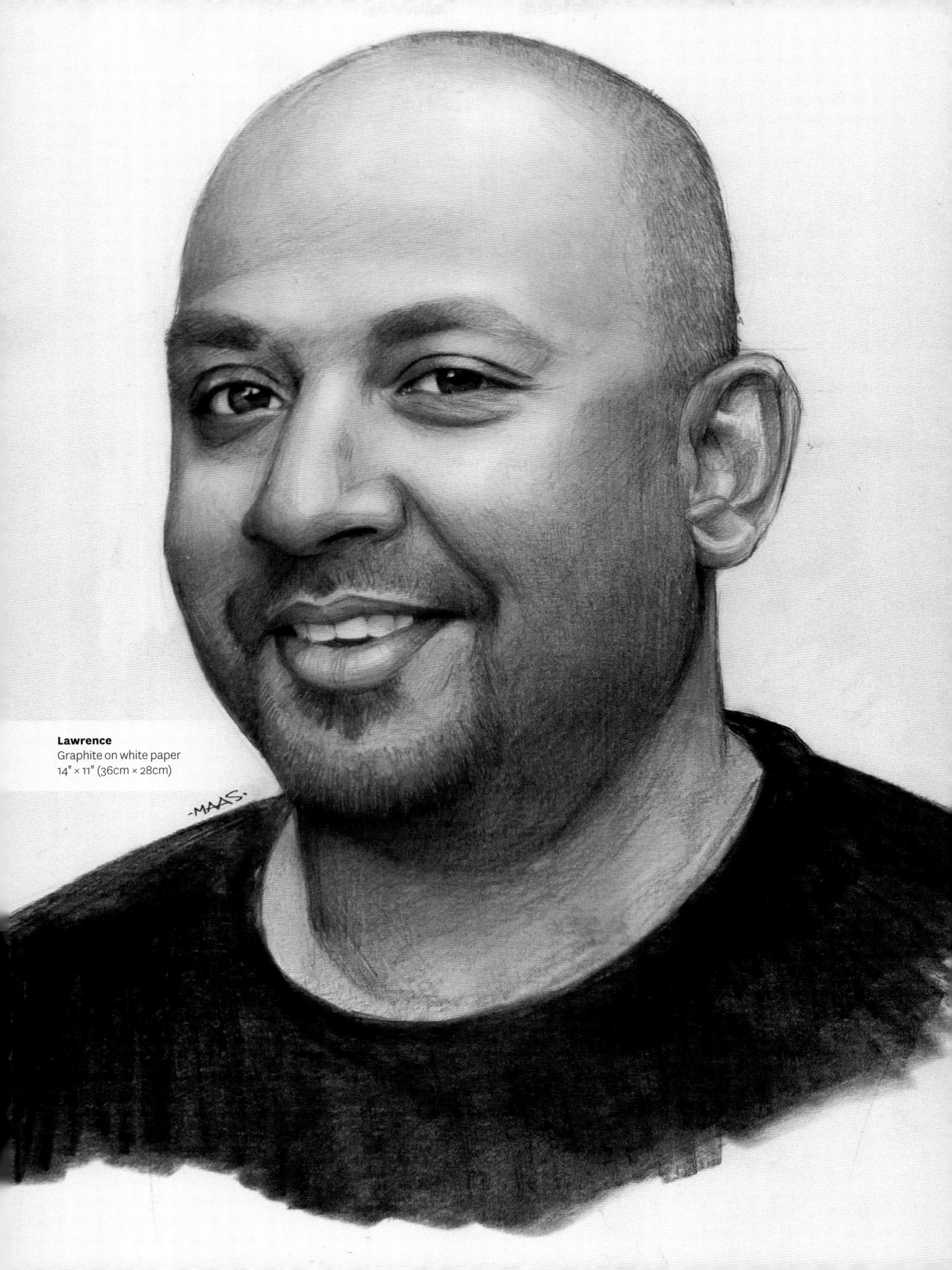

Lawrence
Graphite on white paper
14" × 11" (36cm × 28cm)

DEMONSTRATION

ERIN

Erin Krakow is well known as the star of Hallmark Channel's *When Calls the Heart* but she is also an incredibly sweet and charismatic lady. The first time I met her she seemed more excited to meet me than the other way around. I have drawn Erin many times and for this demo I have decided to use pastel pencils to create a full-color portrait. Some people call pastel works such as this a *painting* since we will be applying the pigment in a painterly fashion (no lines, full coverage). In my opinion, both terms *drawing* and *painting* are correct. This photo of Erin was taken by my friend Janette Stephens and was used as my reference with her permission.

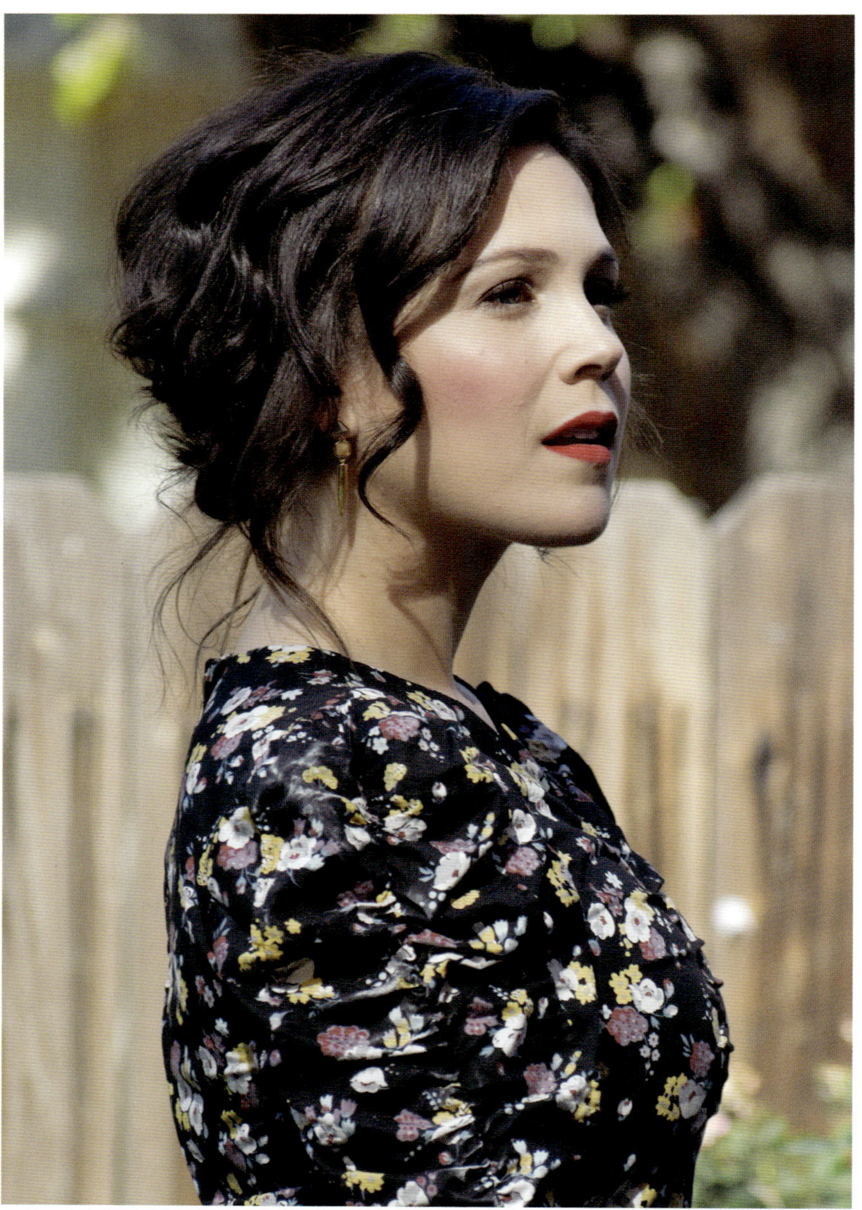

Reference Photo

Materials

DRAWING METHOD

Freehand (transferred onto pastel paper)

TOOLS

16" × 12" (41cm × 30cm) sand-toned Sennelier La Carte Pastel Card paper

tortillon

STABILO CARBOTHELLO PASTEL PENCILS

C726 (Cold Grey 4)

C100 (Titanium White)

C625 (Burnt Umber)

C770 (Payne's Grey)

C680 (Dark Flesh Tint)

C720 (Cold Grey 1)

C610 (Raw Umber)

C706 (Warm Grey 4)

C750 (Neutral Black)

C210 (Orange Yellow)

BRUYNZEEL PASTEL PENCILS

B75 (Light Flesh)

B38 (Carmine)

B45 (Havana Brown)

B41 (Light Brown)

B50 (Ultramarine)

B27 (Yellow Ochre)

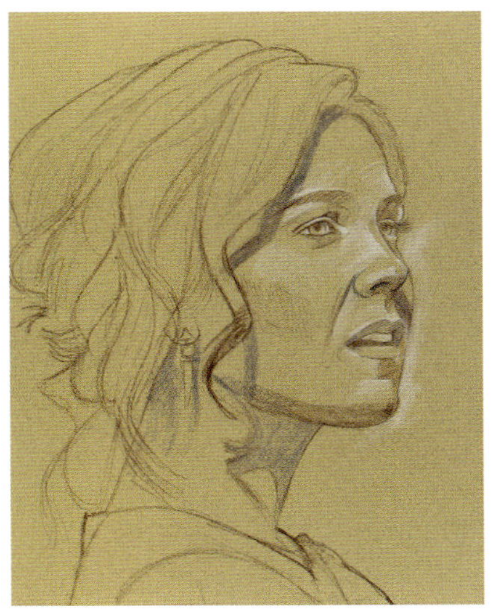

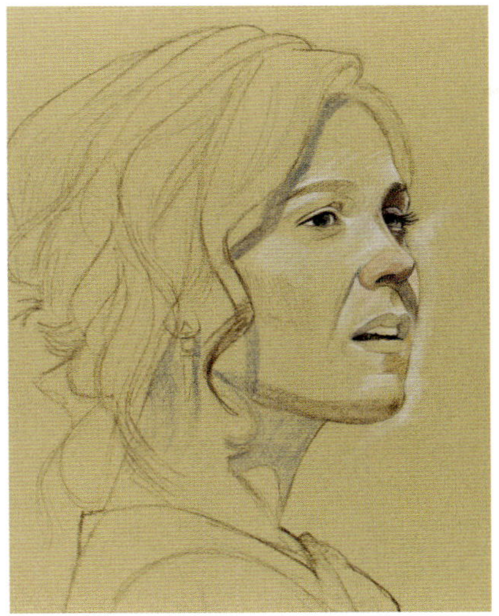

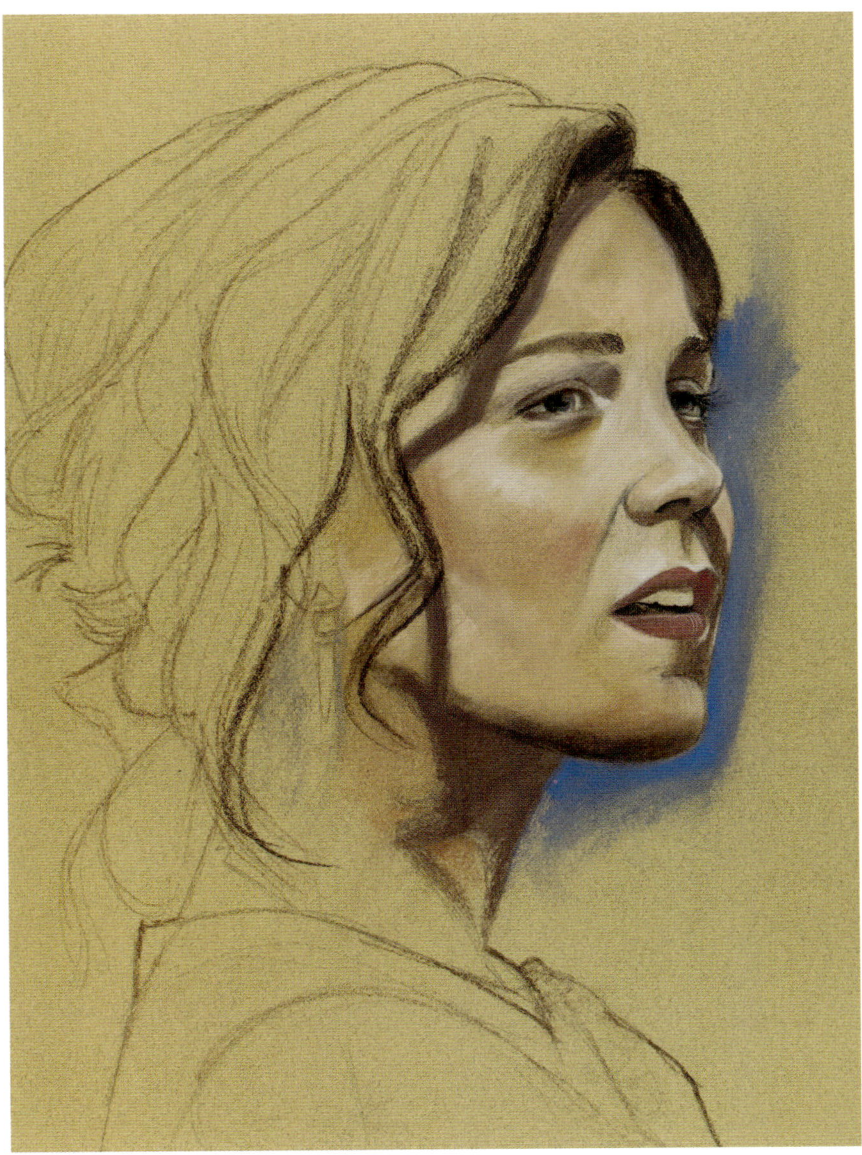

1 *TRANSFER THE SKETCH* Pastel paper—especially sanded paper like we are using here—can be quite expensive, so it is advisable to limit the amount of overworking. By transferring the initial rough sketch using a projector, light table or transfer paper, the paper is left undamaged from the early steps. Using a C726 (Cold Grey 4), C100 (White) and C625 (Burnt Umber), create a contour drawing framework upon which to build the portrait.

2 *IDENTIFY THE KEY FEATURES* Pastels are an opaque medium. Once likeness is achieved in the contour stage, it's important not to lose that, so building the key features first, such as the eyes, nose and mouth, can help keep them established so they aren't lost as other areas are built up.

Using a C770 (Payne's Grey), outline the areas of the eyes, nostril and dark areas in the mouth. Use a B75 (Flesh) and C680 (Dark Flesh Tint) to build up skin tones.

3 *BEGIN BUILDING UP LAYERS* Apply B75 (Light Flesh), C680 (Dark Flesh Tint), C100 (Titanium White), B45 (Havana Brown), B41 (Light Brown) and C770 (Payne's Grey) to create a base layer, paying special attention to the subtle changes in light. Because this is sanded paper, details will not be sharp yet, so do not be discouraged by this rough-looking stage. Light layers of B38 (Carmine) and C720 (Cold Grey 1) are used to establish Erin's bright lipstick. A background color of B50 (Ultramarine) is picked and applied sparingly so it won't be smudged too much but helps develop hard edges between foreground and background.

4 LAY DOWN THE HAIR MASS

The hair in this portrait accounts for roughly the same amount of space as the whole face and approximately one-fifth of the entire piece. It's important to create accurate values and build up the individual sections. Use a B45 (Havana Brown) and C610 (Raw Umber) to lay down midtones and darker areas of the hair. Try to visualize the shapes of the hair as geometric objects rather than strands of hair. This may be easier to do if the artwork is flipped upside down.

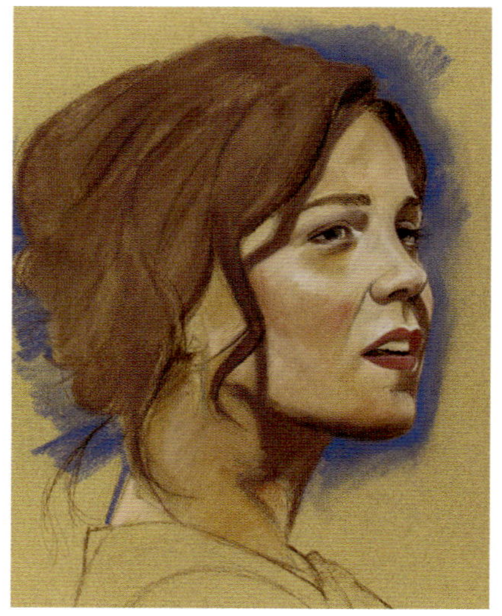

5 DEFINE THE HAIR MASS

Begin to introduce C625 (Burnt Umber) and C770 (Payne's Grey) as well as B45 (Havana Brown) and C610 (Raw Umber). Erin's hair is brown, but sun and shadow introduce many shades and tints. These in turn help define form.

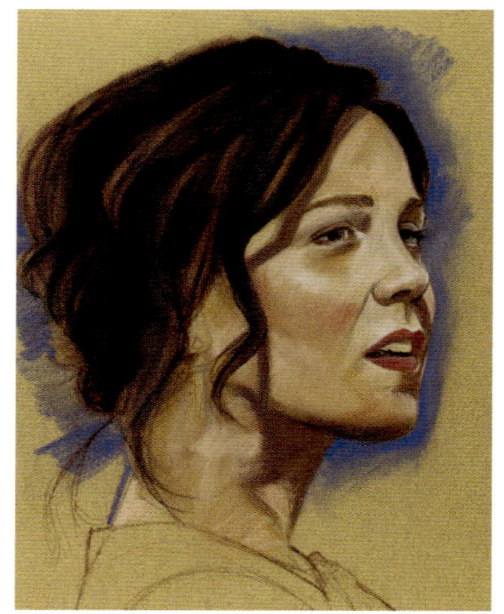

6 REFINE THE HAIR

Using a large, wide tortillon, blend each section of hair. Be careful to move organically, the way the hair does. As each section gets smoother, apply layers of C770 (Payne's Grey) and C625 (Burnt Umber) to darken sections. When the layers are built up nicely, begin adding highlights to the hair using a C706 (Warm Grey 4). Note that even though the highlights appear to be white, they are actually gray.

Build up more volume with a steady pattern of laying down lights and dark masses and by blending with a tortillon. C750 (Neutral Black) can be added to the darkest darks. Do not add any details like individual hairs yet as these will only go on once the hair masses are fully defined.

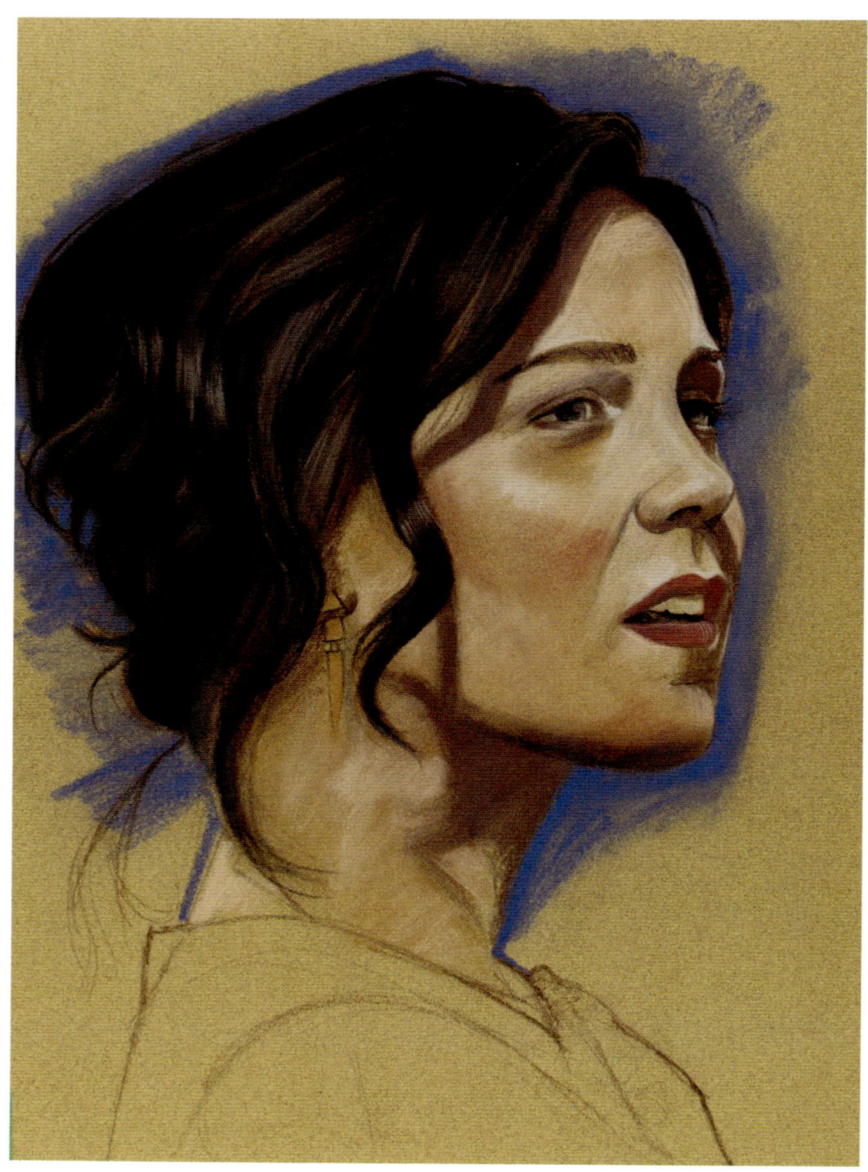

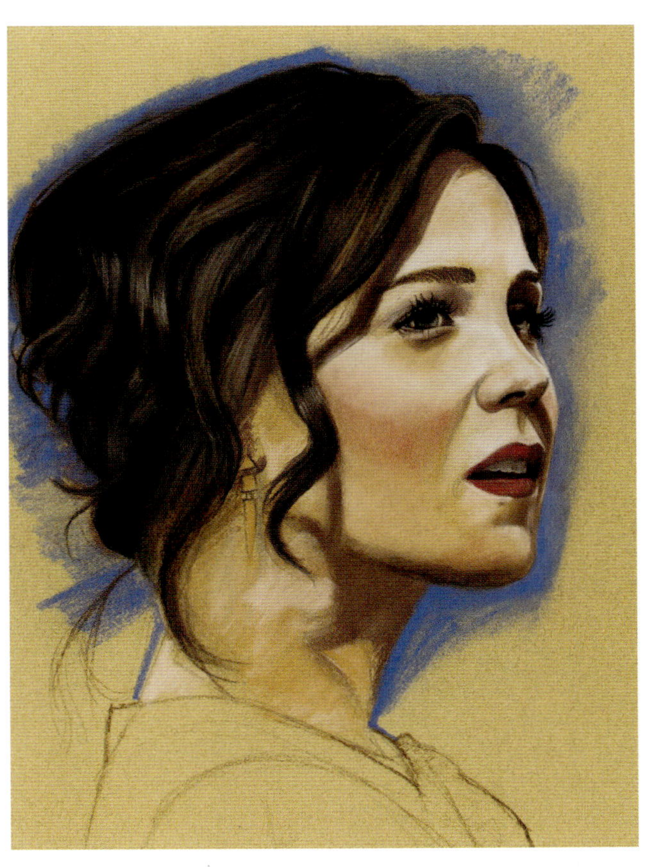

7 BEGIN TO ADD DETAIL TO THE FACE

Now that hair values are established, switch back to the face to further develop the layers. Use a B75 (Light Flesh), B27 (Yellow Ochre), B45 (Havana Brown), C625 (Burnt Umber) and C100 (Titanium White) to add details to the face. Remember that the information to create the portrait comes from the reference. Be careful to study the variations of tone and value on color. Apply a light layer of B38 (Carmine) on the cheeks to give them warmth and volume.

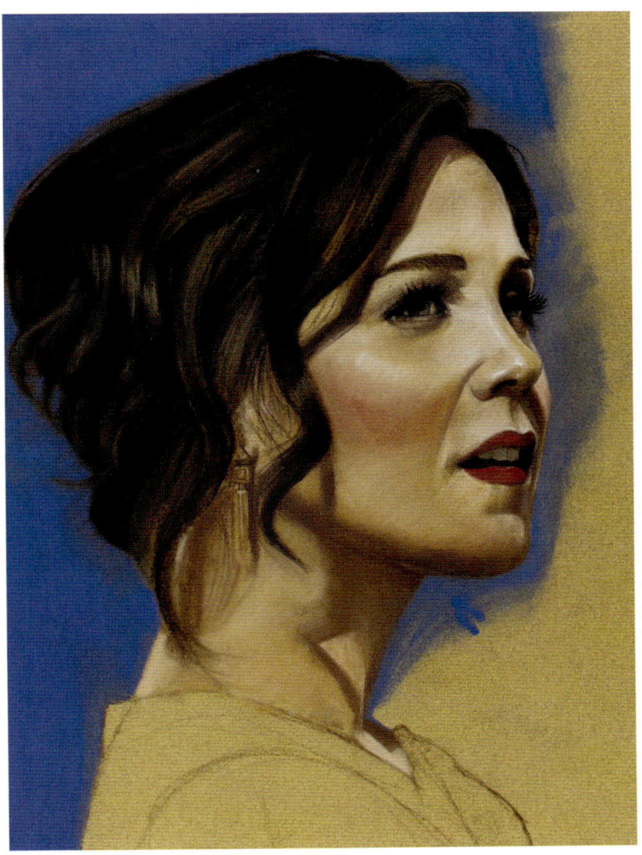

8 COMPLETE THE BACKGROUND

Since there is very little actual background showing in this portrait, we will keep it a single color. This is a good choice because there is a lot of detail in her face, her hair and her dress. Use the B50 (Ultramarine) for the remainder of the background. The section at right is left unfilled so that it doesn't get too smudged. Don't worry about individual hairs right now; they will be developed once the background is finished. Add more value to the face using a B45 (Havana Brown) and C610 (Raw Umber). Continue to compare the darks and lights of the face to the darks and lights of the hair. Each will relate on the value scale.

9 BRING OUT THE DARKS AND MAKE ADJUSTMENTS

Using a C750 (Neutral Black), begin bringing out darks throughout the piece. Darken sections of the hair, add black in the dress and add more background using B50 (Ultramarine). Using confident but tapering strokes, begin applying flyaway hairs. This is an important stage because it ties the foreground to the background and helps soften the sharp edges. Add just enough wisps for visual interest.

As the drawing progresses, it's quite common that some features will change slightly or get a little muddled. Carefully study the reference and determine if any features need correcting. Often it is something very subtle—in this case, Erin's cheekbones needed more defining (raising) and her lips/mouth needed slight adjustment. This is the most difficult part of rendering a portrait—especially in color—because the slightest nuance will usually indicate that something isn't quite right.

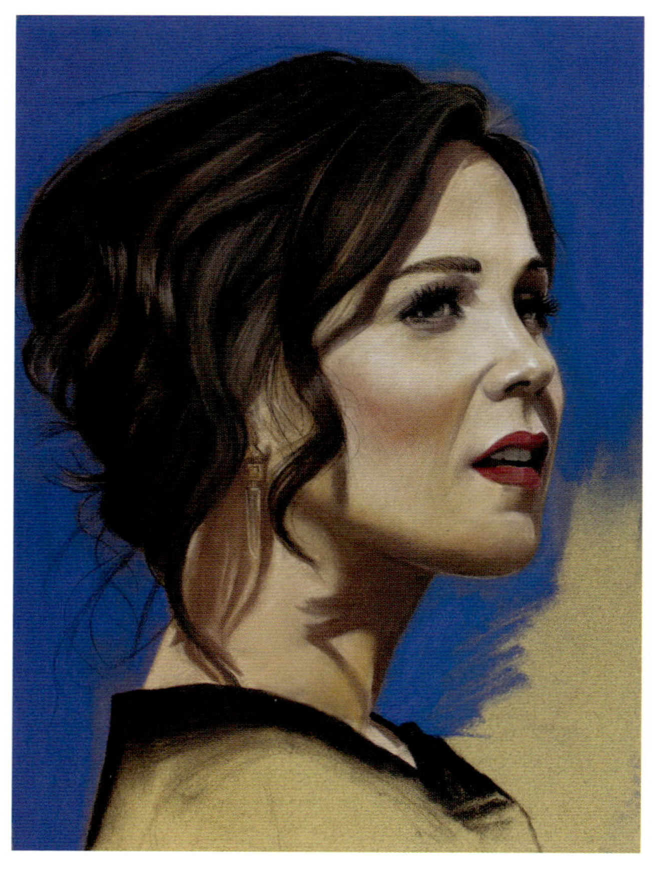

10 ADD CLOTHING

Apply a layer of C750 (Neutral Black) and C770 (Payne's Grey) to create the shoulders of her dress. Because the actual pattern is quite complex, we can choose to simplify it. Use just enough detail to give the sense of the original dress, but not too much to detract from the main focal points in the portrait. Using C100 (Titanium White), C210 (Orange Yellow) and B38 (Carmine), render flowers on Erin's dress. Render the farthest flowers with a C726 (Cold Grey 4) to help indicate depth.

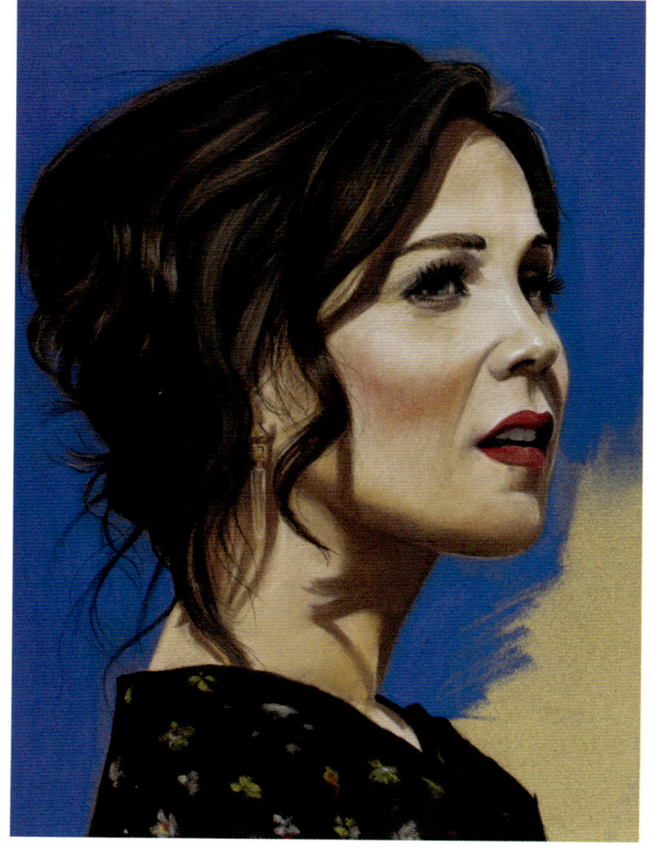

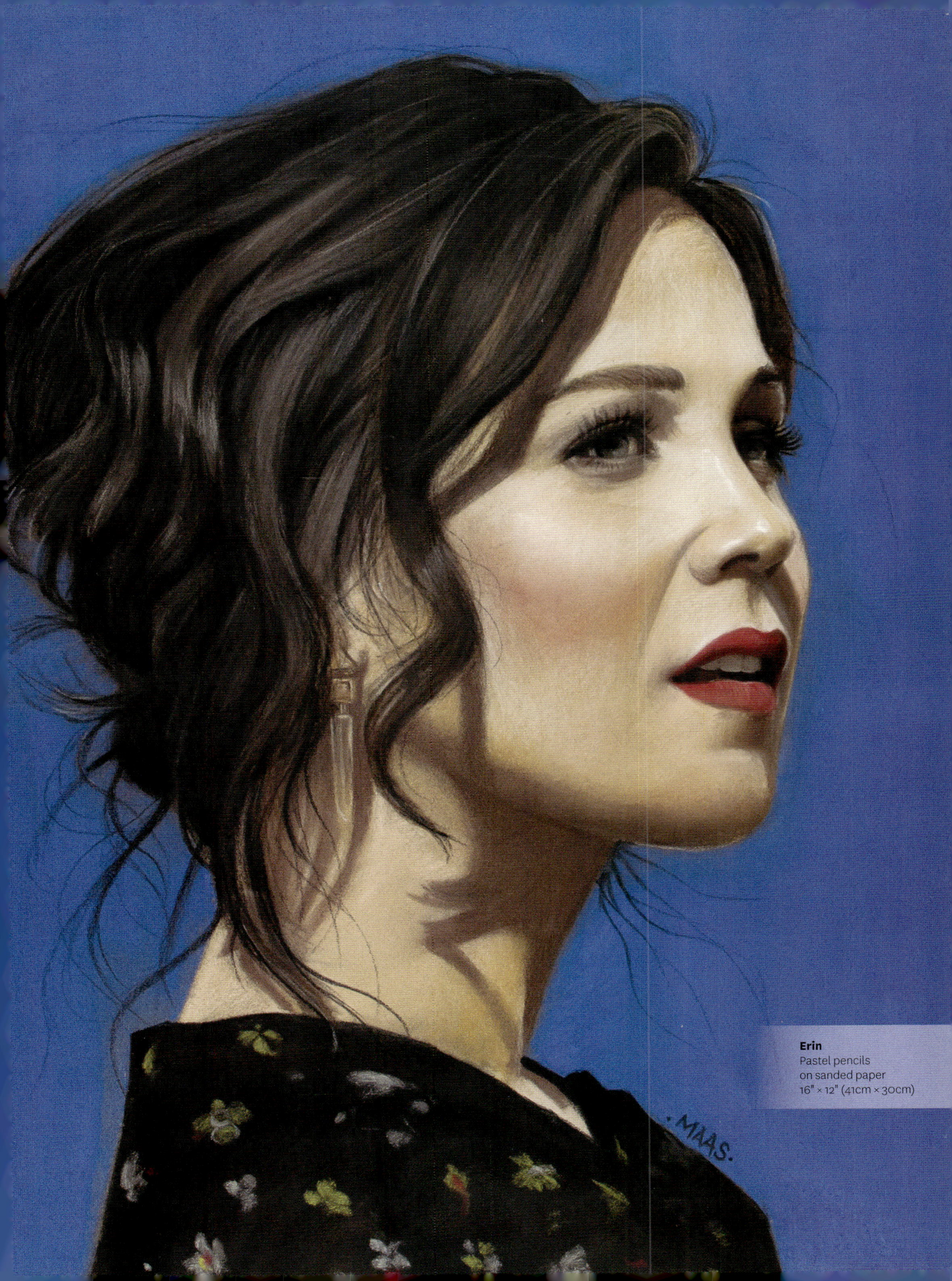

Erin
Pastel pencils
on sanded paper
16" × 12" (41cm × 30cm)

GALLERY

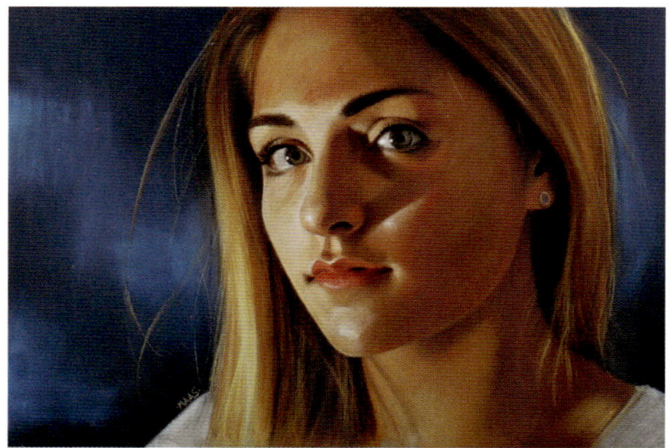
I've Just Seen a Face
Pastel on sanded paper
12" × 16" (30cm × 41cm)

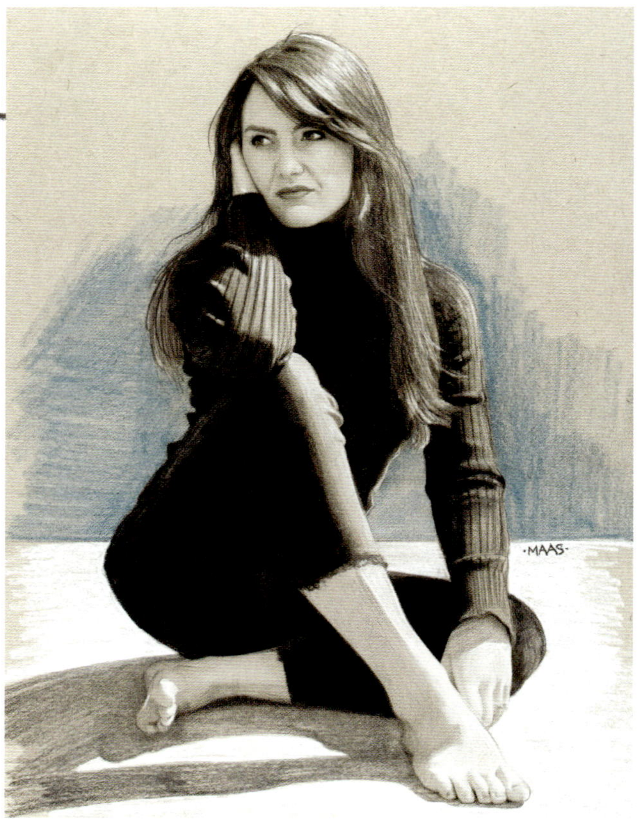
Darby
Graphite, white charcoal and blue pencil on toned paper
14" × 11" (36cm × 28cm)

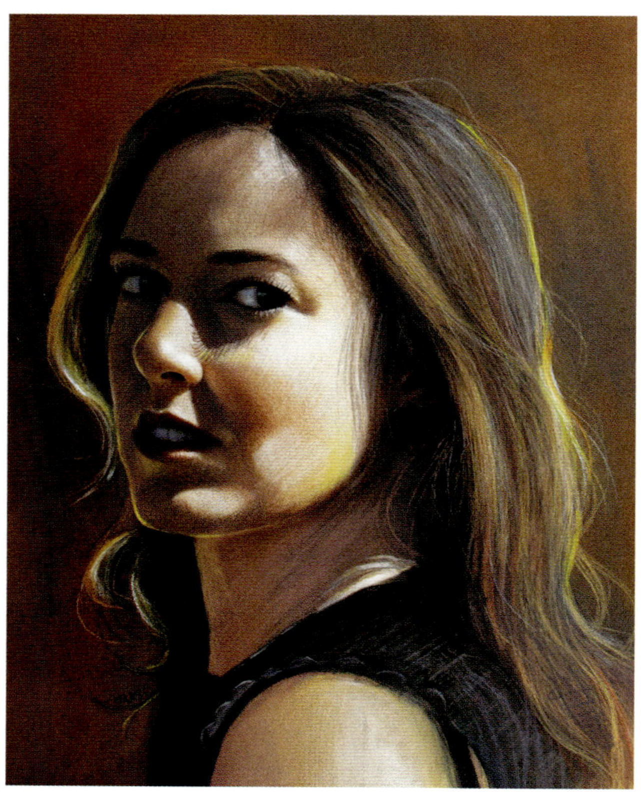
Incognito
Pastel on sanded paper
16" × 12" (41cm × 30cm)

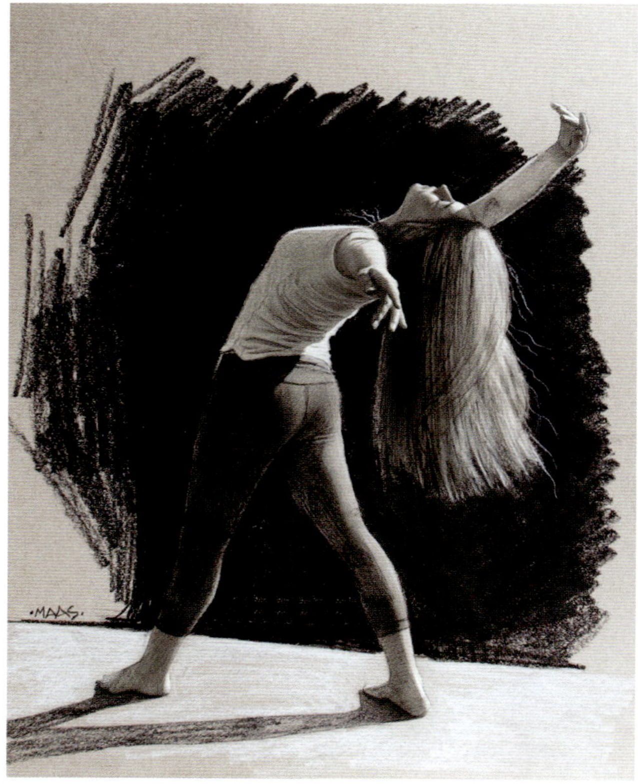
Dance Series #3
Graphite and white charcoal on toned paper
14" × 11" (36cm × 28cm)

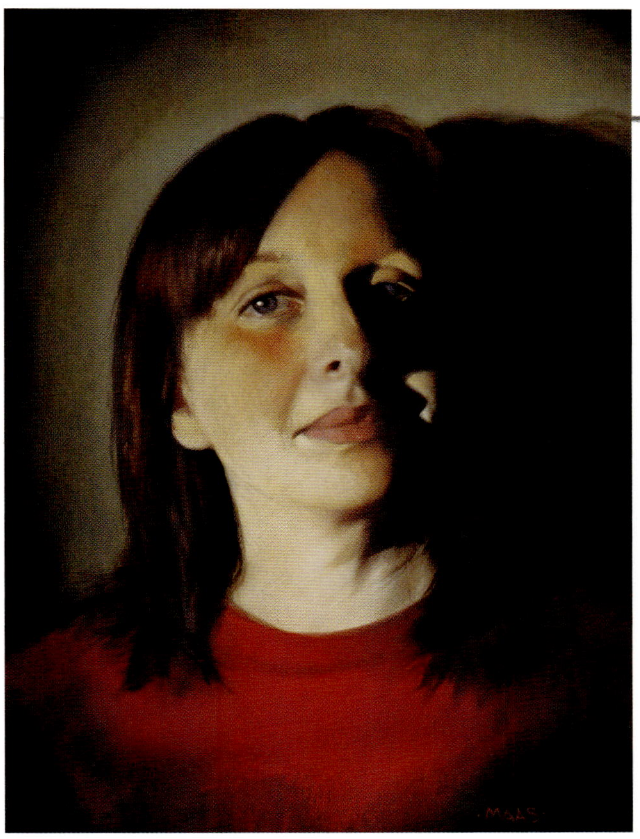

Little Wing
Pastel on paper
24" × 15" (61cm × 38cm)

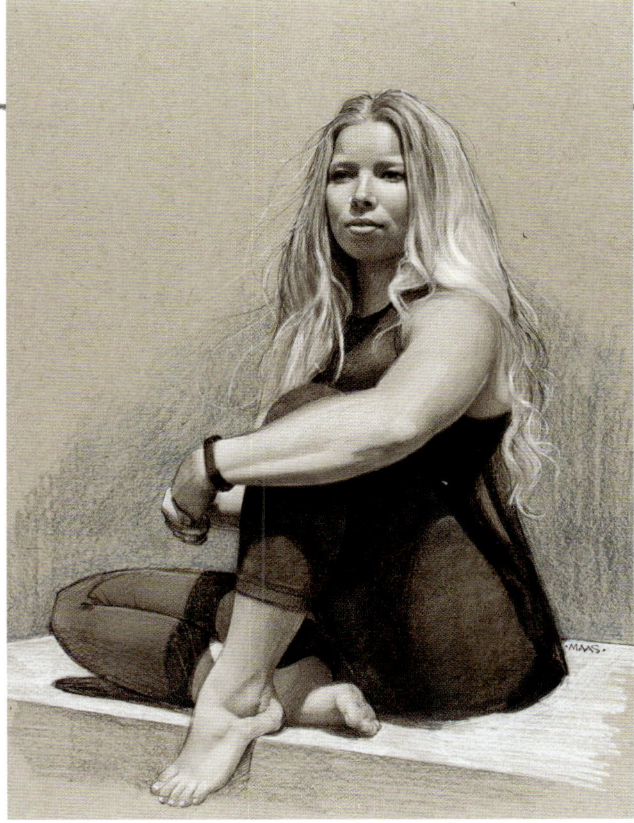

Elise
Graphite, white charcoal and blue pencil on toned paper
14" × 11" (36cm × 28cm)

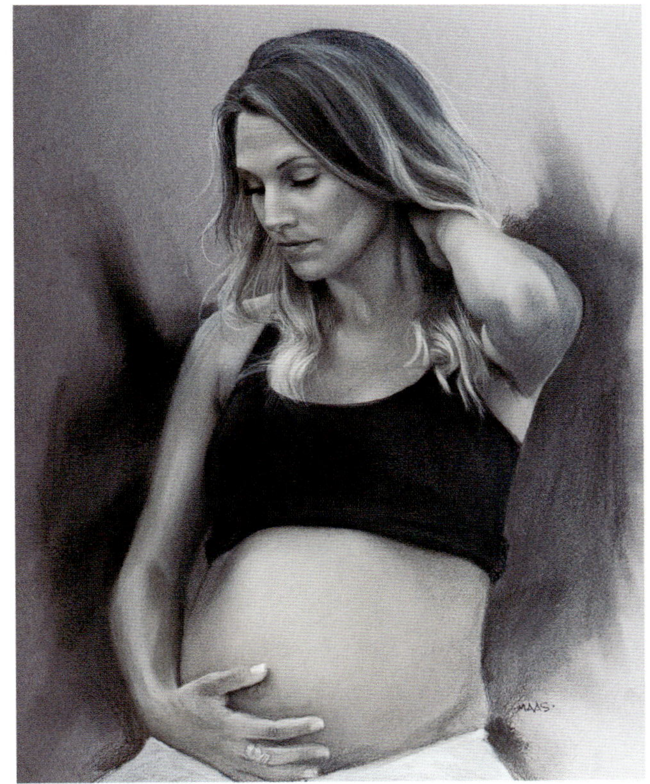

Lost Together
Pastel on sanded paper
16" × 12" (41cm × 30cm)

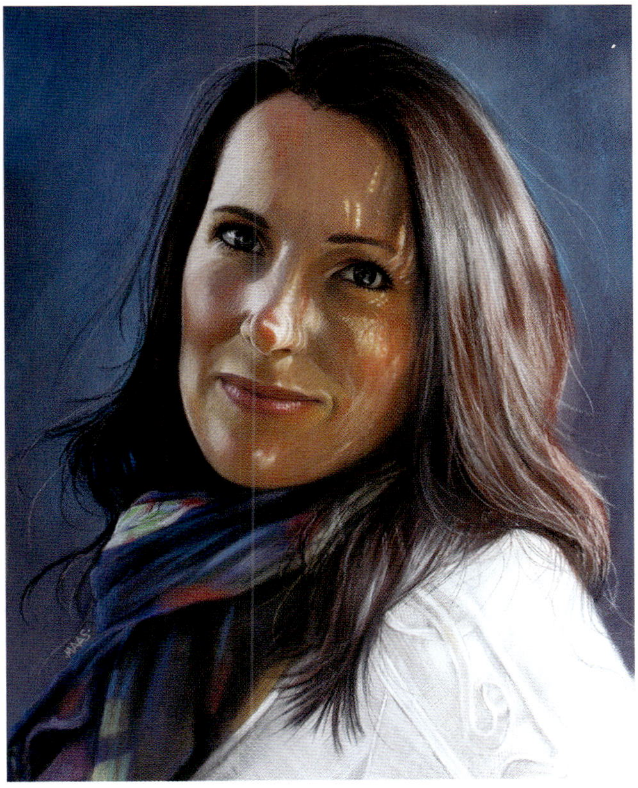

I'll Follow the Sun
Pastel on sanded paper
16" × 12" (41cm × 30cm)

CONCLUSION

Drawing is a lifelong adventure, a means of expression and, at times, the most personal form of self-contemplation. Drawing is one of the universal forms of communication that spans not just the globe, but time as well. As long as humans have been alive, we have drawn—in every corner of the earth.

I hope this book has been helpful to you. Whether you are a novice or an experienced portraitist, my goal is to help impart some of the skills and techniques that I have learned to assist you on your journey.

Where will your drawings take you? Will they be a (crucial) stepping stone for larger painted works? Or will you develop them in such a way that they will be grand works of art in their own right? Perhaps your only goal is to draw your grandchildren or the people and the things that you love.

Whatever your reason, I hope you find some guidance within these pages. A couple of pencils, some paper and a subject. That's all you need to make magic.

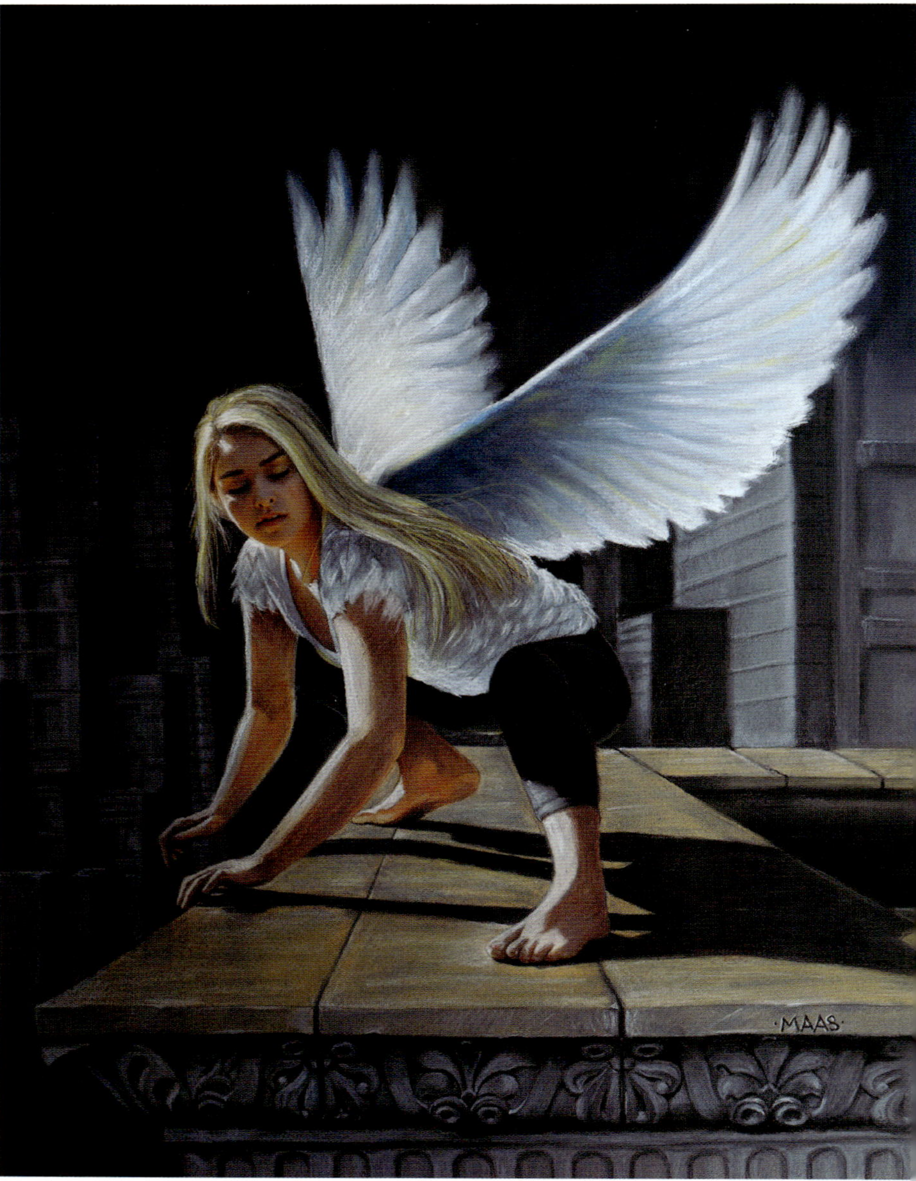

Hear My Train a-Coming
Pastel on paper
28" × 16" (71cm × 41cm)

INDEX

ABOUT THE AUTHOR

Justin Maas was born in the 1970s in Hartford, Connecticut. His parents moved to Canada before his third birthday, and it is the country he has called home ever since, becoming a Canadian citizen roughly seven years later. Justin studied at the Art Institute of Chicago and the University of British Columbia, and he received a degree in visual communications from the Alberta College of Art & Design. Justin has worked full time as a professional illustrator, fine artist and graphic designer for over twenty years. Justin works primarily in pastel, graphite and charcoal.

His work is on display in private collections all over North America, Europe and parts of South America.

Justin is a Signature Member of the Federation of Canadian Artists (FCA) and an Elected Member of the Society of Canadian Artists (SCA).

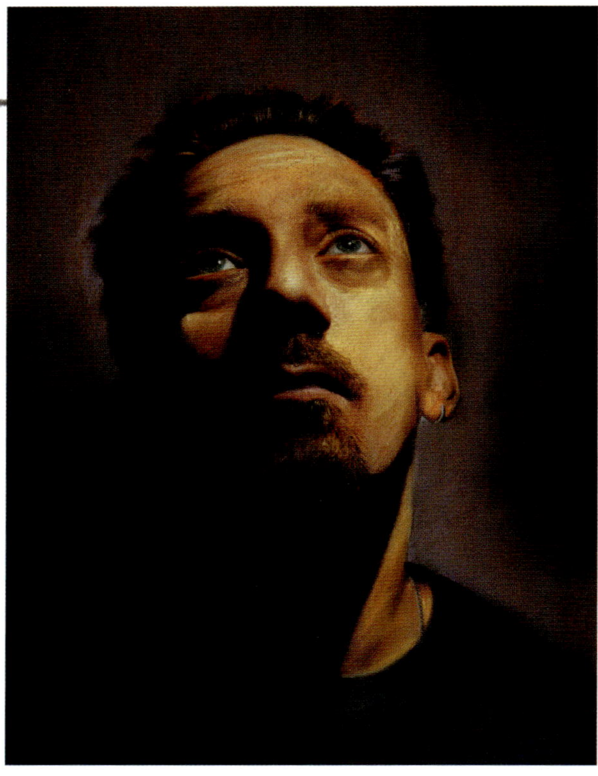

Behind Blue Eyes
Pastel on paper
25" × 15" (64cm × 38cm)

ABOUT MY WORK

While many would describe my work as realistic or traditional, the main focus of my paintings and drawings is the concept of light. Technical skill is certainly a part of my craft, but I believe that the real key to creating art is to elevate it beyond pure ability or skillful mark-making.

Regardless of the subject, style or media, the one thing that ties any of my paintings or drawings together is an attempt to translate what we see as lights (and darks) into a two-dimensional piece. I hope that my work communicates to you.

ACKNOWLEDGMENTS

Thank you to my father for being the voice of reason all these years. Mom sugarcoated things, but your honesty helped me learn and grow. You were my greatest teacher—in all things—and my hero. I will always be grateful.

Thank you to each and every one of my models for putting up with my demands and being a constant source of inspiration.

Thank you to Noel, Sarah, Christina and Clare, who took my messy submission and made something great out of it.

And finally, thank you, dear reader. May your pencils be blessed.

DEDICATION

This book is dedicated to the four most important women in my life:

To my mother, Pat: I am saddened you were not around to see this book come to life, but I can feel your pride, which is with me to this day. You were my biggest supporter, my first champion and the kindest person I ever met.

To my wife, Maggie: You are the love of my life, the energy that drives me—my forever muse. I could not have done it without you, nor would I have wanted to.

To my daughters, Jada and Ashley: You inspire me daily and make me more proud with every passing year.

Drawing Realistic Pencil Portraits Step by Step.

Published by North Light Books, an imprint of F+W Media, Inc. 10151 Carver Road, Suite 300, Blue Ash, Ohio, 45242. (800) 289-0963. First Edition.

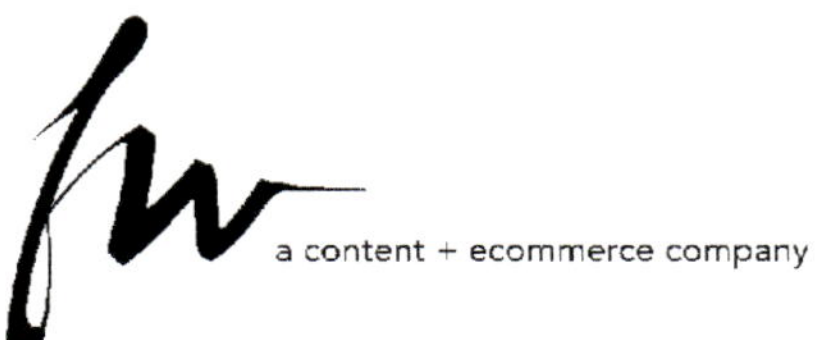

Other fine North Light books are available from your favorite bookstore, art supply store or online supplier. Visit our website at fwmedia.com.

23 22 21 20 19 5 4 3 2 1

DISTRIBUTED IN THE U.K. AND EUROPE
BY F&W MEDIA INTERNATIONAL LTD
Pynes Hill Court, Pynes Hill, Rydon Lane, Exeter, EX2 5AZ, United Kingdom
Tel: (+44) 1392 79680
E-mail: enquiries@fwmedia.com

ISBN 13: 978-1-4403-5461-8

PROJECT MANAGER: Noel Rivera

EDITOR: Sarah Laichas

COVER DESIGN: Clare Finney

INTERIOR PAGE DESIGN: Charlene Tiedemann

PRODUCTION MANAGER: Debbie Thomas

METRIC CONVERSION CHART

To convert	to	multiply by
Inches	Centimeters	2.54
Centimeters	Inches	0.4
Feet	Centimeters	30.5
Centimeters	Feet	0.03
Yards	Meters	0.9
Meters	Yards	1.1

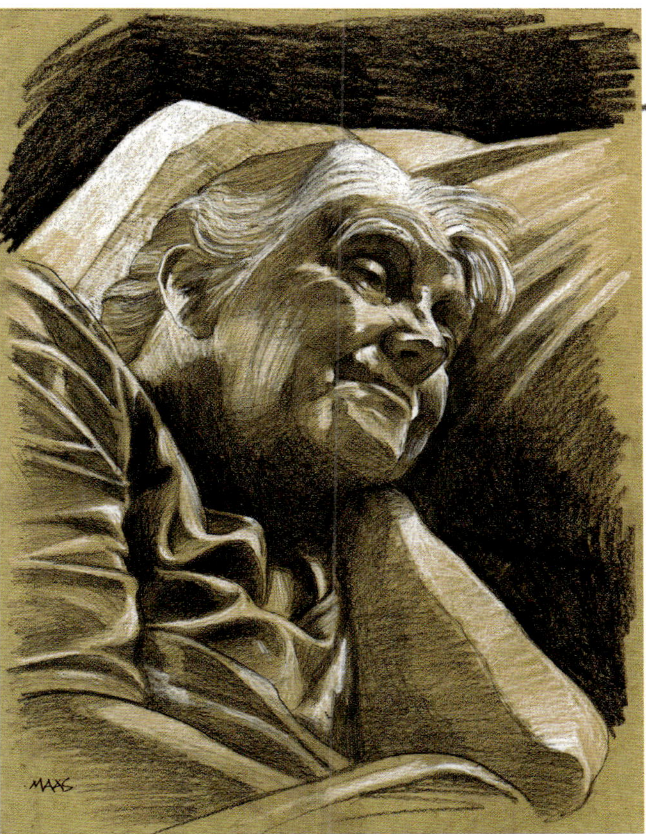

Memory Fades but Love Remains
Graphite and white charcoal on toned paper
14" × 11" (36cm × 28cm)

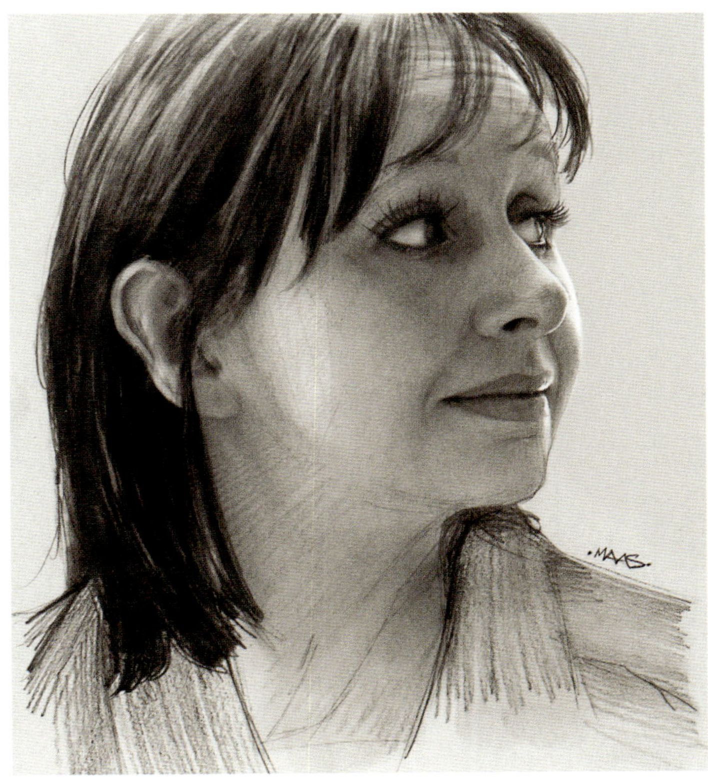

Maggie
Graphite on white paper
9" × 8" (23cm × 20cm)

IDEAS. INSTRUCTION. INSPIRATION.

Receive FREE downloadable bonus materials when you sign up for our FREE newsletter at artistsnetwork.com/Newsletter_Thanks.

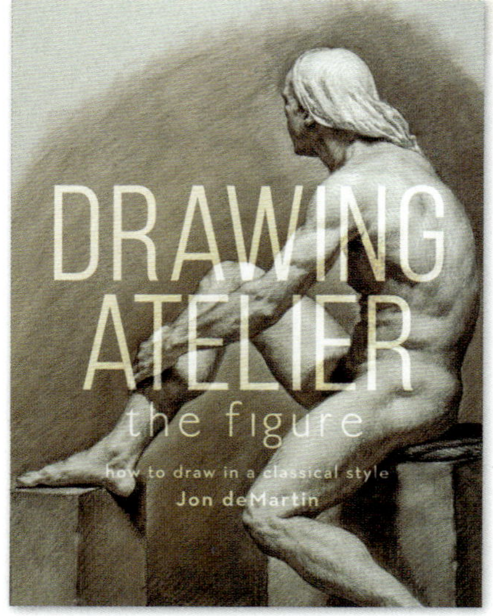

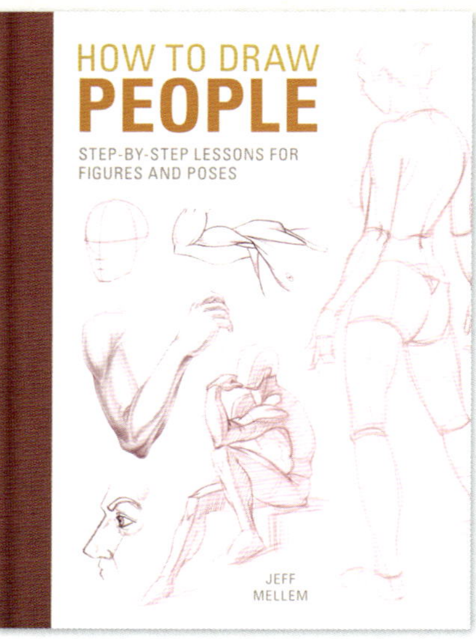

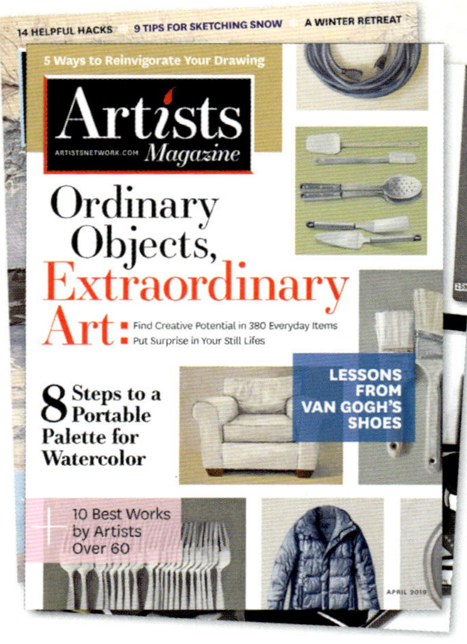

Find the latest issues of *Artists Magazine* on newsstands, or visit artistsnetwork.com.

These and other fine North Light products are available at your favorite art & craft retailer, bookstore or online supplier. Visit our websites at artistsnetwork.com and artistsnetwork.tv.

Follow Artists Network for the latest news, free wallpapers, free demos and chances to win FREE BOOKS!

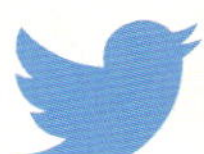

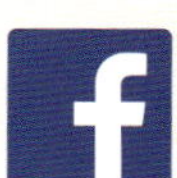

GET YOUR ART IN PRINT!

Visit **artistsnetwork.com/competitions** for up-to-date information on *Strokes of Genius: The Best of Drawing* and other North Light competitions.

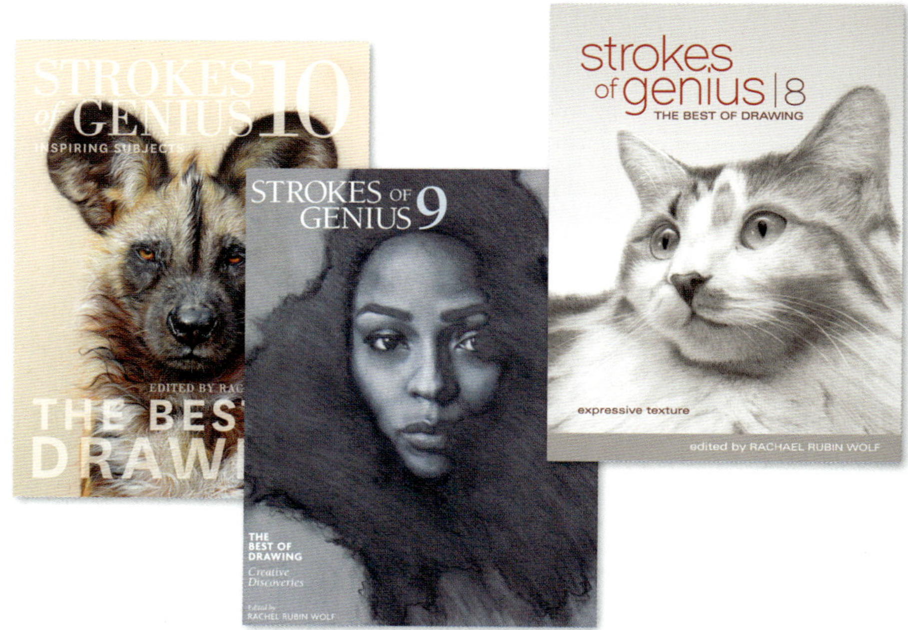